ANALECTA BIBLICA

INVESTIGATIONES SCIENTIFICAE IN RES BIBLICAS

13

CHRIST'S RESURRECTION
IN PAULINE SOTERIOLOGY

ROMAE

E PONTIFICIO INSTITUTO BIBLICO

1961

David Michael Stanley, S.J.

Christ's Resurrection in Pauline Soteriology

REEDITIO PHOTOMECHANICA (1963)

ROMAE
E PONTIFICIO INSTITUTO BIBLICO
1961

IMPRIMI POTEST
Romae, 21 iunii 1961
Ernestus Vogt S. I.
Rector Pontificii Instituti Biblici

IMPRIMATUR
E Vicariatu Urbis die 22 iunii 1961
Aloysius Card. Provicarius

REPRINTED IN AUSTRIA

Stabilimento Tipografico « Pliniana » - Selci Umbro (Perugia)

TABLE OF CONTENTS

SELECT BIBLIOGRAPHY

ALLO, E.-B.,   *L'Apocalypse et l'époque de la parousie* in *RB* 24 (1915) 393-455.

—   *S. Paul et la « double résurrection » corporelle* in *RB* 41 (1932) 187-209.

—   *Sagesse et Pneuma dans la première épître aux Corinthiens* in *RB* 43 (1934) 321-346.

—   *L'évolution de l'Évangile de Paul* in *Vivre et Penser* (1941) 48-77 ; (1942) 165-193.

ARGYLE, A. W.,   *The New Testament Doctrine of the Resurrection of Our Lord Jesus Christ* in *ExpT* 61 (1949-50) 187-188.

AULEN, G.,   *Christus Victor*, transl. by A. G. HEBERT (London, 1931).

BARRETT, C. K.,   *New Testament Eschatology I. Jewish and Pauline Eschatology* in *ScotJT* 6 (1953) 136-155 ; 225-243.

BENOIT, P.,   *La Loi et la Croix d'après saint Paul (Rom. VII, 7-VIII, 4)* in *RB* 47 (1938) 481-509.

—   *L'Ascension* in *RB* 56 (1949) 161-203.

BEYSCHLAG, W.,   *Neutestamentliche Theologie* [2], (Halle, 1896).

BLACK, M.,   *The Pauline Doctrine of the Second Adam* in *ScotJT* 6 (1953) 170-179.

BLAKELY, H. B.,   *The Gospel of Paul, a study in the Prison Epistles* in *TT* 3 (1946-47) 354-357.

BOISMARD, M.-E.,   *Constitué Fils de Dieu (Rom., I, 4)* in *RB* 60 (1953) 5-17.

BONNARD, P.,   *Mourir ou vivre avec Jésus-Christ selon saint Paul* in *RHPhilRel* 36 (1956) 101-112.

BONSIRVEN, J.,   *Le Judaïsme palestinien au temps de Jésus-Christ* [2] (Paris, 1934).

—   *Exégèse rabbinique et exégèse paulinienne* (Paris, 1939).

—   *L'Évangile de Paul* (Paris, 1948).

—   *Théologie du Nouveau Testament* (Paris, 1951).

BORNKAMM, G.,   *Taufe und Neues Leben bei Paulus* in *TB* 18 (1939) 235-242.

BOUSSET, W.,   *Kyrios Christos* [2] (Göttingen, 1921).

BOUYER, L.,   *ARPAGMOS* in *RSR* 39 (1951) 281-288.

BOVER, J. M.,   *De paulinae theologiae duplici gradu* in *G* 3 (1922) 254-258.

—   *Christus, Novus Adam* in *VD* 4 (1924) 299-305.

BOWEN, C. R.,   *The Meaning of* συναλιζόμενος *in Acts* 1,4 in *ZNT* 13 (1912) 247-259.

BRAUN, F.-M.,   *Où en est l'eschatologie du Nouveau Testament?* in *RB* 49 (1940) 33-54.

BROMILEY, G. W.,   *The Significance of Death in relation to the Atonement* in *EQ* 21 (1949) 122-132.

BROWN, R. E.,   *The Semitic Background of the New Testament Mysterion* in *Bib* 39 (1958) 426-448 ; 40 (1959) 70-87.

—   *The Pre-Christian Semitic Concept of « Mystery »* in *CBQ* 20 (1958) 417-443.

BULTMANN, R.,   *Theologie des Neuen Testaments* (Tübingen, 1948).

CAIRNS, D. S.,   *Some Thoughts on the Atonement* in *ExpT* 52 (1940-41) 16-20 ; 60-64.

—   *Anselm's Cur Deus Homo : a critical essay* in *ExpT* 51 (1939-40). 415-419.

CAMFIELD, F. W.,   *The Idea of Substitution in the Doctrine of the Atonement* in *ScotJT* 1 (1948) 282-293.

CASEL, O.,   *Mysteriengegenwart* in *JL* 8 (1929) 145-224.

—   *Art und Sinn der ältesten christlichen Osterfeier* in *JL* 14 (1938) 1-78.

—   *Zur Kultsprache des heiligen Paulus* in *Archiv für Liturgiewissenschaft* 1 (1950) 1-64.

CAZELLES, H.,   *À propos de quelques textes difficiles relatifs à la Justice de Dieu dans l'Ancien Testament* in *RB* 58 (1951) 169-188.

CERFAUX, L.,   *La voix vivante de l'Évangile* (Tournai-Paris, 1946).

—   *La théologie de l'Église suivant saint Paul* [2] (Paris, 1948).

—   *Le Christ dans la théologie de saint Paul* (Paris, 1951).

—   *Kyrios* in *VDBS V* 200-228.

—   *Recueil Lucien Cerfaux* (Gembloux, 1954) 2 vols.

—   *La théologie de la grâce selon saint Paul* in *VSp* 83 (1950) 5-19.

—   *La résurrection du Christ dans la vie et la doctrine de saint Paul* in *LumVi* § 3 (1952) 61-82.

—   *La mystique paulinienne* in *VSp Suppl* 23 (1952) 413-425.

COOLS, J.,   *La présence mystique du Christ dans le Baptême* in
                       Mémorial Lagrange (Paris, 1940) 295-305.

COPPENS, J.,   *L'état présent des études pauliniennes* in *ETL* 32 (1956)
                       363-372.

—   *La christologie de saint Paul* in *L'Attente du Messie*
                       (Bruges, 1954) 139-153.

COUTTS, J.,   *The Relationship of Ephesians and Colossians* in *NTS*
                       3 (1957-58) 201-207.

CULLMANN, O.,   *La signification de la sainte Cène dans le Christianisme
                       primitif* in *RHPhilRel* 16 (1936) 1-22.

—   *Le retour du Christ, espérance de l'Église* [3] in *CTAP*
                       8 (Paris-Neuchâtel, 1948).

—   *Le baptême des enfants et la doctrine biblique du Bap-
                       tême* in *CTAP* 19-20 (Paris-Neuchâtel, 1948).

—   *Christ et le temps* (Paris, 1947).

—   *Die Christologie des Neuen Testaments* [2] (Tübingen,
                       1958).

DAHL, N.,   *Anamnesis* in *ST* 1 (1948) 69-95.

DANIÉLOU, J.,   *Théologie du Judéo-Christianisme* (Paris, 1958).

DAVIES, W. D.,   *Paul and Rabbinic Judaism* [2] (London, 1955).

DECOURTRAY, A.,   *Renoncement et amour de soi selon saint Paul* in *NRT*
                       74 (1952) 21-29.

DEHAES, P.,   *De morte Domini tamquam sacrificio expiatorio in
                       theologia paulina* in *ColMech* 40 (1955) 690-699.

DEISSMANN, A.,   *Die neutestamentliche Formel « In Christo Jesu »* (Mar-
                       burg, 1892).

—   *Paulus* [2] (Tübingen, 1925).

DENIS, A.-A.,   *L'élection et la vocation de Paul, faveurs célestes* in
                       RThom 37 (1957) 405-428.

—   *La fonction apostolique et la liturgie nouvelle en Esprit:
                       Étude thématique des métaphores pauliniennes du culte
                       nouveau* in *RSTP* 42 (1958) 401-436 ; 617-656.

DENNEY, J.,   *The Death of Christ* (London, 1903).

DODD, C. H.,   *The Mind of Paul : a Psychological Approach* in
                       BJRylL 17 (1933) 91-106.

—   *The Mind of Paul : Change and Development* in *BJRylL*
                       18 (1934) 69-110.

—   *The Apostolic Preaching and Its Developments* (London,
                       1936).

DRUMMOND, J.,   *Occasion and Object of the Epistle to the Romans* in
                       HibJ 11 (1912-13) 787-804.

DUBOSE, W. P.,   *The Gospel according to Saint Paul* (London, 1907).

DUPERRAY, J.,   *Le Christ dans la vie chrétienne d'après saint Paul* [5]
                       (Paris, 1928).

DUPONT, J.,   *Filius meus es tu ...* in *RSR* 35 (1948) 522-543.

—   *Gnosis : la connaissance religieuse dans les épîtres de saint Paul* (Louvain-Paris, 1949).

—   *Le chrétien miroir de la gloire divine d'après 2 Cor* 3,18 in *RB* 56 (1949) 392-411.

—   *La réconciliation dans la théologie de saint Paul* in *Estudios Biblicos* 11 (1925) 255-302.

—   ΣΥΝ ΧΡΙΣΤΩΙ : *L'union avec le Christ suivant saint Paul* (Saint André-lèz-Bruges, 1952).

DURAND, A.,   *Le Christ premier-né* in *RSR* 1 (1910) 56-66.

DURRWELL, F.-X.,   *La résurrection de Jésus, mystère de salut* [2] (Le Puy-Paris, 1954).

EASTON, W. B. JR.,   *The Crucifixion, the Resurrection and Christian Living :* *an Interpretation* in *TT* 7 (1950-51) 54-67.

FEINE, P.,   *Theologie des Neuen Testaments* [1] (Leipzig, 1922).

FESTUGIÈRE, A.-J.,   Πνεῦμα *en Paul* in *RSR* 15 (1930) 385-415.

—   *L'enfant d'Agrigente* (Paris, 1941).

FEUILLET, A.,   *L'Homme-Dieu considéré dans sa condition terrestre de Serviteur et de Rédempteur* in *Vivre et Penser* (1942) 58-79.

—   *Le plan salvifique de Dieu d'après l'épître aux Romains* in *RB* (57 (1950) 336-387 ; 489-529.

—   *Le mystère Pascal et la résurrection des chrétiens d'après les épîtres pauliniennes* in *NRT* 79 (1957) 337-356.

DE FINANCE, J.,   *La Sophia chez S. Paul* in *RSR* 25 (1935) 385-417.

FORSTER, A. H.,   *The Meaning of Power for St Paul* in *AnglTR* 32 (1950) 17-7185.

FRIDRICHSEN, A.,   *The Apostle and his Message* (Uppsala, 1947).

GAECHTER, P.,   *Zur Exegese von Rom. VI, 5* in *ZKT* 54 (1930) 88-92.

GOGUEL, M.,   *Le caractère, à la fois actuel et futur, du salut dans la théologie paulinienne* in *The Background of the New Testament and its Eschatology* (ed. W. D. DAVIES, D. DAUBE) (Cambridge, 1956) 322-341.

—   *Paulinisme et Johannisme* in *RHPhilRel* 11 (1931) 1-19 ; 129-156.

—   *Le caractère et le rôle de l'élément cosmologique dans la sotériologie paulinienne* in *RHPhilRel* 15 (1935) 335-359.

—   *L'Évangile et la Loi* in *RHPhilRel* 17 (1937) 19-30.

GUIGNEBERT, C. H.,   *Quelques remarques d'exégèse sur Phil. 2,6-11* in *RHPhilRel* 3 (1923) 512-533.

HÄUSER, P.,   *Der Gottessohn « geworden unter dem Gesetze »* (*Gal.* 4,4) in *BZ* 11 (1913) 178-184.

HAHN, W. T.,   *Das Mitsterben und Mitauferstehen mit Christus bei Paulus : Ein Beitrag zum Problem der Gleichzeitigkeit des Christen mit Christus* (Gütersloh, 1937).

HASPECKER, J., Vestigia Evangelii Oralis in S. Pauli ad Corinthios Epistolis in VD 27 (1949) 129-142 ; 206-213.

HATCH, W. P., The Pauline Idea of Faith in its relation to Jewish and Hellenistic Religion in Harvard Theological Studies 2 (Cambridge, 1917).

HAVET, J., Christ collectif ou Christ individuel en I Cor. XII, 12 in ETL 23 (1947) 449-520.

HÉRING, J., Saint Paul a-t-il enseigné deux résurrections ? in RHPhil-Rel 12 (1932) 300-320.

— Kurios Anthropos in RHPhilRel 16 (1936) 196-209.

— Le Royaume de Dieu et sa venue (Paris, 1937).

— Les bases bibliques de l'humanisme chrétien in RHPhilRel 25 (1945) 17-40.

HEITMÜLLER, W., Zum Problem Paulus und Jesus in ZNT 13 (1912) 331-337.

HITCHCOCK, F. M. R., The Atonement and Modern Thought (London, 1911).

HOCEDEZ, E., Notre solidarité en Jésus-Christ et en Adam in G 13 (1932) 373-403.

HOLTZMANN, H. J., Lehrbuch der Neutestamentlichen Theologie ² (Tübingen, 1911).

HUBY, J., La Vie dans l'Esprit d'après S. Paul (Romains, c. 8) in RSR 30 (1943) 5-38.

— Mystiques Johanniques et Pauliniennes (Paris, 1946).

HUGHES, T. H., Recent Trends of Thought on the Atonement in ExpT 50 (1938-39) 250-253.

HULSBOSCH, A., Conceptus paulini vitae ac mortis in DTP 47-49 (1944-46) 35-55.

— Resurrectio Christi in doctrina soteriologica S. Pauli ibid. 193-206.

— Passibilitas et mors Christi in doctrina soteriologica S. Pauli ibid. 207-227.

HUNTER, A. M., Interpreting Paul's Gospel (London, 1954).

— The Hope of Glory : The Relevance of Pauline Eschatology in Int 8 (1954) 131-140.

IACONO, V., Il Battesimo nella dottrina di S. Paolo (Roma, 1935).

JEREMIAS, J., Zwischen Karfreitag und Ostern in ZNT 42 (1949) 194-201.

— Zum Problem der Deutung von Jes. 53 im palästinischen Spätjudentum in Aux sources de la tradition chrétienne (Neuchâtel-Paris, 1950) 113-119.

JOÜON, P., Notes philologiques sur quelques versets de l'épître aux Philippiens in RSR 28 (1938) 89-97; 223-235; 299-311.

JOURDAN, G. V., Koinonia in I Corinthians 10,16 in JBL 67 (1948) 111-124.

KAFTAN, J.,   *Jesus und Paulus* (Tübingen, 1906).
KÄSEMANN, E.,   *Eine urchristliche Taufliturgie* in *Festschrift für Rudolf Bultmann* (Stuttgart, 1949) 133-148.
KIRK, K. E.,   *The Atonement* in *Essays Catholic and Critical* (London, 1926).
KITTEL, G.,   *Jesus bei Paulus* in *Theologische Studien und Kritiken* 85 (1912) 366-402.
KNOX, W. L.,   *The Acts of the Apostles* (Cambridge, 1948).
—   *The « Divine Hero » Christology in the New Testament* in *HTR* 41 (1948) 229-249.
KÜMMEL, W. G.,   *Römer 7 und die Bekehrung Paulus* (Leipzig, 1929).
KURZINGER, J.,   Συμμόρφους τῆς εἰκόνος τοῦ υἱοῦ αὐτοῦ (*Rom* 8,29) in *BZ* 2 (1958) 294-299.
LABOURT, M.,   *Notes d'exégèse sur Phil. 2,5-11* in *RB* 7 (1898) 402-415 ; 553-563.
LAGRANGE, M-J.,   *Les origines du dogme paulinien de la divinité du Christ* in *RB* 45 (1936) 5-33.
LEBRETON, J.,   *Études sur la contemplation dans le Nouveau Testament : I. La contemplation dans la vie de S. Paul* in *RSR* 30 (1943) 81-108.
—   *La foi en Jésus-Christ, vie du Chrétien : l'origine et le développement de cette foi dans l'Église primitive* in *RSR* 30 (1943) 17-69.
LEENHARDT, F.-J.,   *Le Baptême chrétien : son origine, sa signification* in *CTAP* 4 (Paris-Neuchâtel) 1946.
LEMONNYER, A.,   *Théologie du Nouveau Testament* (Paris, 1928).
—   *Notre baptême d'après S. Paul* (Paris, 1935).
LESTRINGANT, P.,   *Essai sur l'unité de la révélation biblique* (Paris, 1942).
LIETZMANN, H.,   *Messe und Herrenmahl* (Bonn, 1926).
LOHMEYER, E.,   Σὺν Χριστῷ in *Festgabe für Ad. Deissmann zum 60. Geburtstage* (Tübingen, 1927) 218-257.
—   *Kyrios Jesus* in *SHAW* (1927-28) 4 Abhandlung 1-89.
—   *Grundlagen paulinischer Theologie* (Tübingen, 1929).
—   *Probleme paulinischer Theologie* (Stuttgart, 1955).
LOWE, J.,   *An Examination of Attempts to detect Developments in St. Paul's Theology* in *JTS* 42 (1941) 129-142.
LYONNET, S.,   *De « Justitia Dei » in Epistola ad Romanos 1,17 et 3,21-22* in *VD* 25 (1947) 23-34.
—   *De « Justitia Dei » in Epistola ad Romanos 10,3 et 3,5 ibid.* 118-121.
—   *De « Justitia Dei » in Epistola ad Romanos 3,25-26 ibid.* 129-144 ; 193-203 ; 257-264.
—   *S. Cyrille d'Alexandrie et 2 Cor 3,17* in *Bib* 32 (1951) 25-31.

LYONNET, S.,	*De Christo summo angulari lapide secundum Eph* 2,20 in *VD* 27 (1949) 74-83.
—	*Propter remissionem praecedentium delictorum (Rom* 3,25) in *VD* 28 (1950) 282-287.
—	*Note sur le plan de l'épître aux Romains* in *RSR* 39 (1951) 301-316.
—	*La Morale de saint Paul* in *Catéchistes* (1953) 149-159.
—	*Liberté du chrétien et loi de l'Esprit selon saint Paul* in *Christus* 1 (1954) 6-27.
—	*Le sens de* ἐφ'ᾧ *en Rom* 13 *et l'exégèse des Pères grecs* in *Bib* 36 (1955) 336-356.
—	*Le péché originel et l'exégèse de Rom* 5,12-14 in *RSR* 44 (1956) 63-84.
—	*Conception paulinienne de la Rédemption* in *LumVi* § 36 (1958) 35-66.
—	*La valeur sotériologique de la résurrection du Christ selon Saint Paul* in *G* 39 (1958) 295-318.
—	*La Sotériologie paulinienne* in *Introduction à la Bible II* (Tournai, 1959) 840-889.
MACAN, R. W.,	*The Resurrection of Jesus Christ* (London, 1877).
MAGNIEN, P. M.,	*La Résurrection des morts dans I Thess IV,* 13-V, 3 in *RB* 16 (1907) 349-382.
MALEVEZ, L.,	*L' Église dans le Christ* in *RSR* 25 (1935) 257-291 ; 418-439.
—	*L' Église corps du Christ* in *RSR* 32 (1944) 27-94.
—	*Quelques enseignements de l' Encyclique « Mystici Corporis »* in *NRT* 67 (1945) 385-407.
MANSON, T. W.,	*St Paul in Ephesus : The Date of the Epistle to the Philippians* in *BJRylL* 23 (1939) 182-200.
—	*St Paul in Ephesus : The Problem of the Epistle to the Galatians* in *BJRylL* 24 (1940) 59-80.
—	*St Paul in Ephesus : The Corinthian Correspondence* in *BJRylL* 26 (1941-4) 101-120 ; 327-341.
—	*St Paul in Greece : The Letters to the Thessalonians* in *BJRylL* 35 (1953) 428-447.
—	ΙΛΑΣΤΗΡΙΟΝ in *JTS* 46 (1945) 1-9.
MASSON, C.,	*L' Hymne christologique de l'épître aux Colossiens, I,* 15-20 in *RThéolPhil* 36 (1948) 138-142.
MacKEOWN, W.,	*Paul at Athens* in *ExpT* 42 (1930-31) 382-383.
MACKINTOSH, R.,	*Recent Thought on the Doctrine of the Atonement* in *ExpT* 37 (1925-26) 198-203.
MacLEAN, J. H.,	*St Paul at Athens* in *ExpT* 44 (1932-33) 550-553.
McGRATH, B.,	*« Syn » Words in St Paul* in *CBQ* 14 (1952) 219-226.
McNEILE, A. H.,	*St Paul, his Life, Letters and Christian Doctrine* (Cambridge, 1925).

McNeile, A. H.,   *New Testament Teaching in the Light of St Paul's.* (Cambridge, 1923).

Médebielle, A.,   *Christus Dominus* in *VD* 4 (1924) 86-90 ; 117-119 ; 135-139.

Mehl-Koehnlein, H.,   *L'homme selon l'apôtre Paul* in *CTAP* 28 (Paris-Neuchâtel, 1951).

Ménégoz, E.,   *Le péché et la rédemption d'après S. Paul* (Paris, 1882).

Menoud, P.-H.,   *Le sort des trépassés* in *CTAP* 9 (Paris-Neuchâtel, 1945).

—   *Révélation et Tradition. L' influence de la conversion de Paul sur sa théologie* in *VC* 7 (1953) 131-141.

Michaelis, W.,   *Rechtfertigung aus Glauben bei Paulus* in *Festgabe für Ad. Deissmann zum 60. Geburtstage* (Tübingen, 1927) 116-138.

Milligan, W.,   *The Ascension and Heavenly Priesthood of Our Lord,* Baird Lectures for 1891 (London, 1901).

—   *The Resurrection of Our Lord,* Croall Lectures for 1879-80 (London, 1905).

Minear, P. S.,   *The Truth about Sin and Death. The Meaning of the Atonement in Romans* in *Int* 7 (1953) 142-155.

de Montcheuil, Y.,   *Signification eschatologique du repas eucharistique* in *RSR* 33 (1946) 10-43.

Morgan, W.,   *The Religion and Theology of Paul* (Edinburgh, 1917).

Mouroux, J.,   *Remarques sur la foi dans S. Paul* in *RA* 65 (1937) 129-145 ; 281-300.

—   *Le Corps et le Christ* in *RSR* 30 (1947) 140-169.

Munck, J.,   *Paulus und die Heilsgeschichte* (Kopenhagen, 1954).

Mundle, W.,   *Der Glaubensbegriff des Paulus* (Leipzig, 1932).

Nélis, J.,   *L'antithèse littéraire* ΖΩΗ-ΘΑΝΑΤΟΣ *dans les épîtres pauliniennes* in *ETL* 20 (1943) 18-44.

—   *Les antithèses littéraires dans les épîtres de saint Paul* in *NRT* 70 (1948) 360-387.

Orchard, B.,   *A New Solution of the Galatians' Problem* in *BJRylL* 28 (1944) 154-174.

Orr, J.,   *The Resurrection of Jesus* in *EX* (1908) 420-437.

Peake, A. S.,   *The Quintessence of Paulinism* in *BJRylL* 4 (1917-18) 285-311.

Pfleiderer, O.,   *Der Paulinismus²* (Leipzig, 1890).

—   *Lectures on the Influence of the Apostle Paul on the Development of Christianity,* Hibbert Lectures 1885 (London, 1897).

Pherigo, L. P.,   *Paul and the Corinthian Church* in *JBL* 68 (1949) 341-350.

Prat, F.,   *L' idée-mère de la théologie de S. Paul* in *E* 83 (1900) 203-223.

PRAT, F.,   La Théologie de Saint Paul I⁸ (Paris, 1920) ; II⁷ (Paris,
                     1923).

PRÜMM, K.,   Die pastorale Einheit des I. Korintherbriefs in ZKT
                     64 (1940) 202-214.

—   Zur Struktur des Römerbriefes. Begriffsreihen als Einheits-
                     band in ZKT 72 (1950) 333-349.

RAMSEY, A. M.,   The Resurrection of Christ² (London, 1946).

—   The Glory of God and the Transfiguration of Christ
                     (London, 1949).

REICKE, Bo,   The Law and This World according to Paul in JBL 70
                     (1951) 259-276.

RIDDLE, J. G.,   Recent Thoughts on the Doctrine of the Atonement in
                     ExpT 47 (1935-36) 246-250 ; 327-332.

RICHARD, L.,   La Rédemption, mystère d'amour in RSR 13 (1923)
                     193-217 ; 397-418.

RIESENFELD, H.,   La descente dans la mort in Aux sources de la tradi-
                     tion chrétienne (Paris-Neuchâtel, 1950) 207-217.

RIVIÈRE, J.,   Le dogme de la Rédemption (Paris, 1905).

—   La Rédemption devant la pensée moderne in RCF 70
                     (1912) 161-180 ; 278-305.

—   Où en est le problème de la Rédemption ? in RScRel
                     3 (1923) 211-232.

ROBINSON, J. A. T., The Body. A Study in Pauline Theology (London,
                     1952).

ROBINSON, J. M.,   A Formal Analysis of Col 1,15-20 in JBL 76 (1957)
                     270-287.

ROSE, V.,   Études sur la théologie de S. Paul, I. Comment il a
                     connu Jésus-Christ in RB 11 (1902) 321-346.

—   II. Jésus-Christ Seigneur et Fils de Dieu in RB 12
                     (1903) 336-361.

ROUSSELOT, P.,   La grâce d'après S. Jean et S. Paul in RSR 23 (1928)
                     87-204.

SAHLIN, H.,   The New Exodus of Salvation according to St Paul
                     in The Root of the Vine (Westminster, 1953) 81-96.

SASSE, H.,   Jesus Christ the Lord in Mysterium Christi, ed. G. K.
                     A. BELL and A. DEISSMANN (London, 1930).

SCHLIER, H.,   Die Verkündigung im Gottesdienst der Kirche (Köln,
                     1953).

SCHMIDT, H. W.,   Das Kreuz Christi bei Paulus in ZSystTheol 21 (1950)
                     145-160.

SCHMIDT, T.,   Der Leib Christi (Σῶμα Χριστοῦ) (Leipzig, 1919).

SCHMITT, J.,   Jésus ressuscité dans la prédication apostolique (Paris,
                     1949).

                     Petra autem Christus erat in La Maison-Dieu 29 (1952)
                     18-31.

SCHNACKENBURG, R.,   *Das Heilsgeschehen bei der Taufe nach dem Apostel Paulus* (München, 1950).

SCHULZE, B.,   *La nuova soteriologia russa* in OCP 9 (1943) 406-430 ; 11 (1945) 165-215 ; 12 (1946) 130-176.

SCHWEITZER, A.,   *Die Mystik des Apostels Paulus* (Tübingen, 1930).

SELWYN, E. G.,   *The Approach to Christianity* (London, 1925).

—   *The Resurrection* in *Essays Catholic and Critical* (London, 1926).

SHARP, D. S.,   *For Our Justification* in ExpT 39 (1927-28) 87-90.

SHAW, J. M.,   *The Resurrection of Christ* (Edinburgh, 1920).

—   *The Problem of the Cross* in ExpT 47 (1935-36) 18-21.

SMITH, S. F.,   *The Atonement* in M 133 (1919) 241-249.

—   *The Atonement theologically explained* in M 133 (1919) 348-359.

SPARROW SIMPSON, W. J.,   *The Resurrection and Modern Thought* (London, 1911).

SPICQ, C.,   *L'origine johannique de la conception du Christ-prêtre dans l'épître aux Hébreux* in *Aux sources de la tradition chrétienne* (Paris-Neuchâtel, 1950) 258-269.

STAAB, K.,   *Pauluskommentare aus der griechischen Kirche* in NTA 15 (Münster, 1933).

STEVENS, G. B.,   *The Theology of the New Testament²* (Edinburgh, 1911).

STORR, H. V. F.,   *The Development of English Theology in the nineteenth Century* (London, 1913).

SWALLOW, F. R.,   ' *Redemption* ' in St Paul in Scr 10 (1958) 21-27.

TASKER, R. V. G.,   *St Paul and the Earthly Life of Jesus* in ExpT 46 (1934-35) 557-562.

TAYLOR, T. M.,   ' *Abba, Father* ' *and Baptism* in ScotJT 11 (1958) 62-71.

TAYLOR, V.,   *Great Texts Reconsidered* : *a commentary on Rom 3,25* in ExpT 50 (1938-39) 295-300.

—   *The Atonement in New Testament Teaching²* (London, 1945).

—   *The Unity of the New Testament* : *the doctrine of the Atonement* in ExpT 58 (1946-47) 256-259.

TOBAC, E.,   *Le Christ nouvel Adam dans la théologie de saint Paul* in RHE 21 (1925) 249-260.

—   *Le problème de la justification dans saint Paul* (Louvain, 1908).

TONER, P. J.,   *The Soteriological Teaching of Christ* in IrTQ 2 (1907) 89-109.

TRESMONTANT, C.,   *Saint Paul et le Mystère du Christ* (Paris, 1956).

VENN, J.,   *St. Paul's Three Chapters on Holiness* (London, 1877).

VISSER'T HOOFT, W. A.,   *Jesus is Lord* : *the Kingship of Christ in the Bible* in TT 4 (1947-48) 171-189.

VITTI, A.,   *Comprehensus sum a Christo* in *VD* 4 (1924) 353-359.
—   *Christus-Adam. De Paulino hoc conceptu interpretando eiusque ab extraneis fontibus independentia vindicanda* in *Bib* 7 (1926) 121-145 ; 270-285 ; 384-401.
—   *La resurrezione di Gesù e la soteriologia di s. Paolo* in *CC* 81² (1930) 97-109 ; 298-314.
VOSTÉ, J.-M.,   *Studia Paulina* (Romae, 1932).
VÖGTLE, A.,   *Die Adam-Christus Typologie und « Der Menschensohn »* in *TrierTZ* 60 (1951) 309-328.
WARREN, M.,   *In Christ the New has come* in *TT* 3 (1946-47) 472-485.
WEBER, V.,   *Wann und wie hat Paulus « Christum nach dem Fleische » erkannt ?* in *BZ* 2 (1904) 178-188.
WEISS, B.,   *Lehrbuch der biblischen Theologie des Neuen Testaments*⁷ (Stuttgart-Berlin, 1903).
WESTCOTT, B. F.,   *The Gospel of the Resurrection* (London, 1879).
—   *The Revelation of the Risen Lord* (London-Cambridge, 1881).
WHALE, J. S.,   *The Resurrection of the Body and the Life Everlasting* in *ScotJT* 2 (1949) 127-138.
WHITELEY, D. E. H.,   *St. Paul's Thought on the Atonement* in *JTS* 8 (1957) 250-255.
WIKENHAUSER, A.,   *Die Christusmystik des Apostels Paulus*² (Freiburg, 1956).
WILSON, W. E.,   *The Development of Paul's Doctrine of Dying and Rising again with Christ* in *ExpT* 42 (1930-31) 562-565.
WORDEN, T.,   *Christ Jesus who died, or rather who has been raised up (Rom 8,34)* in *Scr* 10 (1958) 33-43 ; 11 (1959) 51-59.
XAVERIUS A VALLISOLETO,   *« Christus-Adam »* in *VD* 15 (1935) 87-93 ; 114-120.

INTRODUCTION

§ 1. - **Aims of This Investigation**

The present essay will attempt to present an aspect which I believe to be central to the whole of Paul's thought on the role of Christ as Redeemer : the function assigned to Christ's resurrection in Pauline soteriology. The purpose of this inquiry is not merely to determine the place held by Christ's resurrection in the maturer expression of Paul's theology, but also to observe how the progressively deeper understanding of this central Christian truth enabled Paul to arrive at the definitive expression of his conception of Christian salvation. Consequently, it will be necessary to investigate the resurrection of Christ as a formative factor in Paul's development as it is found reflected in the authentically Pauline epistles preserved in the New Testament canon.

I have employed the term « soteriology » in preference to expressions like « theology of the redemption » or « theology of the atonement » because, as its etymology suggests, « soteriology » embraces the whole gamut of the divine activity in the salvation of mankind. Moreover, the word is not coloured by those juridical overtones which these other terms appear, rightly or wrongly, to possess in modern theological language. By « Pauline soteriology », I understand the theological thought of the Apostle concerning the definitive, universal salvific work effected by God the Father and the incarnate Son in the latter's sacred humanity which, by transforming that humanity into a perfect instrument for the salvation of man in his entire corporate personality [1], made possible a new and intimate union, in the Holy Spirit, of man with God.

---

[1] Pauline soteriology is dominated by that realistic view of man, characteristic of the Semitic mentality, which does not content itself with an investigation of the « salvation of man's soul » (a Greek viewpoint only too common among occidental theologians). It conceives Christian salvation as something which affects man in his bodily, no less than in his spiritual, aspect.

§ 2. - The Concept of Biblical Theology

Since the ultimate purpose of this study is to make a small contribution to the biblical theology of the NT, it may not be out of place
here to state my own view of the nature of this branch of positive
theology, which in recent years has been the object of considerable
discussion and to which so many valuable contributions have been made
since the close of the second world war.

NT biblical theology is that sacred science which analyses the Christian reality as attested and interpreted by the various NT writers according to the manner in which it was revealed to them, and which
seeks, whilst remaining within biblical thought-categories, to realize a
synthesis which those authors did not formulate.

Biblical theology is, therefore, truly a branch of theology, and must,
in consequence, be distinguished from the history of religion as also from
exegesis. It cannot be regarded simply as a profane science, nor does
its function consist in supplying the systematic theologian with the
scriptural raw materials out of which he can create scholastic theology.
This point is of some importance, since it was not admitted, until fairly
recently, even by the authors of NT biblical theologies. Not only liberal
critics like H. J. HOLTZMANN [2], W. BEYSCHLAG [3], B. WEISS [4], PAUL
FEINE [5], and RUDOLF BULTMANN [6], but also Catholic exegetes like FER-
DINAND PRAT [7] and JOSEPH BONSIRVEN [8] have denied the « theological »
nature of NT biblical theology.

With MAX MEINERTZ [9], a change of attitude amongst Catholics is
perceptible, while recent articles by Catholic scholars like C. SPICQ [10],

---

[2] HEINRICH JULIUS HOLTZMANN, *Lehrbuch der Neutestamentlichen Theologie
I*[2] (Tübingen, 1911) 20-22.
[3] WILLIBALD BEYSCHLAG, *Neutestamentliche Theologie I*[2] (Halle, 1896) 1-2.
[4] BERNHARD WEISS, *Lehrbuch der biblischen Theologie des Neuen Testaments*[7]
(Stuttgart-Berlin, 1903) 1-5.
[5] PAUL FEINE, *Theologie des Neuen Testaments*[4] (Leipzig, 1922) 1-3.
[6] RUDOLF BULTMANN, *Theologie des Neuen Testaments* (Tübingen, 1948) 1-2.
[7] F. PRAT, *La Théologie de Saint Paul I*[8] (Paris, 1920) 1.
[8] JOSEPH BONSIRVEN, *Théologie du Nouveau Testament* (Paris, 1951) 7-9.
[9] MAX MEINERTZ, *Theologie des Neuen Testaments I* (Bonn, 1950) 1-7.
[10] C. SPICQ, *L'avènement de la théologie biblique* in *RSPT* 34 (1951) 561-574 ;
also *Nouvelles réflexions sur la théologie biblique* in *RSPT* 42 (1958) 209-219.

VIKTOR WARNACH [11], F. M. BRAUN [12], S. LYONNET [13], and R. A. F. MAC-
KENZIE [14], have laid down the principles governing the creation of a
proper NT biblical theology as the work of *fides quaerens intellectum*.
The biblical theologian, as these authors insist, must regard the NT
not merely as a human, historical document, but as the divine-human
testimony to the Christian reality [15]. To name but one fundamental
contribution to this new conception of the purpose of biblical theology,
F. P. MUÑIZ [16] has shown that it must be considered as a necessary
and integral part of positive theology.

The aim of NT biblical theology, accordingly, is not only to establish and to synthesize the theological data formally expressed by the
sacred writers of the NT. In other words, it cannot remain merely a
« theology of the NT », but must become a « theology created out of the
NT ». It will accomplish this by developing the doctrinal deposit found
upon the sacred page which will serve the spiritual life of the Christian.
At the same time, such a NT biblical theology will be distinguishable
from scholastic theology by its structure and method, which are governed
not by Aristotelian philosophy but by the thought-patterns peculiar to
the NT itself.

Thus the NT biblical theologian must take account of the various
modalities of Christian reality which appear in the theological viewpoint of each evangelist, of each author of the NT letters and of the

---

[11] VIKTOR WARNACH, *Gedanken zur neutestamentlichen Theologie* in *Gloria
Dei* 7 (1952) 119-122.

[12] F. M. BRAUN, *La théologie biblique. Qu'entendre par là ?* in *RTh* 53 (1953)
221-253.

[13] S. LYONNET, *De Peccato et Redemptione I : De Notione Peccati* (Romae,
1957) 7-25 ; see also his article, *De notione et momento theologiae biblicae* in *VD*
34 (1956) 42-53.

[14] R. A. F. MACKENZIE, *The Concept of Biblical Theology* in *The Catholic
Theological Society of America : Proceedings of the Tenth Annual Convention* (New
York, 1955) 48-66. The literature on this subject is already large : one might also
consult H. SCHLIER, *Über Sinn und Aufgabe einer Theologie des Neuen Testaments*
in *BiblZ NF* 1 (1957) 6-23 ; C. GAMBLE, *The Literature of Biblical Theology : a Biblio-
graphical Study* in *Int* 7 (1953) 466-480 ; KARL RAHNER, V. HAMP, H. SCHLIER,
Biblische Theologie in *Lexikon für Theologie und Kirche* 2 (Freiburg, 1958) 439-451.

[15] J. DE FRAINE, *L'Encyclique Humani Generis et les erreurs concernant
l'Écriture Sainte* in *ScEcc* 5 (1953) 7-28.

[16] F. P. MUÑIZ, *De diversis muneribus S. Theologiae secundum doctrinam D.
Thomae* in *Ang* 24 (1947) 93-123.

Apocalypse, tracing the development of Christian doctrine through each
inspired writer of the NT, in order to present a complete synthesis of
the divine reality, whose many facets are depicted in the various books
of the NT.

The realization of such a programme is obviously not easy, and
much preliminary investigation is required into the historically ascer-
tainable stages through which, both in its conception as well as in its
expression, the body of Christian truth progressed. In the case of at
least one NT author, St Paul, as we hope to show, it is possible (and
indeed necessary) to gain some insight into the evolution of his theological thought and its expression.

§ 3. - Some Modern Views of Pauline Resurrection-Soteriology

Since the present work is an investigation into the function of the
Pauline conception of Christ's resurrection in Paul's theological development, it may be useful to examine some of the previous studies in
this field.

H. J. HOLTZMANN found two irreconcilable sets of texts dealing with
the redemption in the Pauline epistles[17] : the first series, of Jewish theological provenance, reflected a *juridical* point of view in terms of reconciliation (2 Cor 5,18 ff ; Col 1,20 f ; Eph 2,16 ; Rom 5,10), expiatory
sacrifice (Rom 3,25 ; Gal 3,10 ; 4,5), vicarious atoning death (Gal 3,13 ;
Col 2,14 f) ; the second series, stemming from Hellenistic syncretism,
revealed a *mystical* outlook and provided a palliative for the idea of
vicarious atonement (Rom 6-8 ; 2 Cor 5,14 ff). While these two totally
divergent viewpoints could not, for Holtzmann, be integrated into any
sort of synthesis, still the mystical aspects of Paul's thought (despite
their objective presentation) might be considered the subjective coun-
terpart to the objective *Rechtshandel*[18].

---

[17] HEINRICH JULIUS HOLTZMANN, *Lehrbuch der neutestamentlichen Theologie
II*[2] (Tübingen, 1911) 105-131.

[18] Speaking of Pauline mysticism, Holtzmann says (*op. cit.* 131), « Sie schliesst
sich an keinen Vorgang an und ist eigentlich nur unter Begleitung des sinnlich
empfindbaren Momentes, welches sich in die Anschauung vom Absterben des zu
Tod getroffenen Fleisches kleidet verständlich. Sofern dieses Moment in der Sphäre
des subjektiven Erlebnisses zu liegen kommt, lässt sich die mystische Theorie als
die subjektive Kehrseite der anderen bezeichnen, obschon des beschriebenen Her-

W. J. SPARROW SIMPSON devoted a lengthy study to the discussion of the many problems, both apologetic and dogmatic, which Christ's resurrection presents to the modern mind [19]. He insisted upon its unique character in contrast with the resurrection of other men [20], and stressed the importance of the instrumentality of Christ's glorified humanity [21] in effecting the justification of the individual Christian in what he calls his « moral » resurrection [22].

The work of another member of the English school, A. M. RAMSEY, reveals a deeper insight into the meaning of NT soteriology, which must take Christ's resurrection as its point of departure, both from the historical and the theological point of view [23]. The double perspective of Christ's death and resurrection is reflected in all the apostolic writings [24]. Indeed, to grasp the significance of the OT as something more than an object of comparative religion, it is necessary to concede to Christ's resurrection its proper place in biblical theology [25].

---

gang gerade so objektiver Bestand zugeschrieben wird, wie dem Rechtshandel ». An article by MAURICE GOGUEL, *Ce que l'Église doit à l'Apôtre Paul* in *RHPhilRel* 31 (1951) 157-180, shows how far many non-Catholic scholars have retreated from a position like that of Holtzmann. Paulinism, for Goguel, represents the reorganization of Jewish theology in view of Christ's coming and his effecting the redemption through his death and resurrection. Paul conceived Christ's work not only in terms of God's justice but also of his power. Hence, the redemption comprises both the expiation of sin and the transmutation of the life of the flesh into that of the spirit : that is to say, it includes not only Christ's death but also his resurrection. Still, GOGUEL holds that Pauline soteriology is constructed on two different levels, and to some extent, those two lines of thought which HOLTZMANN had set in opposition must run parallel in his estimation.

[19] W. J. SPARROW SIMPSON, *The Resurrection and Modern Thought* (London, 1911).

[20] *op. cit.* 291.

[21] *op. cit.* 293.

[22] *op. cit.* 298.

[23] A. MICHAEL RAMSEY, *The Resurrection of Christ²* (London, 1946). In an earlier work, *The Gospel and the Catholic Church* (London, 1936), Ramsey developed an ecclesiology in terms of dying and rising with Christ.

[24] *op. cit.* 12. In a later passage (95), he remarks, « Cross and Resurrection are the grounds of the Church's origin, the secret of the Church's contemporary being, the goal of the Church's final self-realization on behalf of the human race ».

[25] *op. cit.* 120, « Read in its own light, the Bible has the Resurrection as its key. Its God is the God who raised up Jesus Christ from the dead, and in so doing vindicated His word in the Old Testament and in the Cross of Christ. It is only in virtue of the Resurrection that the Bible is one, and that the message of the Bible is coherent and true ».

ALBERT SCHWEITZER's study of the mystical elements in Pauline
theology was a serious effort to dislodge Protestant thought on the redemption from the position created for it by HOLTZMANN [26]. Pauline soteriology is essentially eschatological : redemption through Christ's atoning
death is a pure *hors d'oeuvre* inherited from the primitive Christian tradition [27]. Paul's Christ-mysticism is simply this eschatological redemption
« von innen her geschaut » [28].

Unless we grasp the eschatological character of Paul's mysticism,
we cannot understand it. Just as Jesus attained his position in the
Kingdom by his death and resurrection, so those who are to share in
the Kingdom must, by passing through the same experience, acquire the
resurrection-existence. While the rest of the apostolic Church believed
that faith in Christ's messiahship was the only link with him, Paul
asserted that the union of the « elect » with Christ was made possible
by a present participation in his dying and rising [29].

In attempting to reconcile such realistic mysticism with his own
conception of Pauline eschatology, Schweitzer, as his critics have pointed
out [30], has attempted the impossible. The weakness in his position is
his failure to grasp the metahistorical character of Christ's death and
resurrection.

It is this very point that W. T. HAHN has sought to clarify in his
monograph on the Christian's participation in Christ's death and resurrection according to Paul, a book which some Catholic reviewers consid-

---

[26] ALBERT SCHWEITZER, *Die Mystik des Apostels Paulus* (Tübingen, 1930).

[27] *op. cit.* 214 ff. It is important to grasp the meaning SCHWEITZER gives
to the term « eschatological ». It is applied to the liberation from servitude in the
period subsequent to the parousia, but intermediate between that event and the
Endzeit, i. e. to a Messianic reign of the elect with Christ.

[28] Pauline mysticism is not mythical like that of the Hellenistic mystery
religions, but is « geschichtlich-kosmisch ». It is orientated not to the « Vorzeit »,
but to the « Endzeit » (*op. cit.* 23).

[29] On SCHWEITZER's view, eschatology dissolves the natural world in the
supernatural, the world of the present in that of the future ; and Paul's mysticism asserts the possibility of escape from the present, natural world into the future,
supernatural state. Unless, says Schweitzer, we realize that Paul postulated his
mysticism because of his concept of the Messianic kingdom, we miss the eschatological quality of Pauline mysticism and fail to understand it (*op. cit.* 98). In consequence, Schweitzer's interpretation of Paul rests upon the validity of his exegesis
of the texts regarding the Messianic Kingdom.

[30] Cf. the review of SCHWEITZER's book by KARL ADAM in *ThQ* III (1930)
and that by M.-J. LAGRANGE in *RB* 42 (1933).

ered as a step towards the Catholic position [31]. Hahn discusses two principal aspects of the problem as answered by Paul.

In the first place, both the rising as well as the dying with Christ occur during the present existence of the Christian. It might seem, from Rom 6, that the rising with Christ is reserved to the future life, but this impression, says Hahn, is due to the question Paul is answering. His adversaries do not deny the reality of the new life, but the necessity of practising virtue in order to preserve it. Paul states that the « indicative » of the life of grace has a corresponding « imperative ». This is not to say that it is merely an ethical life which is inaugurated by Baptism, for the new life is given « als ganzes » by that sacrament [32]. The passage in Col 2,12 ff enuntiates the same conception of Baptism in the face of the opposite error. The gnostics of Colossae have misunderstood the « indicative » of Christian existence [33]. Accordingly, Paul consistently asserts that the Christian life is an actual possession of the believer.

The second question Hahn discusses is the Pauline concept of Christian life itself; and he finds it expressed in the Pauline formula of dying and rising with Christ. Paul is aware of the twofold character of the *Christusgeschehen*: for him, it is at once historical and also *heilsgeschichtlich*[34]. The result of this double quality is a tension in Christian existence, which can be solved only at the parousia: *Mitsterben* and *Mitauferstehung* are at once the constitutive elements of Christian life and an object of Christian hope [35]. Through preaching, Baptism, and the Eucharist, the Christian is drawn into a « contemporaneity » with Christ. That is to say, through Christian faith, the believer is transported

---

[31] WILHELM TRAUGOTT HAHN, *Das Mitsterben und Mitauferstehen mit Christus bei Paulus* (Gütersloh, 1937).

[32] *op. cit.* 38.

[33] HAHN cites other Pauline passages to prove his point: *op. cit.* 43.

[34] *op. cit.* 81 : « Beide Seiten müssen, soll Paulus verstanden werden, klar zu Ausdruck kommen, dürfen aber nicht als zwei unzusammenhängende Hälfte verstanden werden, so dass man einmal nur die eine Seite vornehmen und von der anderen absehen könnte. Beide stehen in einem Wechselverhältnis. Nennen wir das zur Geschichtlichkeit hinzutretende zweite Charakteristikum die ' Heilsgeschichtlichkeit ', so kann diese Einheit etwa folgendermassen umschreiben werden : Es handelt sich um ein geschichtliches Ereignis, das heilsgeschichtlich qualifiziert ist ... um Heilsgeschichte, die in der Geschichte Ereignis geworden ist ».

[35] The « indicative » and the « imperative » of this Christian existence make it at once « ein Gegebenes und zugleich Aufgegebenes », *op. cit.* 88.

back to Calvary and made a sharer in the power of the resurrection [36]. The weakness of Hahn's conception appears in the difficulty of discovering texts in Paul which show convincingly that this notion of « contemporaneity » was ever actually in Pauline thought [37].

This question of the « contemporaneity » of the Cross and the resurrection in the life of the modern Christian is a major issue in the writings of RUDOLF BULTMANN, and it may be said to play a major role in his proposals for the *Entmythologisierung* of the NT [38].

In the section of his synthesis of NT biblical theology [39] in which he deals with the Pauline conception of the salvation-occurrence, Bultmann asserts that this *Heilsgeschehen* consists in Christ's death and resurrection conceived as a single unity. This doctrine Paul had received from apostolic tradition. He received it moreover, formulated in a series of mythological representations, which may be reduced to three categories. Firstly, there is a group of texts which describe it under the myth of Jewish sacrificial practice and Jewish juridical thought : as a propitiatory sacrifice (Rom 3,25 f ; 5,9 ; 1 Cor 15,3 ; 2 Cor 5,14) ; as a vicarious sacrifice (Gal 3,13 ; 2 Cor 5,21 ; 2 Cor 5,14 ; Rom 8,3 etc.) ; as a « redemption », i. e. at once a cancellation of the debt incurred by sin and a release from the powers of Law, sin and death (Gal 3,13 ; 1,4 ; 1 Cor 6,20 ; 7,23). Secondly, the *Heilsgeschehen* is depicted by analogy with the death of the god in the Mystery cults. Here Bultmann equivalently admits that he is unable to find any precise textual examples [40]. Finally, Christ's death is interpreted by means of the gnostic Myth ; and thus the salvation-

---

[36] Paul understood this most realistically, HAHN claims. This « Gleichzeitigkeit » for Paul signifies « das reale Hineingenommenwerden in das einmalige, konkrete, geschichtliche Leiden, Sterben und Auferstehen Christi. Er ist die Einbeziehung der ganzen Existenz des Christen in dieses Heilsereignis », *op. cit.* 96.

[37] Cf. the criticisms levelled at the theory by R. SCHNACKENBURG, *Das Heilsgeschehen bei der Taufe nach dem Apostel Paulus* (München, 1950) 145-149 ; also P. BONNARD, *Où en est l' interprétation de l'épître aux Romains ?* in *RTheolPhil* Ser 3 1-2 (1951-1952) 233.

[38] Since I have discussed this whole question elsewhere, I take the liberty of referring the reader to my article : *Rudolf Bultmann : A Contemporary Challenge to the Catholic Theologian* in *CBQ* 19 (1957) 347-355. For a more thorough treatment of the question, see L. MALEVEZ, *Le message chrétien et le mythe* (Bruxelles-Bruges-Paris, 1954), and R. MARLÉ, *Bultmann et l' interprétation du Nouveau Testament* (Paris, 1956).

[39] RUDOLF BULTMANN, *Theologie des Neuen Testaments* (Tübingen, 1948) 287-301.

[40] *op. cit.* 293.

event takes on a cosmic character, which it has in the early Christian hymn cited in Phil 2,6-11 (2 Cor 5,14 ; 1 Cor 15,20-22). Paul was forced to express his soteriological thought by means of these last two classes of myth because the strictly Jewish mythological framework did not bring out the salvific meaning of Christ's resurrection.

How, for Bultmann, does the *Heilsgeschehen*, presented thus mythologically in the Pauline texts, become actual or capable of experience by man today ? By its being made contemporary in the preached word, which does not represent Christ's death and resurrection as past events but makes of them a present, eschatological happening. Moreover, it is by faith that man is enabled to give an affirmative response to the decision-question of the kerygma, and so makes the *Heilsgeschehen* a reality for himself.

Since Bultmann's attempt to « demythologize » the NT has been universally criticised and, on several of its key notions, judged unacceptable by Protestant no less than Catholic theologians [41], it is scarcely necessary here to repeat arguments which are familiar to all students of Scripture. One may simply ask whether Bultmann's exposé of Pauline soteriology, as summarized in the preceding paragraphs, which appears to centre the whole reality of Christ's redemptive death and resurrection in the preached word and to make its appropriation by the individual Christian the result of a Lutheran act of faith, gives an adequate or indeed a true picture of Paul's thought [42].

Thus far, we have been considering non-Catholic studies of Pauline soteriological thought and the place which Christ's resurrection occupies in it. We must now review the work of the Catholic theologians and scriptural scholars. Here, a rather curious fact is to be noted : with one or two exceptions, most Catholic writing on the subject is of quite recent origin. Indeed, it would not be an exaggeration to say that it comes from the last ten or twelve years.

---

[41] For the Protestant side, cf. *Kerygma und Mythos I : ein theologisches Gespräch* (Hamburg-Volksdorf, 1951) ; IAN HENDERSON, *Myth in the New Testament* (London, 1952) ; G. CASALIS, *Le problème du mythe* in *RHPhilRel* 31 (1951) 330-342. For the Catholic views, cf. RENÉ MARLÉ, *Bultmann et l' interprétation du Nouveau Testament* (Paris, 1956) ; *Kerygma und Mythos V : Die Theologie Bultmanns und die Entmythologisierung in der Kritik der katholischen Theologie* (Hamburg, 1955).

[42] Cf. the review of PIERRE BENOIT of Bultmann's *Theologie des Neuen Testaments* in *RB* 59 (1952) 93-100.

A possible explanation of this rather striking phenomenon may be found, I believe, in the great emphasis which Catholic post-Reformation theology has placed upon the satisfactory nature of Christ's redemptive death. The exigencies of controversy led to the formulation of apologetic arguments against the errors of Socinianism and Modernism ; and as a result, the treatise *De Deo Redemptore* has tended to be confined within juridical categories. The redemptive work of Christ is discussed in terms of merit, satisfaction, and sacrifice [43]. Such a conception is of course a valid one, and, given the need of defending Catholic doctrine, a very necessary one.

However, as becomes evident when we recall the larger frame of reference within which the thought of ST THOMAS on Christ's redemptive activity moves, this conception of the redemption as a meritorious or satisfactory work, which is concerned almost exclusively with the death of the Redeemer, gives only one aspect of the salvation-event [44]. While it does not fall within the scope of our present study to discuss St Thomas' soteriology [45], we wish to remark in passing that by examining Christ's salvific work in terms of efficient (as well as of meritorious) causality, Aquinas has been able to show how Christ's resurrection is related to his death as a « complementum salutis » [46].

In his classical work on Pauline theology, F. PRAT has consecrated several pages to the place which Christ's resurrection holds in Paul's soteriology [47]. Through his death, Christ accomplished but half his redemptive work [48]. Hence it is necessary also to consider the influence of his resurrection upon our justifying faith, of which the resurrection is the principal object, and upon the meaning and efficacy of Christian Baptism. As Père Prat makes clear, it is in the *application* of the redemp-

---

[43] Cf. J. FILOGRASSI, *De Christo Verbo Incarnato et Redemptore* (Roma, 1942) ; PAULUS GALTIER, *De Incarnatione et Redemptione* (Paris, 1947).

[44] Christ's resurrection enters into this conception as the consummation of the sacrifice of the Cross : cf. P. GALTIER, *op. cit.* 426, who devotes a brief *scholion* to the place of the resurrection in the redemption.

[45] The place of the redemptive resurrection in Thomistic thought has been recently discussed by S. LYONNET, *La valeur sotériologique de la résurrection du Christ selon saint Paul* in G 39 (1958) 301-304, and by F. HOLTZ, *La valeur sotériologique de la Résurrection du Christ d'après saint Thomas* in ETL 29 (1953) 609-647.

[46] *Summa Theologica* III, 53, 1.

[47] F. PRAT, *La Théologie de Saint Paul* II⁷ (Paris, 1923) 250-256.

[48] *ibid.* 252.

tion to the individual Christian that the resurrection exercises its causality. By his resurrection, Christ became « vivifying Spirit », i. e. received the power which he did not previously possess during his mortal life, of communicating the fulness of life to men [49].

Thus, on Prat's view, there is a double aspect to Christ's redemptive work, of which Paul is very much aware : what he did for all men, and what he continues to do for each individual. The first was effected by his redemptive death : the second is caused through his resurrection. This twofold function, described in the Pauline letters, is what explains the double series of texts which HOLTZMANN had found contradictory [50]. The work of Christ on Calvary Paul often describes in juridical and sacrificial terms : the work of the risen Christ is described in the so-called mystical passages.

While there can be no doubt that, for Prat, Christ's resurrection forms an « integral part of the redemption itself » [51], still he appears to restrict its causality (in Paul's writings) to what is often called the « subjective » redemption, the application to the individual of the fruits of Christ's « objective » redemptive work.

Here we must mention an early attempt on the part of a Catholic at writing a biblical theology of the redemption. R. G. BANDAS has reserved slightly less than ten pages to the place occupied by Christ's resurrection in the large volume he composed on Pauline redemption-theology [52]. Since in his treatment of the subject he follows the work of Père PRAT very closely, without going beyond it, it is unnecessary to summarize Bandas' position.

ALFREDO VITTI, in an article which criticised the theories of SOMMERLATH, MÉNÉGOZ, and CORNELIUS A LAPIDE, underscored the role of the risen Christ as « operatore efficiente » of man's justification, thus restricting the efficient causality of Christ's resurrection to the application of the fruits of his redemptive work [53]. He describes this operation of the risen Lord, first, in terms of Christ's sacerdotal mediation as presented by the epistle to the Hebrews, and secondly, by means of

---

[49] *ibid.* 253.

[50] *ibid.* 254-256.

[51] *ibid.* 256.

[52] RUDOLPH G. BANDAS, *The Master-Idea of Saint Paul's Epistles, or the Redemption : A Study of Biblical Theology* (Bruges, 1925).

[53] ALFREDO VITTI, *La Resurrezione di Gesù e la Soteriologia di S. Paolo* in *CC* 120 (1930) 97-109 ; 298-314.

Christ's activity as the new Adam or « vivifying Spirit » which began
« nel momento della sua Resurrezione ».

A. JANSSENS discussed the soteriological value of Christ's resurrection first with regard to Baptism, which depends on it as well as on
Jesus' redemptive death for its efficacy and its signification [54]. We owe
our solidarity with Christ to his risen humanity as well as to his sacrifice. Moreover, Christ's resurrection has, properly speaking, effected our
salvation « quantum ad inchoationem et exemplar bonorum » [55]. Thus
Janssens would appear to admit that the resurrection exercised a kind
of exemplary causality in the « objective » redemption.

A somewhat similar position was adopted by A. VAN HOVE, who
finds a « valor completivus » in the mysteries of the resurrection and
the ascension with respect to Christian salvation [56]. While it is only
Christ's work as a « viator » which is meritorious, one cannot deny all
redemptive significance to these acts which followed his death. Van Hove
suggests a twofold interpretation of Rom 4,25 : first, in the line of exem-
plarity, then, in terms of the application of the redemption to the
Christian.

A. HULSBOSCH has, in three articles [57], provided a more thorough-going
treatment of the place assigned to Christ's resurrection in Paul's thought.
He begins by analysing the Pauline notions of death and of life.
Where the scholastic theologian will describe the relation between sin
and death as one of *culpa* to *poena*, Paul posits an ontological connection between physical death and the loss of grace. He connects corporeal
resurrection with grace-glory in a similar way. For Paul, physical death
and bodily resurrection are symbols of the absence or presence of the
life of grace [58]. By a careful exegetical examination of Rom 5,12-15 and
Wis 2,23-24, Hulsbosch shows that life and death are the visible manifestation in man of his greatest good or greatest penalty [59].

---

[54] A. JANSSENS, *De valore soteriologico resurrectionis Christi* in *ETL* 9 (1932)
225-233.

[55] *ibid.* 228.

[56] A. VAN HOVE, *De valore soteriologico resurrectionis et ascensionis Christi*
in *ColMech* 6 (1932) 191-194.

[57] A. HULSBOSCH, *Conceptus paulini Vitae ac Mortis* in *DTP* 47-49 (1944-
46) 35-55 ; *Resurrectio Christi in doctrina soteriologica S. Pauli, ibid.* 193-206 ;
Passibilitas et Mors Christi in doctrina soteriologica S. Pauli ibid. 207-227.

[58] *ibid.* 36.

[59] *ibid.* 45. A further proof that such is Paul's mentality is offered by a
consideration of the notion of « life » in 2 Cor 4,16 ; 3,18 ; 1,22 ; 5,4 f ; Eph, 1,13 f.

Hulsbosch now applies these concepts to Christ's resurrection [60]. On the characteristically Semitic view of Paul, salvation affects man in his entire corporeal personality and is to be found, consequently, in its fulness only in bodily resurrection [61]. Paul's conception of Christ's death is also typically Jewish. While it cannot, as in other men, denote a lack of grace, still Christ in death is *like* a sinner ; and hence, he appears, in his risen state, as the first of the redeemed. Indeed, Christ's resurrection, which is an essential part of the redemption, constitutes « that very messianic salvation » which men had so long sought [62].

In a final article, Hulsbosch discusses the meaning of God's « condemnation of sin in the flesh » (Rom 8,3). From the fundamental Pauline soteriological principle of man's solidarity with Christ (the fruit of Paul's Damascus experience) [63], it follows that Christ's *transitus* to the state of glory is equivalently his redemption as « first man » and becomes, in consequence, the possession *de jure* of all humanity. The Father's « condemnation of sin in the flesh » was (to the mind of Paul) not accomplished by the incarnation, which is rather a « concessio erga peccatum » [64]. Nor does the death of Christ fully account for this condemnation [65]. One may rightly speak of a « condemnation of sin in the flesh »

---

[60] Cf. the important prenote (*ibid.* 193) in which HULSBOSCH states that he is not considering the meritorious aspect of Christ's death.

[61] Friendship with God in this life is of course possible, but full salvation can be had only by the whole man. HULSBOSCH does not refer to Eph 2,5.8, where Paul states that God has already saved us.

[62] *ibid.* 199. It is primarily 1 Cor 15 which enables HULSBOSCH to demonstrate the function of Christ's resurrection in the redemption. In the Pauline opposition set up between Christ and Adam (1 Cor 15,44b-45), Adam is not considered as a sinner, but merely as first parent as he came from God's creative hands. It is thus as two proto-parents that Adam and Christ are contrasted, not as author of sin and its vanquisher (*ibid.* 204). Moreover, the human nature which Christ received from Adam appears entirely restored, so that it cannot now be called by its old name : it is henceforth designated necessarily as spirit, since the Spirit has taken full control of Christ's humanity (*ibid.* 206). Although Christ personally possessed the fulness of the Spirit from the moment of his conception, he is nevertheless only the source (for men) of the Spirit after his resurrection.

[63] *ibid.* 207-208.

[64] *ibid.* 217.

[65] *ibid.* 218 : « Non enim intelligitur quomodo peccatum per mortem alicuius damnaretur ; e contrario est doctrina certissima S. Pauli mortem esse stipendium peccati ... mors ergo Christi potius est dominatio ab ipso peccato exercita quam damnatio eidem inflicta ». HULSBOSCH appears here to neglect that idea which is

only when that flesh, in which sin has in a certain sense exercised its
dominion, is changed into something better. This was accomplished in
Christ's sacred humanity through his rising from death [66].

W. GOOSSENS considers Christ's resurrection and ascension as the
« complementum redemptionis » because they comprise the Redeemer's
own exaltation and manifest God's approval of his redemptive work [67].
The risen Christ is the exemplary cause, the pledge, and the « princi-
pium resurrectionis justorum » [68]. As we have already noted, this is the
most common view of Catholic theologians.

JOSEPH BONSIRVEN may, I believe, be rightly considered to have
made a really new and most important contribution to Catholic thought
regarding the position of Christ's resurrection in the « objective » redemption [69]. Bonsirven's innovation consisted principally in the re-orientation
which he gave to Catholic soteriology by providing a new conception of
the « objective » redemption, as the following definitions will illustrate.
The word « redemption » for Paul does not necessarily connote the idea
of ransom, which its etymology might suggest. It signifies the more comprehensive process by which God in Christ grants man those supernatural
gifts which are to culminate in eternal happiness [70]. The Pauline term,
« salvation », embraces all the spiritual goods which are given to the
Christian in Jesus Christ [71]. « Grace » is simply the common element in
those various acts whereby God raises man to himself [72]. According to
Bonsirven, the « objective » redemption may be described simply as a
triumph in positive terms of divine grace. God exalts his Son and with
him the people he has acquired for himself, reconciling them to himself
and giving them his Spirit [73]. Christ's part in this process consists of a

---

also characteristically Pauline, that Christ, by dying, has changed the very nature
of death for the Christian ; cf. however *ibid.* 220.

[66] Thus there is a close connection between Christ's death and resurrection
in the entire work of the redemption. HULSBOSCH understands the « justifying »
of Christ mentioned in 1 Tm 3,16 as due to his resurrection ; he is also aware
of texts like Rom 4,25 ; 2 Cor 5,15 ; Eph 2,4f ; Col 2,12 ; 3,1.

[67] W. GOOSSENS, *De Valore soteriologico Resurrectionis et Ascensionis Christi*
in *ColG* 24 (1937) 9-17.

[68] *ibid.* 15.

[69] JOSEPH BONSIRVEN, *L' Évangile de Paul* (Paris, 1948). We refer here particularly to ch. 4 : *Le Christ, Médiateur, reçoit la grâce*, 143 ff.

[70] *ibid.* 145.

[71] *ibid.* 146.

[72] *ibid.* 147.

[73] *ibid.* 156.

series of « gestes rédempteurs » : his incarnation, his mortal life, and especially his death, his resurrection (« aussi comme déterminante ») [74]. Any synthesis of Pauline thought on the redemption must take cognizance of all these redemptive « gestures » [75].

JOSEPH SCHMITT devotes a chapter of his study of the place of the risen Jesus in the apostolic preaching to St Paul's thought on Christ's resurrection [76]. For Paul, the passion and the resurrection are simply two acts of the same redemptive work (2 Cor 5,15 ; Rom 4,25). The risen Christ is source of justice by the fact that he is object of faith (1 Cor 15,13-14), confers life upon the believer (1 Cor 15,17-18.45). This last text contains the central idea of Pauline soteriology : the contrast of Christ with Adam. As « vivifying Spirit », Christ is at once the source and the type of our salvation [77]. The Christian life which consists of union with the risen Christ and to which the Christian is admitted by Baptism has three aspects : an « objective » aspect, incorporation into Christ ; a « subjective » aspect, the possession of the Spirit ; and a « mystical » aspect, the presence of Christ in the believer. There are three Pauline formulae which correspond to this threefold view of Christian existence : « in Christo », « in Spiritu », « Christus in nobis » [78]. In addition, Paul views the work of salvation as a collective grace [79]. Hence the prominence of the Pauline themes of Christ as « last Adam » and of the Church as « Body of Christ », the second being a corollary of the first.

One regrets the brevity and consequent vagueness of Schmitt's remarks on the function of Christ's resurrection in Paul's soteriological thought. However, it was obviously to go beyond the limits of his sub-

---

[74] I find it impossible to agree that Paul really included Christ's incarnation in the actual work of the redemption. Texts like Gal 4,4 ff and Rom 8,3 appear to give the customary Pauline view of the incarnation as a prerequisite for, rather than a constitutive element of, Christ's salvific activity.

[75] *ibid* 156.

[76] JOSEPH SCHMITT, *Jésus ressuscité dans la prédication apostolique* (Paris, 1949), *Le Christ ressuscité, principe de vie spirituelle*, 216-240.

[77] *ibid.* 228.

[78] « In Christo » connotes the objective aspect of the Christian life : our incorporation into Christ ; « In Spiritu », the subjective : the possession of the Spirit ; « Christus in nobis », the mystical : the presence of the Lord in the faithful. Of this insight, PIERRE BENOIT in his review of Schmitt's book, *RB* 57 (1950) 270, remarks, « Voilà qui est bien vu et bien dit ».

[79] *ibid.* 235-6.

ject to give more than the broad outline of Paul's view of the redemption.

F. X. DURRWELL has undertaken a more thorough-going development of Pauline soteriology in his study of Christ's resurrection as the mystery of salvation [80]. The scope of this book, as a biblical theology of Christ's resurrection based on the entire NT, goes far beyond the limits of our present study. Accordingly, we shall refer only to those sections dealing with Paul's theology. Moreover, the monograph is presented as a synthesis, and the question of Paul's doctrinal development is left unexplored [81]. The first three chapters deal with the salvific character of Christ's resurrection, its relation to the incarnation and death of Jesus, its meaning as the outpouring of the Spirit. The next four chapters discuss the effects of the resurrection in Christ, in the Church, in her life and history. The two final chapters describe the sacraments in their relation to the resurrection and the heavenly consummation of the supernatural life which the resurrection bestows.

In contrast with John, whose soteriology has the incarnation of the Son as its *point de départ*, Paul regards the risen Christ as an absolute beginning and considers that the Christian salvation-principle is constituted by his resurrection. The proper understanding of Rom 4,25 lies « en pleine efficience salutaire » [82]. The glorified Christ is man's only means of access to the justice of God [83]. The baptismal texts of Romans and Colossians show that our act of justifying faith, uniting us to Christ's death and resurrection, is a single act. So too is the Father's justifying

---

[80] F. X. DURRWELL, *La Résurrection de Jésus, mystère de salut*[2] (Le Puy-Paris, 1954).

[81] DURRWELL outlines his method on pp. 10-11 of his book. One cannot help but feel, however, that the value of this study would have been enhanced considerably by some attention to the historical development of this most important NT theme.

[82] *op. cit.* 41. The part played by the Father in man's justification is analogous to his role in the destruction of sin. While death expiates sin, justice is given to man only in consequence of the resurrection (*ibid.* 42). This is precisely the point to be elucidated if Ambrosiaster's error is to be avoided : for the details of this interpretation, cf. our study *Ad historiam exegeseos Rom* 4,25 in *VD* 29 (1951) 262.

[83] *op. cit.* 46. It is to be observed that, although DURRWELL implies that Christ's resurrection forms part of the act of man's redemption with Christ's death, his ultimate explanation of this text appears to be in terms of the application of the fruits of the redemption .

act through Baptism. Hence it would appear that Christ's act of dying and rising is also somehow one act. The formula « in Christo » connotes our vital union with the glorified Christ, not with Christ in his earthly life. While it is true that the baptismal texts speak of our union with Christ's death and burial, still the death we put on in Baptism is found in the Christ of glory. « Cum Christo » identifies the Father's justifying act in Baptism with his raising of Christ.

For Paul, the redemption is a drama enacted first and foremost in Christ himself. It is a sanctifying transformation from the state of sinful flesh to that of the holiness of the divine life. The kenosis described by Phil 2,6 ff is not to be identified with the incarnation (even in his glorified state, Christ remains man), nor with the passion precisely, but with a condition of physical existence modelled upon the life of ordinary human beings, which is closely bound up with sin. The terms « flesh » and « death », like « sin » denote separation from God. Death can only be the termination of sinful flesh when it is consummated in the glorification produced by the resurrection. Hence this transformation, which is the redemption effected by death and glorification, is a single mystery. Thus Christ's resurrection is also the mystery of the incarnation in the fulness of its glory [84].

The redemptive character of the resurrection may best be described as an outpouring of the Spirit. The relation of the glorified Christ to the Spirit is a triple one : he is raised by the Spirit, is transformed by the Spirit, and becomes source of the Spirit for the Christian [85].

The effects of the resurrection for Christ himself may be seen by Paul's use of the titles « Lord » and « Son of God in power ». It is in the Pauline letters that the title *Kyrios* expresses, more exactly than in more primitive Christian formulae, the divinity of Christ as revealed in his resurrection and the universal nature of his sovereignty. « Son of God » attains its full theological meaning with the event of Christ's resurrection since it is really a birth to a new life.

The birth of the Church occurred in the resurrection of Christ inasmuch as thereby (1) Christ became head of the Church, as the new Adam, and (2) his glorified Body is the principle of the Church as « Body of Christ » [86]. The Church's life « in Christo » means that the faithful

---

[84] *op. cit.* 78.
[85] *ibid.* 115-131.
[86] *ibid.* 200-220.

2. - D. M. STANLEY.

share « a community of being and of life with the glorified Christ » [87], without however « realizing complete identity » with him [88]. The Church possesses her life also « in Spiritu », since it is the Spirit who works man's salvation by « including our humanity in that of the risen Saviour » [89]. The formula « cum Christo » tells us that the Church is the Body of Christ « in the act of his death and resurrection » [90].

The effects of Christ's resurrection may be also seen in the means whereby the Church grows : the apostolate, Baptism, and the Eucharist, are the risen Christ's instruments ; faith, Christian effort, suffering, and death constitute the Church's means of assimilating the paschal mystery [91].

This splendid NT theology of the resurrection has justly won the praise of reviewers [92]. It constitutes an important milestone in the progress of Catholic thought on the Christian mystery of salvation.

Attention to the developmental aspects of Paul's theology and a presentation of that theology in its historical phases, features which were entirely absent from Durrwell's study, are the outstanding qualities of LUCIEN CERFAUX's masterly study of Pauline Christology [93]. Since however, this book has a much wider range than the question which is the object of our own present study, we shall content ourselves with giving only a broad outline of Cerfaux's conception of the position of Christ in Paul's theology.

Cerfaux finds three stages in the development of this theology. The first, the period prior to the founding of the Corinthian community, was a re-thinking of the theology of the primitive (Jerusalem) community. It represents Christ as the « agent of salvation » in which the resurrection holds the central place as prelude to the parousia, on the one hand, and, on the other, as the introduction into the present Christian existence of the sanctifying forces of the future life. The antitheses which

---

[87] *ibid.* 253.
[88] *ibid.* 255.
[89] *ibid.* 261.
[90] *ibid.* 263.
[91] *ibid.* 358-361 ; 366-368 ; 372-380.
[92] Cf. the following reviews of the first (1950) edition : SPICQ in *RSPT* 35 (1951) 53 ff ; DE WAILLY in *VSp* 84 (1951) 541 ff ; LEVIE in *NRT* 73 (1951) 659 ff ; BRINKMANN in *S* 26 (1951) 659 ff. One dissenting voice was that of JOSEPH BONSIRVEN in *Bib* 32 (1951) 458 ff.
[93] L. CERFAUX, *Le Christ dans la théologie de saint Paul* (Paris, 1951).

form the axes of Paul's thought at this period are parousia-resurrection and death-life. This initial stage is represented by the two Thessalonian letters and the final section of 1 Corinthians which deals with the problem of the resurrection of the just.

Paul's experience at Athens and his work in Corinth led to the second stage of his theological evolution. These crises inspired a new theology of the passion. This period, represented by 1,2 Corinthians, Galatians and Romans, is a controversial one, in which Paul battles with the Judaizers and with paganism. Against the first group of adversaries, the Apostle insists that Christ has put an end to the Mosaic Law and is author of Christian justice : against the effects of paganism still remaining in the minds of his Corinthian Christians, he asserts that Christianity is not to be equated with Greek philosophy or Greek Mystery religions. Christ now appears as God's gift to men, as justice, wisdom, holiness, life. The literary antitheses, Cerfaux finds, which are characteristic of this stage, are Christ-Abraham, Christ-Adam [94], and flesh-spirit. The orientation of this theological period is best described by the term « mystical ».

In the final stage, which Cerfaux connects with Paul's Ephesian ministry, the idea of « mystery » holds the centre of interest. This, the most properly Christological period in Pauline theology, is reflected in the Capitivity epistles (among which Cerfaux appears to consider Philippians as contemporary with Colossians and Ephesians) and is best described as « cosmic » The presence of certain hymns in these letters indicates that the Christian mysteries are now contemplated in connection with Christian cult. There is emphasis placed upon the idea of knowledge in Christian faith.

Such a brief summary of this most important book scarcely does justice to the wealth of erudition and careful analyses of key-texts which it contains. We have wished simply to point out some of the main ideas presented by Cerfaux which have been of considerable help in our present study [95].

---

[94] With regard to this theme and its place in Paul's thought, CERFAUX (op. cit. 401 f) remarks : « Le Christ mystique serait un Christ collectif : autre formule que l'on combine avec celle du second Adam et de l' Église corps du Christ. Sans nier que la pensée paulinienne touche à sa périphérie à ces thèmes, nous ne voyons pas que l' intelligence de la théologie historique gagne à élaborer une synthèse en les plaçant au point de départ ».

[95] At the same time, we must admit that we cannot follow CERFAUX on certain important points. Thus we feel that Phil was written before 1 Cor. Also,

BRUCE VAWTER has sought to determine the place which Christ's resurrection holds in the work of man's redemption [96]. From a consideration of 1 Cor 15, 13-17, which is to be understood in relation with 1 Cor 15,45, where the risen Christ is called « life-giving Spirit », and from Rom 4,25, which connects man's spiritual regeneration with Christ's resurrection, Vawter concludes that there is a direct causal relation between the resurrection and the forgiveness of sins.

The most recent article bearing on our theme is by STANISLAS LYON-NET, who discusses the soteriological value of Christ's resurrection according to Paul [97]. Actually the principal aim of this study is to convince the dogmatic theologian that, to do justice to Pauline thought, he must consider Christ's resurrection as forming an integral and essential part with Christ's death in the « objective » redemption. Lyonnet reviews the history of the exegesis of Rom 4,25 to conclude that Paul affirms that Christ's resurrection exerts a real causal effect in man's justification. According to the modern, juridical view of the redemption, which confines itself to the category of merit, only the death of Christ can be said to constitute the « objective » redemption ; and hence, on such premises, any causality attributed to Christ's resurrection must form part of the « subjective » redemption.

Lyonnet solves this difficulty by re-defining « objective » and « subjective » redemption in terms of efficient causality. The first is simply the sacred humanity of Christ become capable of justifying men, i. e. of being used as instrument by his divinity for this purpose. This stage comprises all Christ's mysteries, especially his death and glorification. The second definition is verified when this instrumental causality is effectively exercised upon the individual Christian by faith and the sacraments.

While Paul never thought in terms of instrumental causality, still it is possible to find a conception of the redemption in Paul's letters

---

we find it difficult to accept his view (*op. cit.* 120 ff) that Paul began to insist upon the Cross only at Corinth. The Apostle's first encounter with judaizing Christian pharisaism was, after all, at Antioch (Acts 15,1 ff). We find the same difficulty with his explanation of the *Sitz im Leben* of Col, Eph : why does Paul's experience of Jewish or Jewish Christian thought not appear in the « greater » letters which are more or less contemporary with his Ephesian sojourn ? Cerfaux (*op. cit.* 8) has apparently felt this difficulty himself.

[96] BRUCE VAWTER, *Resurrection and Redemption* in CBQ 15 (1953) 11-23.
[97] S. LYONNET, *La valeur sotériologique de la résurrection du Christ selon saint Paul* in G 39 (1958) 295-318.

which corresponds to it. Paul represents the redemptive work of Christ essentially as man's return to God from whom sin had irrevocably separated him. This « return » was effected by Christ who underwent death and resurrection as first fruits of the human race (1 Cor 15,20). It was effected in each Christian who dies and rises, in turn, with Christ in Baptism (Rom 6,3-4).

This « return » of humanity to God in Christ did not operate as a kind of biological process, but inasmuch as it was Christ's supreme expression of obedience to the Father and love for men. This shows the indivisible unity of the mystery of our redemption : Christ's death as an expression of his divine love (which by definition is simply divine life) implies the resurrection, since it is supremely efficacious and life-giving, firstly with regard to Christ's own humanity, and secondly with regard to all who are drawn into solidarity with him.

It is to be regretted that the narrow limits of a single article did not permit Père Lyonnet to illustrate in more detailed fashion the excellent principles for a solution of the problem which Pauline thought on the redemption has presented to so many exegetes and theologians, insofar as Paul appears to assign a place of paramount importance to Christ's resurrection in his redemptive work.

We may say quite frankly that the present study is nothing more than an attempt to fill in the details omitted by Père LYONNET, to verify in our own way the conception of Pauline soteriology which he has sketched, and to show, by tracing Paul's development through the various stages reflected by his epistles, how his grasp of the entire Christian reality was undoubtedly helped by an ever deepening understanding of the function of Christ's resurrection.

Before we can attempt to deal with texts in the Pauline letters which are germane to our subject, we must endeavour to situate our problem historically : firstly, within the general milieu of apostolic Christianity, which provided Paul with the Christian doctrinal tradition to which he so closely adhered ; secondly, within the Christian experiences of the Apostle himself, that is, his conversion, his work as a preacher of the Gospel.

Moreover, we must attempt to situate chronologically those Pauline epistles whose authenticity is more commonly admitted, viz. 1,2 Thes, Phil, 1,2 Cor, Gal, Rom, Col, Eph [98]. We shall also discuss their rela-

---

[98] Since the soteriological texts which appear in 1,2 Tm, and Ti do not appear to us to represent any notable advance beyond the development reflected in

tionship to the various crises through which their author passed, since
these events will, we feel, be found to have been a formative influence
on the growth of Paul's theology.

Although the authorship of the Pastoral epistles is so frequently
denied to Paul, we consider it necessary to devote a chapter to the
discussion of certain passages found in these letters which appear to
be citations of, or allusions to, credal formulae antedating the Pastorals.
These may well be Paul's own compositions. At any rate, they seem to
reflect his characteristic theological outlook.

We begin our study with three preliminary chapters, which are concerned respectively with (1) the position occupied by Christ's resurrection
in the primitive apostolic preaching, (2) the nature of the Gospel as
Paul habitually preached it, and (3) the general lines along which Paul's
soteriological doctrine developed in the course of his epistles.

---

the commonly accepted Pauline epistles, we feel justified in prescinding from the
very delicate and difficult question of their authenticity, i. e. whether they come
from Paul's pen immediately, or only mediately (being composed by one of Paul's
companions who was allowed an unusual amount of liberty in writing them).

CHAPTER I

CHRIST'S RESURRECTION IN THE PRIMITIVE PREACHING

Just as Israelite religion was born of the experience of the living God which the *qahal* of Israel was privileged to undergo in the deliverance out of Egypt and, perhaps pre-eminently, in the theophany-promulgation of the Sinaitic covenant [1], so the faith of the apostolic community was awakened to life by the Pentecostal experience of the living Spirit [2]. Accordingly, in attempting to sketch the salient features of the apostolic preaching from the data provided us in Acts, we shall begin by endeavouring to form some estimate of the revolutionary change which the coming of the Holy Spirit worked in the hearts of the first Christians.

§ 1. - The Pentecostal Revolution

For forty days after his resurrection, Christ had visited the little group of disciples to convince them of the reality of his risen body, to

---

[1] GERHARD VON RAD, *Das erste Buch Mose : Kap.* 1-12/9 [2] (Göttingen, 1950) 34. D. M. STANLEY, *The New Testament Doctrine of Baptism : an Essay in Biblical Theology* in TS 18 (1957) 179 : « However, the OT view was that the covenant was primary in God's self-revelation to Israel. The point of departure of OT religion was, historically speaking, summed up in the dictum, ' You shall be my people, and I will be your God ' (Jer 31, 33 ; Ex 19,5) ».

[2] The fourth evangelist, who records Jesus' promise of the Spirit who was to « lead them along the way to the complete truth » (Jn 16,13), insists that this gift of Christian understanding was the consequence of Jesus' glorification (Jn 7,39). Luke underscores the same connection by his reiteration of the command to remain in Jerusalem (Lk 24,49 ; Acts 1,4). Moreover, as we have pointed out elsewhere, it is only after, and as a result of, the Spirit's descent (according to NT evidence) that the disciples are permitted to collaborate in Jesus' mission of *teaching* : cf. *Didache as a Constitutive Element of the Gospel-Form* in CBQ 17 (1955) 223-244.

« speak with them of the Kingdom of God » (Acts 1,3), to instruct them
in the meaning of his death by « opening their minds to the understanding of the Scriptures » (Lk 24,44-49), and to assure them of the gift
of the Holy Spirit, the promise of the Father (Lk 24,49 ; Acts 1,5.8).

Acts describes the little group of disciples, who returned to Jerusalem
after the Lord's ascension, as already sufficiently large to form, according to Jewish law, a distinct community (Acts 1,15), with a « sanhedrin » composed of the apostles [3]. The latter appear to be fully aware
of their commission, which is to witness to Christ's resurrection both to
the Jews and within the community of believers [4]. Indeed it is with
this in mind that they elect a twelfth member to the apostolic college as
a replacement for the unfortunate Judas (Acts 1,25-26).

Yet the limitations of the apostles' realization of the nature of Christ's
work as Saviour and of his plans for their future ministry appear clearly
in Luke's account. Their question put to the ascending Christ, « Lord,
is it at this time that you will restore the sovereignty to Israel ? » (Acts
1,6), betrays a crassly material view of the Kingdom of God. It may
well be, as WIKENHAUSER has pointed out [5], that Matthias' election
was motivated by the apostles' concern to fill each of the twelve thrones
which, as Jesus had promised, they were to occupy in the great eschatological judgment of Israel. Moreover, it may well be also that the
disciples conjectured that their own baptism with the Spirit was to usher
in his parousia, the glorious second Coming of the Lord, of which the
angels has spoken on the day of his ascension (Acts 1,11).

The descent of the Holy Ghost transformed this little nucleus of
ignorant, timid Jews into the Christian Church. St. Luke has taken pains
to underscore the revolutionary character of the event. Two facts emerge
clearly from his *récit* (Acts 2,1-13) : the community was caught up in
ecstasy and began to pray « in other tongues » ; they were moreover
endowed with the gift of prophecy [6], a charism which is exemplified in

---

[3] As Dom JACQUES DUPONT remarks in his note on this verse : cf. L. CERFAUX,
J. DUPONT, *Les Actes des Apôtres*[2], *BJ* (Paris, 1958) 39.

[4] L. CERFAUX, *La communauté apostolique*[2] (Paris, 1953) 26 ff.

[5] A. WIKENHAUSER, *Die Apostelgeschichte*[2] (Regensburg, 1951) 30.

[6] This charism is, I believe, to be distinguished from the gift of « tongues »,
which was essentially a form of ecstatic prayer (cf. the accounts of a repetition of
the phenomenon at Caesarea, Acts 10,46, and at Ephesus, Acts 19,6). Luke has so
closely interwoven the data of two sources in composing his *récit* of the first Pentecost
(one describing the charism of « tongues », another referring to Peter's discourse)

the Petrine discourse to the assembled multitude (Acts 2,14-36). In other words, the beginning of Christianity, at least on Luke's view, must be traced back to this tremendous experience of the living Spirit.

The most palpable change in the disciples' attitude is their new-found awareness that the messianic times have been inaugurated *by the descent of the Spirit and not by Christ's second Coming.* Peter voices this conviction when he declares that it was of this hour that Joel had spoken in prophesying that Yahweh's Spirit would be poured forth, prophecy would again return to Israel, and salvation would come to all men through the Name of the Lord, that is, of the risen Christ. Joel had also foretold the creation of the messianic community, filled with the Spirit, which was to constitute « the little remnant of Israel » (Jl 2,32b,c) [7].

On the evidence of Peter's speeches in Acts, it appears that the disciples fully realized the redemptive character of Christ's passion, death, and resurrection only as a consequence of the coming of the Holy Ghost. Part of the Pentecostal revelation, it appears, was that this ineffable experience of the advent of the Spirit was the direct result of Christ's celestial exaltation to the Father's right hand (Acts 2,33). This divinely-communicated knowledge of Jesus' *sessio ad dexteram Patris* was, genetically, the foundation of the Christian faith in his divinity and also in his mission as Saviour of the world. The second of Peter's discourses reported by Luke contains a remark which has not perhaps received the attention it deserves. « Having raised his Servant, God has sent him to you, first and foremost, to bless you by turning each one of you from his evil ways » (Acts 3,26). This remarkable statement sheds much light upon the psychological process by which the apostles came to conceive the redemptive character of Jesus' death and resurrection. *They first learned to recognize him as Redeemer through his sending of the Spirit* (God sends his risen Servant, Peter declares, to bless them in the person

---

as to give the (unwarranted) impression to not a few of the ancient commentators that when Peter preached he spoke « in tongues ». On the interpretation of this latter gift, cf. S. Lyonnet, *De glossolalia Pentecostes eiusque significatione* in *VD* 24 (1944) 65-75 ; also A. Wikenhauser, *op. cit.* 34 ff., *Das Reden in Zungen* (« Zungenreden »).

[7] It is instructive to observe that Luke, with his characteristic interest in the universality of the Christian Church, does not cite this part of the prophecy. He was probably already aware of the exclusivist tendency which the Remnant-doctrine could produce in Jewish-Christian communities.

of the Spirit). They were led by this mission of the Holy Ghost to recognize Jesus' exaltation « to God's right hand » : that is, they acknowledged fully, for the first time, Jesus' divinity. Further reflection revealed to them the salvific character of the two principal acts of Jesus' career amongst them : his death and resurrection. At first, as we shall observe in considering the Jerusalem kerygma, the expression of these great mysteries was halting and imperfect. The full thinking-out of Christian soteriology must await the conversion of Saul of Tarsus.

We must now turn to the accounts of Peter's preaching in Acts, in order to study in detail the modalities of the message proclaimed by the Jerusalem community.

§ 2. - The Kerygma of the Jerusalem Community

Before investigating the role assigned to Christ's resurrection in the earliest examples of the apostolic preaching, we must say a word about the *authenticity* of the speeches in Acts [8], and also about the distinction between *preaching* and *teaching* which, as C. H. DODD has pointed out [9], is made by the writers of the NT.

The essential authenticity of these speeches is nowadays admitted amongst critics [10]. By this we mean that if, on the one hand, the view that the discourses are simply free compositions by Luke is more and more being abandoned, the tendency is to consider the sermons to « represent, not indeed what Peter said upon this or that occasion, but the *kerygma* of the Church at Jerusalem at an early period » [11]. This nuanced opinion, which is not unacceptable to the Catholic critics, we may make our own inasmuch as it sufficiently safeguards the question of authenticity as far as our present purposes are concerned. JOSEPH SCHMITT

---

[8] In speaking of authenticity here, two extremes must be avoided : on the one hand, it is historically implausible that these speeches recorded by Luke are verbatim accounts of what was said on this or that occasion ; on the other hand, it is an exaggeration to maintain that the Lukan discourses are the same genre as those found in Thucydides.

[9] C. H. DODD, *The Apostolic Preaching and Its Developments*[2] (London, 1950).

[10] Cf. the nuanced statements of PIERRE BENOIT, *Les origines du Symbole des Apôtres dans le Nouveau Testament* in *LumVi* § 2,39-60 ; also BERTIL GAERTNER, *The Areopagus Speech and Natural Revelation* (Uppsala, 1955) 7-36.

[11] C. H. DODD, *op. cit.* 21.

in his splendid study of the primitive preaching defends a stricter authenticity [12]. However, as he has admitted, in a more recent article [13],
the presence of Hellenistic elements, even in the Pentecostal address of
St. Peter, it seems better to leave room for this broader interpretation
of the historical character of these discourses.

The question of the distinction made throughout the NT between
preaching and *teaching* we have discussed elsewhere [14]. Consequently, it
will be sufficient here to draw attention to the conclusions arrived at,
insofar as they apply to the discourses of Acts and the letters of St.
Paul. *Preaching* may be defined, after DODD, as « the public proclamation
of Christianity to the non-Christian world » [15]. It is centred upon the
redemptive death and exaltation of Jesus as the inauguration of the
messianic era ; and to this essential kerygma there is prefixed a survey
of Jesus' public ministry, introduced by the work of John the Baptist.
The preaching ends with a call to μετάνοια, which is specified as
Christian by the act of faith in Jesus' divinity and messiahship, and
concretized in the aggregation to the Christian community by the reception of Baptism.

Teaching (διδαχή) gives to the convert, who has already responded
to the preaching by an act of faith, a deeper theological insight into
the meaning of the kerygmatic proclamation. It bears a close relation
to the full Christian understanding of « the Scriptures » [16]. It explains
the nature of the Kingdom which has come in the messianic community
and instructs the disciple in the salvific meaning of the events of Jesus'
life which brought it about. The Pauline epistles furnish one of the best
examples of this *teaching*, inasmuch as they contain abundant instances
of a more profound explanation of the truths of the Christian faith,
which results in the living of these dogmas in a fully fruitful manner.

This distinction between κήρυγμα and διδαχή will be particularly
useful in helping us reconstruct the *Gospel* of Paul as distinguished from
his *teaching*. But it will also be necessary to apply the distinction to

---

[12] JOSEPH SCHMITT, *Jésus ressuscité dans la prédication apostolique* (Paris,
1949) 19 ff.

[13] JOSEPH SCHMITT, *Les sources et les thèmes de la naissante foi apostolique au
Christ Sauveur* in *LumVi* § 15 (1954) 314-16.

[14] This is the article referred to already in n. 2 : *CBQ* 17 (1955) 223-244. It
will be noted that I have differed from the interpretation of Dodd.

[15] DODD, *op. cit.* 3.

[16] KARL HEINRICH RENGSTORF, διδάσκω *TWNT II*, 148.

the discourses in Acts which represent the Jerusalem version of the Gospel. For, while it remains true that preaching and teaching signify different activities, still very rarely, if ever, will the kerygma be found in a pure state without some admixture of διδαχή.

What are the principal points of the Jerusalem preaching ? The answer to this question lies in an analysis of Peter's sermons in Acts (Acts 2,14-36 ; 3,12-26 ; 4,8-12 ; 10,34-43).

The Petrine address on the day of Pentecost begins with an explanation, based on a citation of Joel, of the phenomenon of the glossolaly, suited to the occasion. It contains however a point which is capital to the kerygma : the « last times », that is, the messianic period, have arrived (Acts 2,14-21) [17]. Peter next recalls the miracles of the public life (v. 22) : Jesus proved himself, like the prophets his predecessors, a « man accredited by God ». His death by crucifixion at the hands of pagans is laid at the door of the Jews, although it was admittedly « according to the determined will and foreknowledge of God » (v. 23). God raised Jesus from the dead « delivering him from the horrors of Hades » (v. 24). Ps. 16 gives testimony to the impossibility of Christ's experiencing death's ultimate victory over man, corruption (vv. 25-28). Moreover, David was permitted to foresee Jesus' resurrection because God had sworn that the Messias should be of his line and should sit upon his royal throne (vv. 29-31). The apostolic testimony to the resurrection is solemnly given (v. 32)[18]. Finally, Peter dwells upon Jesus' exaltation to God's right hand, attested both by his pouring forth of the Spirit in a perceptible manner, and by Ps. 110 (vv. 33-35). The conclusion : God has made the crucified Jesus Lord and Messias ; and this message, now proclaimed for the first time, is intended for « all the house of Israel » (v. 36). In a kind of epilogue to the sermon (vv. 38-39),

---

[17] This point is capital because it means that God's definitive act of salvation has been accomplished through Jesus Christ : more specifically, through his death and resurrection (hence their redemptive character is undoubtedly implied, even if it is not expressly mentioned). DODD has seen this clearly : he remarks, *op. cit.* 33, « The main burden of the *kerygma* is that the unprecedented has happened : God has visited and redeemed his people ». He adds, *ibid.* 34, « the *eschaton*, the final and decisive act of God, has already entered human experience ». For the place of Eschatology in modern criticism, cf. H. A. GUY, *The New Testament Doctrine of the ' Last Things '* (London, 1948) 8 ff.

[18] On the nature of this testimony, cf. our remarks in *The Conception of Salvation in Primitive Christian Preaching* in *CBQ* 18 (1956) 248 ff.

Peter adds the exhortation to repentance and to Baptism with the accompanying gift of the Spirit.

The speech delivered on the occasion of the healing of the man crippled from birth (Acts 3,12-26) covers basically the same material as the Pentecostal discourse. However, there are some points of the kerygma which appear for the first time. The introduction (3, 12-16) gives an explanation of the miracles : it is the result of an intervention of the glorified Jesus. The God of the Christians, who is also the God of the patriarchs, has glorified « his Servant » Jesus, put to death by the Jews. Jesus is described as the « Holy One », « the Just », « the Prince of life », titles which imply his divine mission (vv. 14-15) [19]. The apostles are the official witnesses to the resurrection (v. 15).

In the second part of the discourse, we find a more benign interpretation of the Jews' part in Jesus' death : it was done « through ignorance » (v. 17) and in order to fulfil the prophetic utterances concerning a suffering Messias (v. 18). The invitation to repentance is given new motivation : the glorious second Coming of Christ is contingent upon the conversion of the Jews (vv. 20-21). This reference to the parousia (the only one in the Petrine sermons) [20] is of particular interest, since it reveals a re-thinking of the old Jewish eschatology very early in the apostolic era, a re-thinking necessitated by the ascension of Christ and the descent of the Spirit [21]. Vv. 22-24 contain a new testimonial from the prophetic

---

[19] With regard to the title, « the Holy », O. PROCKSCH (*TWNT* I 102) remarks that it is both « altertümlich und inhaltreich ». JOSEPH SCHMITT, *op. cit.* 187, says it is not a synonym for « just », but rather that « il souligne, mieux que l'appellation ὁ δίκαιος, la place décisive du fait pascal dans la révélation du Christ ... Glorifié, il participe à la sainteté de Dieu, est doté de sa vertu sanctificatrice. De ce chef, il mérite d'être appelé ' le Saint ' par excellence ». The title, « the Just », belongs to the terminology of the Suffering Servant theology : cf. OSCAR CULLMANN, *Die Christologie des Neuen Testaments*[2] (Tübingen, 1958) 72 n. 1. The title ἀρχηγός was probably current in primitive Christianity. A propos of it, JOSEPH SCHMITT, *op. cit.* 223 remarks : « Exalté, Jésus est ' le Chef du salut ' (*Heb.*, II, 10). Non seulement il en est l'auteur, mais surtout, il le préfigure ... Ressuscité, il est ' le Chef de la vie ' (*Act.*, III, 15) ».

[20] This probably indicates the position which this future event of the salvation-history held in the minds of the apostolic group. In other words, it was not the obsession that some modern critics would have us think. J. A. T. ROBINSON, *Jesus and His Coming* (London, 1957) 143-148, considers this passage an example of the most primitive Christology, according to which Jesus did not become the Christ, even at his resurrection, but is to *return* as the Christ.

[21] On this point, cf. OSCAR CULLMANN, *Christ et le Temps* (Neuchâtel-Paris, 1947) 56-65.

writings for the initiation of the messianic age [22]. The conclusion contains a reference to the Abrahamitic pact : the blessing promised to Abraham has been realized in God's sending the risen Jesus as Saviour to Israel.

In the brief résumé of Peter's speech to the Sanhedrin (Acts 4,9-12), we have a recapitulation of the main points of the kerygma : Jesus' death was caused by the Jews ; his resurrection is due to God alone (v. 10) ; he is the stone of stumbling spoken of by the psalmist (Ps 118, 22) [23], yet the unique redeemer of mankind (v. 12).

The proclamation of the good news given to Cornelius' household at Caesarea (Acts 10,34-43) is similar in outline to the Synoptic Gospels, particularly that of St. Mark. The brief introduction, appropriate to the occasion (the speech is considered by St. Luke as an example of Peter's preaching to pagans), states Peter's newly discovered belief [24] in the complete universality of the divine salvific will (vv. 34-35). « Jesus Christ » [25] is the bearer of God's definitive revelation to Israel, and he is also Lord of pagans no less than Jews (v. 36). The Gospel begins with the baptism preached by John (v. 37) and refers to the Galilean and Judaean ministry of Jesus, witnessed by the apostles. His miracles and exorcisms prove his anointing « with the Spirit and power », the fact that « God was with him » (vv. 38-39a). Jesus' death upon the cross is the crime of the Jews (v. 39b). God raised him « the third day » [26], and permitted him to show himself to a chosen group of witnesses, the apostles (vv. 40-41). The risen Christ gave to the Twelve a mandate to preach and witness to him : he is the divinely-appointed Judge of both living and dead (v. 42). The sermon closes with a reference to the prophetic argument and the promise of forgiveness to those with faith (v. 43).

Since the kerygma is by definition the announcing of the good news

---

[22] On the fortunes of this title, « the Prophet », as applied to Jesus, cf. OSCAR CULLMANN, *Die Christologie des Neuen Testaments*, 11-49 ; cf. also F. GILS, *Jésus prophète d'après les évangiles synoptiques* (Louvain, 1957).

[23] This text is employed again in 1 Pt 2,4-8.

[24] The result of Peter's vision at Joppa (Acts 10,9 ff.).

[25] The use of this title here is interesting, since it is generally regarded as coming into use much later, during the period of Paul's evangelization of the Hellenistic centres in Asia Minor and Europe. It may, of course be due to Luke's redaction of his sources ; but he is generally rather scrupulously faithful in citing them.

[26] The importance of this point in the apostolic kerygma may be seen in Paul's grammatically awkward use of it in 1 Cor 15,4. Cf. J. DUPONT, *Ressuscité « le troisième jour »* in *Studia Biblica et Orientalia* II (Roma, 1959) 174-193.

of salvation in Jesus Christ, we may, from the data of Peter's sermons, summarize the contents of the Jerusalem preaching under the following points :

1) *the proclamation of the consummation of Israel's religious history.* — The Gospel is essentially an eschatological message. It is the proclamation of prophecy fulfilled. The much-abused term « eschatological » is employed here to connote God's definitive visitation of his people : the ἔσχατον has entered human history, thereby giving it its ultimate purpose and fundamental meaning [27]. In other words, the messianic era is announced as inaugurated by the descent of the Spirit and by Jesus' exaltation at God's right hand as Saviour of Israel, Lord of all, and Judge of the living and the dead. Yet in this newly-revealed scheme of things there is a moment that remains in the future. The glorious coming of the exalted Christ in « the times of refreshment », of « the restoration of the universe » (Acts 3,20-21) [28], is still the object of Christian hope. It is conceived as dependent upon the conversion of Israel as a people to their Christ, — an event which, in view of the marvellous growth of the community during the first years, must have seemed very near to realization. On Peter's view, Pentecost is « the day of the Lord » (Acts 2,20), or at least part of the immediate *prodromos* to its dawning. We shall observe Paul adding further precision to this primitive conception as a result of his experience with the Thessalonian parousiac expectation [29], and, later, of his intercalation of the conversion of the Gentiles into this original theology of salvation [30].

2) *the proclamation of the apostolic testimony, supported by the dynamic witnessing of the Holy Spirit* (Acts 5,32). — The apostles announce in the first place their testimony to Jesus' resurrection, the central object

---

[27] This awareness of the consummation of Israel's religious history in the events of Jesus' death and resurrection was a formative factor in the production of the primitive kerygma : cf. *The Conception of Salvation in Primitive Christian Preaching* in *CBQ* 18 (1956) 241-248.

[28] It is the parousia which divides the « last times » into two principal moments : one, the time in which salvation is offered to all men, is the period of the Church's activity upon earth ; the other is the final consummation, described by Paul in 1 Cor 15,28.

[29] For the moment, it is sufficient to recall the apodictic statement in 2 Thes 2,1-2.

[30] Cf. Rom 11, 25-27.

of their μαρτύριον (Acts 2,32 ; 1,8 ; 3,15 ; 5,32 ; 10,41 ; cf. also 13,31). They also witness to the divinely ordained public ministry of Jesus in Galilee and in Judaea (Acts 2,22 ; 10,38-39). They testify that Jesus' death at the hands of the Jews was « according to the determined will and foreknowledge of God » (Acts 2,23 ; 3,18). The apostolic testimony includes as well the mission of John the Baptist (Acts 10,37 ; cf. also 13,24-25). The testimony to Jesus' resurrection extends moreover to his exaltation to the throne of God's majesty as revealed by his sending of the Spirit (Acts 2,33) and by the miracles wrought in his newly-conferred Name and by his invisible power (Acts 3,16 ; 4,10.30). The titles which the apostles attribute to the exalted Jesus are a summary of their testimony : he is *the Christ* (Acts 2,36), *the Lord* (Acts 2,21.36 ; 10,36), the *'Ebed Yahweh* (Acts 3,13 ; 4,30 ; 10,38), *the Holy, the Just* (Acts 3,14), *the Prince of life* (Acts 3,14 ; 5,31), *the Judge of the universe* (Acts 10,42).

3) *the invitation to repentance and to the reception of Christian Baptism.* — This announcement of « the good news of peace through Jesus Christ » (Acts 10,36) is proclaimed first to Israel (Acts 2,36 ; 3,20b. 25-26 ; 10,36) then to the God-fearing lovers of justice or holiness amongst men of all nations (Acts 10,35).

It will be helpful at this point to note certain signal omissions in this primitive schema of the Jerusalem Gospel. First of all, Jesus is nowhere referred to as « Son of God », the title so characteristic of Paul's preaching and teaching [31]. St. Luke will take care to note in Acts that Paul is the first of the early preachers to proclaim Jesus as Son of God (Acts 9,20). In the second place, there is no mention of the incarnation or of the pre-existence of the son (although, as we have seen, Jesus' divinity was expressed in various rudimentary ways). The absence in these speeches of such Christological data testifies to the archaic nature of Luke's sources, which antedate the elaboration of these facets of the dogma which a later age will call the hypostatic union. Thirdly, there is no theological treatment, such as we find in Paul or John, of the divine « motives » for the redemption. Implicit, of course, in the many references to the fulfilment of « the Scriptures » and to the promise given Abraham (Acts 3,25) is the motive Paul will insist upon in the first section of Romans : the « justice of God », that is, God's faithfulness to his promise of salva-

---

[31] In this connection, cf. the significant remark of Luke : Acts 9,20, as well as his reference to the Pauline use of Ps 2,7 (Acts 13,33).

tion. There is no reference to the divine love of the Father or of Christ. Finally, there is a certain timidity and *malaise* observable in the apostolic testimony regarding the death of Christ. That sureness of touch, so clearly felt in the Pauline treatment of Jesus' death, the result of its integration into a higher synthesis, is somehow wanting in the primitive preaching. There is no need to exaggerate this point however, as some critics have done, by insisting that the death of Christ was not considered salvific in the Petrine preaching [32]. It is clear that the death is implicitly proclaimed as salutary, that is « for our sins », else it would not appear with such regularity in all the examples of the early kerygma (Acts 2,23.36 ; 3,13-15.17-18 ; 4,10-11 ; 5,30 ; 10,40 ; cf. also 4,27-28), where it is described as part of the divinely-predestined plan for man's salvation. Still for all that, it must be admitted that Jesus' death appears as a « scandal » which must be apologized for and defended by resorting to the testimony of « all the prophets, that his Christ should suffer » (Acts 3,18) [33]

§ 3. - Hellenistic Influence in the Jerusalem Kerygma

Another point which must be considered is the influence of the Hellenistic section of the Jerusalem community in the creation of the kerygma. The evidence for this influence by Jewish Christians, whose mother-tongue was Greek rather than Aramaic, and whose culture derived in part

---

[32] Cf. for example P. LESTRINGANT, *Essai sur l'unité de la révélation biblique* (Paris, 1942) 68. M. GOGUEL, *Les premiers temps de l'Église* (Neuchâtel-Paris, 1949) 54, expresses a more nuanced view in speaking of Acts' Petrine discourses : « On rencontre ici la première expression d'une idée qui trouvera dans la suite un grand développement, celle de la réalisation d'un plan divin par la mort du Christ. » Speaking of the significance of the title of Suffering Servant for primitive Christian theology, OSCAR CULLMANN (*Die Christologie des Neuen Testaments* 81) states : « Ja, man kann sogar sagen, das dies der urchristlichen Theologie, ihrem Geschichts- und Zeitverständnis, nach welchem der Tod Christi die Mitte der gesamten Heilszeit darstellt, in besonders glücklicher Weise entsprochen hätte ».

[33] This was due, in part at least, to the polemic and apologetic pre-occupations of the early years which resulted in the obscuring of the Father's part in « handing over » his Son to death. The Palestinian kerygma highlighted the part played by the Jews in the *traditio* of Jesus to the pagans. It will be only in the Pauline soteriology, once anti-Jewish propaganda is left aside, that the « handing over » is explicitly and consistently attributed either to the Father (Rom 8,32 ; 4,25) or to Jesus himself (Gal 2,20 ; Eph 5,2.25).

3. - D. M. STANLEY.

at least from the Hellenistic civilization with which they lived surrounded, has long been remarked by the critics [34]. More recently, JOSEPH
SCHMITT [35] and JACQUES DUPONT [36] have drawn attention to this Hellenistic element in the early part of Acts. Indeed, it is the presence of certain traces of this influence in Peter's Pentecostal discourse which has led
us to define the authenticity of these speeches in the more general terms
of the Jerusalem kerygma. At the same time, it would be faulty historical
method to ignore the fact that some of these Hellenistic elements are
found, in the very earliest sources at Luke's disposal, in close combina-
tion with the Aramaic, Palestinian elements. Consequently, to oppose the
one to the other is to fly in the face of evidence. It is more in accord
with the documentary sources to admit that the Hellenistic developments were but an explicitation of the Palestinian, Aramaic tradition and were elaborated very early in Jerusalem itself (and hence under
the supervision of Peter and the Twelve). That they should appear in the
Lukan *précis* of the Jerusalem kerygma need not surprise anyone. As a
Gentile Christian, a Hellenist, Luke was naturally not uninterested in
setting forth the traditional nature of this Hellenistic Gospel.

What are the discernible traces of such Hellenistic currents of thought
in the Petrine discourses ? The first of these elements may be classified as
polemical. They appear not only in the anti-Jewish sentiment occasionally
perceptible in the speeches (Acts 2,23.36 ; 3,13-15.17 ; 4,10-11 ; 5,29-30 ;
10,40-41), but more particularly in the arguments constructed of proof-
texts taken from the Greek Bible (Acts 2,17-21.25-28.31.34-35 ; 3,25 ;
4,11.25b-26). The second trend which owes its development, if not
its origin, to Hellenistic elaboration is *theological*, and is concerned primarily with the theme of the *'Ebed Yahweh* and its application to the
work of Christ [37].

---

[34] JOACHIM JEREMIAS, *Untersuchungen zum Quellenproblem der Apostelgeschichte* in *ZNW* 36 (1937) 205-221 ; WALTER GRUNDMANN, *Das Problem des hellenis-
tischen Christentums innerhalb der Jerusalemer Urgemeinde* in *ZNW* 38 (1939) 45-73 ;
WILFRED L. KNOX, *Some Hellenistic Elements in Primitive Christianity* (London,
1944).

[35] JOSEPH SCHMITT, *Les sources et les thèmes de la naissante foi apostolique
au Christ Sauveur* in *LumVi* § 15 (1954) 309-332.

[36] The reader is referred to Dom DUPONT's notes on the discourses in Acts
in the volume already referred to in n. 3.

[37] D. M. STANLEY, *The Theme of the Servant of Yahweh in Primitive Christian
Soteriology, and its Transposition by St. Paul* in *CBQ* 16 (1954) 385-425.

An illustration of this Hellenistic interest in the Servant theology is provided by the incident concerning Philip, one of the Hellenistic deacons (Acts 6,5), and the eunuch of the Queen of Ethiopia (Acts 8,26-40). The vizier demands to be informed of the identity of the suffering Servant described in the passage he has been reading (Is 53,7-8). Luke states that Philip « gospelled Jesus to him, beginning with this passage » (Acts 8,35). However fortuitous the reading of the Isaian passage may have been on the chamberlain's part, Acts' account of the episode indicates that Philip was quite prepared to present the message of salvation in terms of Jesus' work as the 'Ebed Yahweh. Such a preparedness presupposes, surely, a previous thinking-out of the Gospel along the lines of the Servant theme. This is implied moreover by the fact that the catechumen was ready to receive Baptism at the close of the instruction. Indeed, Luke's inclusion of this incident would seem to indicate that it was particularly the Hellenistic branch of the primitive community which had exploited the theological possibilities of the Servant *motif*, perhaps specifically for use in pre-baptismal instruction [38].

Another interesting sidelight on Hellenistic influence is provided by the much-disputed v. 37, which contains Philip's reply to the eunuch's request for Baptism. « ' If you believe with your whole heart, it is possible '. And he replied : ' I believe that the Son of God is Jesus Christ ' ». If A. C. CLARKE is right in including this verse in the original text of Acts [39], it would appear that it was the Hellenists who were accustomed to apply the epithet « Son of God » to Jesus. This would also help to clarify Luke's observation that Saul, upon his conversion, began to preach the divine Sonship of Christ (Acts 9,20) [40].

The greatest representative of the early Hellenistic group is St. Stephen, to whose *apologia pro vita sua* Luke devotes more space than to any other speech in Acts. While Stephen omits any reference to the theology of the Servant, his great *plaidoyer* for the truth of Christianity exemplifies another contribution to the primitive preaching, important for its influence on Paul's theology, made by the Hellenists : the Christian interpretation of the OT.

---

[38] Thus, for instance, 1 Pt 2,20-25 makes use of the theme : cf. the comments of E. G. SELWYN, *The First Epistle of St. Peter* (London, 1949) 30.

[39] ALBERT C. CLARKE, *The Acts of the Apostles : A Critical Edition with Introduction and Notes on Selected Passages* (Oxford, 1933) *in loc.*

[40] In other words, the title « Son of God » would be characteristic of the Hellenists' preaching, which stemmed from Stephen and of which Philip was the outstanding representative known to Luke.

Stephen's significance lies in the fact that he was the first great figure of the apostolic age with the foresight to realize the fundamental incongruity between the new religion and Judaism. If Christianity were to fulfil the divine mission bequeathed her by her founder, she could not allow her light to remain hidden under the bushel-measure of the Jewish code and cult. She must assert her individuality, become a *visible* Church,[41] which, if the heir of Judaism, could never rightly be regarded as a sect of that religion. The basic reason for such a declaration of independence, Stephen saw clearly, lay in Israel's intransigent refusal to regard as relative what the divine will had never intended as the definitive form of revealed religion [42]. In other words, the Judaism contemporary with apostolic Christianity had blinded itself to the ephemeral nature of the Mosaic legislation, despite the warning of Jesus' public preaching and the clear manifestation of his messianic character through his resurrection from death.

While Christ's resurrection is nowhere mentioned in the résumé of Stephen's speech, still, as CÉLESTIN CHARLIER has remarked [43], this mystery is the key to its understanding. Stephen's study of the OT had revealed to him the infallible triumph of Yahweh's plan of redemption over every obstacle that human malice might devise to thwart its execution. That is to say, he had discovered upon almost every page of Israel's sacred history the prophetic adumbration of the central truths of the apostolic kerygma : Christ's death at the hands of the Jews and his resurrection by the power of God the Father.

Abraham's faith in leaving his homeland to follow his monotheistic vocation, his confidence in the divine promise of a heritage in Palestine despite the fact that he was to die without possessing so much as a *pied-à-terre* in the Holy Land, his fidelity in observing the alliance of circumcision which Yahweh had made with him, all of this proves the error of attaching the divine presence to a particular region and the need of spiritualizing and universalizing the conception of « the land ».

---

[41] L. CERFAUX, *La Communauté apostolique* [2] (Paris, 1953) 63-70.

[42] D. M. STANLEY, *Kingdom to Church* : *The Structural Development of Apostolic Christianity in the New Testament* in *TS* 16 (1955) 13 : « In the context of Acts, Stephen's *plaidoyer* is addressed to his Jewish judges, and as such it insists upon Israel's characteristic sin, the clinging to what is of passing value in code and cult as if it were definitive ».

[43] CÉLESTIN CHARLIER, *Le Manifeste d'Étienne (Actes 7)* : *essai de commentaire synthétique* in *BiViChrét* § 3 (1953) 83-93.

Joseph's triumph in Egypt despite, or rather, because of, the jeal-ousy of his brothers, and his ultimately saving his family from extinction by famine, are due to the fact that « God was with him » (Acts 7,9) — a remark made with regard to Jesus in Peter's preaching (Acts 10,38).

Moses' story (vv. 17-43) illustrates once again the divine victory over mere human might. He is, despite the Hebrews' refusal to acknow-ledge him, the divinely-established « chief and judge » (v. 27), and so a type of the risen Christ [44]. In fact, he is the divinely-sent « chief and redeemer » (v.35) [45] who leads God's chosen people through the Red Sea and the desert (vv. 36-37) and who receives the Law from the angel on Sinai, « the words of life » for Israel (v. 38), yet who is, for all that, dis-obeyed by « our fathers » and rejected (v. 39) [46]. Stephen implies that the Law, given more than « four hundred years » after Abraham had founded the religion of Israel, can hardly be considered essential to the worship of the true God or incapable of abrogation.

The same holds for the cult of Yahweh and its liturgical centre, the Temple. In the desert, the « tent of witness » had been designed by Moses ac-cording to the heavenly model of which he had been given a vision (v. 44). David, the king who enjoyed God's favour to a pre-eminent degree, was not allowed to build the Temple ; and the fact that it was erected by Solomon, a man of very questionable virtue, proves how little in con-formity with God's will the construction of this edifice was [47]. God does not dwell in buildings of human construction (v. 48). Israel's history also contains abundant examples of the way the people « resisted the Holy Spirit » (v. 51) : the persecution of the prophets, the infraction of the

---

[44] The title ἄρχων is only given to the risen Christ in Ap 1,5 ; however ἀρχηγός was a common primitive appellation for him : Acts 3,15 ; 5,31 ; Heb 2,10 ; 12,2. The office of judge belongs to the glorified Christ : cf. Acts 10,42 ; 17,31 ; Rom 2,16 ; Jn 5,22.

[45] Nowhere in the OT was the title « redeemer » given to Moses, so this may be an instance where the anti-type has influenced the description of the type. The term is freely applied to Moses, as type of the Messias, in rabbinic sources, beginning with the Jerusalem Targum. See R. Bloch, *Quelques aspects de la figure de Moïse dans la tradition rabbinique* in *Cahiers Sioniens* 8 (1954), 211-285. « La phrase stéréotypée ' comme le premier libérateur (Moïse), ainsi le dernier libérateur ' revient comme un *leitmotiv* dans les textes », 274, n. 197.

[46] Paul will refer to this disobedience of the generation of the Exodus in 1 Cor 10,5 ff.

[47] This is, of course, only one aspect of the question : Heb 8,5 takes another view.

heaven-sent Law, have been climaxed by the betrayal and murder of God's Christ (v. 52).

This speech is a precious example of the way in which one section of the early Church understood the OT. It is also significant as the first manifesto of Christianity's necessary autonomy with respect to Judaism. And yet Stephen has only worked out the logical conclusions already present in the teaching for which Jesus had suffered death : he had set himself above the Temple and had proposed to replace the Mosaic Law with a new code of perfection. In Stephen's eyes, the history of Israel provides types of Christ the redeemer. It also justifies the rejection of the Jewish people by God in the new dispensation. These elements were destined to find their way into the kerygma of the apostolic age and into the written works of the NT, of which the best example is perhaps the canonical Gospel of St. Matthew [48].

The discourse also suggests that much of the reflection upon the salvific nature of Christ's death was undertaken by the Hellenistic branch of the community. It is the *betrayal* of Joseph by his brethren that effects their salvation in time of famine. It is the *rejection* of Moses by his own people that leads to his vocation as their leader and redeemer. It is with these suggestions of a theology of the redemption that Paul will come into contact in the Antiochian church, whose founders were the Hellenistic heirs of Stephen's genius. These pregnant ideas will, under the creative power of Paul's mind, fructify in a soteriology such as we find exposed in the letter to the Roman church.

One final contribution of Stephen deserves mention, although it may have made no more than a subconscious impression upon the attitude of the Hellenists towards the parousia. Stephen dies before the Lord's return. Not all the first generation Christians would survive until that greatly longed-for event, even the holiest of them. This may have led to a deeper appreciation of the « word of the Lord » cited in 1 Thes 4,15 : the living were to have no advantage over the dead at the Lord's coming. How could they hope to take precedence over the protomartyr St. Stephen ?

---

[48] Cf. the excellent discussion of the theme of Matthew's Gospel by PIERRE BENOIT, *L'Évangile selon Saint Matthieu*[2] (Paris, 1953) 31-37.

CHAPTER II

THE PREACHING OF PAUL

We have examined the kerygma of the Jerusalem community as set forth in Acts. The present chapter is intended as a companion-piece to the last. In it, an *exposé* of the preaching of Saul of Tarsus will be sketched in such a way as to bring out the points of comparison and of contrast with the apostolic preaching we have just reviewed. As a necessary preliminary to this study of Paul's Gospel, indeed to the whole study of Pauline theology, we shall begin with a discussion of Paul's conversion and its influence upon his conception of Christ and Christ's redemptive work. A propos of ALBERT SCHWEITZER'S *Die Mystik des Apostels Paulus*, MAURICE GOGUEL remarks that any study of Paul's thought must take into account the psychological element in his life, which, ultimately, forms part of Pauline history, since it explains the manner in which Paul arrived at Christianity [1].

§ 1. - The Significance of Paul's Conversion

With the exception of the Pentecostal descent of the Holy Spirit, the most momentous event in the life of the nascent Christian community was undoubtedly the victory of the risen Christ over Saul of Tarsus. Such a statement may appear strange when it is realized that this conversion was never permitted to become *immediately or directly* a formative influence upon the Jerusalem church. Always, the terrible memories of Saul's overzealous bigotry would remain too exquisitely painful for that. Indeed, it is not improbable that to the end of Paul's career the Pales-

---

[1] MAURICE GOGUEL, *La mystique paulinienne d'après Albert Schweitzer* in *RHPhilRel* 11 (1931) 185-210.

tinian Christians never quite rid themselves of their suspicions of him
(Acts 22,20-21). The fanaticism with which Saul had played the grand
inquisitor of Judaism had made his name a cause of terror as far away as
Damascus (Acts 9,13). In consequence, fully three years after his conversion, upon his return to Jerusalem, Saul needed to invoke the powerful
patronage of Barnabas before he could gain admittance to fellowship
in the Christian community (Acts 9,26). Even so, the stigma attaching to
his reputation ultimately forced Saul to leave the evangelization of Judaea
to less controversial figures than himself (Acts 22,18-19). Thus it was
that he came to follow the strangest vocation that ever Pharisee received, that of christianizing the pagan peoples of the Mediterranean world.

Herein lies the real significance for Christianity of Saul's capitula-
tion to Jesus of Nazareth. Under the impulse of his missionary zeal, the
new religion was, in a relatively short time, to emerge as a predominantly
Gentile Church. Inspired by Paul's theological genius, the apostolic Christians were to comprehend the meaning of « the Mystery », hidden in the
beginning as long as they remained within the orbit of the Temple : the
admission of pagan converts on a basis of equality with their Jewish
brethren into the new Israel.

If the conversion of Saul of Tarsus produced such a metamorphosis
in the life of the early Church, it is not difficult to conjecture the transformation which that conversion wrought in the life and character of the
convert himself. To appreciate the change in Saul, we have only to recall
the picture he has drawn of himself before his meeting with the glorified Jesus.

The most fervent of Pharisees (Gal 1,14), a sect notorious for their
isolationism [2], Saul was, on his own admission (Phil 3,6), irreproachable
according to the standards of legalistic righteousness. A zealot, he was
naturally fitted to lead the persecution of the Hellenistic Christians in
Palestine (Acts 8,3 ; 9,1 ; 22,4.19-20) and beyond its borders (Acts 26,11).
To the end of his life, the mere recollection of his frenzied hatred of « the
Church of God » was to inspire bitter regret in his soul (1 Cor 15,9 ; Gal
1,23 ; Phil 3,6 ; 1 Tm 1,13). If we are to assess the distance which sepa-

---

[2] The sectaries of Qumran reflect this same attitude : cf. J. SCHMITT, *Les
écrits du Nouveau Testament et les textes de Qumran : bilan de cinq années de recher-
ches* (2) in *RScRel* 30 (1956) 61-62. On the Pharisees, cf. J. WELLHAUSEN *Die Pha-
risäer und die Sadducäer* [2] (Hannover, 1924) ; LOUIS FINKELSTEIN, *The Pharisees,
Their Origin and Their Philosophy* in *HTR* 22 (1929) 185-261.

rates Saul the persecutor from Paul the apostle, we must grasp the significance of the momentous meeting between Saul and Christ on the Damascus road. Accordingly, it will be necessary to review the accounts of Saul's conversion given in Acts as well as the references to it made by the apostle himself in his letters.

It may be objected that in either case we are dealing with *interpretations* of the event. Yet this very quality of the evidence to be dealt with will prove an aid rather than a hindrance in evaluating the impact of this unique experience upon Paul's thought. Luke, dearly loved companion of the apostle (Col 4,14 ; Phlm 24), for whom Paul was so manifestly one of the heroic figures of the apostolic age, was ideally situated to assess the importance of that conversion. As for Paul himself, his own conception of this first meeting with Christ can be relied upon to provide an invaluable clue to his theology. We shall first examine the three passages in Acts which deal with Paul's conversion (Acts 9,3-19 ; 22,6-16 ; 26,12-18), then the four references to it in the epistles (Gal 1,15-16 ; 1 Cor 15,8-9 ; 2 Cor 4,6 ; Phil 3,12).

The accounts in Acts occur at three important junctures in that book and have a functional purpose in the structure of the whole story. With that purpose we are not concerned here [3]. Our interest lies rather in the light they throw upon various aspects of Paul's conversion.

Before taking up each account in detail, it will be helpful to note the elements common to all three narratives. There is a striking verbal agreement in the dialogue between Christ and Paul as recorded in each *récit*. « Saul, Saul, why do you persecute me ? » — « Who are you, Lord ? » — « I am Jesus, whom you are persecuting ». In accounts which display such a wealth of variation, such word-for-word agreement is no chance occurrence. It underscores the impact upon Saul of two essential points in the revelation.

« *I am Jesus* ». The glorified Lord, surrounded by the light which is a sign of his celestial origin, discloses his identity with that Jesus of Nazareth whom Paul knew to have been put to death as « a curse » upon the cross (Gal 3,13). Hence in his first intuition of Christian faith, Saul learns to know Christ *as One risen from death*. Given his firm Pharisee faith in the resurrection of the dead, this truth would find a ready re-

---

[3] We have elsewhere discussed this point : cf. *Paul's Conversion in Acts : Why the Three Accounts ?* in *CBQ* 15 (1953) 315-338.

ception in the soul of Saul [4]. As a result, he recognizes also the redemptive character of Jesus' death and resurrection [5].

« *Jesus, whom you are persecuting* ». The second great supernatural truth imparted to Saul is that in attacking the Christian community he has *somehow* caused suffering to this exalted personage. For in some mysterious way, the risen Jesus is still at work in the world of men through the instrumentality of his followers. Does this mean that Paul received with this insight a revelation of the Church as the « Body of Christ » of which he will write so illuminatingly in his letters (1 Cor 12,12-28 ; Rom 12,4-6 ; Eph 4,11-16) ? This question is disputed amongst modern commentators [6]. While it seems an exaggeration to claim that Paul here received the doctrine of the « Mystical Body », it might be admitted that the seeds of this truth were planted in his mind on this occasion. For its full development however, a further revelation of the Christian's intimate union with Christ and a certain experience of the Church as she existed upon earth seem to be necessary. Similarly, it may be said that the Pauline conception of Christian suffering (and death), which will also develop through personal experience in the course of Paul's apostolate, is *germinally* present in this insight.

The first account (Acts 9,3 ff.) of Paul's conversion is Luke's own reconstruction of what happened, composed with the help of various sources [7]. Luke informs his reader of Ananias' role in Paul's reception into the faith (vv. 10-19). To the head of the Damascus church [8] is con-

---

[4] That it did so is borne out by the passages in Acts and in Paul's own letters in which he describes Christ as One risen from death : Acts 13,33.37 ; 17,3.18.31 ; 23,6 ; 24,15 ; 26,8.23 ; 1 Thes 1,10 ; 4,14 ; 1 Cor 15,20 ; 2 Cor 4,14 ; 13,4 : Rom 1,4 ; 4,25 ; 6,9 ; 8,11.34 ; 10,9 ; 14,9 ; Phil 2,8-9 ; Col 1,18 ; 2,12 ; Eph 1,20.

[5] This would appear to be suggested by Paul's remarks in Gal 1,16 (« to reveal his Son *in me* ») and in 2 Cor 4,6, where he refers to this experience as giving him « the illuminating knowledge of the divine glory ». We shall discuss these texts later in this chapter.

[6] For an affirmation that Paul here learned the truth of the « Body of Christ », cf. E.-B. ALLO, *L'évolution de l'Évangile de Paul* in *RB* (*Vivre et Penser*) (1941) 48-77 ; (1942) 165-193. L. CERFAUX, *La Théologie de l'Église suivant saint Paul* [2] (Paris, 1948) 201 n. 1, denies Allo's contention ; as does also J. HAVET, *Christ collectif ou Christ individuel en I Cor.*, XII, 12 in *ETL* 23 (1947) 516-517.

[7] Cf. our article *Paul's Conversion* 325-328.

[8] This conjecture seems plausible in view of the whole story ; cf. also Paul's description of him in Acts 22,12, which suggests he was a man of some prominence.

fided the work of restoring Paul's sight, of baptizing him, and of conferring the Holy Spirit, after instruction in the essentials of the apostolic kerygma. Ananias' intervention serves to underscore two qualities of Saul's meeting with Christ. Firstly, — a fact of great significance — it is *not the risen Christ* who admits the neophyte into the community of the faithful *but a mere man to whose care the community of Damascus has been confided by the apostles.* This point (the case of Cornelius is analogous, Acts 10,48) illustrates an important consequence of the incarnation : sacramental admission to the Church is, by the will of Christ, left to the care of other men. Far from proving a barrier to the soul's union with the Lord, the divinely-appointed leaders of the Christian community constitute an essential link effecting and ensuring that union. In this respect, the incident indicates the necessarily *visible* nature of the Church by showing the necessity, even for members favoured with remarkable graces of conversion, of some externally perceptible aggregation to the community. When Paul comes to choose a metaphor to describe this character of the institution founded by Christ, he will employ a figure of speech which adequately expresses this tangible quality, « the Body ».

In the second place, Ananias' part in Saul's admission to the Church helps distinguish Saul's meeting with Christ from the Pentecostal experience of the first disciples. Saul's Christian life begins, not with an experience of the living Spirit, but *with an experience of the living Christ.* In this respect, it is more closely allied to the post-resurrection appearances with which the apostles were favoured, as Paul himself will assert (1 Cor 15,5-8)[9]. This factor explains the emphasis in Paul's sermons and letters upon the resurrection of Christ rather than, as in the Jerusalem kerygma, upon the *sessio ad dexteram Patris,* as point of departure for the salvific activity of the glorified Lord.

A subsidiary element in Luke's own account which will be clarified further in the third *récit* may be noted here (cf. Acts 26,12 ff.). Paul's future vocation is hinted at : he is « to carry my Name to the Gentiles and kings » (v. 15), and he is destined to « suffer for my Name's sake » (v. 16).

The second account (Acts 22,6-16) purports to be a résumé of Paul's speech in Aramaic to the infuriated Jews in the Temple area in Jerusalem. To this narrative is appended Paul's statement (vv. 17-21) that he received, in a subsequent vision, more precise information about his future

---

[9] Cf. *Paul's Conversion* 328-329.

vocation : he must leave Jerusalem, since his testimony to Christ there is unacceptable to Jews and Christians alike, and he is to be sent « afar to the pagans ».

The most important contribution to the meaning of Saul's conversion made by this discourse is the religious interpretation which is given in it of Saul's blinding. This new factor points up one notable difference between Christ's appearance to Saul and those to the disciples after the resurrection : *it is the risen Christ exalted in divine glory who manifests himself to Saul.* Nowhere in the NT is there any record of a similar revelation of his glorified humanity to the disciples during the forty days preceding Christ's ascension. As PIERRE BENOIT has remarked, Luke's description of the ascension itself is remarkable for the absence of any mention of the light of glory [10]. In this respect, his description of the departure of Christ from this earth differs from other more theological accounts of it in the NT as Jesus' *coelestis exaltatio* [11]. Paul then, on his own testimony, was privileged to enjoy a post-resurrection appearance of Christ which is unparalleled by the apostolic experience.

It is to be noted that Paul here depicts this revelation as one of *seeing* rather than of *hearing*. Paul does not, of course, describe *what* he saw. That would be to attempt the impossible. Indeed, it is only indirectly that he asserts he saw Christ, in quoting Ananias' words to himself (v. 14) [12]. Paul does however contrast the effect of the « heavenly vision » upon himself with that on his companions in terms of visual perception. His fellow-travellers *see the light* (they hear nothing) without being affected, as he himself is, by his miraculous illumination. They are neither blinded, nor do they receive the supernatural light of faith. Thus the physical effects of the light radiating from the risen Lord (Paul's blindness) are symbolic of the spiritual effects of the light (Paul's faith). That Paul is himself aware of this significance may be gathered from the precise formulation of this description : it was « the *glory* of that light » (v. 11) which struck him blind. The term δόξα is technically employed by the LXX and the NT writers as equivalent to the Hebrew *kabōd*, the sensible manifestation of the divine presence amongst men [13]. Hence it becomes clear why Saul's sight was restored at his Baptism into the Christian

---

[10] PIERRE BENOIT, *L'Ascension* in *RB* 56 (1949) 161-203.
[11] Acts 2,33-34 ; 5,30-31 ; Eph 4,10 ; 1 Tm 3,16 ; Heb 1,3.13 ; 2,7 ff ; 12,2 etc.
[12] The Lukan account in Acts 9,17 also mentions this fact.
[13] Paul will connect this δόξα of the Father with Christ's resurrection : cf. Rom 6,4.

Church. It is symbolic of the « new creation » effected in him by the gift of faith.

In the third account (Acts 26,12-18), Paul presents Christ's appearance to him as his own *inaugural vision*. In v. 16, the Lord's words echo those heard by the prophet Ezekiel during the vision which constituted his call to the prophetic office (Ez 2,1 ff), while v. 17 contains a phrase taken from the *récit* of Jeremias' inaugural vision [14]. A little later in this speech before Agrippa, Paul refers to his meeting with Christ in a manner wholly unprecedented elsewhere in his writings [15]. He calls it a « heavenly vision » and sees in it the beginning of his apostolic activity. Paul wishes to convince the half-pagan potentate whom he is addressing that he, Paul, is called by God to continue the line of OT prophets [16].

However, a noteworthy addition to this description of Paul's prophetic vocation specifies it still more exactly. The apostle states that he is called to fill the role of the Servant of Yahweh. Christ has appeared to him to constitute him « a servant and a witness » (v. 16) and his future office is described in terms borrowed from the first of the Servant songs (Is 42,7.16) : « to open their eyes [17], to turn (them) from darkness to light, and from Satan to God, so that they may receive the remission of their sins and an inheritance amongst those consecrated by faith in me ».

As we have attempted to show elsewhere [18], this transposition of the

---

[14] Cf. Jer 1,7.

[15] H. B. SWETE, *The Appearances of Our Lord after the Passion* (London, 1908) 130 f : « But the appearance on the Damascus road was unique ; it came to an unbeliever and turned him to faith. He classes it with the appearances of the forty days ... It was the only vision which he regarded in the light of evidence that could be produced if the Resurrection were denied ; he never appeals in this way to visions received during an ' ecstasy '... ».

[16] Paul explicitly identifies his message with that of the OT prophets by declaring that it contains « nothing beyond what the prophets had declared would come to pass and Moses : namely, that the Christ was to suffer ; was, as first of the resurrection of the dead, to proclaim light both to the People and to the Gentiles » (Acts 26,22). There is, of course, an essential difference between the message of the OT prophets and that of Paul : the former had *foretold* the events of Christian salvation, the latter declares that they have occurred.

[17] It is interesting to note that, while Mt 12,18 ff applies this passage to Christ, the third evangelist does not quote it ; but in his description of the scene in the Nazareth synagogue (Lk 4,18 f) cites Is 61,1 ff, which is similar. Thus Luke is aware of Paul's conception of himself as heir of Christ's role as the Servant of Yahweh.

[18] *The Theme of the Servant of Yahweh in Primitive Christian Soteriology, and its Transposition by St. Paul* in *CBQ* 16 (1954) 385-425.

Servant theology by Paul is a hall-mark of his view of the Christian apostleship. It may well be that this insight into his role as a preacher of the Gospel was given to him with the revelation, made to him by Christ through Ananias (Acts 9,16), of the great sufferings he was to endure. At any rate, this conception of himself as the Suffering Servant probably explains why this theme does not play as significant a part in Paul's presentation of Christ's work for man's redemption as it did in the earlier Palestinian soteriology [19].

It remains to consider the passages in the Pauline epistles which contain Paul's reflections upon his conversion.

The first of these occurs in the autobiographical sketch which serves as introduction to Galatians. « When he, who chose me from my mother's womb and called me by his loving favour, deigned to reveal his Son in me that I might gospel him among the pagans, straightway, without seeking instruction from any mere man, or without even journeying up to Jerusalem to consult] my predecessors, the apostles, I went off into Arabia, returning later to Damascus » (Gal 1,15-17). Paul's use of phraseology borrowed from the second Servant song [20] to describe his vocation to Christianity shows how closely, in his mind, his call to the faith is related to his call to perform the work of the ' Ebed Yahweh in the apostolate. Noteworthy also is his qualification of his conversion as the Father's revelation of « his Son in me ». By the expression « in me », instead of the simple dative « to me », he underscores the personal, interior nature of the experience [21]. What is most striking here is Paul's characterization of that experience as *the Father's disclosure of the divine Sonship of Jesus*. We have already noted that Christ primarily revealed himself to Saul as One risen from death. This other aspect of the revelation is equally

---

[19] It would be an exaggeration to say that this Servant soteriology which occupied a place of honour in the most ancient Christian traditions was unknown to Paul, ignored by him, or had no influence in Paul's own theological thinking on the redemption. Even if, as we are convinced, Phil 2,5-11 is a hymn of Palestinian origin cited by Paul, it still remains true that he cites it. Moreover, the theme of Christ's « handing himself over » (I Cor 11,23 ; Gal 2,20 ; Rom 4,25 ; 8,32 ; Eph 5,2), belongs to the Servant motif, as does Paul's characterization of the work of the Second Adam as « obedience » (Rom 5,19). Still, when all this is admitted, it is noteworthy that this conception of Christ as the Suffering and Glorified Servant of Yahweh does not occupy the first place in Pauline soteriology.

[20] Is 49,1.

[21] S. Lyonnet, *Les Épîtres de Saint Paul aux Galates, aux Romains* ², BJ (Paris, 1959) 24 n. *a*).

basic and one which will exert a great influence upon Pauline theology :
the risen Lord is God's own Son [22].

It is significant that Paul should mention his role as Servant of Yahweh in a paragraph where he insists upon his independence as an evangelist with respect to the rest of the apostles [23]. His renunciation of the
Servant theme as a vehicle for his conception of Christ's redemptive work
is one of the most striking ways in which Pauline theology is distinguished from that of Jerusalem [24].

The second reference Paul makes to his conversion is found in 1
Cor 15,8. « Last of all, he appeared also to me as to one prematurely
born ». In reciting the list of those favoured by appearances of the risen
Christ (vv. 5-7), Peter, the apostolic college, the disciples, James, etc.,
Paul adds his own experience by the Damascus road. He puts himself
in last place as unworthy of the name of apostle because he had perse-
cuted the Church of God (v. 9). The more fundamental reason for his self-
deprecation however is the fact that he is an ἔκτρωμα, an « abortion ». Like
Macduff, Paul « was from his mother's womb untimely ripped ». Judaism,
mother of all the apostolic group, was dead by the time Saul received the
gift of Christian faith. In this respect, he may rightly be called « the least
of the apostles ». Since Paul had had no personal experience of the events
of Jesus' public life or of his death, he had, in preaching the kerygma, to
rely upon the traditions handed down to him by the Twelve (1 Cor 11, 23 ;
15,3).

At the same time, he was constituted a witness of Christ's resurrection
by the unique experience which effected his conversion to Christianity.
Paul was convinced that his meeting with the risen Jesus on the Damascus
road was on a par with the earlier post-resurrection appearances cited
in the apostolic preaching [25].

Thus, while Paul's grasp of the Mystery of Christ was fundamentally
the same as that of the other apostles, and while he preached the one

---

[22] Pauline theology will underscore the role of the Father in the redemption
and the aspect of adoptive filiation in the Christian life.

[23] The Jerusalem kerygma commonly employed the Servant soteriology :
cf. C. H. DODD, *The Apostolic Preaching and Its Developments* 47 ; also W. L.
KNOX, *The Acts of the Apostles* (Cambridge, 1948) 72.

[24] L. CERFAUX, *Saint Paul et le Serviteur de Dieu d'Isaïe* in *StAns* 27-28
(1951) 351-365.

[25] This is clear from the context where Paul enumerates his experience of
the risen Christ after those of the apostolic college.

« Gospel of Christ » apart from which « there is no other » (Gal 1,7), still the fact that he never knew Jesus « according to the flesh »[26] and that he had not participated with the first disciples in the events of the first Pentecost undoubtedly played some part in shaping the distinctive character of Pauline theology. To · recall, for instance, the contrast between Paul's introduction to Christ and that of John is to appreciate more deeply the varying modalities in the distinctive theologies of these two apostolic writers[27].

There is a third reference to Paul's conversion in 2 Cor 4,6. « Because the God who had said ' Light shine out of the darkness '   is he] who caused light to shine in our hearts [to effect] the illuminating knowledge of the divine glory in the face of Christ ». In his defense of the apostolic ministry, Paul insists that the preaching of the Gospel is of itself a source of ʻthe divine light of faith for his hearers, since God the Creator of light has illumined the hearts of the apostles (who, as a result, preach not themselves but Christ the Lord) and so has enabled them to communicate the light of faith to others. The sentence is overcharged, in characteristic Pauline fashion, with expressions drawn from the metaphor of light with the result that, while its general meaning is clear, some of the details remain obscure. The gift of faith is clearly compared with the divine act of creation of light (Gn 1,3) ; and this may be applied to any conversion to Christianity. Moreover, Paul asserts that belief in Christ's divinity is essential to that faith (Christ has been called the image of God in v. 4)[28]. The apostle, however, in considering the *initium fidei* in the hearts of all believers, is led inevitably to recall the dynamic experience of his own conversion ; and so introduces the very concrete detail, which remains ever vivid to him, of that light of God's glory which radiated from the countenance of the glorified Christ he had beheld. This recollection explains the figure of light as symbol of faith. Nothing is so characteristic of the accounts in Acts of Saul's conversion as the insistence upon the light which shone round the risen Lord.

This passage highlights an important quality of the Damascus road experience of Saul. It was *an act of creation*, analogous to the divine creation

---

[26] This is probably the meaning of 2 Cor 5,16 b.

[27] For a résumé of Johannine soteriology, cf. D. M. STANLEY, « *From his Heart will flow rivers of living water* » (*Jn* 7,38) in *Cor Jesu : Commentationes in Litteras Encyclicas « Haurietis aquas »* I (Rome, 1959) 510-515.

[28] In 2 Cor 3,18, Paul has described the Christian existence in this world as a progressive transformation into the image of the Son.

of light. Paul twice employs this phrase to describe the mystery of man's elevation to the life of grace (Gal 6,15 ; 2 Cor 5,17). To this same cycle of ideas also belongs the Pauline presentation of the risen Christ as the new or second Adam (1 Cor 15,21-22.45-49 ; Rom 5,12-21), as well as Paul's view of the cosmic effects of Christ's death and resurrection (Rom 8,18-22).

The last reference to his conversion appears in Phil 3,12 : « Not that I am already arrived at the goal or am as yet perfect ; but I am [still] in pursuit in the hope that I may capture, since I was myself captured by Christ Jesus ». Here Paul speaks of his experience near Damascus as a seizure by the risen Christ. It is *the great grace* [29] in his life and the supernatural motive-power of all his apostolic activity. From that experience he has received the impulse to strive for the prize, « the heavenly call of God in Christ Jesus » (v. 14).

In the passage immediately preceding, Paul has described the revolutionary character of this capturing by Christ. All the advantages he possessed as a member of the race of Israel and the tribe of Benjamin he considers a disadvantage « with respect to Christ » and « the high privilege of the knowledge of Christ my Lord » : his faithful adherence to Pharisaism, the preservation of his ancestral tongue, the perfect observance of the Law. All this is « rubbish » compared with the gaining of Christ. « My own righteousness which is all the Law can bestow » is infinitely inferior to that righteousness by faith in Christ which comes from God alone.

We may now sum up the significance of Paul's Damascus experience as *point de départ* for his theological thought as follows [30] :

1) *the primary intuition of Jesus Christ as the Son of God risen from death*. The religious experience undergone by Paul at his conversion was essentially an experience of the living Christ. It was only three days later (Acts 9,9) that he received the Holy Spirit on the occasion of his Baptism at the hands of Ananias. All his life, Paul remained acutely con-

---

[29] PHILIPPE-HENRI MENOUD, *Révélation et Tradition* : *L' influence de la conversion de Paul sur sa théologie* in *VC* 7 (1953) 2-10. Speaking of Paul's conversion, Menoud says : « Il a compris alors que le salut est l'oeuvre de Dieu et non celle de l'homme ; chrétien, il est devenu par suite plus sceptique qu' il ne l'avait été quand il était Pharisien à l'égard de la possibilité qu'aurait l'homme de vivre par ses propres forces selon la volonté de Dieu » (6-7).

[30] MENOUD (*art. cit.*) points out two consequences for Pauline theology of the experience by the Damascus road : the *revelation* of God's Son, and Paul's realization of the Church's already existing *tradition*.

4. - D. M. STANLEY.

scious of the fundamental meaning of Christ's appearance to him, which
was underscored by the religious significance he attached to his blindness :
he had seen the Christ in glory, recognized him as divine, indeed as the
exalted Son of God (Gal 1,16).

2) *the realization that the risen Jesus was somehow present and active
in the world of men through his disciples.* This second moment in Paul's
initial Christian experience is found reflected in the words of the divine
Lord who appeared to him, and also in the fact that it was one of the disciples, Ananias, and not Christ himself who was to inform him of the
Master's will, who baptized and conferred the Spirit on him.

3) *the origin of Paul's vocation as apostle to the pagans, more specifically, of his role as Servant of Yahweh.* Paul received with the Christian
faith the call to be an apostle (Rom 1,1) ; and this vocation was revealed
to him as an extension of Christ's own ministry as the Servant of Yahweh
(Acts 9,15-16 ; 26,16-18 ; Gal 1,15 ; 1 Cor 9,1 ; 15,8). This double vocation
is on Paul's view a « new creation », an entirely gratuitous, wholly divine
transformation of a zealot Pharisee into an apostle (2 Cor 5,17 ; Phil 3,12).

§ 2. - The Gospel preached by Paul

In Acts, Luke gives two lengthy examples of Paul's preaching : one
to the Jews in Pisidian Antioch (Acts 13,16-41), the other to pagans at
Athens (Acts 17,22-31).

The discourse at Pisidian Antioch, which Luke intends to be taken
as typical of Paul's approach to Jews, is a carefully constructed speech,
whose triple division is clearly set out by the use of three apostrophes.[31]
The first section consists of a recitation of the divine *gestes rédempteurs* in
the OT and reveals the existence of an already carefully elaborated typology, in which the anti-type — God's action in raising Jesus from death —
has influenced the description of the OT types. Paul calls attention to the
divine election of the Hebrews (v. 17) and their « exaltation » during their
Egyptian enslavement [32] ; their exodus and entry into the heritage of

---

[31] F. PRAT, *La Théologie de Saint Paul* I [8] (Paris, 1920) 63 n. 1.
[32] The word ὑψοῦν belongs to the vocabulary of Christian resurrection theology ; cf. Acts 2,33 ; 5,31 ; Jn 3,14 ; 12,34 ; 8,28 ; 12,32 ; Phil 2,9.

the promised land as an effect of the divine power (v. 19) [33]. After the divine « gifts » of the judges (v. 20b) and of a king (v. 21), God « raised up » David (v. 22) [34]. The promise of a Davidic Messias was fulfilled by God's « bringing Jesus as Saviour for Israel » (v. 24). The section ends with a reference to the preaching of John the Baptist, precursor of Christ (vv. 24-25) [35].

The second section (vv. 26-37) contains essentially the kerygma of Jerusalem [36], which Paul describes as « the account of this salvation » (v. 26 ; cf. Acts 10,36) and in which the Jerusalem Jews and their leaders failed to perceive the fulfilment of the OT prophetic utterances (v. 27). The Jews were instrumental in accomplishing « the Scriptures » by demanding that Pilate pass sentence of death upon the innocent Jesus (vv. 28-29). God raised him from death (v. 30) and he appeared to those who are now witnesses to his resurrection (v. 31) [37].

The remainder of this section is devoted to the mystery of the resurrection, and it is here we find some traces of Paul's *cachet personnel*. His Gospel is the Gospel of the divine promise realized in Jesus' resurrection (v. 33a) [38]. He interprets Ps. 2,7 (« You are my Son : this day have I begotten you ») in function of the resurrection (v. 33b) [39]. Paul insists, as Peter had done, upon the fact that Jesus' sacred body was not subjected to corruption (vv. 34-37) [40].

---

[33] It is effected by the divine δύναμις like Christ's resurrection in Pauline theology : cf. Phil 3,10 ; 1 Cor 1,24 ; 5,4 ; 6,14 ; 15,43 ; 2 Cor 13,4 ; Rom 1,4 ; Eph 1,19 ; 3,7.

[34] The term ἐγείρειν also belongs to the vocabulary of the resurrection.

[35] John's function is to bridge the gap between OT and NT ; hence it was always the first point in the primitive preaching and was retained in the written Gospels.

[36] PIERRE BENOIT, *L'horizon paulinien de l'épître aux Ephésiens* in *RB* 46 (1937) 342-361 ; 506-525 ; M. GOGUEL, *Esquisses d'une solution nouvelle de l'épître aux Ephésiens* in *RHR* 112 (1935) 95 f. More recently, HEINRICH SCHLIER, *Der Brief an die Epheser*, 22-28, defends the Pauline authenticity of this epistle. So also, after a scrupulously careful examination of the problem, does L. CERFAUX, *Introduction à la Bible II*, 505-508.

[37] Note that Paul does not include himself amongst these apostolic witnesses in this section.

[38] This quality of Paul's Gospel, as we have attempted to show elsewhere, is particularly to the fore in his letter to the Galatian community : cf. *Theologia « Promissionis » apud S. Paulum* in *VD* 30 (1952) 129-142.

[39] The idea is similar to that later expressed in Rom 1,4.

[40] The point was capital in the primitive kerygma as the constant references to « the third day » show. As JACQUES DUPONT (*Actes des Apôtres* [2] 126 f) points

The final section (vv. 38-41) contains the exhortation to repentance after the manner of the Jerusalem preaching. Here again Paul's personal touch is perceptible in the references to justification by faith rather than by the Mosaic Law (v. 38) and to a section of Habacuc which appears as a favourite commonplace in the Pauline letters [41].

The address delivered in Athens before the council of the Areopagus appears, from the evidence in 1 Corinthians [42], to have been a unique experiment in presenting Christianity in the cultural capital of the ancient world, and consequently not altogether typical of Paul's approach to pagan audiences. In addition, it was an experiment which failed to gain many adherents to the new faith and was, as a result, replaced by the « folly of the cross ». However, Luke presents it as an example of preaching to pagans, and in many respects it may be considered as such.

The exordium (vv. 22-23), somewhat in the classical grand style, ably introduces the theme of Paul's discourse : the unknown God of the Athenians is the living God of Israel and of the Christians. The body of the speech sketches the principal divine attributes. God the Creator of the universe, its supreme Lord, unique source of all life, is set in contrast with the idols which dwell « in temples made by human hand » (vv. 24-25) [43]. His providence directs the destinies of the nations (v. 26a). The « argument from design » is invoked to show that the knowledge of God is attainable by all (vv. 26b-28), a *confirmatio* being added in the form of citations from Greek literature (vv. 28-29).

Only towards the end of the sermon is there question of a supernatural revelation : God's mercy, his universal offer of pardon (v. 30), his eschatological judgment, the carrying-out of which he has confided to « a Man » whom he has constituted Judge and accredited by raising him from death (v. 31). This is reminiscent of certain features in Peter's address to the pagans at Caesarea : the universal offer of salvation (Acts 10,34-35), the risen Jesus' role as Judge of the living and the dead (v. 42).

---

out, the inclusion of Is 55,3 here is a typically rabbinical argument. The Septuagintal text however speaks of the διαθήκη ἀιώνιος which Yahweh had made with the Davidic dynasty and which is referred to also in Ps 2,7.

[41] Heb 1,5. In Gal 3,11 and Rom 1,17 (cf. Heb 10,38), Paul cites this section (Heb 2,4).

[42] Cf. Paul's insistence (1 Cor 2,1 ff) that he used no rhetoric or human philosophy in his preaching to the Corinthians.

[43] DOM GREGORY DIX, *Jew and Greek* : *A Study in the Primitive Church* (London, 1953) 12-13. The author draws a striking contrast between the « formless » character of the Israelite aniconic cult and the Greek devotion to « form ».

At Athens, Paul had, from the very first (Acts 17,18), insisted strongly upon Christ's resurrection [44], but he had evidently said little about the « folly » of his death. His efforts were rewarded with slight success, and accordingly, upon his entry into Corinth, he was to change his tactics. The failure at Athens was caused by that rationalism which had vitiated the religious sense of the Greeks. Resurrection from the dead they would not accept because it contradicted their rigid conception of a cosmos tidily regulated by inexorable « laws » of nature, which permitted no intrusion of the divine. Paul learned his lesson well ; and the result was a direct assault upon this « wisdom of the world » at Corinth by means of a kerygma which proclaimed the definitive entry of God into the scheme of human history. Yet Paul never became anti-intellectual. There is a Christian wisdom (1 Cor 2,6-16), and the human intellect, like the rest of man, is susceptible of redemption, provided it obey the Gospel's summons to μετάνοια [45].

There are no other full-length discourses in Acts which present examples of Paul's preaching [46]. There are frequent references to it however, both in Acts and in the epistles. Immediately upon Paul's conversion in Damascus, he set out to preach Jesus as « the Son of God » (Acts 9,20) ; he preached « in the Name of Jesus » (Acts 9,27) ; and three years later in Jerusalem, he preached « in the Name of the Κύριος » (Acts 9,28). Of his preaching to Gentiles during the year he spent with Barnabas at Antioch (Acts 11,25), we have almost no record (cf., however, Acts 15,35). Here he came into contact with the form of the kerygma adopted by the Hellenists and had perhaps his first taste of proclaiming the Gospel to the Gentiles. This pattern of preaching he later exposed before Peter in Jerusalem and had it approved by him (Gal 2,1-9).

Of the sermons preached on the first missionary journey together with Barnabas, we possess, in addition to that in Pisidian Antioch already alluded to, a brief discourse on the living God delivered to the pagan

---

[44] Cf. Acts 17,32 f : Paul's mention of the resurrection which ran counter to the Greek philosophy (and to Greek religion, which tolerated no miracles) was clearly the cause of his failure at Athens. Cf. ALAN RICHARDSON, *An Introduction to the Theology of the New Testament* (New York, 1958) 51-52.

[45] L. CERFAUX, *L'Église des Corinthiens* (Paris, 1946).

[46] The discourse to the elders of the Ephesian church (Acts 20,18-35) must be considered rather as an example of the Pauline *teaching* : cf. *Didache as a Constitutive Element of the Gospel-Form* in *CBQ* 17 (1955) 225-226.

Lycaonians at Lystra (Acts 14,15-17). We know that Paul's Gospel also proclaimed the « Kingdom of God » (Acts 14,22).

On the second journey, at Philippi, Paul's preaching is characterized as an announcement of « the way of *salvation* » (Acts 16,17) and as « the word of *the Lord* » (v. 32). Both these expressions (σωτηρία, Κύριος) indicate the transposition of the kerygma into terms comprehensible to the Greek-speaking pagans, a task already undertaken to a degree by the Hellenistic evangelists. Luke tells us that at Antioch they had tried the experiment of turning to « the Greeks » and « preaching the Gospel of Jesus as Κύριος » (Acts 11,20 ; cf. 15,35) with great success. Instead of preaching Jesus as the Messias, a title which would mean nothing to non-Jewish audiences, the Hellenists proclaimed him as Κύριος to the Gentiles, a term which connoted for them his universal lordship and his divinity, and which had been given already a traditional Christian meaning [47].

Luke gives a brief summary of Paul's preaching to the Jews at Thessalonica. Bible in hand, the apostle had proved to them « the Messias had to suffer and rise from the dead » ; and he testified that Jesus was the Messias (Acts 17,2-3). That he also preached the Kingdom in which sovereignty belongs to Jesus [48] is proven by the account of the accusation made against him (v. 7).

In Corinth, Paul states that he preached the traditional kerygma which he himself « had received » : Christ died for our sins, was buried, was raised the third day, as the Scriptures had foretold ; and subsequently appeared to those entrusted with the office of witnessing to his resurrection (1 Cor 15,1-9).

At Ephesus, Paul preached the Kingdom of God to the Jews [49], but without success (Acts 19,8). Paul refers to the evangelization of Ephesus in his discourse to the seniors of that church as a testimony before pagans and Jews concerning the « turning to God and belief in Jesus as our Lord »

---

[47] Cf. the hymn cited in Phil 2,9-11.

[48] The charge is that Paul claimed that Jesus was a βασιλεὺς ἕτερος ; this is reminiscent of the discussion between Jesus and Pilate in Jn 18, 33-19,16.

[49] Luke states that this sustained attempt by Paul to win over those of his own race lasted for three months ; nowhere else in Acts is there mention of such a long and fruitless effort on Paul's part. It is all the more curious, since on Paul's first visit the Jews had asked for a fuller explanation of the Gospel (Acts 18,20-21). This frustration was undoubtedly a contributing factor to the change which Paul's outlook underwent at Ephesus during these years. We shall refer to this crisis again in the following chapter.

(Acts 20,21), as a witnessing to « the Gospel of the loving favour of God » (v. 24b), and a proclamation of « the Kingdom of Jesus » (v. 25) [50].

During his arraignment before the Sanhedrin in Jerusalem, Paul declares that he is a Pharisee, that « it is for our hope, the resurrection of the dead, that I am on trial » (Acts 23,6). Before Felix the governor, he professes his faith in the Law and the prophets and his confident hope « that there will be a resurrection of the just and of sinners » (Acts 24,15). Festus, Felix' successor, tells Agrippa of Paul's quarrel with the Jews « concerning a certain Jesus who is dead, whom Paul declared to be alive » (Acts 25,19). Paul himself tells Agrippa that he has been jailed « because of my hope in the promise made by God to our fathers » (Acts 26,6-8) — God's raising of the dead —, a hope to which the Jewish cult itself witnesses. He describes his kerygma as concerned with the need of repentance and a return to God by means of « works worthy of repentance » (Acts 26,20). His testimony includes only what is already contained in the predictions of Moses and the prophets, « that the Messias must suffer, and, as the first to be raised from death, he must announce light for the people and the pagans » (Acts 26,22-23).

Arrived in Rome, Paul preached first to the Jews ; and by witnessing to the Kingdom of God tried to persuade them about Jesus from the Law and the prophets (Acts 28,23). When his message was rejected by them, he turned to the pagans, « proclaiming the Kingdom of God and teaching what concerns Jesus as Κύριος » (Acts 28,31).

There are occasional references in Paul's letters to his preaching, which, if sporadic, still serve to discover points of emphasis in his kerygma.

Two such points, which he insisted upon at Thessalonica, were the service of the living God in place of idolatry, and the expectation of « his Son from heaven, whom he raised from death, Jesus, our rescuer from the wrath that is coming » (1 Thes 1,10). At Corinth, he also preached the expectation of « the revelation of our Lord Jesus Christ » (1 Cor 1,7) ; and he stressed « Jesus as crucified » (1 Cor 1,23 ; 2,2) in the way he had already done in Galatia (Gal 3,1). He proclaimed the sovereign lordship of the glorified Christ (2 Cor 4,5), his divine sonship revealed in his resurrection, and his Davidic lineage (Rom 1,4 ; 2 Tm 2,8), his role as

---

[50] Thus it is clear how closely Paul must have followed the pattern of the kerygma which we can rediscover from the Synoptic Gospels, where the notion of the Kingdom is a dominant theme.

supreme Judge at the end of time (Rom 2,16). His preaching concerned
itself with at least the principal mysteries of Jesus' life included in the
apostolic tradition : the account of the Last Supper (1 Cor 11,23-26),
the details of the passion (1 Tm 6,13-14), as well as the death, burial and
resurrection (1 Cor 15,3).

There is little doubt that Paul's preaching had certain characteristic
themes which were not present in the Palestinian kerygma. The most
notable perhaps of these is the proclamation of « the Mystery » *par excellence* : the admission of pagans into the Church on a footing of absolute
equality with Jewish Christians (Rom 16,25-26 ; Col 1,24-27 ; Eph 3,1-13).

It is to be recalled that the distinction between *preaching* and *teaching* referred to in the last chapter [51] is clearer in Paul than in the other
NT writers, and that the greater part of his letters fall within the category
of *teaching* rather than preaching in the technical sense. Consequently,
it is necessary to guard against the inclusion in the Pauline kerygma of
elements which belong to διδαχή. At the same time also, since the evidence for *what* Paul *preached* is limited, one must beware of using the
term in too exclusive a sense [52]. Moreover, Paul's constant concern for
uniformity of doctrine in the churches committed to his care, and his deep
loyalty to the apostolic tradition as it came from the Jerusalem community must be borne in mind [53]. With these *caveats* before us, we may
summarize Paul's preaching under the same three divisions used in resuming the Jerusalem kerygma, in order that the points of comparison and
of contrast may be kept to the fore.

1) *the sacred history of Israel has reached its consummation*. In the
résumé of his Gospel which Paul exposes to the Roman church, he includes
the whole OT revelation (Rom 1,1-2). This factor is abundantly illustrated
by the Pisidian Antioch sermon (Acts 13,16-25). The principle underlying

---

[51] Chapter I p. 27.

[52] It is a highly dangerous, if somewhat alluring, method to assume that Paul's
kerygma was substantially different from that emanating from Jerusalem under
the aegis of Peter. While Paul undoubtedly preached the Gospel in a manner that
was quite personal, one can safely assume that it was not basically different from
that of the apostolic college.

[53] Cf. Paul's remarks in 1 Cor 15,3 ; in 1 Cor 11,23 there is no reason to think
that Paul is insisting upon the immediacy of what « I received from the Lord ».
Paul's denial of the possibility of there being any Gospel different from that which
he preached (Gal 1,7-9) lends further support to this contention.

THE PREACHING OF PAUL 57

the harmony of the two testaments is one very dear to the apostle : God's method of dealing with mankind is constantly the same whether in the old or the new dispensation [54]. The Antiochian sermon demonstrates the function of this axiom in the development of a Christian hermeneutics of the OT. God's intervention in the lives of Abraham, Joseph, the kings and prophets, are so many examples of the divine pedagogy, preparing the minds of the Chosen people for the coming of Jesus Christ. The kerygmatic recital of such *gestes salvifiques* is calculated to imbue the hearers with a sense of the consummation of this prophetic history in the present age.

The evangelist when preaching to pagan audiences sought to produce this same sense of fulfilment by insisting that God, in times past, while overlooking the sins of those who did not know him, offered this knowledge of himself and his essential attributes through the manifestation of his provident care of the human race in his creation (Acts 14,15-17 ; 17,24-31 ; cf. Rom 1,18-32 ; 2,16). The future judgment of mankind through the mediation of the risen Jesus was also dwelt upon (1 Thes 1,10). Paul's repeated insistence upon the lordship of the risen Christ is another illustration of this same point in his kerygma (Acts 9,28 ; 15,35 ; 16,17 ; cf. Rom 10,9 ; 14,9).

One theme which appears to have been preached both to Jewish and to pagan audiences is that of the coming of the Kingdom. Paul preached it on his first missionary journey (Acts 14,22). It is mentioned also in the sermons to the Jews and pagans of Thessalonica (Acts 17,7), and at Ephesus to the Jews first (Acts 19,8), then to the pagans (Acts 20,25). We find Paul in Rome still preaching the same doctrine to the Jews (Acts 28,23) and to the pagans (Acts 28,31). It is not without significance for the central place held by the Kingdom in Paul's preaching that in Acts the proclaiming of the Kingdom is only mentioned in connection with his activity.

2) *the message of salvation.* Jesus' death for our sins (cf. 1 Tm 1,15-16) and his resurrection « according to the Scriptures » lie at the heart of Paul's kerygma as in the Jerusalem preaching. A difference however is observable : Paul preached Jesus' resurrection as witnessed to by the apostles (cf. Acts 13,31), not by himself. It may well be, however, that

---

[54] Note that in resuming his Gospel in Rom 1,1-4, Paul explicitly mentions the OT prophecies and promises as forming part of the Christian kerygma.

some reference to his seeing the glorified Christ on the Damascus road was included in his sermons [55]. Was Jesus' public ministry part of Paul's preaching? As FERDINAND PRAT remarks [56], it is scarcely credible that Paul omitted it entirely ; and the fact that he did include the work and preaching of John the Baptist (Acts 13,24-25) confirms this view. Still it is curious that Luke nowhere gives any hint that Christ's earthly life was touched on by Paul. While it is not likely that he omitted it altogether, still, as he was not himself an eye-witness to the events and had not come to a knowledge, at least a supernatural knowledge, of Jesus by means of the Galilean ministry (cf. 2 Cor 5,16b), it is conceivable that Paul felt less at home with this section of the Gospel-message and tended to stress it less. In any event, we know that his *teaching* (as distinct from his preaching) did not proceed along the lines of the Jerusalem διδαχή , which popularized the theology of the ' *Ebed Yahweh*. This favourite vehicle of the apostolic preaching (and teaching) was not much employed by Paul who had forged the Servant theme into a theology of the Christian apostolate [57].

   3) *the call to repentance*. As in the Jerusalem kerygma, this was the final point preached by Paul (Acts 13,38-41 ; 17,30 ; 1 Thes 1,10). Its particular importance in Pauline theology is shown by the great stress which the apostle places upon justification by faith in his letters.

   While Paul thus faithfully followed the general lines of the Gospel as outlined by the Palestinian preachers, still several points are characteristic of his presentation of Christ. Jesus is depicted by him as Son of God (Acts 9,20 ; 13,33 ; Rom 1,4) ; the resurrection of Christ accomplishes specifically the promise of salvation made to Abraham (Acts 13,23. 32-33). With Paul, it would seem that the divine motives for the redemp-

---

   [55] One might infer this from 1 Cor 15, 1-8, which resumes certain points of Paul's preaching at Corinth.

   [56] F. PRAT, *op. cit.* I 36 ff. Cf. also JULES LEBRETON, *Les origines du dogme de la Trinité* [3] (Paris, 1910) 289 ff.

   [57] « ... Paul's utilization of the Servant theme as applied to his own missionary activity led to a new dogmatic development, which in its turn was of the greatest importance. It produced a characteristically Pauline thesis : the mystical conception of the Apostolic vocation. Aware of his Divine appointment as the Servant of Yahweh, Paul perceived, more deeply perhaps than any other inspired New Testament writer, that in carrying on the work of his Lord as the Servant in gospelling to the Gentiles, he was in a very real sense identified with Him » : *The Theme of the Servant of Yahweh* 420.

tion find more explicit enunciation than in the Jerusalem kerygma : there is God's fidelity to his own promise, that is his « justice » (cf. Rom 1,17-4,25), and God's love for men (Rom 5,8 ; 8,39 ; Col 1,13 ; Ti 2,11 ; 1 Tm 1,15-16), as well as his mercy (Acts 17,30).

As Paul himself remarks, it is this *preaching* which gives the stamp to the teaching we call Pauline : the Gospel is the τύπος of Paul's διδαχή (Rom 6,17). This teaching, which we shall presently study in detail, insofar as it is concerned with Christ's resurrection, is simply a further development of his kerygma. The points he has picked out for emphasis in his teaching are those he will deepen in his theology. Moreover, it is to be expected that, as Paul's διδαχή evolved in the course of his missionary life, this would have repercussions upon his preaching.

CHAPTER III

THE DEVELOPMENT OF PAULINE DOCTRINE

The question of the evolution of Paul's theology has received more nuanced answers in recent years than it did half a century ago[1]. Yet the critics are far from agreement on this subject. BERNARD ALLO insists that all the essential points of Paulinism were revealed to the apostle in the light of the Damascus experience[2]. C. H. DODD considers the mysterious θλῖψις, which brought Paul face to face with death in Ephesus as the cause of a very significant change in Paul's eschatology, in his evaluation of the human institutions of this world, in his concept of universalism, and in the notion of reconciliation[3]. MAX MEINERTZ, while denying any « essential or contradictory evolution » in Paul's teaching, admits development in the doctrine of justification between Galatians and Romans, and in the conception of the Mystical Body of Christ, which received its fullest expression in Ephesians as a result of the spread of the Church and the time for reflection afforded by Paul's Roman captivity[4]. LUCIEN CERFAUX finds three periods which mark Paul's theological growth : the first (eschatological) was inspired by the primitive community in Jerusalem ; the second (mystical) was the result of Paul's experience in the mission-field and his personal meditation ; the third (cosmic) grew out of Paul's contacts in Asia Minor with

---

[1] The earlier Pauline criticism was concerned in large measure with the question of the authenticity or inauthenticity of the letters ascribed to Paul : cf. ALBERT SCHWEITZER, Geschichte der Paulinischen Forschung (Tübingen, 1911).

[2] E.-B. ALLO, L'évolution de l'Évangile de Paul in Vivre et Penser RB (1941) 48-77 ; (1942) 165-193.

[3] C. H. DODD, The Mind of Paul : a Psychological Approach in BJRylL 17 (1933) 91-106 ; The Mind of Paul : Change and Development in BJRylL 18 (1934) 69-110.

[4] MAX MEINERTZ, Theologie des Neuen Testaments (Bonn, 1950) II, 3.

the Jewish-Christian milieu [5]. The late WILFRED L. KNOX took a more radical view of the evolution of Paul's theology. Faced with the task of evangelizing the pagan world, the apostle discarded the eschatological presentation of the Gospel in favour of a cosmological view more in keeping with Hellenistic speculation, an adaptation in which the Alexandrian Greeks had preceded him (especially in the personification of wisdom). Thus in 1 and 2 Corinthians, Paul revises his eschatology : the resurrection of a spiritual body replaces that of the material body, and such a conception of resurrection is later replaced by a spiritual immortality of the soul liberated by suffering from its earthly prison. In Galatians and Romans, with a Jewish-Christian audience in mind, Paul talks of the redemption in terms of justification, speaks of the descent from Abraham and the new creation. Colossians marks the last step in the metamorphosis of Paulinism. Here the language of gnostic illuminism is adopted, and while asserting Jesus' superiority over the spiritual beings that inhabit the heavenly spheres, Paul does not deny their reality. The most serious consequence of this last stage in Paul's evolution is the identification of the historical Jesus with eternal divine wisdom, which no longer occupies the secondary place it held in 1 Corinthians, but assumes the primacy in his Christology. Jesus is not merely the head of the social body, the Church, but of the cosmos, and as such, can reconcile not merely men but the celestial powers with God. Philippians, the last authentically Pauline epistle, written from the Roman captivity, adds nothing to Paul's theological development [6].

We may say once that there is some truth in each of these opinions. Nor can we hope to present a solution to the problem of Paul's development which does not borrow elements from several of these conceptions. What we propose here is to determine the order of Paul's letters as exactly as possible by the use of historical, not doctrinal, data provided by the NT [7], and then to seek formative influences upon Paul's

---

[5] L. CERFAUX, *Le Christ dans la théologie de saint Paul* (Paris, 1951). The author states in the Foreword, « Nous supposons qu'elle (la pensée de saint Paul) a été une pensée vivante », 7. In his general Conclusion (399-403), he distinguishes three successive levels of interest in Pauline thought. Cf. also the résumé of this book by J. COPPENS, *La Christologie de Saint Paul* in *L'Attente du Messie* (Bruges, 1954) 139-153.

[6] WILFRED L. KNOX, *St. Paul and the Church of the Gentiles* (Cambridge, 1939).

[7] The distinction between historical and doctrinal data, when it is a question of using Paul's letters as sources, is not always easy to clarify. Thus, for example,

thought amongst the various events of his apostolic life which are known to us. This latter consideration has not, as far as I am able to ascertain, hitherto received the attention it merits in studies concerned with Pauline theology and its development [8].

First of all, it must be admitted that the difficulties raised against the probability of change in the mind of Paul carry a certain weight. Paul was a Christian, with considerable experience in the work of evangelization, for fifteen years before any of the canonical epistles were written. Moreover, the period covered by his extant letters is hardly fifteen years in duration. Can Paul's theological attitude, then, have changed notably in so short a time ? In addition, the great revelation, with which his Christian life began, loomed large in his formation, and it contained, at least germinally, much that was later enucleated in the course of his ministry. This initial experience was completed, more thoroughly perhaps than the earlier Pauline critics suspected, by careful training in the evangelical traditions emanating from the Jerusalem community. Furthermore, there is, as we have already pointed out, a distinction between *preaching* and *teaching*, a distinction which must be borne in mind in the present inquiry. Paul's Gospel must not be confused with his more theological reflection upon the data of the Gospel, such as we find in his letters [9]. Finally, evolution must not be taken to mean that Paul turns from one viewpoint to adopt another without carrying over anything of this earlier theological position. As we shall observe in examining the texts, each centre of interest continues, to a greater or lesser extent, to have repercussions upon the further stages of Paul's thought [10].

---

we would classify as historical Paul's varying attitudes towards his adversaries (which obviously have certain doctrinal aspects).

[8] One ventures to make such a statement with great hesitation and considerable reserve. Many excellent biographies of Paul do this undoubtedly to a certain extent : cf. GIUSEPPE RICCIOTTI, *Paolo Apostolo* (Roma, 1946) ; JOSEPH HOLZNER, *Paulus : Ein Heldenleben im Dienste Christi in religionsgeschichtlichem Zusammenhang dargestellt* (Freiburg im Breisgau, 1937) ; F. PRAT, *Saint Paul* [25] (Paris, 1946) ; MARTIN DIBELIUS, WERNER GEORG KÜMMEL, *Paulus* (Berlin, 1951) ; ANGELO PENNA, *San Paolo* [2] (Alba, 1951).

[9] It is of course understood that the Pauline epistles contain allusions to the kerygma, to credal formulae and to hymns, which belong rather to the genre of the spoken word.

[10] L. CERFAUX, *op. cit.* 399 : « On ne constate pas de véritable évolution dans la christologie paulinienne, en ce sens que les matériaux principaux restent les mêmes à travers les épîtres ».

Granted that there are difficulties attendant upon a study of development in the Pauline teaching, still, when we recall the many and varied experiences which Paul underwent even during this brief period of his literary activity, it should not be surprising that his theology suffered several important modifications. This will seem the more plausible where there is question of a temperament so sensitive and a character so adaptable as Paul's. Moreover, a mind as creative as his could not but react continally to the impressions made on it by its surroundings and the persons with whom he came into contact [11]. Development is an essential property of life ; and there have been few minds so alive as that of the apostle of the Gentiles.

It is true that in his correspondence Paul is usually dealing with particular situations, discussing specific problems. Modern Pauline criticism has become more conscious of the danger of taking a one-sided view of Paul's theology at a given period because of the questions upon which his attention is concentrated. Yet it must be admitted, on the other hand, that these particular situations force the apostle to bring into play the whole of his intellectual and religious genius, and so develop these very phases of his teaching [12]. To assume that Paul's addressees were the only ones to receive a clearer grasp of certain aspects of the Christian Mystery would be to ignore the basic laws of human psychology and to misunderstand Paul's own character and temperament. The errors and the crises to which the communities to whom he wrote were subjected undoubtedly provided Paul himself with new insights into the truths he preached as well as with new and apter formulae for their expression.

Except perhaps for an occasional shift of emphasis, it seems very unlikely that Paul ever changed the basic themes of the kerygma which

---

[11] We may say that there were two principal factors operative in Paul's apostolic career : revelation and experience.

[12] Thus Paul's meeting with the characteristically Greek mentality in Athens and Corinth forced him to re-think the theology of Christ's redemptive work, as also the significance of the parousia, in terms of a more interior causality than that of the divine Will merely, which the Palestinian kerygma had been content to proclaim. The Apostle's struggles with the judaizers clarified his own views of the absolutely universal efficacy of Christ's death. Finally, his missionary activity and the resulting growth of the Church as an institution in this world turned his attention to her nature and function as an external, historical, visible continuation of Jesus' own mission to men, with the result that we have the Pauline conception of the Church as « the Body of Christ ».

he inherited from the apostolic circle in Jerusalem [13]. It must be admitted that on this point we possess very scanty evidence. But that Paul's teaching remained static is, we believe, not supported by the facts which lie under our control. Two factors were continually operative in Paul's theological development : revelation and the experiences of the apostolate. These two necessarily went together, — a fact of which Paul, like Luke [14], was well aware.

§ I. - The Chronological Order of Paul's Epistles

Before proceeding any further, we must attempt to determine the order in which the Pauline epistles were written. The letters ascribed to Paul by the NT we consider to be genuinely his, apart from the epistle to the Hebrews [15]. As regards the Pastoral epistles, we shall prescind from the vexing question of their Pauline authenticity for reasons to be given at the end of the present chapter.

The following is the chronological order we have adopted :

I, 2 Thessalonians
Philippians
I Corinthians
2 Corinthians
Galatians
Romans
Philemon, Colossians, Ephesians
[I Timothy, Titus,
2 Timothy].

The majority of modern critics are agreed that the first letter of Paul's which has survived is I Thessalonians. While the balance of schol-

---

[13] The Lukan attribution to Paul of sermons in Acts (e. g. Acts 13,16 ff) which do not differ essentially from those ascribed to Peter (although they do contain characteristically Pauline expressions and viewpoints) may be validly accepted as evidence of this.

[14] The peculiarly Lukan conception (not evinced by other evangelists) that the experiences of the apostolic Church during her formative years are an integral part of the Gospel (cf. ÉTIENNE TROCMÉ, Le « Livre des Actes » et l'Histoire (Paris, 1957) 47-50) is one that Luke undoubtedly had inherited from his master Paul.

[15] We accept the conclusions of C. SPICQ regarding the relation of Heb to Pauline theology (without however subscribing to his hypothesis that Apollo was its author) : cf. C. SPICQ, L'Épître aux Hébreux I (Paris, 1952) 169-219.

arly opinion does not lean as heavily in favour of the authenticity of 2 Thessalonians, still it is considered sound to accept it also as genuine [16]. Both these epistles were probably written from Corinth, shortly after Paul's arrival there for the first time, towards the end of the year 51 or the beginning of 52 [17].

The next period of Paul's literary activity, of which we have some record, dates from his stay in Ephesus during two to three years (cf. Acts 19,20 ; 20,31) somewhere between the years 55 and 58. The two letters we assign to this very troubled time in Paul's life are Philippians and 1 Corinthians. It seems clear that 2 Corinthians was written during the journey through Macedonia en route to Corinth at the close of 57 or the beginning of 58. Galatians also must belong to this same journey. for reasons we shall enumerate later. It may well be that both 2 Corinthians and Galatians were written from Philippi.

One basic reason for the order we have adopted is drawn from the movements of Timothy. Assuming for the moment that Paul wrote Philippians from Ephesus rather than from Rome, it becomes clear that Philippians is the first of the Ephesian letters. At the moment of writing it, Paul was intending to dispatch Timothy to Philippi in the very near future (Phil 2,19). By the time Paul composes 1 Corinthians, Timothy has departed from Ephesus (1 Cor 4,17), but there is not time enough for Paul to have learned whether he has reached Corinth (1 Cor 16,10) [18]. In 2 Corinthians, we find Timothy once more at Paul's side (2 Cor 1,1). The Apostle has, by this time, left Ephesus after the trouble with the silversmiths (Acts 20,1), journeyed to Troas where he hoped to find Titus returned from Corinth, crossed over to Macedonia (2 Cor 2,12-13), where he meets Titus bearing good news (2 Cor 7,5-7). As Paul writes

---

[16] ALFRED WIKENHAUSER, *Einleitung in das Neue Testament* (Freiburg, 1953) 262-265 ; BEDA RIGAUX, *Les Épîtres aux Thessaloniciens* (Paris, 1956) 121-152 ; WILLIAM NEIL, *The Epistles of Paul to the Thessalonians* (London, 1950) xix-xxvi.

[17] One must insist on the approximate nature of these dates. L. CERFAUX, in his introduction to *Les Actes des Apôtres* [2] 26, places Paul's stay at Corinth between 51-53 ; in the same volume, J. DUPONT states (162) that Paul arrived at Corinth at the end of 50 and left in the summer of 52. B. Rigaux, *op. cit.* 45, dates 1 Thes in the first half of 51 (he is vague on date of 2 Thes, but insists it was not written simultaneously with 1 Thes, 74-75).

[18] In fact, from this last named passage, it is to be assumed that Paul expects the present letter to arrive in Corinth ahead of Timothy, who has been directed to stop along the way to visit Philippi and other Pauline communities.

5. - D. M. STANLEY.

2 Corinthians, Titus is preparing to return to Corinth as the bearer
of the epistle (2 Cor 8,6.16-17.23-24) and the precursor of Paul himself [19].

We must now prove our hypothesis regarding the Ephesian origin
of Philippians, an opinion which has gained favour in recent years [20].
The most cogent reason [21] for postulating Ephesus rather than Rome
as the place of origin for Philippians is the fact that Paul states that he
has received no alms from Philippi since he was in Thessalonica on his
second missionary excursion (Phil 4,16). He gives, as reason for this, the
Philippians' lack of a suitable opportunity (Phil 4,10). We know, however
(Acts 20,2 ; 20,6), that by the time Paul was imprisoned in Rome *he
had twice visited the Philippian church,* and consequently on either of
these occasions he could have been given financial support. To assume
that his allusion to a lack of opportunity is sarcasm or irony would
appear to contradict the evidence for the unusually cordial relations
between Paul and his Philippian Christians [22].

The main objection against this view of the origin of Philippians
is the silence of Acts regarding any imprisonment of Paul at Ephesus.
This argument *ex silentio Lucae* loses its cogency however when it is
recalled that Luke does not mention the very serious threat to Paul's
life at Ephesus (2 Cor 1,8-9). Consequently, it seems reasonable to admit
that Paul was imprisoned at Ephesus, whatever Luke's reason for omit-
ting any reference to it [23].

---

[19] Titus was probably the bearer of 1 Cor ; hence he stayed on in Corinth
after Timothy's departure to see that Paul's orders were carried out there, returning only when he can bring word of some progress in Christian practice on the
part of the Corinthians.

[20] J. HUGH MICHAEL, *The Epistle of Paul to the Philippians* [5] (London, 1948)
xiii-xxi. Among Catholic authors, this opinion is held by PAUL GAECHTER, *Summa
Introductionis in Novum Testamentum* (Innsbruck, 1938) 204-206 ; PIERRE BENOIT,
Les épîtres de Saint Paul aux Philippiens, etc (Paris, 1949) 11-13, and (it would seem)
by STANISLAS LYONNET, *Bulletin d'exégèse paulinienne (IV)* in *Bib* 32 (1951) 569-586.

[21] For other reasons, cf. PIERRE BENOIT, *op. cit.* 11-12 ; also A. WIKENHAUSER,
op. cit. 311-312.

[22] Paul's attitude appears constantly throughout the epistle : cf. Phil 1,3-11 ;
1,21-26 ; 2,12 ; 4,1-20.

[23] For a good discussion of this whole point, cf. GEORGE S. DUNCAN, *St.
Paul's Ephesian Ministry* (London, 1929) 95-107. We wish to add some considerations of our own to this question. Acts 19,8-12 would seem to give us a clue to the
period of Paul's incarceration at Ephesus. We learn that after vainly trying to preach
to the Jews and convert them, Paul broke with them and set up a catechetical
centre in the school of Tyrannos. Now the motive given by Phil 1,12-13 for Paul's

The relative position of 1,2 Corinthians and Galatians, letters written sometime in this same period, must now be determined [24]. First of all, Galatians would appear to have been written later than 1 Corinthians [25], since Paul refers to his organization of the Jerusalem collection in Galatia without giving any hint of a judaizing crisis in that region (1 Cor 16,1) [26]. Indeed it seems fairly obvious that at the date of 1 Corinthians the judaizing tendencies, which were to harass the apostle in some of the churches he had founded, were not yet a real issue. He views the various « parties » at Corinth as stemming from personal loyalties rather than from doctrinal differences (1 Cor 1,11 ; 3,5.21-22). He can still speak of making himself a Jew with Jews (1 Cor 9,20-22), a policy he must certainly have abandoned in the period of the judaizing crisis. As J. B. LIGHTFOOT has pointed out, there is a sharp contrast between Paul's attitude of indifference towards circumcision when writing 1 Corinthians (cf. 7,18) and the view he expresses in Galatians (cf. 5,2.11) [27].

Having established the priority of 1 Corinthians over Galatians, it remains to discuss the relative chronology of Galatians and 2 Corinthians. Modern critics, impressed by the striking similarity between Romans and Galatians, place the composition of these letters at approximately the same period [28]. As far as the question of doctrinal development is concerned, the date of Galatians relative to 2 Corinthians is of slight importance, once it be granted that Galatians is posterior to 1 Corinthians. M. GOGUEL [29] advances an argument for placing Galatians after 2 Corin-

---

imprisonment is the preaching of the Gospel, and one suspects (cf. Phil 3,2-6) it was Paul's Jewish adversaries (Phil 1,28) who had him jailed. Moreover, Acts 19,12, which speaks of miracles worked by the application of articles of clothing which had touched Paul's body, is the more easily understood on the hypothesis that Paul was, at the time, in jail, and so unable to heal the sick personally. Finally, Paul's imprisonment at Ephesus would explain why Epaphras founded the communities of Colossae, Laodicaea, and Hierapolis (Col 1,7 ; 4,12-13), when the Apostle himself was so near at hand, a departure from Paul's customary habit (cf. Rom 15,20).

[24] We do not believe that the celebrated « South Galatian » theory has been satisfactorily proved ; hence Gal belongs to this period. Cf. STANISLAS LYONNET, *Les épîtres de Saint Paul aux Galates, aux Romains* [2] (Paris, 1959) 10-15.

[25] From the literary and doctrinal point of view, of course, the parallels existing between Gal and Rom form a most suasive argument on this point.

[26] From this, it would seem fairly certain that Paul has as yet no suspicion of what is going on in the Galatian churches.

[27] J. B. LIGHTFOOT, *St. Paul's Epistle to the Galatians* [3] (London, 1869) 53.

[28] STANISLAS LYONNET, *op. cit.* 15.

[29] In his review of Oepke's commentary on Gal in *RHPhilRel* 18 (1938) 535-

thians, which appears to be valid. When writing 2 Corinthians, Paul does not seem as yet to have understood that his adversaries are not merely attacking him personally, but are opposing his doctrine (cf. 2 Cor 2,5-10 ; 3,5 ; 5,12 ; 10,2.10-18 ; 11,5.13.22-23 ; 12,11). M.-J. LAGRANGE [30] has observed that, while the judaizing opposition appears to have evolved further in Galatians than in 2 Corinthians, this may be due to the fact that in Galatia such opposition was more deep-seated than at Corinth. However, GOGUEL's view, which is also that of J. B. LIGHT-FOOT [31], carries much weight ; and it seems to provide a sufficient reason for placing the composition of Galatians soon after 2 Corinthians.

By the time Paul wrote Romans, the judaizing danger appears to have passed. Paul is now able to include the Jewish Christians among the « weaker » brethren (Rom 14,1 ff). The whole letter breathes a serenity rarely equalled by any of the other Pauline epistles [32]. It is generally considered to have been composed at Corinth during Paul's three months' stay in Greece (Acts 19,2-3) [33]. In the concluding chapters, Paul is on the point of leaving Greece because of a plot against him by the Jews there (Rom 15,18 ; Acts 20,3). Phoebe, deaconess of the church at Cenchraeae, is to take the letter to Rome with her (Rom 16,1-2). Paul left Corinth some time before Easter in the year 58, as he celebrated that feast with the Christians in Philippi (Acts 20,6).

To the Roman captivity belong most probably the letters to Philemon, to the Colossians and to the Ephesians [34]. There are very few historical data in these letters, which provide a basis for dating them [35]. The strongest argument for placing Colossians after Romans is the more developed theology of the cosmic aspects of the redemption which it contains [36]. The authenticity of Ephesians is still frequently questioned.

---

[30] M.-J. LAGRANGE, Épître aux Galates (Paris, 1918) xxviii.

[31] J. B. LIGHTFOOT, op. cit. 55. For other explanations of the nature of these Pauline adversaries, cf. A. WIKENHAUSER, op. cit. 282.

[32] Rom is more like a theological treatise than any other letter from the pen of Paul.

[33] STANISLAS LYONNET op. cit. 51.

[34] PIERRE BENOIT, op. cit. 9-10.

[35] In Phlm and Col, Paul appears to have the same missionary companions (Col 4,7-14 ; Phlm 23-24), and the mission of Onesimos (Col 4,9 ; Phlm 12) seems to be a contemporary event. Mark's presence (Col 4, 10 ; Phlm 24) would suggest, as BENOIT has noted, that Rome (possibly Caesarea) is the place of origin of these letters.

[36] ERNST PERCY, Die Probleme der Kolosser- und Epheserbriefe (Lund, 1946) 135-136.

However, the majority of commentators now admit that the refusal to regard it as Pauline raises at least as many serious difficulties as does the view which attributes it to Paul [37]. From the doctrinal aspect, Ephesians represents a synthesis of the teaching of Colossians and Romans [38]. Accordingly, it seems best to regard it as later than either of these letters.

The letters to Timothy and to Titus belong to a period of Paul's missionary activity after his release from prison in Rome, which is probably implied by Acts 28,30 [39]. They would appear to have been written in the year or two preceding Paul's death, traditionally dated about 67 [40]. The first letter to Timothy is said to have been written from Macedonia (1 Tm 1,3), the second from prison in Rome (2 Tm 1,17 ; 2,9). The epistle to Titus seems to be contemporaneous with 1 Timothy [41].

§ 2. - The Crises in Paul's Life which bear upon his Doctrinal Development

In the preceding chapter, Paul's conversion and the events immediately connected with it have been dealt with at some length [42]. We wish now to take cognizance of the significant events during Paul's apostolic career which may be considered formative factors in the evolution of his theology.

These periods of development appear to be associated with Paul's relatively lengthy stays in Antioch, Corinth, and Ephesus respectively. At the beginning of his missionary life, Paul lived with the Antiochian community for a year (Acts 11,26) ; and, if the period of his first missionary journey be also included, the time extends to almost two years (Acts 14,28 ; 15,35). At Corinth, on the occasion of his first visit, Paul stayed at least eighteen months (Acts 18,11). Paul's sojourn in Ephesus, which marked his second visit to that city, lasted from two to three years (Acts 19,10 ; 20,31). Finally, at Rome, during his imprisonment,

---

[37] PIERRE BENOIT, L'horizon paulinien de l'épître aux Éphésiens in RB 46 (1937) 342-361 ; 506-525. M. GOGUEL, Esquisse d'une solution nouvelle de l'épître aux Éphésiens in RHR 112 (1935) 95 f.

[38] PIERRE BENOIT, op. cit. 10.

[39] Cf. J. DUPONT, op. cit. 219 n. e.

[40] A. WIKENHAUSER, op. cit. 256.

[41] Cf. the discussion by SPICQ in his commentary, pp. LXXIII-LXXXVIII.

[42] Cf. infra p. 39-50.

Paul was forced to remain at least two years (Acts 28,30). It is the experiences of these first three periods of Pauls' life we now wish to examine insofar as they may aid us in tracing the development of Paul's theological thought.

Paul was brought to Antioch by Barnabas from Tarsus where he had gone into a kind of retirement after his first visit to Jerusalem as a Christian (Acts 11,25). On that occasion, a vision had revealed to him the impossibility of his preaching in the Palestinian church (Acts 22,17-21). At Antioch, Paul witnesses a novel experiment in Christianity, where the community appears for the first time in history distinct from Judaism as well as from paganism (Acts 11,26). Owing to the distance from the Temple, where the « wall of separation » would have divided Jewish and Gentile Christians, both sections of the Church live in harmony. In fact, the community is predominantly pagan in origin. Moreover, the « breaking of the bread » assumes its due liturgical place at the centre of the community's life, since it is no longer overshadowed by the gorgeous ritual of Jerusalem (Acts 13,1). As a result of these local conditions, Antiochian Christianity emerges as an autonomous institution in the world, with a distinctive name and a new cultic life. The community's leaders were drawn from the Hellenists (Acts 13,1) and, as such, were the heirs of Stephen's spirit. Here Paul imbibed the broader outlook of these men : their universalist preoccupations with the conversion of the pagans, their somewhat anti-Jewish sentiments, their theological development of the kerygma with its emphasis on the ' Ebed Yahweh theme, which manifested itself most probably in the eucharistic liturgy which they had created [43], their use of the Greek Bible, their development of OT typology [44], their demonstrations of the attributes of the living God [45].

The most decisive event during this period for Paul occurred one day during the celebration of the eucharistic liturgy (Acts 13,1 ff). The Holy Spirit disclosed to the community the Christian ideal of the missions. Nothing perhaps so clearly differentiates the Antiochian formula

[43] D. M. STANLEY, *Liturgical Influences on the Formation of the Four Gospels* in *CBQ* 21 (1959) 24-38 ; also *The Divinity of Christ in Hymns of the New Testament* in *Proceedings* : *Fourth Annual Convention of the Society of Catholic College Teachers of Sacred Doctrine* (Notre Dame, Indiana, 1958) 12-29.

[44] Stephen's speech (Acts 7,2 ⁻:) is the classic example, as is also Heb 11,1-40.

[45] BERTIL GAERTNER, *The Areopagus Speech and Natural Revelation* (Uppsala, 1955) 170-202.

of Christianity from that of Jerusalem as the birth of the missionary spirit. The descent of the Holy Ghost on the first Pentecost, when the Jews of the diaspora had come in large numbers to Jerusalem on pilgrimage [46], was seen as the fulfilment of the Isaian prophecy which had placed the mountain of Sion as a focal point for the gathering of the messianic people (Is 2,3). Accordingly, it had seemed that the growth of the new faith was to be the result of a centripetal movement of which Jerusalem was the centre. But at Antioch, the Holy Spirit had clarified the issue by unleashing the dynamic centrifugal force, which was to carry the Gospel to the « end of the earth » (Acts 1,8).

The experience of the first missionary journey under Barnabas' guidance taught Paul a great deal about methods of evangelizing. The Gospel must be preached first to the Jews, and only when they had rejected it, to the Gentiles (Acts 13,5-12 ; 13,42-48 ; 14, 1 ff). This pattern had been provided through Peter's teaching that the second Coming of Christ was dependent upon Israel's conversion (Acts 3,19-21), a doctrine which the Hellenists appear to have adopted [47].

Paul's preaching of the Kingdom of God retained its full eschatological significance (« it is by many tribulations that we must enter the Kingdom of God », Acts 14,22). Paul was also engaged in organizing the local churches on this evangelical tour of southern Asia Minor (Acts 14,23). The Church was simply « the Way » to the Kingdom.

Another experience which was to have its repercussions upon the preaching of Paul was the crisis created by the judaizing Pharisees at Antioch, which appears to have occurred shortly after the return of Paul and Barnabas from their missionary journey (Acts 15,1 ff). These men preached circumcision and the observance of the Mosaic law as a necessary means of salvation for the Christians converted from paganism. While this issue was definitively settled by the council of Jerusalem (Acts 15,25 ff), still it was to leave its mark on Paul's manner of preaching the « scandal of the cross ». He seems to have perceived in this Judaeo-Christian insistence upon Mosaic customs a certain hesitancy in admitting the universal efficacy of Christ's death for man's redemption. Paul

---

[46] A. CAUSSE, *Le pèlerinage à Jérusalem et la première Pentecôte* in *RHPhilRel* 20 (1940) 120-141.

[47] Despite their revolutionary experiment in evangelizing Antioch (Acts 11,19-21), the Hellenists (to judge by Barnabas and Saul) customarily preached first to the Jews in the Diaspora, and only when these refused to accept the Gospel, to the pagans.

sensed that somehow, despite their conversion to Christianity, Christ's death had remained a « scandal » for them [48]. At any rate, we find that in the evangelization of Galatia, Paul insisted very much upon the crucified Christ (Gal 3,1) [49]. This doctrine becomes henceforth the touchstone of orthodoxy in the Pauline kerygma.

The painful episode between Peter and Paul at Antioch, which probably occurred after the council of Jerusalem [50], only served to confirm Paul in his opinion on this point. To return to the Law was tantamount to admitting oneself guilty of transgressing it. The Christian is dead to the Law (Gal 2,19) and that by the very force of the Law itself (Gal 3,13) [51]. Paul's experience already at Antioch had brought the issue into sharp focus for him : any judaizing tendency was a voiding of the gift of God ; « for if justice comes from law, then Christ died uselessly » (Gal 2,21).

The next transitional point in Paul's theological development occurs around the time of his first visit to Corinth. He approached that city full of dread and fear (1 Cor 2,3). He had come fresh from his first signal failure in Athens, the city that symbolized the quintessence of the Greek spirit. This first contact with Greek superficiality had frightened Paul. It was something he had never before encountered, and he was at a loss as to how to deal with it.

His previous attempts at preaching the Gospel, on the other hand, during his second missionary expedition, of which we know something, in Galatia, at Philippi, and Thessalonica, had been somewhat in the nature of a triumph. He had found the Galatians sunk in idolatry (Gal 4,8-11), ravaged by impurity (Gal 5,21). Yet, though he himself was ill at the time, though he had confronted them with the cross, the Galatians had received him affectionately and welcomed him « as Christ himself » (Gal 4,13-14). Nor had the testimony of the Holy Spirit failed to accompany his preaching (Gal 3,3-5) ; the neophytes had had an inner experience of their adoptive filiation (Gal 4,6).

In Philippi, where Paul had gone in obedience to the vision inviting him to Macedonia (Acts 16,9), he had succeeded in founding a community whose charity followed him after his departure (Phil 4,15-16). His very sufferings in Philippi had redounded to the triumph of the kerygma

---

[48] Gal 5,2.11-12 ; 6, 12-15.
[49] L. CERFAUX, op. cit. 147.
[50] STANISLAS LYONNET, op. cit. 14.
[51] ibid. 28 n. d.

(Acts 16,19-39) ; and after an appeal to his Roman citizenship [52] had struck fear into the hearts of his persecutors, Paul had had the satisfaction of being allowed to depart with dignity.

In Thessalonica, numbers of pagans had forsaken idolatry to profess the Christian faith (1 Thes 1,10). Once again, Paul's preaching was accompanied by « works of power, the action of the Holy Spirit », which gave him « absolute confidence » (1 Thes 1,5). Paul's letter witnesses to the great affection he felt for this community (1 Thes 2,7-12). And if Paul was forced by Jewish connivance to flee the city, his newly-won converts assisted his flight (Acts 17,5-10), and their subsequent perseverance in the face of persecution was to prove his greatest consolation at Corinth (1 Thes 2,13-14).

At Athens however Paul was to feel frustration to a degree perhaps never again equalled in his life. Deprived even of the human consolation of companionship (1 Thes 3,1), he failed to arouse more than a polite, sceptical interest in his sophisticated audience (Acts 17,18-20). His official hearing before the council of the Areopagus [53] met with only thinly-veiled cynicism. Whether Paul felt afterwards that he had betrayed the message of the cross by attempting to render the kerygma more palatable by quoting tags from the Greek poets, we do not know. We do know that he came to appreciate the truth that only by « the folly of the cross » could the kerygma save the Greek-educated mind, which had been made the measure of all things (1 Cor 1,18-25 ; 3,18-20). Paul had formerly realized the need of insisting upon Christ's death with Jews who demanded miracles as the price of their acceptance of Jesus Christ. To the Greeks he must preach « the folly » which is divine wisdom : Christ must be announced as « our wisdom from God » (1 Cor 1,30 ; 2,6-9), once they had been brought, through belief in his redemptive death, to admit the limitations of mere human philosophical wisdom. Paul appreciated the lesson thus painfully learned at Athens, and he acknowledges his indebtedness to the Greeks in writing to the Roman church (Rom 1,14).

At Corinth also Paul was forced to re-evaluate the eschatological setting of his kerygma by the crisis which an over-eager expectation of Christ's second Coming had produced in Thessalonica. At first, there was disquiet over the fate of those Christians who had met death, possi-

---

[52] HENRY J. CADBURY, *The Book of Acts in History* (New York, 1955) 65-82.
[53] As to whether this was an official investigation by the council or not, cf. BERTIL GAERTNER, *op. cit.* 52-65.

bly as a result of persecution (1 Thes 4,13-16). It was necessary to insist on the lack of revelation concerning the time of the parousia (1 Thes 5,1-3). Finally, Paul had to declare that «the day of the Lord» had not yet dawned (2 Thes 2,1-3). This statement shows how the earlier opinion about «the day of the Lord» had undergone refinement (Acts 2,20). Paul also reminded the Thessalonians of what he had already told them concerning «the obstacle» to the parousia of «the adversary» (2 Thes 2,6) [54].

These crises with which Paul had to deal before and during his stay in Corinth were not without their repercussions upon his theological development. In the correspondence with Thessalonica we may still discern the role played by Christ's resurrection in the earlier Pauline theology. At first, as was natural, it evoked the hope of the general resurrection of all Christians which was to occur at the Lord's second Coming (1 Thes 4,14). The completely apocalyptic description of these eschatological events, which is the same as that subsequently recorded by the Synoptics [55], indicates that the Pauline teaching of this era was a very careful reproduction of the Jerusalem kerygma. As in the primitive preaching, the risen Christ, rather than the crucified Christ, appears as Saviour (cf. Acts 3,26), as «our rescuer from the wrath that is coming» (1 Thes 1,10). As a result, the Christian life is measured against this eschatological background : conversion (1 Thes 1,10), supernatural vocation (1 Thes 2,12 ; 2 Thes 2,13), progress in perfection (1 Thes 3,13 ; 5,9.23), hardships and persecution (1 Thes 2,18 ; 2 Thes 1,5).

But the difficulties which the parousiac expectation evoked in the Thessalonian church and, to an even greater extent, the soulsearing experiences of Paul's introduction to the vagaries of the Greek spirit with its sceptical rejection of any resurrection from the dead, forced the apostle to reconsider the key-points in his kerygma. This transition in Paul's thinking is reflected in the first letters he wrote upon leaving Greece.

---

[54] The opinion identifying «the obstacle» with the Roman imperial power, which found such favour amongst the patristic writers, would explain quite satisfactorily one factor which was undoubtedly influential in changing Paul's view regarding the parousia. On the evidence of Acts, it was the Roman officials who constantly protected Paul and saw that justice was done, despite the calumnious accusations of the Diaspora Jews, in whose malice the Apostle could scarcely fail to recognize the evil work of «the adversary» (cf. for example 1 Thes 2,18).

[55] BERNARD ORCHARD, *Thessalonians and the Synoptic Gospels* in *Bib* 19 (1938) 19-42. Orchard's view, viz. of Paul's *literary* dependence upon the Greek Mt, is not supported, we believe, by the evidence.

Gradually his mind turns from the relation *resurrection-parousia* to a newer synthesis *death-resurrection*. In Philippians, the values of the Christian life are still reckoned in terms of « the day of Jesus Christ » (Phil 1,6.10.19.28-29 ; 2,16 ; 3,11.14.20-21 ; 4,1.5). In 1 Corinthians, there is considerably less insistence upon this criterion (1 Cor 1,8 ; 3,13 ; 5,5). Already Paul thinks of the knowledge of Christ in terms of « the power of his resurrection and fellowship in his sufferings » (Phil 3,10). The points of the kerygma upon which Paul insists with the Corinthians concern the death and resurrection of Christ (1 Cor 15,3-4). He conceives the eucharistic liturgy as a heralding of the death of the risen Christ (1 Cor 11,26). The further development of this newer resurrection-theology must await the phase of Paul's career during his stay of almost three years at Ephesus.

On his first visit to Ephesus, Paul had been well received by the Jews (Acts 18,20) and had left Priscilla and Aquila there (Acts 18,19), after promising to return. Upon his return, he received a group of John the Baptist's disciples into the Christian faith. The event was accompanied by a Pentecostal outpouring of charisms (Acts 19,1-7). Paul then spent three months arguing with the Jews about the Kingdom of God. But his efforts were doomed to failure (Acts 19,8-9). During the next two years, he taught in the academy of Tyrannos, and his preaching was accompanied by many extraordinary miracles (Acts 19,11). Yet this period was, on the whole, a time of great suffering both physical and spiritual for Paul. He describes it to the Corinthians as a fight with « wild beasts » (1 Cor 15,32). He was, it appears [56], imprisoned, and some time after writing 1 Corinthians, he certainly came face to face with death (2 Cor 1,8). His beloved Corinthian church was torn with party factions (1 Cor 1,10 ff). Paul was obliged to write them an extremely painful letter (2 Cor 2,3 ff ; 7,8 ff) and to make an even more painful visit to them (2 Cor 2,1 ; 13,1-2), which had ended most unsatisfactorily for Paul. During this period also, Paul became aware that there was much personal opposition to himself in the churches he had founded (Phil, 1,15-17 ; 2,20-21 ; 2 Cor 10,10-11). On the eve of his departure from Ephesus, he received word of opposition amongst the Galatians to his collection for Jerusalem (cf. Gal 6,7-10) and of their imminent danger of succumbing to the solicitations of the judaizers.

All this suffering was to bear fruit. First of all, about this time, Paul

---

[56] Cf. n. 23 p. 66-67.

arrived at a new theology of history which he exposes in his letter to the
Roman church (cf. Rom 11,25 ff). He came to the very important conclusion that the conversion of the Gentiles was destined, in God's plan,
to precede the collective return of Israel. This new insight enabled Paul
to fill out the simpler view, expressed earlier by Peter (Acts 3,19-21), that
Christ's parousia was attendant upon the conversion of the Jews to Christianity, an event which had naturally seemed close to fulfilment. The
factor which Paul introduced into the original schema did not prove it
false. But it had the very important effect of lengthening out indefin-
itely the primitive view of Christian history. Once the call of the Gentiles
was known to precede that of the Jews, the second Coming of the Lord
was removed far into the future ; and for the first time, perhaps, it was
borne in upon Paul that he likely would not live to witness the Master's
parousia.

It is also probable, as C. H. DODD believes [57], that the crisis which
brought Paul close to death had something to do with this new view. However, two other causes also present themselves. Firstly, it would appear that
Paul had spent more time and effort than usual in attempting to convert
the Ephesian Jews. This had resulted only in signal ill-success (2 Cor
3,14-15) and in active Jewish hostility to him (Phil 3,18-19). This bitter
experience taught Paul that Israel's time of believing was not yet. A
second reason, which may have confirmed this opinion, came from the
machinations of the judaizers within the Christian fold. Paul divined the
real threat to the Gospel which lay behind this movement. It was an
attempt to nullify the message of the cross. Thus he must have become
aware that in converting the Jews to the Church there was always the
possibility of increasing the judaizing faction.

The second important effect of Paul's Ephesian tribulations was to
direct his attention to the nature of the Church herself and to what is
commonly called the mysticism of the apostolate. With the disappear-
ance of his hopes for a proximate parousia and the increased probability of his death before that event, Paul was forced to reconsider the nature
and the meaning of the institution which was steadily growing in this
world and which represented the Kingdom of God's Son (Col 1,13), the
Church. His attention was also directed to the significance of his own
labours and sufferings for the spread of that Kingdom, particularly since

---

[57] C. H. DODD, *The Mind of Paul : a Psychological Approach* in *BJRylL* 17
(1933) 103 ff.

the validity of his own apostleship was being called into question at this time.

Consequently, in the letters written during this period and shortly after it (Phil, 1 Cor, 2 Cor, Gal), Paul is taken up with ecclesiastical problems : unity of doctrine, unity amongst the faithful, pastoral questions, dangers of heresy and persecution. He begins to sketch a theology of the Church as the « Body of Christ » (1 Cor 10,17 ; 12,12-30).

With 2 Corinthians there is a new shift of viewpoint. Paul has been « under sentence of death » (2 Cor 1,9) ; and while he thinks occasionally of the parousia (2 Cor 1,14 ; 5,10), still he now conjectures that he himself will have died before that « day » (2 Cor 4,14-18 ; 5,1-10). Moreover, his attention is concentrated upon the presence of Christ in his community (2 Cor 13,3-6), upon Christ's action in his own ministry (2 Cor 4,11-12 ; 5,20 ; 6,1-10), and upon his sharing the sufferings of his Lord (2 Cor 1,5 ; 4,10). Confronted with the serious possibility of his own death, Paul begins to view death *as a normal experience of the Christian life*, an integral part of the drama of salvation that must occur in each Christian. With 2 Corinthians, we do not find any further reference to the « transformation » of those still alive at the parousia. The sorrows, sufferings, the encounter with death itself, which form part of Christian existence now appear related to the notion of salvation (2 Cor 1,6 ; 7,10).

By the time Paul writes Galatians, he makes astonishingly little use of the sobering thought of the « day of the Lord » (cf. Gal 1,4 ; 5,21), although such considerations might have proven an efficacious deterrent to the fickle Galatians. One veiled reference to the last judgment reflects Paul's changed attitude (Gal 6,9-10) [58]. His appeal in this letter is rather to the personal experience of the Spirit (Gal 2,19-21 ; 3,3-5 ; 5,16-25 ; 6,14). The central theme of his letter is the Gospel of the promise (3,6-4,31) at whose centre stands the great mystery of the Christian's adoptive filiation (3,26-29 ; 4,4-7 ; 4,28-31).

An important result of this judaizing crisis is Paul's new view of Christ's death as a dying to the Mosaic Law. Actually this conception was only the enunciation of a truth Paul had long been aware of : to accept the Law was to render the cross null and void (Gal 2,19-21 ; 5,2). No compromise was possible : the Christian must remain « co-crucified with Christ »

---

[58] Note that in this passage the whole attention is concentrated upon the possibilities for good in the present time, while the phrase καίρῳ ἰδίῳ appears to suggest not only the complete ignorance of the Apostle but a feeling of resignation (and hence a muted sense of its immediacy).

(Gal 2,19) and Christ had, once for all, become « a curse » for the sake
of those he had redeemed from the Law (Gal 3,13). Judaizing was in reality
nothing but an attempt to escape « persecution for the cross of Christ »
at the hands of fellow Jews (Gal 6,12), whereas the Christian is by definition one who is « crucified » (Gal 5,24 ; 6,14). In these considerations,
we perceive Paul striving to express more fully the *positive effects* of
Christ's death, a line of thought which reaches its culmination in Rom
5,1-7,25.

Another theme, which Paul is sketching during this period, is that
of the « new creation ». Already in his earlier preaching to pagans, Paul
had dwelt upon the attributes of the living Creator of the universe (Acts
14,15-17 ; 17,22-31) and upon the universal parenthood of Adam (Acts
17,26) [59]. It seems clear from the very numerous references in his letters
to the creation-accounts of Genesis that Paul was not content with preaching a sort of Hellenistic theodicy, but was accustomed to combine the
arguments from reason with the biblical notion of the creation of the
world [60].

The phrase « new creation » appears only twice in Paul's letters (2 Cor
5,17 ; Gal 6,15) but the concept is outlined in Rom 8,18-22, and it will
be developed more fully in the Captivity epistles (Col 1,15-20 ; 2,9-10.15 ;
3,5-24 ; Eph 1,9-10.20-23 ; 2,1-2 ; 3,10.18-19 ; 4,7-10 ; 5,21-6,12). The
conception of Christ as the new or second Adam is touched upon briefly
in 1 Cor 15,20-22.45-49. It is exploited fully in Rom, 5,12-21, and is
the basis of the conception of the Church as the « Body of Christ ».

The letter to Rome which Paul wrote from Corinth in 58 is the most
complete expression of Paul's mature theological thought on the redemption, the product of his whole apostolic experience. The degree to which
Paul's soteriology is developed in Romans may be measured by the com-

---

[59] STIG HANSON, *The Unity of the Church in the New Testament* (Uppsala,
1946) 103-104.

[60] We give here a list of references or allusions in Paul's letters to the opening
chapters of Gn : 2 Thes 3,10 = Gn 3,19 ; Phil 2,6 = Gn 1,27 ; 3,5 ; 1 Cor 6,16 =
Gn 2,24 ; 1 Cor 11,3 = Gn 3,16 ; 1 Cor 11,7 = Gn 1,27 ; 1 Cor 11,8 = Gn 2,22-23 ;
1 Cor 11,9 = Gn 2,18 ; 1 Cor 14,34 = Gn 3,16 ; 1 Cor 15,21 = Gn 3,17-19 ; 1 Cor
15,38 = Gn 1,11 ; 1 Cor 15,45 = Gn 2,7 ; 1 Cor 15,47 = Gn 2,7 ; 1 Cor 15,49 =
Gn 5,3 ; 2 Cor 4,6 = Gn 1,3 ; 2 Cor 11,3 = Gn 3,4.13 ; Gal 4,4 = Gn 3,15 ; Rom 5,12
= Gn 2,17 ; 3,19 ; Rom 6,12 = Gn 3,7 ; Rom 7,11 = Gn 3,13 ; Rom 7,18 = Gn
6,5 ; Rom 8, 20 = Gn 3,17-19 ; Rom 14,2 = Gn 1,29 ; Rom 16,20 = Gn 3,15 ;
Col 1,15 = Gn 1,27 ; Col 2,10 = Gn 1,26-27 ; Eph 4,24 = Gn 1,26-27 ; Eph
5,30-31 = Gn 2,24 ; 1 Tm 2,14 = Gn 3,8.13 ; 1 Tm 4,4 = Gn 1,31.

pleteness with which the divine « motives » for man's redemption are therein expressed. Indeed, the plan of the epistle is governed by them : God's justice or fidelity to his OT promises of salvation, God's love [61]. Here too we find a fully evolved theology of history (Rom 9-11).

While the parousia retains its importance as the cause of « the redemption of our bodies » (Rom 8,23), it is mentioned but rarely in this letter (Rom 13,11-12). In the principal soteriological passages of this letter, Paul's attention is concentrated upon the significance of Christ's death and resurrection in effecting man's salvation (Rom 1,4 ; 3,21-26 ; 4,25 ; 5,8-11 ; 8,3-4 ; 14,7-9) [62]. This accentuation of the redemptive causality of these two events is most probably the result of Paul's controversy with the judaizers, whose championing of the necessity for salvation of Mosaic observance, was in effect a denial of the universal and absolute efficacy of Christ's death.

Paul's first Roman imprisonment around the years 61-63, during which he assisted the communities of Asia Minor to withstand the dangers of a serious crisis which threatened the purity of the Christian faith, leads to a new, and, we may say, final phase of Paul's development [63]. His attenion is directed to the Person of the risen Lord, the pre-existent Son, who intervened in the creation of the world, who descended into human history to effect man's salvation, and who, by « ascending to the height of heaven » (Eph 4,10), has wrought the new creation. Here for the first time, Paul distinguishes the exalted Christ, as Head, from his Church, which is his Body (Col 1,18, etc.). Towards the close of his letter to the Roman community, Paul sounded the first notes of a theme which is fully orchestrated in these letters written from his Roman captivity. He calls it « the Mystery » : « the Good News I announce in the preaching of Jesus Christ, the revelation of a Mystery wrapped in silence during countless aeons, but now revealed and made known through the prophetic Scriptures, according to the design of the eternal God, to all Gentiles, in order to bring them to the obedience of faith » (Rom 16,25-26). In these letters, and particularly in that to the Ephesians, which contains the mature expression of Paul's soteriology and ecclesiology, we shall find that the Christian liturgy appears as a new focus of interest.

The Pauline authenticity of the letters to Timothy and Titus was

---

[61] STANISLAS LYONNET, *Note sur le plan de l'épître aux Romains* in *RSR* 39 (1951) 301-306.
[62] C. H. DODD, *The Apostolic Preaching and Its Developments* 42-44.
[63] C. SPICQ, *L'Épître aux Hébreux I* 165.

accepted without question in the early Church. The Apostolic Fathers cite them frequently : only the heretics, Marcion and Basilides, appear to have rejected them. This tradition, maintained by Catholic scholars of the present day [64], was first seriously questioned in the nineteenth century. While exegetes outside the Church for the most part continue to deny that Paul wrote these Pastoral epistles, a number of prominent Protestant critics have tended to accept them as Pauline [65].

Since these letters simply repeat soteriological formulae which are obviously traditional, and since Christ's resurrection is mentioned explicitly only once in what appears to be part of an ancient credal formula (2 Tm 2,8), it is unnecessary to reopen here the discussion of arguments for or against their Pauline authorship. While they unquestionably reflect Pauline doctrine, they do not represent any notable development in his thought, whether by Paul himself or another [66]. Their insistence upon safeguarding the apostolic teaching as a « deposit » (1 Tm 6,20 ; 2 Tm 1,14) suggests they are the work of an old man, who, faced with death, is concerned about the continuance of the work to which he has devoted his life [67].

---

[64] For the latest Catholic reiteration of the traditional position, cf. L. CERFAUX, *Les Épîtres Pastorales* in *Introduction à la Bible II* (Tournai 1959) 529.

[65] *ibid.* 528 f where CERFAUX names W. MICHAELIS, J. BEHM, J. JEREMIAS, as among Protestant critics who hold the traditional view regarding the Pauline authenticity of these epistles.

[66] Cf. the study of the conception of Christ found in the Pastorals by H. WINDISCH, *Zur Christologie der Pastoralbriefe* in *ZNT* 34 (1935) 213-238.

[67] In ch. IX, we shall review the principal passages which deal with the concept of Christian salvation found in the Pastorals. Their main interest for our investigation, however, lies in the fact that they witness to the traditional elements in Christian soteriological teaching, whether Pauline or Palestinian.

CHAPTER IV

THE EARLIEST CORRESPONDENCE : FIRST AND SECOND THESSALONIANS

Bibliography : JOHN LILLIE, *Lectures on the Epistles of Paul to the Thessalonians* (Edinburgh, 1863). J. B. LIGHTFOOT, *Notes on Epistles of St. Paul* (London, 1895). G. MILLIGAN, *St. Paul's Epistles to the Thessalonians* (London, 1908). E. VON DOBSCHÜTZ, *Die Thessalonicherbriefe* (Göttingen, 1909). J. M. VOSTÉ *Commentarius in Epistolas ad Thessalonicenses* (Rome-Paris, 1917). ALFRED PLUMMER, *A Commentary on St. Paul's First Epistle to the Thessalonians* (London, 1918). MARTIN DIBELIUS, *An die Thessalonicher I II. An die Philipper*[3] *HNT* 11 (Tübingen, 1937). F. AMIOT, *Épître aux Galates, Épîtres aux Thessaloniciens, VS* 14 (Paris, 1946). D. BUZY, *Épîtres aux Thessaloniciens, SBP* 12 (Paris, 1946). J. E. FRAME, *Epistles of St. Paul to the Thessalonians*[2], *ICC* (Edinburgh, 1946). ALBRECHT OEPKE, *Die Briefe an die Thessalonicher*[4], *NTD* 8 (Göttingen, 1949). L.-M. DEWAILLY, B. RIGAUX, *Les Épîtres de Saint Paul aux Thessaloniciens, BJ* (Paris, 1954). B. RIGAUX, *Les Épîtres aux Thessaloniciens, EB* (Paris-Gembloux, 1956).

PRAT points out that the Thessalonian epistles present a faithful reflection of Paul's preaching at this stage of his missionary career, with their allusions to Christ as judge and Saviour, to the Kingdom, eschatological basis of Christian hope, to the divine wrath to come upon all unbelievers, and to the second coming of Jesus Christ[1]. CERFAUX also admits that these letters give a good deal of space to eschatology[2]. He suggests that the spirit of the Macedonian Christians was more recep-

---

[1] F. PRAT, *La Théologie de Saint Paul I*[8] (Paris, 1920) 85-86.

[2] L. CERFAUX, *Le Christ dans la théologie de saint Paul* (Paris, 1951) 230 : « C'est un fait que les épîtres aux Thessaloniciens font large place à l'eschatologie. Le Messie était venu, le salut annoncé se manifestait, le Christ entré dans la gloire y convoquait ses fidèles. En Macédoine, saint Paul trouva des esprits préparés à l'entendre et à se tourner vers des promesses glorieuses ».

tive of the call to prepare to meet the parousiac Christ than was that of the Corinthians, who appear to have had a lively interest in the immediate enjoyment of the charismatic blessings brought by Christianity.

It is clear of course that Paul's attention in these two letters is directed to the parousia because of the peculiar problems which arose amongst his addressees. But, while granting that such is the *Sitz im Leben* of Paul's remarks upon the redemption to the Thessalonians, we think it clear that at this point in his missionary activity Paul preached a kerygma closely modeled upon the Palestinian tradition in which the eschatological concept of the « last times » played a predominant role. His fidelity in using imagery borrowed from Jesus' logia for his own descriptions of Christ's second Coming (1 Thes 4, 13-17 ; 2 Thes 2,3-12) and in insisting upon the lack of revelation concerning the date of the parousia (1 Thes 5,1-3 ; 2 Thes 2,2) is proof of that fact. As we progress in our study of Paul's letters, we shall have occasion to remark upon the gradual reorientation of the apostle's kerygmatic viewpoint which we believe is clearly shown in 2 Corinthians and in the epistles which follow it.

§ 1. - The Pauline Kerygma to the Pagans. 1 Thes 1,9-10

The first half of the letter reviews the events connected with the foundation of the Thessalonian church (1 Thes 1,1-3,10). Paul first depicts his evangelization of Thessalonica (1,2-10) ; its success forms the subject of his thanksgiving (2-3) ; the charisms which accompanied it are proof of the Thessalonians' predestination (4-5) ; their splendid example to Macedonia and Achaia (6-7) is heralded everywhere by Paul's Thessalonian guides (8) [3] ; and their report resumes Paul's kerygma at Thessalonica (9-10).

9 For, in regard to us, they continue to broadcast what kind of entry to you we gained, and how you turned to God from idols to serve a living God, alone

---

[3] RONALD A. KNOX, *A New Testament Commentary for English Readers II* (New York, 1954) 298 : « And there was no question of rumours reverberating through the civilized world about the success of St Paul's preaching in Thessalonica. Wherever he went, in Macedonia and in Achaea and everywhere else (which probably means Illyria), the story of his preaching in Thessalonica and the miracles which attended it was told, not by this or that casual traveller, but *by the Macedonian guides who were conducting St Paul himself*. Their existence is implied by Acts 17.10, and mentioned explicitly in Acts 17.15 ».

worthy of the name, 10 and to await his Son from heaven, whom he has raised
from death, Jesus our rescuer from the wrath to come.

[9 a. The reading ὑμῶν (Vat.) is a correction based on a misunderstanding of Paul's
intended contrast in these lines.
10 a. ἐκ νεκρῶν (Alex., Ephr. rescript.) is more typically Pauline than ἐκ τῶν νεκρῶν
(Sin., Vat., D) : cf. Col 1,18 ; Eph 5,14.]

v. 9. Paul's expression, *the entry to you we gained*, is a strange one and a
hapax in the Greek bible (FRAME). Εἴσοδος means the *act* of entering, not the reception, or « door » (LIGHTFOOT) [4]. Paul stresses his act
of entering Thessalonica because it means the advent of salvation (cf.
2 Cor 6,1-2) for his hearers. Where Paul enters, the gospel enters, Christ
enters. Hence the rest of the sentence summarizes his preaching. The
very brief résumé is valuable as evidence of the general tenor of the Pauline kerygma at this point.
You turned to God from idols. In preaching to pagans, Paul did not aban-
don the traditional Gospel-schema, but merely prefixed to it a brief instruction in monotheism [5] after the manner of the Jewish religious propaganda in the Diaspora [6] as a necessary prelude to the Christian message in
a pagan world (OEPKE). The term *idols* [7], applied to the statues of pagan
gods, signifies, as in the LXX, what is void of reality [8] in contrast with
a living God. This expression, like that of the *service* of God, an OT
religious ideal (Jer 23,7-8), reveals the Jewish flavour of Paul's preaching [9].

---

[4] WILHELM MICHAELIS, εἴσοδος, *TWNT V*, 110 : « Die Konstr mit πρός,
die ... beim Zutritt zu Personen eingebracht ist, findet sich 1 Th 1,9 ; 2,1. Dabei
zeigt die Aussage 2,1 ... dass εἴσοδος auch hier den actus ingrediendi meinen
muss, denn nur dann ist die Verwendung von κενός am Platz. »
[5] L. CERFAUX, *op. cit.* 269-270 : « La propagande dans le monde païen ne
brisa pas avec le schème initial. Elle atteignit d'abord des prosélytes, qui croyaient
déjà en Dieu et avaient à accepter la foi spécifiquement chrétienne. Quand elle
s'adresse directement aux paiens, elle se fait en deux temps : une préparation rapide
au monothéisme (quitter les idoles et adorer le vrai Dieu) et croire au Christ que
Dieu a ressuscité des morts et qui nous sauvera de la colère à venir ... C'est la
relation avec le Christ qui spécifie la foi de l'Église ».
[6] R. BULTMANN, *Theologie des Neuen Testaments* (Tübingen, 1948) 69.
[7] GREGORY DIX, *Jew and Greek* (Westminster, 1953) 13.
[8] JOHN L. MCKENZIE, *The Hebrew Attitude towards Mythological Polytheism*
in *CBQ* 14 (1952) 323-335.
[9] JACQUES DUPONT, *Gnosis : la connaissance religieuse dans les épîtres de saint
Paul* (Louvain-Paris, 1949) 333 : cf. also *ibid.* 376.

For the Christian, as for the Jew, the living God is the only *real* God. He is moreover the one who can raise the dead.

v. 10. *to await his Son from heaven*. The divine filiation of the lowly, suffering Jesus of Nazareth was the principal datum of Paul's initial Christian experience on the Damascus road : through his resurrection, Jesus had « become » Son of God. Such was Paul's psychological approach to the mystery of the incarnation, and it always coloured his conception of Christ's divinity (Gal 1,16 ; 4,4 ; Rom 1,4 ; 8,3 ; Acts 9,20 ; 13,33). It is noteworthy that from Paul's earliest letters « Son of God » is employed in its full theological sense [10]. The expectation of the parousiac Christ, which also dominated the apostolic preaching (Acts 3,19-21), is undoubtedly the Christian truth most characteristic of this stage of Paul's theological development (LIGHTFOOT, AMIOT). The intensity with which the apostolic age awaited the returning Christ is not only indicative of these Christians' devotion to the person of Jesus Christ and their complete renunciation of the world [11], but also of the commonly accepted hope in the proximity of the parousia, so characteristic of the apocalyptic genre employed in this letter [12]. « One who looks for Christ » is an authentic NT definition of the Christian (LILLIE).

his Son, whom he has raised from death. Christ's resurrection is central in Paul's preaching, as it was in that of the Jerusalem community [13]. Christ's death is certainly implied [14], although it may not have received the prominence given the resurrection. What is of particular interest is the orientation of this dogma along the axis of the parousia [15] : Jesus, raised from death, will return to judge and to save [16]. To become a Christian essentially means to hope in Christ's return on the basis of his resurrection [17]. Without this hope, the practice of religion is lacking

---

[10] JOSEPH BONSIRVEN, *L'Évangile de Paul* (Paris, 1948) 54 ; JOSEPH SCHMITT, *Jésus ressuscité dans la prédication apostolique* (Paris, 1949) 209, 214.

[11] JULES LEBRETON, *La Vie et l'Enseignement de Jésus-Christ, II* (Paris, 1931) 225-228.

[12] F. PRAT, *op. cit. I*, 89 ; cf. also JEAN CALÈS, *Un maître de l'exégèse contemporaine : le P. Ferdinand Prat, S. J.* (Paris, 1942) 162-169.

[13] JOSEPH BONSIRVEN, *op. cit.* 149.

[14] MAX MEINERTZ, *Theologie des Neuen Testaments II* (Bonn, 1950) 94.

[15] L. CERFAUX, *op. cit.* 47.

[16] R. BULTMANN, *op. cit.* 79.

[17] JOSEPH BONSIRVEN, *op. cit.* 178 n. 2.

an important factor [18]. There is a striking similarity between this kerygma and the conclusion of Paul's Athenian discourse (PLUMMER), as well as Peter's sermon to Cornelius (Acts 10,40-42). Thus we are justified in concluding that the evangelization of Thessalonica was a faithful echo of the primitive preaching.

Jesus our rescuer. The vagueness of the Greek participle is to be noted [19] : Paul does not here specify whether he thinks of the deliverance as in part accomplished in the past or in the present, or to be accomplished at the second Coming, as he states in later letters (Gal 1,4). What is clear however is his belief in the character of the risen Christ as Saviour (PLUMMER) [20], signified by the name, Jesus (LIGHTFOOT).

the wrath to come. The anthropomorphism, common in the OT, expresses the divine sanctity with its consequent hatred of sin [21]. The infallibility of the punishment is indicated by the word « coming » (VOSTÉ). Jesus delivers us from God's wrath by freeing us from sin. Thus Paul's moral precepts flow from this eschatological conception of Christ (DEWAILLY-RIGAUX).

These verses provide a brief but enlightening *raccourci* of Paul's preaching to pagans (AMIOT) at this period in his career. It is of the greatest interest insofar as it constitutes a *point de départ* for estimating Paul's later adaptation of his preaching and teaching. If the « central Pauline conceptions » (DIBELIUS) appear to be missing from this résumé, it may be for the very good reason that they have not yet become central. While Paul must obviously have taught more than is implied in these verses, still it may be said that they do present the highlights of his kerygma at the time of the founding of the Thessalonian church. The subsequent difficulties and doubts at Thessalonica which centred upon the parousia constitute proof of that.

§ 2. - Eschatological Orientation of Christ's Resurrection. 1 Thes 4,14

The next text which interests our theme is found in the second part of Paul's epistle, where he treats two problems connected with the Lord's parousia (1 Thes 4,13-5,11). The first question concerns the order of

---

[18] MAX MEINERTZ, *op. cit. II* 215.
[19] MAX ZERWICK, *Graecitas Biblica*[2] (Romae, 1949) § 264.
[20] JOSEPH BONSIRVEN, *op. cit.* 155 ; MAX MEINERTZ, *op. cit. II*, 105-106.
[21] MEINERTZ, *op. cit. II*, 33-34.

events at the second Coming (4,13-18). Here Paul's faithfulness in adhering to the apocalyptic sections of the Synoptic tradition is manifest [22]. But he also communicates to his converts a piece of information about the precedence of the dead over the living which he bases upon « a word of the Lord » (15) [23].

14 Since if we believe that Jesus died and rose, so also will God bring those who have fallen asleep through Jesus together with him.

[Vat. and the Harclean Syriac read οὗτως ὁ θεὸς καί which makes the point clearer : « as God raised Jesus, so will God also ... »]

If we believe. Paul begins with one of the most fundamental formulae of the Christian creed : *Jesus died and rose* [24]. The use of the name Jesus would indicate the Palestinian origin of the expression [25], even if Paul did not assert elsewhere that he received it from the apostolic tradition (1 Cor 15,3-4). Paul's creative mind, however, transforms everything it receives. Accordingly, here the datum is made the basis of faith in the general resurrection of the just [26]. As such, the sentence illustrates the note of trust which is a constant element in Pauline faith [27]. The conditional form of the statement does not imply doubt about this object of Christian belief [28] : *non dubitantis est, sed praesupponentis* [29]. On the other hand, the hypothetical structure of the argument suggests that we are assisting at the formulation of a truth until now only implicit in the *depositum fidei*, a step occasioned by the problem presented by the Thessalonians. Paul had evidently taught them the dogma of the resurrection of the just (cf. Acts 24,15). That is the origin of their difficulty : *how* could

---

[22] J. B. ORCHARD, *Thessalonians and the Synoptic Gospels* in *Bib* 19 (1938) 19-42. Dom Orchard's conclusion to a *literary* dependence of Paul upon the Matthean discourse on the destruction of the Temple is not warranted by the evidence. What it does prove is Paul's acquaintance with *the oral traditions* reproduced by the author of the Greek Mt.

[23] F. PRAT, *op. cit. I*, 86-89.

[24] The varying of the more common technical word ἠγέρθη here with ἀνέστη is probably not too significant : MAX ZERWICK, *Graecitas Biblica*, § 175.

[25] L. CERFAUX, *op. cit.* 374-375.

[26] J. BONSIRVEN, *op. cit.* 318.

[27] MAX MEINERTZ, *op. cit. II*, 126.

[28] MAX ZERWICK, *Analysis, ad. loc.*, calls this a « condicio realis ».

[29] The phrase is that of GULIELMUS ESTIUS, *In omnes D. Pauli Epistolas, item in Catholicas, Commentarii II²* (Moguntiae, 1859) 578, § 13.

the dead share in the glories of the second Coming ? OEPKE rightly conjectures that Paul had not made clear the connection between Christ's resurrection and that of the faithful already dead. It is very probable that Paul himself had not until now developed the link between the two events. The fact that he hastens to support his newly-discovered theologoumenon with a « word of the Lord's » seems to imply this. The middle term in Paul's argument is not the one which would be employed in one of the later epistles, the solidarity of the disciples with Christ as second Adam (1 Cor 15,20 ; Rom. 6,4 ff. ; Col. 1,18). Nor is it the doctrine of « the Body of Christ » (vs. MILLIGAN). The link is the divine will which, in the resurrection of Christ, has set in motion the great eschatological forces which will one day effect the general resurrection of the just [30].

The arresting phrase, *those who have fallen asleep through Jesus*, has caught the attention of almost every commentator. The conception of death as a sleep was a commonplace of ancient literature, and is found in the Gospels (Mt 9,24 ; Jn 11,11) [31]. The expression *to die through Jesus* is certainly startling (LIGHTFOOT, VON DOBSCHÜTZ). Hence some critics have construed the phrase *through Jesus* with the principal verb, thus making it refer to the mediation of Christ in the resurrection of the believer (DIBELIUS). The chief argument in favour of this interpretation is the need of avoiding a *hapax* in Paul's writings. Against it may rightly be urged the resultant tautology (FRAME). A more convincing argument derives from the required balance of the whole period (VOSTÉ), and the fact that Paul is speaking only of the resurrection of the just. Thus to the phrase *Jesus died* corresponds *those who have fallen asleep through Jesus* ; to *He arose, He will bring with him*. That the nature of death itself has undergone a change in the Christian dispensation by reason of Jesus' death is a notion still latent in Paul's thought and will be explicitly expressed only at a later period (1 Cor 15, 54-55 ; 2 Cor 5,14 ; Rom 6, 10-11). *He will also bring ... with him.* The verb ἄγω is used in the NT of the divine action upon men in the supernatural order (Acts 13,23 ; Lk 4,1 ; Rom 2,4 ; Gal 5,18 ; Rom 8,14 ; Heb 2,10). It is frequently almost synonymous with ἐγείρω (Acts 13,22 and the l. var. 13,23). Here ἄγω is used instead of ἐγείρω since Paul is thinking of the parousia (DIBELIUS) and of those who will still be alive then (PLUMMER).

---

[30] L. CERFAUX, *op. cit.* 68. Cf. also P. -M. MAGNIEN, *La Résurrection des Morts dans I Thess IV,13-V,3* in *RB* 16 (1907) 349-382.

[31] MAX MEINERTZ, *op. cit. II*, 220-221.

With him. The phrase σὺν Χριστῷ is employed by Paul in contradistinction to ἐν Χριστῷ (cf. 1 Cor 15,18) in order to underscore the intimacy of the Christian's relation to Christ[32], either after death or in consequence of the mystical death of Baptism[33]. The final recompense of the Christian is to be with Christ, a doctrine which clearly implies belief in his divinity[34].

He will also bring. Paul considers the Father's act of handing Jesus over to death and raising him, as prolonged, through Christ's mediation, in the resurrection of the just (cf. 2 Cor 4,14). In his later letters, a series of verbs compounded with σύν will illustrate how this divine act effects the *present* status of the Christian (Phil 3,10 ; Gal 2,19 ; Rom 6,3-5 ; 8,17 ; Col 2,12 ; 3,1 ; Eph 2,6 ; cf. also 2 Tim 2,11-12 ; and perhaps 2 Cor 7,3). At the time of writing 1 Thessalonians, the whole perspective is dominated by the hope of future reunion with Christ at his parousia (AMIOT). If Paul thinks of Christ here as somehow the « mediating link between His people's sleep and their Resurrection at the hands of God » (MILLIGAN), still he does not appear to have worked out the connection except in terms of the apocalyptic principles of the power and will of God.

Thus we are dealing with an expression of Paul's soteriology which is surely primitive. The « disturbing density » (BUZY) of the formula, which will be set forth more clearly only later on (cf. 1 Cor 15 ; Rom 14,7-8), suggests that Paul has not had time to work out all its implications. Moreover, the illative argument from Christ's resurrection to that of the just is more elementary and obvious than that which concludes to the function of his resurrection « for our justification » (Rom 4,25). Paul does assert here a causal connection between Christ's resurrection and that of the Christian (DIBELIUS) ; but the connecting link does not appear as anything intrinsic to the risen Christ. It is rather the infallible will of God (cf. the same soteriology in 2 Cor 4,14). Also noteworthy is the liaison between Christ's death and those who have died « through Jesus ». It is the death of *Jesus* (the name is significant) which has created Christian death, henceforth orientated towards an « awakening »[35].

---

[32] ERNST LOHMEYER, Σὺν Χριστῷ in *Festgabe für Adolf Deissmann zu 60. Geburtstag* (Tübingen, 1927) 218-257.

[33] J. BONSIRVEN, *op. cit.* 240 n. 1.

[34] *ibid.* 56.

[35] It was primarily the idea of a resurrection which led, in the NT, to the use of the metaphor « sleep » to describe Christian death.

THE EARLIEST CORRESPONDENCE : FIRST AND SECOND THESSALONIANS

§ 3. - The Purpose of the Redemption. 1 Thes, 5,9-10

Paul treats now (1 Thes 5,1-11) of the second question posed by Christ's parousia : the time of the second Coming. Concerning this point, Paul has no revelation to offer [36], but exhorts his flock instead to the watchful practice of a virtuous life, and bids them remember the divine plan of predestination.

9 Because God has not destined us for wrath but for an acquisition of salvation through our Lord Jesus Christ, 10 who died for us, in order that whether we wake or whether we sleep, we may live in companionship with him.

[9 b. Χριστός is omitted by Vat. and the Ethiopic version.
10 a. περὶ ἡμῶν is attested by Vat. and Sin., the majority of mss. reading ὑπὲρ· ἡμῶν.]

This text is of great interest as it contains the only enunciation of the redemption in the whole epistle. There is a parallel text in the second letter (2 Thes 2,13-14) which we shall examine later [37].
v. 9. *God has destined us*. The Father is author of salvation which is accomplished *through our Lord Jesus Christ*. The title here bestowed upon Christ, as CERFAUX rightly remarks [38], is a heritage from Palestinian Christianity and its natural context is the parousiac theology (cf. the invocation *Maranatha*, 1 Cor 16,22 ; Ap 22,20). It denotes Jesus as God's Messias, who through his resurrection has been acclaimed Lord. Christ's redemptive mediation of which Paul speaks here has been efficaciously exercised through his resurrection and (as v. 10 immediately adds) through his death.
An acquisition of salvation. The LXX phrase εἰς περιποίησιν (Mal 3,17) translates the Hebrew *segullah* : the new Israel destined to be acquired by Yahweh as his own property. This prophecy appears to be present to Paul's thought : the Christian is not fated to be an object of the divine wrath, but is predestined as a possession of God's acquiring *through our Lord Jesus Christ*. The parallelism between ὀργή and περιποίησις σωτηρίας shows clearly that both are the work of God, just as both are intended in

---

[36] F. PRAT, *op. cit. I*, 87.
[37] LIGHTFOOT *in loc.* is wrong in remarking that this present text contains the only allusion in the Thessalonian letters to the redemption.
[38] Cf. his informative discussion of this title, *op. cit.* 379-381.

an eschatological sense [39]. On Paul's view, then, it is not the Christian
who acquires his own salvation, but God who acquires it for him. Or rather, God's acquisition of the believer *is* his salvation (with LIGHTFOOT,
BUZY, AMIOT, vs. FRAME, VOSTÉ, PLUMMER, OEPKE, DEWAILLY-RIGAUX [40]).
Paul takes the OT view that the winning of salvation is God's work,
through of course the mediatorial activity of Christ (Acts 20,28 ; 2 Thes
2,14 ; Eph 1,14) [41].

v. 10. *who died for us.* The phrase may contain an echo of Is 53 [42]. Yet it
is remarkable that this Servant motif is never *developed* for its own sake
in Pauline soteriology. It is Paul's initial conception of Christ as One
risen from death which is operative here and directs the line of his thought.
The characteristic Pauline antithesis, death-life, appears for the first
time (BUZY) [43]. The risen Lord *died for us* in order that *we may live in
companionship with him.* Just what sort of union with Christ in the future
life will be enjoyed is not specified. MAX ZERWICK suggests [44] that ζήσωμεν
is an inchoative aorist (= « that we may rise to the new life with him »).
Paul however is content to state that the Christian is somehow involved
in a movement initiated by the risen Christ [45]. The clause whether *we
wake or whether we sleep* is obviously to be understood here in the context
of 4,13-17. Consequently, it refers to the condition of Christians at the
parousia, who will belong either in the category of « those who sleep »
(4,13), i. e. « the dead in Christ » (4,16), or of « the living » (4,17). It is
to be noted that the affirmation prescinds from the relation between
the Christian in this life and Christ. Paul's attention here is directed,

---

[39] MAX MEINERTZ, *op. cit. II*, 34, 139.

[40] CERFAUX, *op. cit.* 16, likewise appears to be in error when he remarks :
« Il faut ' faire son salut ' (*I Thess.*, V, 9 ; *Phil.*, II, 12) ». In the second text cited
here, Paul adverts to man's cooperation, but in the verse which follows it immediately, he returns to the notion that God is principal author of our salvation.

[41] C. SPICQ, *L'Épître aux Hébreux II* (Paris, 1953) 333.

[42] L. CERFAUX, *op. cit.* 105. — Paul inherited the Servant theme from the
apostolic preaching of the Jerusalem community ; and he undoubtedly repeated
the formulation of the redemptive death of Christ in his preaching. In his theology,
which appears in his letters, the Apostle tended to incorporate the important elements of this Servant theology into his more characteristic view of Christ as the
Second Adam.

[43] MAX MEINERTZ, *op. cit. II*, 93.

[44] MAX ZERWICK, *Graecitas Biblica* § 185.

[45] L. CERFAUX, *op. cit.* 240.

not to the present status of the Christian, but to the eschatological existence with Christ which he will acquire at the parousia [46].

§ 4. Further Precision of Paul's Soteriology. 2 Thes 2,13-14

This passage, taken from the second letter to Thessalonica, is parallel to the pericope just discussed and throws new light upon Paul's conception of salvation at this period of his career.

13 Our duty it is to thank God at all times on your account, brethren beloved of the Lord, because God has chosen you as firstfruits for salvation through the sanctification by the Spirit and faith in the truth, 14 to which he has called you through our preaching for an acquisition of the glory of our Lord Jesus Christ.

[13. We read ἀπαρχήν with Vat., the Vulgate, Harclean Syriac versions, instead of ἀπαρχῆς (Sin., D, the Peshitto and Bohairic versions).
14. With Vat., Alex., the Antiochian recension and the majority of mss., we omit καί. Ὑμᾶς is preferable to ἡμᾶς (Vat., Alex., D first corr.)]

v. 13. *God has chosen you.* Paul is always conscious of the divine election to the Christian faith which leads ultimately to salvation. The rare word εἵλατο (*hapax* in the NT) which here occurs is used of the election of Israel in Dt 26,18. This suggests that Paul is thinking of the collective aggregation of the Thessalonian community to the « Israel of God ». With the Philippians (Phil 4,15), they constitute the « firstfruits » of Paul's Macedonian ministry (cf. 1 Cor 16,15 ; Rom 16,5). As « firstfruits », the converts give promise of further success (AMIOT is scarcely justified in turning the expression into an argument for a probable delay of the parousia). The purpose of the divine choice is the salvation of the neophytes, which Paul describes in v. 14 as *an acquisition of the glory of our Lord Jesus Christ.* The evidence of God's favour [47] is provided by the Thessalonians' *sanctification by the Spirit*, the presence of charisms, the gift of the Holy Ghost following Baptism (cf. 1 Thes 1,5 ; 4,8) [48]. This sancti-

---

[46] J. BONSIRVEN, *op. cit.* 145, 331. — Paul's use of the expression ἅμα σύν here would appear to indicate that the phrase σύν Χριστῷ has not yet assumed the technical sense it will have in his later writings.

[47] Rather than the means of carrying it out, as FRAME, VOSTÉ, AMIOT, BUZY.

[48] Contrary to what MEINERTZ says (*op. cit. II*, 150), the phrase does not designate Baptism. Cf. I. DE LA POTTERIE, *L'onction du chrétien par la foi* in *Bib* 40 (1959) 12-69.

fication is conceived as closely related to the parousia (1 Thes 3,13 ; 5,23), although it involves something already present in the believer (1 Thes 4,3 ff.) and has a special connection with divine cult (Rom 12,1). It is simply the practice of Christianity [49]. In his correspondence with Thessalonica, Paul frequently describes the Christian life by this term (1 Thes 4,3-4,7 ; 5,23 ; 2 Thes 2,13), while in Galatians and Romans, he speaks by preference of justification[50]. *Faith in the truth* is the second sign of those elected to salvation. The truth is not regarded Greek-fashion by Paul as something abstract, but as the full divine reality, the living God manifested through Jesus Christ [51].

v. 14. *He has called you through our preaching.* The divine choice is revealed historically in the preaching of the Gospel (Rom 10,17). Its final purpose is now described as *an acquisition of the glory of our Lord Jesus Christ.* As in 1 Thes 5,9, the term *acquisition* refers to God's, not man's activity. Here however Paul introduces the notion of δόξα (cf. 1 Thes 2,12), a characteristic theme of his theology. Essentially pertaining to the eschatological frame of reference [52], it is also a property of the Christian life which BONSIRVEN aptly denominates « une ascension continuelle vers la gloire finale » [53].

It remains to point out that in these verses the redemption is depicted as a Trinitarian operation : the Father is source of the Christian's divine election and call to believe in the Gospel ; our Lord Jesus Christ is he

---

[49] L. CERFAUX, *op. cit.* 229-234.

[50] J. BONSIRVEN, *op. cit.* 210. — OTTO PROKSCH, ἀγιασμός, *TWNT I*, 114-115.

[51] MAX MEINERTZ, *op. cit. II*, 61. — In these early epistles, the terms δικαιοσύνη and δικαιοῦν nowhere appear, while δίκη (2 Thes 1,9) and the adjective δίκαιος (2 Thes 1,5.6) are used in connection with God's punishment of sin. Once however the adverb δικαίως is employed as more or less synonymous with ὁσίως (1 Thes 2,10). In 1 Cor 6,11, a somewhat similar parallel is drawn between δικαιοῦν and ἁγιάζειν (cf. also perhaps 1 Cor 1, 30).

[52] GERHARD KITTEL, δέξα, *TWNT II*, 253 : « wenn das NT von dem eschatologischen Teilhaben des Gläubiger an der δόξα weiss, so ist dies nichts als ein Stück des allgemeinen heilsgeschichtlichen Satzes über die kausale Verknüpfung und Parallelität : Auferstehung Christi/Auferweckung und neuer Aeon des Gläubigen. Teilhaben an der δέξα, hier ihrer Hoffnung und dort ihrer Vollendung, heisst : Teilhaben an Christus. Wie erst in der Auferstehung Gottes Handeln mit dem Menschen zum Ziel kommt, so vollendet sich sein καλεῖν erst in der αἰώνιος δέξα, die das eigentliche Ziel (εἰς) seiner Berufung ist (1 Pt 5,4-10 ; 1 Th 2,12 ; 2 Th 2,14 ; 2 K 4,17 ; 2 Tm 2,10). »

[53] J. BONSIRVEN, *op. cit.* 331.

through whom the eschatological glory is conferred ; the Holy Spirit reveals the Christian vocation to the believer and consecrates him to the sanctity required at the parousia [54]. Thus the pericope is the most complete summary of Pauline soteriology at this point in Paul's theological thinking, where Christ's resurrection is related immediately to his parousia and to the resurrection of the just.

---

[54] F. PRAT, *op. cit. II*, Note I, 219.

Chapter V

LETTERS WRITTEN FROM EPHESUS: PHILIPPIANS, FIRST CORINTHIANS

Bibliography : J. B. LIGHTFOOT, *St. Paul's Epistle to the Philippians*[6] (London, 1881). M. R. VINCENT, *Epistles to the Philippians and to Philemon*, ICC (Edinburgh, 1902). M. DIBELIUS, *An die Thessalonicher I II — An die Philipper*[3], HNT 11 (Tübingen, 1937). A. MÉDEBIELLE, *Épître aux Philippiens*, SBP 12 (Paris, 1946). JOSEPH HUBY, *Les Épîtres de la Captivité*[14], VS 8 (Paris, 1947). GERHARD HEINZELMANN, *Der Brief an die Philipper*[4], NTD 8 (Göttingen, 1949). PIERRE BENOIT, *Les Épîtres de Saint Paul aux Philippiens ...*, BJ (Paris, 1949). PIERRE BONNARD, *L'Épître de saint Paul aux Philippiens*, CNT 10 (Neuchâtel-Paris, 1950). ERNST LOHMEYER, *Der Brief an die Philipper*[11] (Göttingen, 1956). F. W. BEARE, *The Epistle to the Philippians* (London, 1959). J. WEISS, *Der erste Korintherbrief*, MK 5 (Göttingen, 1910). A. ROBERTSON, A. PLUMMER, *The First Epistle of St. Paul to the Corinthians*, ICC (Edinburgh, 1911). R. ST. JOHN PARRY, *The First Epistle to the Corinthians*, CGT (Cambridge, 1916). E. -B. ALLO, *Première Épître aux Corinthiens*, EB (Paris, 1934). PH. BACHMANN, E. STAUFFER, *Der erste Brief des Paulus an die Korinther*[4], ZK, 7 (Leipzig, 1936). J. MOFFATT, *The First Epistle of Paul to the Corinthians*, MC (London, 1938). J. HUBY, *Première Épître aux Corinthiens*, VS 13 (Paris, 1946). H. D. WENDLAND, *Die Briefe an die Korinther*,[5] NTD 7 (Göttingen, 1948). C. SPICQ, *Première Épître aux Corinthiens*, SBP 11[2] (Paris, 1948). E. OSTY, *Les Épîtres de Saint Paul aux Corinthiens*, BJ (Paris, 1949). J. HÉRING, *La Première Épître de saint Paul aux Corinthiens*, CNT 7 (Neuchâtel-Paris, 1949). HANS LIETZMANN, *An die Korinther I-II*[4], HNT 9 (Tübingen, 1949).

We have already given reasons for adopting Ephesus as place of origin for Philippians and for considering it the first of Paul's letters from that city[1]. The questioning of the unity of the letter appears to create

---

[1] Chapter III, p. 66.

as great a problem as the one it attempts to solve. Consequently, it seems preferable to regard it as a single epistle rather than a collection of several short notes [2]. It is to be recalled that some four years' time separates the writing of the Thessalonian letters from those of the Ephesian period. These years, as we have pointed out[3], were momentous ones for Paul's apostolic and theological development.

Paul's constant references to Christ's parousia are a reminder that his thought displays much the same eschatological polarity as that evidenced by the Thessalonian letters [4]. The practice of the Christian life is still specified by the « Day of Jesus Christ » (Phil 1,6.9 ; 2,14-17), as is his own ministry (Phil 1,18-19 ; 4,1). The Christian is still regarded as one who awaits the parousiac Christ as Saviour (Phil 3,20 ; cf. 1 Thes 1,10) and who holds citizenship in the heavenly Kingdom. The Church's watchword is still *Maranatha*, although the expression now appears in Greek garb : « The Lord is nigh » (Phil 4,5). Christ's resurrection still evokes the hope of the general resurrection of the just (Phil 3,11) and Paul still speaks of the « transformation » of the bodies of those alive at the parousia (Phil 3,21 ; cf. 1 Thes 4,17).

Yet certain modifications of Paul's outlook are also perceptible. He clearly envisages his own death as a proximate possibility (Phil 1,20-23 ; 2,17 ; 3,10). The term *justification*, nowhere mentioned in the earlier letters but so characteristic of Galatians and Romans, makes its appearance (Phil 1,11 ; 3,9). The same may be said of γνῶσις (Phil 3,8) or ἐπίγνωσις (Phil 1,9).

§ 1. - A Palestinian Soteriological Theme: Christ as 'Ebed Yahweh. Phil 2,6-11

After relating his own situation in prison (Phil 1,12-26), Paul exhorts his Philippians to struggle courageously for the faith (Phil 1,27-30) and to preserve unity and fraternal charity amongst themselves (Phil 2,1-5). To this end, he proposes « Christ Jesus » as a model and cites a hymn

---

[2] Cf. the introductions in the commentaries of LOHMEYER, pp.1-8, of BONNARD, p. 9, of BENOIT, p. 19. BEARE, however, pp.24-29, maintains the letter is a collection of fragments.

[3] Chapter III, pp. 75-77.

[4] J. BONSIRVEN, *L'Évangile de Paul* (Paris, 1948) 340. Speaking of the references to the parousia in the Thessalonian letters, he adds : « L'épître aux Philippiens est proportionnellement plus riche ».

with which they must have been familiar [5], one taken quite possibly from the liturgy.

> 6 Who, while he kept his character as God,
> did not consider his divine equality
> something to be proudly paraded.

> 7 No, he despoiled himself,
> by taking on the Servant's character,
> becoming similar to mortal men.

> 8 And looking outwardly like any other man,
> he carried self-abasement, through obedience,
> right up to death, yes, death by the Cross.

> 9 Therefore did God in turn immeasurably exalt him,
> and graciously bestow on him the Name,
> outweighing every other name,

> 10 that everyone, at Jesus' Name,
> should bow adoring : those in heaven,
> on earth, in the infernal regions,

> 11 and every tongue take up the cry,
> « Jesus is Lord ! » —
> thus glorifying God his Father.

[7 b. ἀνθρώπου, instead of ἄνθρωπον, is found in the Chester Beatty papyrus.
8 c. Sin. adds τοῦ before σταύρου.
11 a. ἐξομολογήσεται is the reading of most mss. except Sin. and Vat. which we follow here with A. Merk].

The strophe-division of the hymn is a disputed point amongst various commentators [6]. The question however is of little moment for our present investigation. The hymn passes in review the whole cycle of mysteries

---

[5] D. M. STANLEY, *The Theme of the Servant of Yahweh in Primitive Christian Soteriology, and its Transposition by St. Paul* in *CBQ* 16 (1954) 420-425 ; also, « *Carmenque Christo quasi Deo dicere ...* » in *CBQ* 20 (1958) 180-182 ; *The Divinity of Christ in Hymns of the New Testament* in *Proceedings* : *Fourth Annual Meeting of the Society of Catholic College Teachers of Sacred Doctrine* (Notre Dame, Indiana, 1958) 12-29.

[6] BENOIT in his commentary divides it into six strophes, while CERFAUX (*Le Christ dans la théologie de saint Paul*, 288) has three strophes. BEARE in his commentary has simply two strophes.

connected with the incarnate Son of God, which are thus seen to have been professed, from the earliest years, within the community, by the apostolic Church [6a] : his divine pre-existence (6), his kenosis through the incarnation (7), the supreme self-abasement of his death (8), his exaltation to God's right hand (9), the hommage paid him by all creation (10), and finally, the new Name, Κύριος, with which he was invested at his exaltation (11) (BENOIT).

v. 6. In his pre-existence, the Son was ἐν μορφῇ θεοῦ, a phrase which is practically untranslatable in modern languages (VINCENT). Μορφή denotes the essential attributes of something insofar as they manifest its inner reality (BENOIT) [7]. Whilst remaining divine, the Son assumes a human nature since he does not consider the prerogatives due his divine state [8] « something already laid hold of », « a prize which must not slip from His grasp » (LIGHTFOOT[9]). Instead the Son prefers to win the homage of the universe by following the path of humiliation and of death [10], thereby giving his disciples the supreme example of humility.

v. 7. *he despoiled himself*. The emphatic position of ἑαυτόν underscores the voluntariety of Jesus' humiliation (LIGHTFOOT). By becoming incarnate, the Son underwent a « kenosis », renounced the divine honour due his person [11]. More specifically, he assumed the role of Servant, that

---

[6a] All these mysteries also appear in the summaries, in Acts, of the apostolic kerygma, with the exception of that relating to the Son's pre-existence, which also is not found in the Synoptic Gospels.

[7] L. CERFAUX, *op. cit.* 290 : « Le substantif μορφή , qui revient deux fois dans notre contexte ... est intraduisible en français. Il exprime la manière dont une chose, étant ce qu'elle est en elle-même, se présente aux regards ».

[8] *ibid.* 289 : « considérer ou traiter quelque chose comme une bonne aubaine ». CERFAUX cites CLEMENT of Rome's interpretation : « Le sceptre de la majesté de Dieu, le Seigneur Jésus-Christ, n'est pas venu en bruit de jactance ni d'arrogance, bien qu' il l'eût pu ».

[9] RONALD A. KNOX, *A New Testament Commentary for English Readers II* (New York, 1954) 268 : « What St Paul says is that our Lord, on coming to earth, did not think of his divine splendor as something which must be clung to at all costs ; he laid it aside. He had the opportunity of impressing the world by appearing in majesty, but he did not grasp it. Just so, St Paul at Philippi had the opportunity of exercising his rights as a Roman citizen, but he did not grasp it. And the Philippians, if and when they get the opportunity of asserting themselves at the expense of their neighbors, are not to grasp it either ».

[10] CERFAUX, op. cit. 292.

[11] J. BONSIRVEN, *op. cit.* 64-68 ; ALBRECHT OEPKE, κενόω , *TWNT III*, 661.

is, of the Isaian *'Ebed Yahweh* [12]. CERFAUX has adequately demonstrated
the influence of Isaias 53 upon this hymn, and his conclusion may be
accepted without further comment. Just as « his character as God »
expresses Christ's divinity, so the expression « the Servant's character »
designates his human nature as subject to suffering and death (HUBY).
The verse lays stress upon Christ's likeness to men in all externals, [13] as
Paul himself will insist in Rom 8,3. This insistence does not deny the reality of his human nature, but « leaves room for the other side of his nature,
the divine » (VINCENT). During his mortal life, the Son of God proved by
his whole way of acting that he was truly man (HUBY, BENOIT) [14].

v. 8. *he carried self-abasement.* In vv. 6-7, the incarnation was described
as a kenosis, which is salvific inasmuch as it forms part of the divine plan
of redemption [15]. Here the passion and death on the cross [16] are presented
as the greatest act of self-surrender, the final act of obedience to the Father's salvific will (cf. Heb 5,8). The verse is a paraphrase of Is 53,2-3 [17].

v. 9. *Therefore did God in turn immeasurably exalt him.* The verb employed
is a NT *hapax.* It not only contrasts Jesus' humiliation with his exaltation,
but indicates the uniqueness of his position as mediator. There is no reference to Christ's resurrection as such. It is rather his enthronement at
God's right hand, the occasion upon which the Name is conferred upon
Jesus [18], that is thrown into relief. This investiture is portrayed as an act

---

[12] L. CERFAUX, *L'hymne au Christ-Serviteur de Dieu, Phil II*, 6-11 = *Is. LII*,
13-*LIII*, 12 in *Miscellanea Historica in honorem Alberti de Meyer, I* (Louvain, 1946)
117-130. In his, *Le Christ....* 290, CERFAUX gives a convincing argument to show
that the formula μορφὴν δούλου was inspired by the text of Deutero-Isaias (as found
in the version of Aquila) ; hence, in our translation, we have rendered it, « the
Servant's character ».

[13] Cf. the Note in LIGHTFOOT, 127-133.

[14] J. BONSIRVEN, *op. cit.* 68 : « D'autre part, les divers thèmes, par lesquels
la catéchèse apostolique représente la Divinité du Seigneur Jésus, laissent supposer
qu'on le considérait, non pas comme un homme élevé après sa mort aux hon-
neurs divins, — ce qui serait retomber dans une mythologie polythéiste, — mais
comme vrai Fils de Dieu, entretenant avec son Père, dès sa vie terrestre, une entière
consubstantialité .... ».

[15] Hence we cannot agree with F. -X. DURRWELL, *La Résurrection de
Jésus : Mystère de Salut²* (Le Puy-Paris, 1954) 62-63, on his interpretation of this
hymn.

[16] Cf. the remarks of DIBELIUS in his commentary, p. 81.

[17] CERFAUX has demonstrated this beyond any doubt : cf. *art. cit.* n. 12.

[18] BONSIRVEN, *op. cit.* 67.

of grace on the Father's part, a bold expression, unique in the NT [19]. The passage illustrates the use of Κύριος as a divine title for Christ [20].

The conception of Christ's exaltation as a personal reward for his obedience in undergoing death is characteristic of the theology of the whole passage. This is the one place in the whole *corpus Paulinum* where Christ's glorification appears in the context of his merit [21]. The Reformation theologians were opposed to the idea that a reward was given Christ, and CALVIN was forced to adopt the useless expedient of translating διὸ by *quo facto* (VINCENT). The fourth century Arians, on the other hand, used the verse to buttress their subordinationist theory. Thus the history of theology witnesses to the paramount importance of the doctrine here set forth.

v. 10. *That everyone, at Jesus' Name, should bow adoring.* The reference to Is 45,23 makes it clear that the divine honours portrayed by the OT as proper to Yahweh alone must now be rendered to the exalted Jesus. All creation is obliged to give divine worship to the Name revealed as his by right [22]. Implicit in the text is the doctrine that adoration is due to Jesus precisely because he has received the divine Name through his exaltation to God's right hand [23]. This theological conception is perhaps the strongest

---

[19] P. HENRY, *art. Kénose, VDBS V*, 35.

[20] L. CERFAUX, *art. Kyrios, VDBS V*, 226 : « On tiendra compte de la spécification royale du titre Kyrios. En tant que souverain messianique, Jésus *doit* porter le titre *marana-κύριος*, désignant spécifiquement le souverain régnant. Mais sa royauté messianique (essentiellement religieuse) n'a été exercée de fait et acclamée par la communauté que lorsque, ressuscité, il a été élevé en gloire à la droite de Dieu. A ce moment — nous entendons un moment historique — le titre Kyrios lui est donné au sens fort, avec un insistance théorique ('Dieu l'a fait Christ et Seigneur') qui donne son impulsion à l'usage chrétien caractéristique. Durant la vie du Christ, les actes de foi à sa messianité n'avaient pas été suffisants pour créer un usage technique de Kyrios ».

[21] This fact shows, I believe, that Pauline thought, in the elaboration of this theme, normally ran in other channels, viz. the conception of the redeemer as second Adam. In this soteriological complex, with its stress upon the solidarity of all men with Christ, the resurrection of the Lord is « propter nos ». — On the other hand, the citation of this hymn by Paul shows that he was aware of the importance which the Servant theme enjoyed in the apostolic preaching ; and it is an indication that *in his preaching* (as distinct from his more personal theological thinking) Paul also proposed Christ as the Servant of God.

[22] The word ἐξομολογήσεται is here used in the LXX meaning of « offer praise, or thanksgiving » (LIGHTFOOT).

[23] L. CERFAUX, *op. cit.* 296.

argument for the Palestinian origin of the hymn, inasmuch as it presents
the belief in Christ's divinity in the way in which the apostolic community came to a knowledge of it at Pentecost [24].

v. 11. *« Jesus is Lord ».* The divine adoration paid to Christ by the
universe finds concrete expression in this primitive credal formula (cf.
Rom 10,9) in which the salient features of the apostolic Christological
belief are summarized [25]. The climax of the whole solemn presentation of
the redemption is reached in the phrase *thus glorifying God his Father*
(DIBELIUS) : all adoration paid to the exalted redeemer redounds to the
glory of him who is the source of Christ's salvific work (HUBY) [26].

The majority of commentators are agreed that this passage is a hymn.
HANS LIETZMANN calls it a « Lied » [27]. J. WEISS speaks of « der vorhandene
Rhythmus » [28]. « Eine Art Rhythmus liegt zweifellos vor », says DIBE-
LIUS [29]. A. DEISSMANN refers to it in similar terms [30]. E. LOHMEYER,
after a thorough examination of the rhythm, vocabulary, and phrasing,
concludes that it is not prose-poetry but « ein carmen Christi im strengen
Sinne » [31].

Is the authorship of this hymn to be ascribed to Paul himself ? LOH-
MEYER considered it an adaptation of a pre-Christian, gnostic hymn [32].
CERFAUX insists that it is Paul's composition, probably intended for use
in the liturgy. [33]. RENGSTORFF considers that the source of such a paral-
netic composition must be the apostolic kerygma [34]. BENOIT believes it
probable that Paul here reproduces an ancient liturgical hymn [35]. More

---

[24] D. M. STANLEY, *The Conception of Salvation in Primitive Christian Preaching* in *CBQ* 18 (1956) 247.

[25] J. SCHMITT, *Jésus ressuscité dans la prédication apostolique* (Paris, 1949)
199 ff.

[26] Thus we cannot agree with PRAT, *La Théologie de Saint Paul I*[8] (Paris,
1920) 373, who translates the last lines of the hymn : « que toute langue confesse
que le Seigneur Jésus-Christ est entré dans la gloire de Dieu le Père ».

[27] HANS LIETZMANN, *Messe und Herrenmahl* (Bonn, 1926) 178.

[28] J. WEISS, *Beiträge zur Paulinischen Rhetorik* in *Theologische Studien* (Göttingen, 1897) 190.

[29] M. DIBELIUS in his commentary, p. 72.

[30] A. DEISSMANN, *Paulus*[2] (Tübingen, 1925) 149.

[31] E. LOHMEYER, *Kyrios Jesus, SHAW* (Heidelberg, 1927-28) 7.

[32] *ibid.* 9-13.

[33] L. CERFAUX, *L'hymne au Christ ...* 129 f ; also *Le Christ ...* 283 f.

[34] KARL HEINRICH RENGSTORFF, δοῦλος, *TWNT II*, 282.

[35] P. BENOIT in his commentary, p. 18.

recently, J. JEREMIAS has stated that the hymn is « vorpaulinisch », and consequently the oldest proof of the teaching concerning the three modes of Christ's existence [36].

The most convincing proof of the pre-Pauline origin of this Christian hymn, however, is to be found in the theology it reflects. The soteriological conception it embodies is characteristic of the Palestinian community : it is not characteristic of Paul [37]. In the first place, Paul never conceives Christ's glorification as a reward for his sufferings. He habitually presents it in terms of the benefits it confers upon the Christian people (1 Cor 6,13 ; 15,20 ; 2 Cor 5,15 ; Rom 4,25). The difference of viewpoint is manifested strikingly in a passage like 2 Cor 8,9, often cited as a parallel to these verses of Philippians : « For you know the liberality of our Lord Jesus Christ, how, for your sakes, he became poor, when he was rich, in order that you, through his poverty, might become rich ». An apparent exception to this soteriological conception by Paul of Christ's resurrection is Rom 14,9, where universal lordship is given as Christ's purpose in dying and rising : « To this end Christ died and came to life that he might become Lord both of the dead and of the living ». Here however the context makes it clear (cf. Rom 14,7-12) that there is question of another theme, already present in the apostolic kerygma : Christ's role as judge of all men at his second Coming.

The second point which argues for a Palestinian origin of this hymn is the presence of the Servant of Yahweh motif which was the dominant theme in the theology of the Jerusalem church. In Paul's letters, as we have shown elsewhere, this theme undergoes a remarkable transposition, and Paul himself appears as the Servant [38]. Because Paul made the theme a vehicle for a theology of the Christian apostleship, he did not develop it in his writing upon the redemption. It is indeed worthy of remark that in those passages of Paul's letters where one might conceivably see a reference to Isaias 53 in connection with Christ's death, the soteriological

---

[36] JOACHIM JEREMIAS, *Zur Gedankenführung in den Paulinischen Briefen* in *Studia Paulina in honorem Johannis de Zwaan* (Haarlem, 1953) 154.

[37] OSCAR CULLMANN, *Die Christologie des Neuen Testaments* (Tübingen, 1958) 79 : « Bei Paulus nimmt Jesu Sühnetod eine zentrale Stelle ein. Allerdings verwendet er den Titel *Ebed Jahwe* nicht. Die beiden wichtigsten christologischen Texte (1. Kor. 15,3 ; Phil. 2,6 ff.), nach denen Jesus die Aufgabe des Gottesknechts erfüllt, hat er aus alter Gemeindetradition übernommen und sich zu eigen gemacht. In Rom. 5,12 ff. sind die auf den *Ebed Jahwe* und sein Sühnewerk bezüglichen Gedanken ebenfalls verwertet ».

[38] Cf. *The Theme of the Servant ...* 415-420.

potentialities of the Servant motif are left unexploited (1 Cor 15,3-4 ;
2 Cor 5,14-21 ; Gal 1,4 ; 2,20 ; 3,13 ; Rom 4,25 ; 5,15 ff. ; 8, 32 ; Eph 5,2.25 ;
1 Tm 2,6 ; Ti 2,14).

How then explain the presence in Philippians of this hymn in which
the redemptive work of Christ is portrayed as the work of the Servant ?
It is to be recalled that the evangelization of Philippi occurred relatively early in Paul's missionary career, and that moreover he was,
in his preaching, very careful to follow the kerygma of Jerusalem where
the conception of Jesus as the Servant was a popular one. We might
venture to suggest, given the liturgical character of the pericope, that
it belonged to the eucharistic liturgy of Antioch which Paul must almost
certainly have introduced at Philippi. For it seems clear that in a letter,
whose tenor, for the most part, is that of a friendly « thank you » note[39],
the presence of such a deeply theological passage as Phil 2,6-11 is best
explained as a citation already familiar to the Philippians. It is also to
be noted that Paul does not use the citation to expound the doctrine of
the redemption, but as motivation for the practice of Christian humility.

These considerations would seem to indicate that the soteriology
of the Servant was never quite congenial to Paul. Or at least, when
he came to express his own theological thought on the redemption,
he adopted by preference the theme of the second Adam, as will be
seen from our examination of the subsequent epistles.

§ 2. - Christ's Resurrection a Force in the Christian Life. Phil 3,10-11

After discussing the missions of Timothy and Epaphras (Phil
2,19-30), Paul warns his converts against the Jewish danger (Phil 3,
1-3) by giving a brief autobiographical sketch which serves to illustrate
the only path to salvation for the Christian (Phil 3,4-17). The two
verses which interest us are dependent grammatically on a phrase in
v. 8 : « Indeed, I rather even consider everything to be loss compared with *the high privilege of the knowledge of Christ Jesus my Lord* ...».

10 that I may come to know him and the power of his resurrection and a fellowship
in his sufferings, being moulded to the pattern of his death, 11 in order to arrive,
if possible, at the resurrection from death.

---

[39] BENOIT calls Phil a letter that is « plus affective que dogmatique » in his
commentary, p. 11.

[10a. τὴν κοινωνίαν is the reading of D and several Greek mss., mostly of the Antiochian recension. We omit the definite article with Sin., Vat., and the Chester Beatty papyrus.

10 b. The correct reading is συμμορφιζόμενος. Some late Greek mss. attest συμμορφούμενος, while two western mss. have συμφορτιζόμενος.

11. The *textus receptus* together with two ninth cent. mss. and the Armenian and Coptic versions read ἐξανάστασιν τῶν νεκρῶν instead of the commonly accepted τὴν ἐξανάστασιν τὴν ἐκ νεκρῶν].

In this passage, Paul attempts to define the knowledge of Jesus Christ which the Christian must strive to attain in this life. In speaking of his own conversion, which was the beginning of such knowledge in his own life, he will use the metaphor of being overtaken in a race or being taken prisoner (Phil 3,12) [40]. This figure emphasizes at once the complete *engagement* of the Christian and the personal nature of the relationship between knower and known. The term γνῶσις (8) *may* be employed here because it was a technical term in the Greek mystery cults (DIBELIUS) [41] and hence familiar to Paul's addressees, but *the conception* of which it is the expression has nothing to do with Greek syncretism. It is, as with the Semites, a knowledge which involves *an experience of Christ*, resulting in a « transforming union » (HUBY). Paul is of course thinking of his own experience by the Damascus road, which was mystical in the proper sense [42]. But he considers the experiential knowledge of Christ which any Christian possesses as analogous to it (Gal 3,3-5 ; Rom 8,14-16) [43].

Three parallel purpose clauses (9-11) express the nature of this knowledge : « in order that ... in union with him, I may be found to possess, not any justice of my own making through the Law, but that which comes through faith in Christ, God's justice based on faith » ; « that I may come to know him and the power of his resurrection and a fellowship in his sufferings » ; « being moulded to the pattern of his death in order to arrive, if possible, at the resurrection from death ». In the first clause, this transforming knowledge is expressed in terms of « justice », — a proof, as DIBELIUS observes, that the « mystische Gedankenreihe » cannot be opposed to the « juristische » in Paul. However, it must be remembered

[40] JACQUES DUPONT, *Gnosis : la connaissance religieuse dans les épîtres de saint Paul* (Louvain : Paris, 1949) 84.

[41] Cf. however the view of DUPONT, *op. cit.* 502, 511.

[42] *ibid.* 522.

[43] MAX MEINERTZ, *Theologie des Neuen Testaments II* (Bonn, 1950). 124.

that the term *juridical* as used in our modern languages and as applied to Pauline « justice » is equivocal. To forget this is to endanger an understanding of much that is central to Paulinism.

The second clause gives Paul's thought greater precision : the Christian's knowledge of Christ in this life is a participation in the mysteries of his resurrection and his passion (HUBY). It is the experience of our new life of union through the Spirit with the risen redeemer which Paul described in the Thessalonian letters by the term ἁγιασμός [44]. In the third clause, this knowledge is conceived as a preparation for the eschatological redemption of the Christian at the parousia, effected definitively by the resurrection of the just. This same line of thought is found in 1 Cor 1,30, a letter which is almost contemporaneous with Philippians : « ... you are in union with Christ Jesus, who has become our Wisdom from God, that is, Justification and Sanctification and Redemption ».

v. 10. *that I may come to know him.* The final infinitive [45] is a further explicitation of the « being found in Christ » or « gaining Christ » (HUBY) or of the « justice of faith » (VINCENT), and implies continual growth in deeper knowledge (HEINZELMANN). *The power of his resurrection* explains αὐτόν (VINCENT) : it is this power of his new supernatural life which gives the Christian the capacity for sharing in Christ's sufferings (MÉDEBIELLE, DIBELIUS), which so unites the Christian's sufferings with Christ's that they are part of his passion [46]. *Being moulded to the pattern of his death.* This phrase, which carries the Christian participation in Christ's passion to its consummation in death, is extremely important as an indication of Paul's changed attitude towards the possibility of his own death before the parousia.

v. 11. *to arrive, if possible, at the resurrection from death.* The condition

---

[44] The term ἁγιασμός however puts the accent rather upon God's action : the ἅγιοι are not « saints » in the modern sense, where stress is laid upon moral excellence, but those whom God has called, consecrated, destined for himself. Where we moderns tend to think of « holiness » in a *subjective* sense, the Bible (and Paul notably) conceives it *objectively*. In other words, a « saint » in the biblical sense is not one who has done great things for God but for whom God has done great things (cf. the *Magnificat*, Lk 1,49).

[45] MAX ZERWICK, *Graecitas Biblica*[2] (Romae, 1949) § 269.

[46] MAX MEINERTZ, *op. cit.* 95 ; J. BONSIRVEN, *op. cit.* 277, calls this the « génitif mystique », which unites two characteristically Pauline points of view : « suivre le Christ en se laissant faire par lui et en se conformant à lui ». Cf. BARNABAS MARY AHERN, *The Fellowship of his Suffering* (Phil 3,10) : *a Study of St. Paul's Doctrine on Christian Suffering*, in *CBQ* 22 (1960) 1-32.

is a virtual interrogative and expresses expectation, not doubt [47]. By *resurrection from death* is meant the eschatological resurrection of the just [48], the consummation of the mystical union with Christ which is, in turn, the fruit of his salutary resurrection [49]. It may seem surprising that Paul should introduce this idea into a context where he is applying the concepts of death and resurrection to the apostolic life. This passage which thus appears as a sort of hybrid [50], is of some moment since it is a transitional step between a text like 1 Thes 4,14 and those of later provenance where the intrinsic causal connection between Christ's resurrection and that of the Christian becomes explicit (1 Cor 6,14 ; 15,20-22), and where the antithesis, death-resurrection, is applied to the present Christian life (2 Cor 1,5 ; 4,10-12 ; 13,4).

§ 3. - The Christian Eschatological Hope of Salvation. Phil 3,20-21

In the earlier part of this chapter (3,3-14), Paul proposed his own conversion and Christian life as the attitude characteristic of the « mature » disciple (15-16), which will guarantee union in the Philippian community. Previously (2,5-11), Paul cited Christ's « attitude » [51] towards his work of redemption as a motive for Christian unity. Now (17) he draws the same lesson from his own practice of Christian perfection : « Remain united in becoming imitators of me, brothers ». « The enemies of the cross of Christ », whose ideals are centred on « the things of earth » (18-19), display the opposite viewpoint. In the hymn-like passage which follows [52],

---

[47] ZERWICK, *op. cit.* § 283.

[48] BONSIRVEN, *op. cit.* 330.

[49] MEINERTZ, *op. cit. II*, 223.

[50] CERFAUX, *op. cit.* 89-90 : « Le texte en question parle de la participation par les souffrances de la vie apostolique. Mais au lieu que l'antithèse se développe dans la sphère de l'apostolat, elle rejoint simplement le thème fondamental de la résurrection ».

[51] The τοῦτο φρονεῖτε of 2,5 is recalled by the phrase τοῦτο φρονῶμεν which is used in 3,16.

[52] Cf. LOHMEYER's remark in his commentary, p. 157 : « Eine Fülle seltener oder einzigartiger Worte begegnet in diesem kleinen sechzeiligen Hymnus ». Also BONNARD's observation on p. 72 of his commentary : « Nous avons de nouveau affaire ici à une sorte d'hymne au Seigneur de l' univers ; il faut bien remarquer, cependant, que l'apôtre ne s'étend pas sur cet aspect cosmique de la rédemption finale ; il en fait seulement mention pour soutenir la doctrine de la résurrection du corps ».

the Apostle directs his Christians' attention to the parousiac Christ and that eschatological salvation which will only be realized at the glorious resurrection of the just.

20 Our [true] city-state, however, exists in heaven. It is from there that we expect as Saviour Lord Jesus Christ, 21 who will transform our wretched body by giving it the character of his glorious body, in keeping with that force enabling him even to subject the universe to himself.

v. 20. *Our* (true) *city-state.* The possessive pronoun is emphatic (LOHMEYER) to contrast the Christian ideal with that of Paul's adversaries. The term πολίτευμα, frequent in Hellenistic Judaism (BONNARD), expresses by a metaphor familiar to Paul's addressees that supernatural reality denoted by the Gospel-phrase « kingdom of heaven » [53]. Paul has already employed the same figure of speech in Phil 1,27. He thinks of this supreme divine dominion as existing in heaven, not inasmuch as heaven is the ultimate goal of the Christian, but, as the following sentence makes clear, because heaven is at present the abode of the glorified Christ, his « capital » (BONNARD). The conception reflects the essentially eschatological orientation of Paul's early theological thinking. The Christian's life here below necessarily transcends the limitations of earthly, human existence, since the risen Christ, its source and inspiration, is in heaven.

The second half of the verse, recalling as it does Peter's remark in Acts 3,20-21, shows that, at this period, Paul is still guided completely by the primitive eschatology of the Jerusalem community. The use of ἀπεκδέχεσθαι to designate the expectation of the End is habitual with Paul (BONNARD). The title, « Saviour », used only here (apart from Eph 5,23) in the Pauline corpus [53a] to designate Christ, has a « strong eschatological accent » (BONNARD). It is at his parousia that Christ will effect the resurrection of the just.

This glorious resurrection is described in some detail by v. 21. It is

---

[53] HERMANN STRATHMANN, πολίτευμα, *TWNT VI*, 535.

[53a] The term σωτηρία however with its predominantly eschatological orientation is used constantly by Paul in the greater epistles (2 Cor 1,6 ; 7,10 ; Rom 1,16 ; 10,1.10 ; 11,11 ; 13,11), as well as in Eph 1,13 (cf. also 2 Tm 2,10 ; 3,15). The verb σώζειν is used even more frequently (I Cor 1,18.21 ; 3,15 ; 5,5 ; 9,22 ; 10,33 ; 15,2 ; 2 Cor 2,15 ; Rom 5,9 ; 8,24 ; 10,9 ; 11,14.26). Eph 2,5.8 reveals a change in Paul's viewpoint. The verb ἀπεκδέχεσθαι, which also belongs to Paul's eschatological terminology, recurs constantly, though less frequently (I Cor 1,7 ; Gal 5,5 ; Rom 8,19.25).

to be noted, as NEAL FLANAGAN has observed [54], that Paul appears to have drawn upon the vocabulary of the hymn cited in 2,6-11 for his terminology here. The hymn described how Christ accomplished man's redemption by appearing in human form and acting « outwardly like any other man » (σχήματι εὑρεθεὶς ὡς ἄνθρωπος). This was the specific form of his « self-abasement » (ἐταπείνωσεν ἑαυτόν). It will be by reversing this process that the parousiac Christ will bring salvation to the Christian. « He will transform (μετασχηματίσει) our wretched body » (σῶμα τῆς ταπεινώσεως) by causing man, in his entire corporeal personality, to enter a new, personal relationship with his Lord (LOHMEYER), viz. by giving man a share « in the character » (σύμμορφον) of Christ's glorified humanity (τῷ σώματι τῆς δόξης αὐτοῦ). The term here translated as « character » was a keyword in the hymn and summed up its theme: while retaining « his character as God » (ἐν μορφῇ Θεοῦ), the pre-existent Lord took on « the Servant's character » (μορφὴν δούλου). The δόξα of Christ was described in the hymn as the Father's « immeasurably exalting him » by giving him the divine Name, Kyrios, and so making him the object of universal adoration on the part of all creatures, an adoration due to the Father and redounding to his « glory » (εἰς δόξαν).

In 3,21 b, man's glorification is ascribed to that very δόξα of Christ, here called ἐνέργεια, since it bestows on him the uniquely divine power of dominating the universe. The text is noteworthy as one of the very rare places in Paul (cf. 1 Cor 6,14) where the power which effects the resurrection of the just is attributed, not to the Father, but to Christ.

While retaining the marked eschatological polarity of Paul's earlier thought, Philippians gives some evidence of a new development in the resurrection theme. *The power of his resurrection* is already conceived as a dynamic force conferred upon the sacred humanity of the risen Christ, in order to produce in the Christian the new life of grace and, ultimately, to bring about his *resurrection from the dead.* For a fuller development of this line of thought, however, we must await the formulae of a later period.

---

[54] NEAL FLANAGAN, *A Note on Philippians* 3,20-21 in *CBQ* 18 (1956) 8-9. We wish to draw attention to the importance of this analysis as a (hitherto unused) proof for the unity of Phil, at least as regards chs. 2,3.

§ 4. - The Risen Christ as Divine Wisdom. 1 Cor 1,30

In contrast with many of the Pauline epistles, 1 Corinthians appears
to consist principally of a series of admonitions concerning division and
and scandals in the community (1,10-6,20), then of a group of *responsa*
(7,1-14,40), and finally of a lengthy apology for the dogma of the resurrection of the just (15,1-58). KARL PRÜMM has shown however that there
is a unity of theme in this letter based upon the conception of Christian
wisdom which Paul uses to combat the fundamental evil at Corinth, dis-
unity [55]. If PRÜMM's contention be correct, the importance of the verse
under consideration becomes apparent : it is a restatement of Pauline
soteriology in terms of Christian wisdom.

Now from him comes your existence in Christ Jesus, who became for us Wisdom from
God, that is, Justice and Sanctification and Redemption.

[30 a. ἡμῖν is placed before σοφία in the Syriac, Coptic, Armenian and Vulgate versions,
as well as in citations by Origen, Augustine, Pelagius and Ephrem. This is probably due to a wish to co-ordinate the four words which are applied to Christ].

In the paragraph to which this verse belongs (1,17-31), Paul speaks
of the λόγος τοῦ σταυροῦ, which he terms the « folly of the kerygma » (21). The object of this « discourse » is « a crucified Christ » (23),
or « Christ as Power of God and Wisdom of God » (24). With delicate tact,
Paul refers to the Corinthian's own vocation to the faith : God has, in
them, made choice of the foolish and weak of this world (26-28) in order
to nullify man's pride in his own natural powers (29). From being nonent-
ities, the Corinthians have come to-be-in-Christ (WENDLAND). The unique source of this « new creation » (2 Cor 5,17) is God the Creator (cf. 1
Cor 8,6 ; Rom 11,36).
Your existence in Christ Jesus. Paul has already referred to this Christian life as a gift of God the Father, a call « into fellowship with his Son,
Jesus Christ our Lord » (1 Cor 1,9). He will later describe it as an effect
of « the Name (or Person) of the Lord Jesus Christ » and of « the Spirit
of our God » (1 Cor 6,11). The formula used in the present text is one of
his own creation, *in Christ Jesus.* It connotes the new mode of Christian

[55] K. PRÜMM, *Die pastorale Einheit des ersten Korintherbriefes* in *ZKT* 64
(1940) 202-214.

existence in union with the risen Christ as Saviour or as second Adam [56]. The meaning of the expression ranges from a maximum, where it signifies the Mystical Body of Christ, to a circumlocution for « Christian ». Here Paul uses the formula in its fullest sense and refers to the existence of the Corinthian community as part of « the Body of Christ ». This is clear from the following clause where Paul is not content to call Christ divine Wisdom, which is all the context requires, but adds three epithets explanatory of the new life. The addition is no mere rhetorical flourish (DIBELIUS), but is necessary to explain the formula *in Christ Jesus.*

who became for us Wisdom from God. Despite his attack on Greek philosophy, Paul is not anti-intellectual. He points out to the Greeks that Christ fulfils their loftiest aspirations for wisdom. Christian wisdom is however primarily a religious experience (MOFFAT). On Paul's view, Christ *became for us Wisdom* in his death and resurrection. The apostle never stops to consider the incarnation after the fashion of John [57]. Christ's act of redemption disproves the basic thesis of Greek philosophy, viz. the impossibility of divine intervention in the cosmos [58]. Paul's experience at Athens and at Corinth had taught him the need of presenting « a crucified Christ » who was risen from the dead as the incarnation of God's Wisdom. But Paul now advances beyond his own thesis and takes occasion to resume the whole work of Christ, who justified us, sanctified us, redeemed us (HÉRING). Paul puts the truth much more graphically however, and for a reason. Christ *became* our *Justice, Sanctification, Redemption* because he first effected this redemptive work in his own sacred humanity through his death and resurrection. Paul always thinks concretely after the Semitic fashion. He does not consider Christ's redemptive work in the category of merit, which is still the most common viewpoint of modern theology.

The Greek difficulty in accepting Christianity was a desire for human wisdom : « a crucified Christ » was « folly » to them. The Jews were in search of miracles : the Cross was « a scandal » (22-23). Paul does not iso-

---

[56] On the formula, « in Christ Jesus », cf. PRAT, *op. cit. II*, 359-362 ; BONSIRVEN, *op. cit.* 239-242 ; CERFAUX, *op. cit.* 376-379 ; MEINERTZ, *op. cit. II*, 135-138.

[57] CERFAUX, *op. cit.* 134 : « On serait encore tenté de ramener au contexte de l' incarnation les formules : ' Le Christ est devenu notre justice, notre sagesse, notre sainteté, notre rédemption ' (*I Cor.*, I, 30). Il est trop évident que ce n'est pas l' incarnation qui est en jeu, mais la rédemption ».

[58] GREGORY DIX, *Jew and Greek* (Westminster, 1953) 9-14.

late the Greek religious problem from that of the Jews, but replies to
both simultaneously [59]. Hence, in proposing Christ Jesus to the Greeks
as *Wisdom*, he appends an explanation which points out Christ to the
Jews as the culmination of the three chief tendencies in the OT search
for God. The Mosaic code and cult strove to impart justice and sanctification. The prophets proclaimed Yahweh's definitive act of redemption.
The sapiential literature strove to teach humano-divine wisdom. Thus
Paul shows that the striving of pagan religion as of the Jewish faith finds
its consummation in Christ Jesus.

who became for us Justice. Paul will demonstrate in the first section
of Romans that Christ is the embodiment of the « Justice of God », i. e.,
God's faithfulness to his promises of salvation (Rom 3,21-30). *he became
for us Sanctification.* The term, as we have seen, is characteristic of Paul's
earlier manner (1 Thes 4,3.4.7 ; 2 Thes 2,13), where it expresses the truth
that the risen Christ is bearer of the Spirit, imparted at Baptism as principle of the new existence in Christ Jesus. For Paul, as BONSIRVEN points
out [60], there can be no sanctity without justification. MAX MEINERTZ
observes that it is un-Pauline to separate justification from union with
Christ : hence there can be no distinction between « juridical » and « mystical » texts in Paul [61]. *He became for us Redemption.* The redemption
is mentioned last, since, on Paul's view, it comes as the last grace bestowed on the Christian at the *resurrectio justorum* (Rom 8,23).

§ 5. - The Paschal Character of the Christian Life. 1 Cor 5,6b-8

The second problem **at** Corinth, a public scandal, was a case of incest
(1 Cor 5,1-13). Paul states the principle that evil condoned, even in the
smallest degree, is destructive of the new life « in Christ Jesus ».

6 b. Are you not aware that a little yeast leavens the whole batch ?
7 Clean out the old yeast that you may be a new batch, unleavened as you are.
And [this is imperative] since our Pasch has been sacrificed — Christ ! 8 Let us then
keep the feast, not with the old yeast of malice and wickedness, but with the unleavened bread of sincerity and truth.

---

[59] CERFAUX, *op. cit.* 224 : « Paul cependant ne consentait pas à séparer le
problème grec du problème juif. Il n'y a qu' un problème religieux : le christianisme
est l'antithèse et l'achèvement des religions anciennes, juive et païenne ».

[60] BONSIRVEN, *op. cit.* 210.
[61] MEINERTZ, *op. cit. II*, 116.

[6 b. The western text has δολοῖ instead of ζυμοῖ , as do the citations of Marcion, Irenaeus, Tertullian ; cf. the Vulg. *corrumpit.*
7 a. Some mss. insert οὖν as an introductory enclitic.
7 c. The Syriac and Sahidic versions and some minuscle mss. read ὑπὲρ ἡμῶν before ἐτύθη].

v. 6. *a little yeast.* In the Gospels (Matt 13,33 ; Lk 13,20-21), yeast is a symbol of the dynamic power of the Kingdom. For Paul, it is a symbol of evil (Gal 5,9). The reference is to the Jewish custom of clearing out the leavened bread in preparation for the Passover (Ex 12,15-16 ; 13,7), a sign of moral renovation (So 1,12). It may be that the time of year suggested these paschal similes to Paul (1 Cor 16,8) [62].
v. 7. *a new batch.* Paul is not thinking of the sin of incest which could hardly be qualified as a *little yeast,* but of the least suggestion of their former pagan standards of morality (PARRY). The Corinthians must *as a community* (individually they are « unleavened ») rid themselves of « the old yeast » (cf. BACHMANN-STAUFFER).
our Pasch has been sacrificed–Christ . Paul is not thinking of the Christian feast of Easter but conceives Christ's death after the Johannine manner (Jn 1,29.36 ; 19,36 ; Ap 5,6 ; 14,1-5 ; for the phrase « sacrifice the pasch », cf. Dt 16,5). The paschal lamb was sacrificed to redeem the first-born, representative of Israel delivered out of Egypt, and, at the annual feast, the new life to which Israel had been called in the desert was commemorated (PARRY). Paul uses this twofold aspect of the Passover as a type of the new Christian reality. He thinks *immediately* however not of the Jewish sacrifice of the paschal lamb which does not appear to have been *primarily* (like *Kippurim*) a sacrifice of atonement, but of that of *our Pasch–Christ* [63]. The emphatic position of the word *Christ* shows that Paul

---

[62] E. SCHWARTZ, *Osterbetrachtungen* in *ZNW* 7 (1906) 1-33. G. RICCIOTTI, *Le lettere di San Paolo* (Roma, 1949) 49.
[63] Cf. the opinion of BACHMANN-STAUFFER, p. 216 : « Diese festliche Schlachtung hatte nicht sowohl den Charakter eines sühnenden Abwendungsopfers, wie die einstige erstmalige, als den einer Opfermahlzeit, bei welcher man der gnädigen Gemeinschaft Gottes mit dem Volke in dankbaren Erinnerung an die Erlösung aus Agypten sich freut ». This statement needs to be somewhat refined : cf. Ez 45,21-24 which prescribes a sin-offering of a bull on the Pasch itself, and a he-goat, sacrificed for the same purpose, on each of the seven days during which the Passover feast was continued. « But when the fourteenth day was come, and all were ready to depart, they (the Hebrews) offered the sacrifice and purified their houses with the blood ... Whence it is that we do still *offer this sacrifice in like manner to this day,* and call this festival *Pascha,* which signifies the feast of the Passover,

thinks of the risen « Lamb who was slain » as the centre of the Christian cult. DE LA TAILLE observes that this is the common patristic interpretation of the new Pasch [64]. The conception of Christ's death as a sacrifice, one of the principal themes of Hebrews, is referred to, in various ways, in the Pauline epistles, although the Apostle does not give any extended development of it [64a].

v. 8. *Let us keep the feast.* The joyful note which the phrase implies (MOFFATT) shows that the Christian commemoration of the redemption must, from apostolic times, have included the resurrection as well as the death of Christ [65].

With the unleavened bread of sincerity and truth. As JACQUES GUILLET remarks [66], the « azymes » used at the Passover were a symbol of the new life to which God had called Israel. The *qahal* in the desert represented, for the later prophets and the NT writers [67], the ideal, messianic community. In consequence, Paul employs the paschal theme as a type of Christ's double redemptive act : his death to the old, his rising to the new existence (Rom 6,10). Yet the *anamnesis* of the Christian Pasch is much more than an annual commemoration. It provides the pattern for everyday Christian living [68]. *Let us keep the feast* is a daily invitation [69].

---

because on that day God passed us over, and sent the plague upon the Egyptians ... » : WILLIAM WHISTON, *The Works of Flavius Josephus* (Edinburgh, 1834), *Antiquities of the Jews*, Book 11, chapter XIV, §6, p. 75.

[64] M. DE LA TAILLE, *Mysterium Fidei* (Paris, 1921) 132 ff. : « Apparet *primo* mens Patrum, dum exponunt Pascha novum. Antitypum enim judaici sacrificii paschalis non reponunt in coena aut passione tantum, sed adjecta resurrectione ». There follow citations from CHRYSOSTOM, THEOPHILUS of Alexandria and the Venerable BEDE.

[64a] As STANISLAS LYONNET (*La sotériologie paulinienne* in ROBERT-FEUILLET *Introduction à la Bible, II,* 875 f) has pointed out, this theme of sacrifice is, in Paul, subordinate to that of divine love.

[65] On the meaning of the paschal observances of the first three Christian centuries, cf. O. CASEL, *Art und Sinn der ältesten christlichen Osterfeier* in *JL* 14 (1938) 1-78.

[66] J. GUILLET, *Thèmes Bibliques* (Paris, 1951) 22 : « De cette nouveauté, trait essentiel de la Pâque dès le judaïsme, l'usage des azymes est le signe ».

[67] *ibid.* 11.

[68] We find a parallel to this idea in the use made in the psalms of the Exodus : cf. GUILLET, *op. cit.* 21 ; CARROLL STUHLMUELLER, *The Influence of Oral Tradition upon Exegesis* in *CBQ* 20 (1958) 299-326 ; THOMAS BARROSSE, *The Senses of Scripture and the Liturgical Pericopes* in *CBQ* 21 (1959) 1-23.

[69] W. T. HAHN, *Das Mitsterben und Mitauferstehen mit Christus bei Paulus* (Gütersloh, 1937) 34. The author is speaking of the meaning of the baptismal texts

§ 6. - Christ's Resurrection, Principle of our Resurrection.
1 Cor 6,13b-15a.

After discussing the question of lawsuits before pagan tribunals (1 Cor 6,1-11), Paul presents his celebrated argument against fornication (1 Cor 6,12-20). The Corinthians seem to have been in danger of adopting the slogans for libertinism employed by some of the Cynic and Stoic philosophers (12). A popular argument was the transcendental relation between organ and function. Just as the relation between the stomach and eating is natural, so too that between the body and the sexual act (13). Paul denies the parity : nutrition pertains to the transitory order and will have no place in the body's future spiritualized existence ; hence it has no religious value. For Paul, only what endures eternally is of value in the spiritual life. The body [70], on the other hand, is destined to be glorified, and has a superlative spiritual value [71]. The evil of fornication consists in setting up a personal relationship which is in direct opposition to the personal relationship between the Christian and the Lord.

13 b But the body is not for fornication, but for the Lord, and the Lord for the body. 14 Because God has both raised the Lord, and he will raise us through his power. 15 Do you not know that your bodies are members of Christ ?

[14. The reading ἐξεγερεῖ (Sin., some western mss., and the Vulg., Syriac, Coptic, Ethiopic versions) is to be preferred to ἐξεγείρει (Alex., D first corr.) and to ἐξήγειρεν (Vat., Chester Beatty papyrus).
15 a. There is some hesitation in the mss. tradition between ἡμῶν (Sin., Alex., Irenaeus) and ὑμῶν, the more commonly attested reading].

v. 13b. *the body is ... for the Lord, and the Lord for the body.* With this passage, we come to one of the most marvellous conceptions in Pauline theology (ALLO). This is the first expression of the notion of « the Body of Christ » in the epistles. That formula is not yet enunciated, but the reality is already present in Paul's thought [72]. It is not so much a question here

---

in Rom 6 : « Zum Indikativ gehört der Imperativ. Nur im vollzogenen Imperativ hat der Indikativ seine Wirklichkeit und nur als vom Indikativ umfangener hat der Imperativ seine Gültigkeit, ist er überhaupt als solcher möglich ».
    [70] The body, for the Semite, includes the whole human personality : BONSIRVEN, *op. cit.* 220, 306.
    [71] Cf. the remarks of J. HÉRING in his commentary p. 47.
    [72] BONSIRVEN, *op. cit.* 220, 241.

8. - D. M. STANLEY.

of the risen Christ's lordship over the Christian (2 Cor 5,15 ; Rom 7,6 ;
14,7-9) as of a *mutual personal* relationship. Not only does the Christian
belong to the Lord, but the Lord bears a relation to the Christian, a person
with a material as well as a spiritual nature. The death and resurrection
of Christ, consequently, concern our bodies no less than our souls (HUBY).
The significance of this doctrine for the Pauline theology of justification
(and grace) will be seen in later epistles (2 Cor 5,17 ; Gal 2,20 ; 6,15 ; Rom
4,25 ; 6,6 ; 7,5-6 ; 8,3 ff.).

v. 14. *God has both raised the Lord and he will raise us through his power.*
It is, in the first place, God's act of raising Jesus which has established the
marvellous new relationship between the risen Lord and the Christian ;
and, in the second place, the future resurrection of the just. One might
ask how this future event can be said to function in the Christian's present
existence. Paul has « interiorized » the causal connection between Christ's
resurrection and that of the Christian at the end of time. The phrase
through his power is to be understood of the divine energy now communicated to the risen Christ. Paul has already called Christ « God's power »
(1 Cor 1,24). This transfer of the divine power has been described as the
communication of the divine Name to the risen Christ (Phil 2,9) and of
the divine glory (1 Cor 2,8) [73]. Our interpretation of the present passage is
consistent with Paul's newer manner of conceiving the link between
Christ's resurrection and that of the Christian (1 Cor 15,21), with the conception of the risen Lord as « Son of God in power » (Rom 1,4) and as bearer of the vivifying Spirit (Rom 8,11 ; cf. 1 Cor 15,45 ; 2 Cor 3,17). It is
by virtue of this communicated power that « he who cleaves to the Lord
is one spirit » (17). Paul uses the term *spirit* here, where the whole context
would lead us to expect *one body* [74], because he is thinking of this spiritualizing force given to the risen Christ, in virtue of which he possesses
the Christian. The notion of possession is stressed towards the conclusion
of the paragraph (19-20) : the Christian in his material personality is a

---

[73] CERFAUX, *op. cit.* 69 : cf. the commentary of HUBY, p. 149, n. 1, for the
opposite view : « ' Par sa puissance ' à lui, Dieu, le même qui a ressuscité le
Christ ... ».

[74] E. PERCY, *Der Leib Christi in den Paulinischen Homologoumena und Anti-
legomena* (Lund, 1942) 14 : « Wenn es nun hier aber heisst, dass er mit dem Herrn
ein Geist ist, so kann dies entsprechend dem, was wir eben über die paulinische
Auffassung von Leib des Menschen ausgeführt haben, nicht anders verstanden
werden, als wenn hier gestanden hätte, dass er mit ihm ein Leib sei ».

sanctuary of the indwelling Spirit ; he has been « bought with a price » [75].
v. 15. *your bodies are members of Christ.* Here we have one of the earliest
formulations of the Pauline doctrine of the Mystical Body. While the doctrine of the Eucharist will also contribute to the final expression of this
truth (1 Cor 10, 17), still it is Paul's conception of the salvific nature of
Christ's resurrection which forms the basis of it.

§ 7. - Typology of the Exodus : Baptism and the Eucharist.
1 Cor 10,1-4.

In his solution of the question concerning the eating of meat offered to idols (1 Cor 8,1-11,1), Paul recalls Israel's experiences in the desert
to counsel against the sin of presumption (10,1-11) : « these happenings
were types of our existence » (6). The idea is not new. Jewish thought
had already perceived in the *qahal* of Israel in the desert a type of the
messianic community (HUBY) [76]. What is new is Paul's interpretation
of the Exodus in terms of Baptism and the Eucharist. Stephen had pointed to Moses as type of Christ the redeemer (Acts 7,20-40) : Paul provides a variation upon the same theme.

1 I will not have you ignorant, brothers, that our fathers — all of them — marched
beneath the cloud. All passed through the sea, 2 and all were baptized into [fellow-
ship with] Moses. 3 And all ate the same spiritual food, 4 and all drank the same
spiritual drink. They drank from a spiritual rock that followed them ; and the
rock was the Christ.

[1 a. γὰρ is attested by the great majority of mss., δὲ by Sin. third corr., two western mss. and the Syriac versions.
2. Μωυσέα is found in the Chester Beatty papyrus. ἐβαπτίσαντο (the reading of
Vat., the Byzantine recension, Chester Beatty papyrus, and Origen) may well be
more primitive than ἐβαπτίσθησαν (Sin., Alex., D., and the majority of Greek
mss.).
3-4. τὸ αὐτὸ is omitted by Alex. and the Chester Beatty papyrus].

v. 1. *I will not have you ignorant.* As elsewhere in Paul (1 Thes 4,13 ;
1 Cor 12,1 ; 2 Cor 1,8 ; Rom 1,13 ; 11,25), the phrase introduces an important communication (HÉRING).

---

[75] What is stressed in this Pauline phrase is *not* the idea of a price, but
the notion of *belonging* henceforth to Christ.
[76] BONSIRVEN, *op. cit.* 129.

our fathers — all of them — marched beneath the cloud. The word *all* is underlined to contrast with *the majority* (5) who merited the divine displeasure. Paul is thinking of the Israelites as a community. *Beneath the cloud.* The tradition is preserved in Ps 104,39 : it differs from that of Ex 13,21 ; 14,19-20, where the cloud precedes or follows the Israelites. *All passed through the sea.* HÉRING (who cites J. WEISS) finds the application of the event as described in Ex 14,22 (the crossing is made dry-shod) to Baptism very difficult. It is the first instance in the paragraph where the anti-type has exerted influence upon the type.

v. 2. *All were baptized into [fellowship with] Moses.* Israel's experience is conceived after the analogy of Baptism « unto Christ ». It can, in consequence, be considered an initiation into Moses' fellowship, enrolment under his leadership, admission to the religion of which he was the founder [77]. To grasp Paul's meaning it is necessary to realize that he employs types in what appears to be almost a reckless manner. GUILLET describes the process very precisely [78]. Paul is formulating in terms of OT history the world-shaking event of Christ's redemptive death and resurrection. If he assigns a typical value to extrinsic analogies which the modern mind finds difficult to accept, it must be remembered that he does so in virtue of his principal assertion. Israel, by leaving Egypt at Moses' word to follow Yahweh in the desert, took a step which, religiously speaking, is analogous to the Christian renunciation of the world in Baptism.

vv. 3-4. *the same spiritual food ... drink.* Israel fed upon manna in the desert (Ex 16,14), which is described elsewhere as « bread from heaven » (Ps 77,24) and « the food of angels » (Wis 16,20). The people drank water from the rock struck by Moses (Ex 17,6 ; Nm 20,11). Paul's repetition of the term *spiritual* indicates the influence of the Eucharist upon the type. He will presently refer to this sacrament as « the chalice *of the Lord* », « the table *of the Lord* » (10,21), as « the body and blood *of the Lord* » (11,27), that is *of the risen Christ* whose body he describes later (1 Cor 15,44.46) as σῶμα πνευματικόν. The use of this same adjective, πνευματικός, in the present passage shows the importance of Christ's resurrection for the Pauline conception of the Eucharist. *They drank from a spiritual rock that followed them ; and the rock was the Christ.* This might be called the extreme case of Pauline typology. The cadre of the

---

[77] CERFAUX, *op. cit.* 252.
[78] GUILLET, *op. cit.* 21 ff ; cf. also GUSTAVE MARTELET, *Sacrements, Figures et Exhortations en* 1 *Cor* 10,1-11 in *RSR* 44 (1956) 323-359 ; 514-559.

OT narrative is too narrow to serve as a type of the Eucharist. Accordingly, Paul widens it by introducing a rabbinic legend [79]. He wishes to teach the two main points in his Eucharistic theology : the fellowship of the Christian with the risen Christ (1 Cor 10,16) really present to nourish him upon his own substance (1 Cor 11,23-27). The tale of the rock which rolled after the Israelites during their years in the desert serves Paul's didactic purpose, and he does not hesitate to use it (cf. ALLO). What is important is Paul's fidelity to the primitive Christian tradition which had seen a connection between the Eucharist and Christ's resurrection [80]. The present passage is sufficient to contradict the thesis of LIETZMANN that the sorrowful Pauline commemoration of the Last Supper and Christ's death superseded the joyous *fractio panis* of the Jerusalem community [81].

§ 8. - The Eucharist and the Parousia. 1 Cor 11,26

This verse occurs at the end of Paul's account of the Last Supper (1 Cor 11,23-25) and constitutes a kind of midrash upon the command of re-iteration, repeated in the Pauline *récit* after each of the formulae of institution.

For as often as you eat this bread and drink of the chalice, you are proclaiming the death of the Lord, until he comes.

[The Chester Beatty papyrus adds τοῦτο after ποτήριον].

Paul explains the reason for Christ's command to repeat the Eucharistic celebration « in memory of me ». It unites the Christian community with the death and resurrection of Christ and directs attention to the joyous reunion with him at his second Coming.
You are proclaiming. The liturgical act of the Eucharist is described by

---

[79] PAUL BILLERBECK, *Kommentar zum Neuen Testament aus Talmud und Midrasch III*, 406-408 ; J. BONSIRVEN, *Textes Rabbiniques des deux premiers siècles chrétiens pour servir à l' intelligence du Nouveau Testament* (Rome, 1955) § 1006.

[80] O. CULLMANN, *La signification de la sainte cène dans le christianisme primitif* in RHPhilRel 16 (1936) 1-22 ; YVES DE MONTCHEUIL, *Signification eschatologique du repas eucharistique* in RSR 33 (1946) 10-43.

[81] HANS LIETZMANN, *Messe und Herrenmahl*, § XV : *Die Ausgestaltung des Herrenmahls* 249 ff.

a term normally used of the act of evangelizing (Acts 13,5 ; 16,17 ; 17,3 ; Phil 1,17 ; 1 Cor 2,1 ; 9,14). On Paul's view then the Eucharist is the Gospel in act, and as such, it is related to the central mysteries of man's redemption. *The death of the Lord.* Paul uses the title *Lord* throughout his narrative of the Last Supper. It sets the tone of the whole recital [82]. Paul, while following the tradition represented also in the Synoptic Gospels, has made a place for Christ's resurrection in his Eucharistic teaching. His phrase « the body of the Lord » (29) indicates that he identifies the Eucharistic body with Christ's risen body [83], even when he is considering the sacrificial aspects of the Eucharist (28). *Until he comes.* The thought of the risen Christ suggests that of his second Coming. The Eucharistic presence is a kind of anticipation of the parousia, which thus contributes to the meaning of this sacrament.

§ 9. - Christ's Resurrection in the Kerygma. 1 Cor 15,3-4

The whole of the fifteenth chapter is concerned with the relations between Christ's resurrection and that of the just. It appears that Paul had heard that the dogma of the general resurrection of the just was questioned by some at Corinth, possibly because of the influence of Platonic philosophy, which tended to regard the body as a prison of the soul and death, consequently, as the soul's liberation [84]. Paul proves *the fact* of the general resurrection from the truth of Christ's resurrection (1-34). Then he discusses the manner of the glorious resurrection (35-53), and concludes with a hymn of triumph (54-58).

3 For I handed on to you, first of all, that tradition which I also received : that Christ died for our sins according to the Scriptures, 4 and that he was buried, and that he has been raised the third day according to the Scriptures.

[4 b. τῇ ἡμέρᾳ τῇ τρίτη, the more emphatic expression, is the correct one (Sin., Alex., Vat., D)].

This piece of Christian tradition is primitive. Paul is simply citing the Palestinian catechesis (WEISS) [85]. He terms it a λόγος (2), that

---

[82] CERFAUX, *op. cit.* 372 n. 1.

[83] *ibid.* 214.

[84] T. W. MANSON, *St Paul in Ephesus* (3) : *The Corinthian Correspondence* in *BJRylL* 26 (1941) 117.

[85] BONSIRVEN, *op. cit.* 26. M. DIBELIUS, *Die Formgeschichte des Evangeliums,* 17, n. 1, asserts that it is the exact reproduction of a definite credal formula.

is, a body of doctrinal elements in a didactic form[86]. The word expresses the double character of the kerygma : dogma and its definitive formulation[87].

v. 3. *I handed on ... that tradition which I also received.* Paul asserts that his preaching was in strict accord with the dogmatic formulations of the apostolic community[88]. His care to preserve the original formulae of the primitive Church is seen by the terms he employs here[89] and by his inclusion of Christ's death and burial which are not directly involved in an argument for the resurrection of the just[90].

First of all. The phrase indicates the great importance, in Paul's eyes, of the apostolic kerygma (ROBERTSON-PLUMMER). It also implies that in his *teaching*, as distinct from his preaching, Paul developed the original datum of tradition according to his own theological conception of the redemption. *Christ died for our sins ... he has been raised.* These two basic truths, so closely connected in the theology of Paul, are essential points in the kerygma. Hence it is clear that the doctrine of Christ's satisfactory death is no Pauline invention.

v. 4. *he was buried.* This event was considered an important article in the kerygma for the evidence it gives of the reality of Christ's death (HUBY). Its main function however was connected most probably with the theme of the incorruption of Christ's body (cf. Acts 2,24-31 ;13, 34-37). *According to the Scriptures.* The principal Scriptural testimony for the salvific death and resurrection of Christ seems to have been drawn from the Isaian Servant songs[91]. We have already remarked that this Servant theology does not appear to have been developed by Paul. Yet his statement in this passage that he used the Scripture proofs found in the apostolic tradition

---

[86] J. SCHMITT, *Jésus ressuscité dans la prédication apostolique,* 52.

[87] GERHARD KITTEL, λέγω, *TWNT IV,* 102, n. 125.

[88] SCHMITT, *op. cit.* 53. CERFAUX, *op. cit.* 62, makes a curious distinction between the formula « God raised Christ from death », which forms part of the act of Christian faith, and the expression « Christ was raised », which (he says) does not pertain to the formulation of the faith but to the recital of those facts on which Christian faith rested. This opinion seems difficult to justify.

[89] *ibid.* 57.

[90] E. STAUFFER, *Die Theologie des Neuen Testaments* (Stuttgart, 1941) 215. Cf. W. HEITMÜLLER, *Zum Problem Paulus und Jesus* in *ZNW* 13 (1912) 331.

[91] W. L. KNOX, *The Acts of the Apostles* (Cambridge, 1948) 72 : « The primary prophecy on which the Church relied was that of Is. liii ... The use of the prophecy is common to all New Testament writers in spite of the fact that Paul uses it only once and then by implication rather than directly ».

and his citation of the hymn in Phil 2,6-11 show that he employed the Servant theme in his *preaching*. The brief allusions he makes, in connection with Christ's death, to Isaias in his letters also indicate this[92]. *He has been raised the third day*. The use of the perfect tense here and throughout this chapter[93] when referring to the resurrection shows that Paul's argument is based upon « the permanent efficacy » of Christ's resurrection (PARRY). The mention of *the third day* here (particularly the unusual use of the phrase in conjunction with the perfect tense) proves that this historical fact was a datum of tradition (HUBY), and of paramount importance for the theme of Christ's incorruption[94].

§ 10. - **Role of Christ's Resurrection in the Kerygma. 1 Cor 15,14-18**

Paul has shown by citing the Palestinian kerygma that Christ's resurrection is part of the deposit of faith (3-4). It is also witnessed to by the apostles and by himself (5-11). The logical consequence of this event is the resurrection of the just. This is proven *negatively* in the paragraph now under consideration : if the resurrection of the dead be impossible, then Christ is not risen, the kerygma is false, and Christianity a delusion (12-19).

14 But if Christ has not been raised, then our kerygma is emptied of its content, and your faith is without object. 15 And we are even detected bearing false witness to God because we have testified against God that he raised Christ, whereas he did not raise him if the dead are not raised. 16 For if the dead are not raised, neither has Christ been raised. 17 But if Christ has not been raised, you have believed without cause : you are still in your sins. 18 Yes, and moreover, those who fell asleep in Christ have perished.

[14b. καί after ἄρα (Sin. first corr., Alex., D) is probably an interpolation, as is δέ after κενή (Sin., Alex., Vat., D first corr.).
14c. ὑμῶν (Sin., Alex., Vulg., Peshitto, Armenian, Coptic versions, Irenaeus, Tertullian, Ephrem) is to be preferred to ἡμῶν (Vat., D first corr.).
15. The last clause εἴπερ .... ἐγείρονται is omitted by D, the Peshitto, Irenaeus, Tertullian, Ambrosiaster, Theodoretus].

---

[92] For instance, 1 Thes 5,10 ; 2 Cor 5,14 ; Gal 1,4 ; 2,20 ; 3,13 ; Rom 4,25 ; 5,8. It is to be noted that such allusions are very general and hence can scarcely be considered more than a point of departure for Paul's theological thinking.

[93] The one exception is found in v. 15, where the aorist active is used.

[94] SCHMITT, *op. cit.* 171 ; J. DUPONT, *Ressuscité « le troisième jour »* in *Studia Biblica et Orientalia II*, 174-193.

v. 14. *our kerygma is emptied of its content.* The preaching of Paul and of the Palestinian church, already described in its essentials, is incontrovertible (LIETZMANN) because based on the apostolic tradition ; and so constitutes an argument *ex absurdo* for the truth of Christ's resurrection. Similarly, the faith of the Corinthians would be *without object.* It is the resurrection, on Paul's view, which thus specifies the whole object of Christian faith. Should it be proven false, then Christ's passion and death would not be salvific but meaningless. At the basis of such an argument is Paul's experience on the Damascus road. It was the risen Christ who gave him his initial insight into the truth of Christianity, and that insight was to function continually in his theological thinking.

v. 15. The apostle is essentially a witness to Christ's resurrection (Acts 10,42) [95]. *We have testified against God.* This strange expression, suggesting perjured calumny ruinous of God's « good name », shows that, for Paul, Christ's resurrection is a source of revelation of the divine nature for men.

v. 16. Paul is *not* attempting to prove the possibility of the resurrection of the just to pagans (OSTY). He insists with his Corinthian Christians that a denial of this article of faith involves a denial of Christ's resurrection. At this stage of the argument, Paul adopts the eschatological viewpoint which we have studied in I Thes 4,14 : both Christ's resurrection and that of the just depend upon the divine will. By raising Christ, God has initiated the general resurrection : he has signified his intention of raising the just. The instrumental causality of Christ's resurrection in this event and the Christian's solidarity with the risen Christ will be developed later (20-22) [96].

v. 17. *You are still in your sins.* Paul views Christ's resurrection as a necessary correlative to his atoning death (LIETZMANN). It is the risen Christ who bestows the Spirit (Rom 1,4 ; 4,25 ; 5,11).

---

[95] L. CERFAUX, *Témoins du Christ d'après le Livre des Actes* in *Ang* 20 (1943) 166-183.

[96] It is not within the scope of Paul's argument to prove anything about the resurrection of the wicked. Some commentators appear to neglect this important point when they assert that the Corinthian error consisted in denying the *possibility* of the general resurrection of *all* men (cf. the commentary of HUBY, p. 368). As a consequence, Paul's counter-argument reduces itself to a simple rebuttal *ab esse ad posse* : if you believe Christ is risen, then resurrection is possible for those who, like Christ, possess a human nature. Paul however is concerned only with the resurrection of such as « died in Christ » ; hence his argument rests upon the *supernatural* solidarity of the just with Christ, not upon a natural solidarity.

v. 18. *Those who fell asleep in Christ*. On the supposition that the risen Christ does not exist, then the « being in Christ » is a delusion (LIETZMANN), and the fate of the dead Christians is the same as that of unbelievers for whom the kerygma was « folly » (1 Cor 1,18 ; Phil 1,28 ; 3,19 ; Rom 9,22).

§ 11. - The Risen Christ as Second Adam (1). 1 Cor 15,20-22

With these verses, Paul begins the more positive aspect of the proof for the resurrection of the just : the solidarity of all Christians with Christ.

20 But on the contrary, Christ has been raised from death as firstfruits of those who have fallen asleep. 21 For, since through a man [came] death, so also through a man [will come] resurrection of the dead. 22 Because just as in Adam all die, so also in Christ all will be brought to life.

[20b. We omit ἐγένετο with the best mss. (Sin., Alex., D first corr.)].

v. 20. *as firstfruits*. Paul now mentions the causality exercised by Christ's resurrection upon that of the faithful for the first time in this chapter[97]. BONSIRVEN points out that the expression *firstfruits* is equivalent to « firstborn from among the dead » (Col 1,18) : Christ is first to rise from the dead, *and* he exerts a causal influence upon those who follow[98]. In the OT, the offering of firstfruits to Yahweh was a solemn obligation (Lev 23,10-14), an acknowledgement of God's exclusive ownership of the land of Israel and of its produce. At the same time, the dedication to Yahweh of firstfruits was a consecration of the whole harvest to him. He then deigned to give it back to his people for their use[99]. The firstfruits were, accordingly, the means of consecrating the entire harvest to God (cf. Rom 11,16 ; Nm 15,18-21).

Christ is *firstfruits* because he has initiated the resurrection of the dead. The metaphor probably suggested itself to Paul because Jesus rose on the very day when the firstfruits of the grain harvest were offered in the Temple to Yahweh (MOFFATT). Inasmuch as he possesses the same nature as the rest of mankind, the risen Christ is cause of man's redemption

---

[97] The idea was implied, of course, in Paul's argument in vv. 14-18.

[98] BONSIRVEN, *op. cit.* 317 ; CERFAUX, *op. cit.* 66, holds that only in vv. 21-22 is there any expression of internal causality, — wrongly, we believe.

[99] Cf. the commentary of CLAMER on Lv in PIROT-CLAMER, *La Sainte Bible II* (Paris, 1940), 169-170.

from death [100]. This verse is the climax of the indirect proof for the resur-rection of the just. By asserting the fact of Christ's resurrection, v. 20a discloses the possibility of that general resurrection. With v. 20b, Paul begins the demonstration of the reality of this future resurrection (LIETZ-MANN).

v. 21. *through a man [came] death - so also through a man [will come] resur-rection of the dead* [101]. Here we have the antithesis, death-resurrection, each member of the antithesis being regarded as due to the instrumentality of two men set in opposition to one another. The verse seeks to justify the application of the title *firstfruits* to Christ (PARRY). There is no solid-ly founded proof that Paul took over the conception of Christ as second Adam from Philo or from the Iranian doctrine of the *Urmensch*. The Pauline doctrine rests substantially upon the Christian *depositum fidei* [102]. Christ possessed the same human nature as Adam [103] and by his resurrection he remedied that death for which Adam had been res-ponsible. In Paul's writing, death, in the context of sin [104], does not mean merely physical death. It signifies as well what we express by the terms « spiritual death » and « eschatological death » [105]. Paul's conception of death, which stems from the earliest OT tradition [106], may be defined as separation from the living God of Israel. To counteract the deleterious influence of Adam upon humanity is the purpose of Christ's work. The future resurrection of the just is considered the antithesis of sin-death.

v. 22. *in Adam all die ... in Christ all will be brought to life*. The use of the definite article indicates that Paul thinks of Adam and Christ as histo-

---

[100] M. DE LA TAILLE, *op. cit.* 134 : « mens Patrum apparet in comparatione inter manipulum sexto decimo die mensis Nisan solitum offerre Deo, primitias frugum terrae, et Christum resurrectione sua eodem die deferentem Deo primitias nostri reparati generis » (the patristic comments on Lv 23,11-14).

[101] The construction of vv. 21-23 is complicated by an anacoluthon. It seems preferable to take v. 22 as a parenthesis, explaining v. 21. This makes Paul's proof that Christ is « firstfruits » much clearer. In any other rendering, the mea-ning of ἐπειδὴ is obscure.

[102] MEINERTZ, *op. cit. II*, 87.

[103] BONSIRVEN, *op. cit.* 58 ; CERFAUX, *op. cit.* 186, n. 1.

[104] R. BULTMANN, θάνατος, *TWNT III*, 15 ; MEINERTZ, *op. cit. II*, 34-35.

[105] S. LYONNET, *Les épîtres de Saint Paul aux Galates, aux Romains* [2] (Paris, 1959) 90 n. b.

[106] THOMAS BARROSSE, *Death and Sin in St. Paul's Epistle to the Romans* in *CBQ* 15 (1953) 438-459 ; HARALD RIESENFELD, *La descente dans la mort* in *Aux sources de la tradition chrétienne* (Neuchâtel-Paris, 1950) 207-217.

rical persons who have influenced human history (ROBERTSON-PLUM-
MER) : death in its plenary sense is due to Adam, life (an equally comprehensive notion) is the gift of the risen Christ. Paul is considering the effects
of Christ's resurrection *primarily* [107] in terms of the Christian's admission to eternal life. In a subsequent and more thorough working-out of
the parallel Adam-Christ (Rom 5,12 ff.), he will dwell upon the change in
man's present status caused by Christ's resurrection. That in this first
sketch of Christ as second Adam Paul's attention is directed mainly to
the eschatological resurrection is of some moment inasmuch as it shows
that Christ receives this title *as risen from death*. Later on, the concept
will be extended to include the suffering Jesus who underwent death for
our sins (Rom 5,12 ff.). The expressions, *in Adam, in Christ*, show that
Paul is considering the causal influence of Adam and of Christ over those
who possess solidarity with them [108].

§ 12. - The Risen Christ as Second Adam (2). 1 Cor 44b-49

In the verses immediately following the last passage studied (23-28),
Paul discusses the hierarchical order of the resurrection of the dead. Although a somewhat different terminology is employed, the pericope exemplifies the same eschatological viewpoint as that expressed in 1 Thes
4,15-18 [109]. Thus the newer conception of the connection between Christ's
resurrection and that of the just expressed in this passage remains imbed-
ded in the same apocalyptic context as the older view [110]. In the subsequent epistles, this context will be abandoned in favour of further development of the intrinsic potential of Christ's resurrection. With 1 Cor
15,35, Paul begins to consider the *manner* of the general resurrection.

44b. If there is a body endowed with natural life, there is also one endowed with
the life of the Spirit. 45 Thus for example it is written : the first man, Adam, became
a living being : the last Adam became a life-giving Spirit. 46 However, it was not
the spiritual organism that was prior, but the natural. The spiritual succeeded it.
47 The first man was from the soil of the earth : the second man from heaven.
48 Those made from the earth are of the same nature as the earthly man : those
who are heavenly possess the same nature as the heavenly man. 49 And just as

---

[107] CERFAUX, *op. cit.* 68.
[108] MAX ZERWICK, *Graecitas Biblica* § 88.
[109] CERFAUX, *op. cit.* 44-45 ; E. STAUFFER, *op. cit.* 195-196.
[110] Cf. also 1 Cor 15,51-53.

surely as we have borne the image of the earthly man, so too shall we bear the image of the heavenly man.

[45a. ἄνθρωπος is omitted by Vat. and a few other Greek mss. 45b. The word Ἀδάμ is omitted by the Chester Beatty papyrus.
47b. ὁ κύριος is inserted by Alex., and the Syriac, Armenian, and Gothic versions before ἐξ οὐρανοῦ, which Tertullian claims is an interpolation of Marcion. The Chester Beatty papyrus reads ἄνθρωπος πνευματικός. The majority of witnesses favour the reading followed in the translation.
49b. The Hesychian and Antiochian recensions as well as the Chester Beatty papyrus and some other mss. read φορέσωμεν. The reading φορέσομεν while less well attested (Vat., the Armenian and Ethiopic versions, Theodoret) seems almost certainly original].

v. 44b. Paul has been explaining the transformation (42-44a) in the risen body by means of an analogy with a seed of grain (37-38). The subject of this transformation is the body endowed with the ψυχή, principle of natural life [111]. In virtue of the resurrection, it becomes a body in which the πνεῦμα replaces the ψυχή. Just as there is *a body endowed with natural life*, Paul asserts, there is also a body endowed with a higher life-principle, that of the Spirit. It is no less a body for being spiritualized.
v. 45. *the first man, Adam, became a living being.* The account of the creation of the first man (Gn 2,7) is interpreted by Paul in function of the present discussion [112]. Adam was given a ψυχή which could do no more than animate his body. On the other hand, Christ, *the last Adam, became a life-giving Spirit.* Paul is thinking of the moment of his resurrection (HUBY vs. ALLO). He is called *last Adam* because, in his glorified humanity, human nature has attained the apogee of its perfection : he belongs to the eschatological stage of existence. After him, there can be no other Adam (HUBY).

These verses (45-49) are a development of the antithesis which Paul suggested earlier in the chapter (20-21). There, Adam and Christ were contrasted within the eschatological framework of the apostolic kerygma : Adam as source of death, Christ as cause of the glorious resurrection. Here, the contrast is worked out in terms of something more intrinsic to each, which lays the basis for Paul's elaboration in terms of justification in Rom 5,12 ff. Christ *became a life giving Spirit.* The risen Lord is made

---

[111] A. - J. FESTUGIÈRE, Πνεῦμα *en Paul* in RSR 15 (1930) 385-415.
[112] Cf. the remarks of LIETZMANN in his commentary, pp 85 f ; J. BONSIRVEN, *Exégèse rabbinique et exégèse paulinienne* (Paris, 1939) 291-292.

bearer of the Spirit, source of the supernatural life of the Christian. In the final analysis, this power is based upon his « Spirit of holiness » (Rom 1,4). It is characteristic of Paul's theology of grace that, although he is clearly aware of the existence and personality of the Holy Ghost (Rom 8,26-27), yet he tends to regard the Lord and the Spirit as one in their work of sanctification (2 Cor 3,17).

v. 46. *It was not the spiritual organism that was prior, but the natural.* This difficult verse possibly ought to stand ahead of v. 45 (WEISS). It may be that Paul is answering some difficulty. Did those who denied the glorious resurrection (12) believe that the spiritualization of the body had already occurred (PARRY) ? It is possible that Paul is thinking of Christ's state before he became a *life-giving Spirit.* LIETZMANN suggests a satisfactory solution. Paul is contrasting the two creation-accounts in Genesis : that of the man « made in God's image and likeness » (Gn 1,26), the « spiritual » man, and that of the man made of « the soil of the earth » (Gn 2,7), the « earthly » man. Contrary to what one might be led to believe from the order of these two *récits* in the Bible, the « earthly », not the « spiritual » man was first in order of time [112a].

v. 47. Adam and Christ are now contrasted as the « earthly » man and the « heavenly » man. HUBY regards this designation of Christ as immediately connected with his resurrection, not his incarnation. It would appear however that Paul is *also* thinking of the parousiac Christ who will come « from heaven » (Acts 3,21) (BACHMANN). The antithesis is not instituted in the natural order of creation [113], but between the old creation, devastated by sin, and the new, effected by Christ's redemptive death and resurrection. Adam's sin is not mentioned explicitly as it will be in Rom 5,12 ff ; but its evil effects are implicit in the contrast. The first man, made of the soil of the earth, was destined by God (Gn 3,19) to return to the soil out of which he was made : the Man, who in his resurrection is become « a new creation », now dwells in heaven, the proper sphere of divine glory and of eternal, imperishable life.

[112a]. It appears that this distinction between the « spiritual » man and the « earthly » man, found in Philo's speculations on the creation-accounts, was probably familiar to Paul in a similar form. Cf. PHILONIS ALEXANDRINI *omnia quae supersunt recognoverunt* LEOPOLDUS COHEN *et* PAULUS WENDLAND (Berolini, 1896), I, 38 ff ; *De opificio mundi* §134 ff.

[113] Thus we cannot agree with the remark of BONSIRVEN, *op. cit.* 103, where, speaking of the present passage (15,44-49), he says, « Le premier passage se tient davantage dans l'ordre naturel de création ... ».

v. 48. The principle of the solidarity of all men in Adam and of all Christians in Christ is here asserted. The first is characterized by corruption (and death) ; the second, by incorruptibility and glory.

v. 49. *the image of the earthly man.* Paul has already stated that man « remains the image and glory of God », but in the context (1 Cor 11,7) he is speaking of the man whose « Head is Christ » (11,3) [114]. Here it is question rather of man's relation to Adam, the sinful first parent, doomed to death and corruption. The term *image* connotes the outward expression of the reality of a thing and implies community of nature [115]. Thus Paul says equivalently that we possess the same corruptible nature as the first Adam, who was made of the soil of the earth. *The image of the heavenly man.* Paul is not thinking of the Christian's present state of conformity to Christ as he will in Rom 5,12 ff. He states that it is through the transformation effected by the glorious resurrection that we shall share in the character of the risen Christ. At the same time, it must be recalled how far Paul has advanced from the *purely eschatological* conception of the resurrection (cf. 1 Thes 4,14). The resurrection of the just is no longer related to Christ's only by the divine will. We shall be transformed into the *image* of the parousiac Christ, who as *last Adam* is empowered to effect that change in us (cf. Phil 3,21).

---

[114] GERHARD KITTEL, εἰδών, *TWNT II*, 394-395.

[115] *ibid.* 393 : « Im NT ist durchweg in dem « Bilde » das Urbild selbst, die abgebildete Gestalt selbst, als in ihrem Wesen sichtbar gedacht ».

Chapter VI

THE MACEDONIAN EPISTLES: SECOND CORINTHIANS, GALATIANS

Bibliography: A. PLUMMER, *The Second Epistle of St. Paul to the Corinthians* (Edinburgh, 1915). H. WINDISCH, *Der zweite Korintherbrief*[9], *MK* (Göttingen, 1924). E. B. ALLO, *Seconde Épître aux Corinthiens* (Paris, 1937). H. D. WENDLAND, *Die Briefe an die Korinther*[5], *NTD* 7 (Göttingen, 1948). C. SPICQ, *Deuxième Épître aux Corinthiens*, *SBP* 11$_2$ (Paris, 1948). H. LIETZMANN, *An die Korinther I-II*[4] (Tübingen, 1949). V. JACONO, *Le Epistole di S. Paolo ai Romani, ai Corinti e ai Galati*, *SBG* (Torino-Roma, 1951). J. B. LIGHTFOOT, *Saint Paul's Epistle to the Galatians* (London, 1896). A. LUKYN WILLIAMS, *Galatians*, *CGT* (Cambridge, 1914). E. DE W. BURTON, *The Epistle to the Galatians*, *ICC* (Edinburgh, 1921). G. S. DUNCAN, *The Epistle of Paul to the Galatians* (London, 1934). M.-J. LAGRANGE, *Épître aux Galates*, *EB* (Paris, 1942). F. AMIOT, *Épître aux Galates* ... *VS* 14 (Paris, 1946). DENIS BUZY, *Épître aux Galates*, *SBP* 11$_2$ (Paris, 1948). HEINRICH SCHLIER, *Der Brief an die Galater*, *MK* (Göttingen, 1949). S. LYONNET, *Les Épîtres de saint Paul aux Galates*[2] ... *BJ* (Paris, 1959). PIERRE BONNARD, *L' Épître de saint Paul aux Galates*, *CNT* 9 (Neuchâtel-Paris, 1953).

The second canonical letter of Paul to the Corinthian church reflects the great difficulties and trials which he underwent during his long stay at Ephesus [1]. Scarcely has he begun to write when he mentions the great crisis during which he was brought face to face with death (2 Cor 1,8-9).

---

[1] The authenticity of 2 Cor has never been seriously questioned by modern critics. Its unity however has, especially since HAUSRATH (*Der Vierkapitelbrief des Paulus an die Korinther*, Heidelberg, 1870), frequently been denied. A number of scholars consider chs. 10-13 as a separate epistle, possibly the « letter in tears » referred to in 2 Cor 2,4. Without entering into a discussion of this hypothesis, we prefer to admit the unity of this epistle with A. WIKENHAUSER, *Einleitung in das Neue Testament* (Freiburg, 1953) 283-284 and with J. HÉRING, *La seconde épître de saint Paul aux Corinthiens CNT VIII* (Neuchâtel-Paris, 1958) 11-13.

But what is even more characteristic of this epistle is the fact that it contains notably fewer references to the parousia than the letters Paul wrote previously (2 Cor 1,14 ; 4,10-14 ; 5,3.10). It may be that DODD is right in stating that Paul no longer viewed the second Coming as possible during his own lifetime once he passed through the harrowing experience of facing death at Ephesus [2]. At any rate, the result of this period of great suffering appears to be that Paul turned his attention to the present status of the Christian in this world, which he conceived both as a participation in the sufferings and death of Christ (2 Cor 4,10-11) and as a transformation into the image of the glorified Lord (2 Cor 3, 18).

§ 1. - Paul's Evaluation of the Crisis at Ephesus. 2 Cor 1,9-10

No letter of Paul's is so full of passion and of eloquence as this epistle [3]. It consists of three main sections : an *apologetic* part (1,12-7,16), in which the apostle dwells on the nature of the ministry to which he has devoted his life ; a section concerned with the organization of the *Jerusalem collection* (8,1-9,15) ; and a *defence of his own good name* against calumny (10,1-13,10). The verses we are considering occur in the thanksgiving (1,3-11).

9 Well, we have carried the death-warrant upon our own head, in order that we might not put our trust in ourselves but in the God who raises the dead, 10 who rescued us from so imminent a death and will rescue us ...

[10 a. τηλικούτων θανάτων is read by the Chester Beatty papyrus and some few Greek mss.
10 b. καὶ ῥύσεται appears as καὶ ῥύεται in some Greek mss. It is omitted by Alex. but attested by Sin., Vat., and the Coptic and Armenian versions.].

v. 9. *Well* (ἀλλὰ) introduces the divine purpose underlying these providential sufferings of Paul (SPICQ). *the death-warrant.* The commentators hesitate between « sentence of death » (PLUMMER, LIETZMANN, SPICQ, OSTY) and « response », as from an embassy, « of death » (VUL-

---

[2] C. H. DODD, *The Mind of Paul : Change and Development* in *BJRylL* 18 (1934) 94-95.
[3] F. PRAT, *La Théologie de Saint Paul I*[8] (Paris, 1920) 168.

9. - D. M. STANLEY.

GATE, JACONO) [4]. In any event, Paul is thinking of a concrete situation which convinced him « that in all human probability his hours were numbered » (PLUMMER). The experience taught him a very precious spiritual lesson, and one which, despite his heroic virtue, he still needed to learn. Given Paul's character, the realization of his total dependence upon God was perhaps the most difficult supernatural truth he ever had to assimilate. His early training as a Pharisee militated against such an act of trust (Phil 3,4-9). His first successes in the Christian mission-field had also possibly tended to make him forget it. To acquire a « real » knowledge of it [5], it was necessary for Paul to be brought close to death itself.

the God who raises the dead. Père BONSIRVEN remarks upon this phrase as a relic of Paul's schooling by Gamaliel [6]. He also notes the importance of this experience in making Paul aware of the possibility of his own death before the Lord's parousia [7]. Paul's insistence on the resurrection, which has been questioned at Corinth, is possibly intentional (PLUMMER). v. 10. *who ... has rescued us.* In the OT, ῥύειν is a technical term expressing deliverance from the peril of death or of sin. Paul spontaneously employs the language of the Greek psalter in his acts of thanksgiving to God (SPICQ). *from so imminent a death.* The rare NT word τηλίκουτος emphasizes the permanent character of the danger which Paul faces (SPICQ). *and will rescue us.* It would seem that the danger is not entirely passed (PLUMMER). More probably however, the thought passes almost unconsciously from the contemplation of physical danger or death, to that of spiritual, eternal death [8]. This is possibly the best explanation of the apparent redundancy (cf. LIETZMANN) at the end of the sentence : « it is in him that our hopes rest that he will deliver us again », that is, through the general resurrection of the just.

The importance of this harrowing experience at Ephesus for Paul's

---

[4] Under ἀπόκριμα, MOULTON-MILLIGAN suggest : « Paul ... may be taken as meaning that he made his distressed appeal to God, and kept in his own heart's archives the answer : 'ἀποθάνῃ· τὸ δέ ἀποθανεῖν κέρδος' as we might reconstruct it. ».

[5] J. H. NEWMAN, *An Essay in Aid of a Grammar of Assent* (London, 1906) 36-97.

[6] J. BONSIRVEN, *L'Évangile de Paul,* (Paris 1948) 72.

[7] *ibid.* 310.

[8] Thus we do not agree with MAX MEINERTZ, *Theologie des Neuen Testaments II* (Bonn, 1950) 34, who interprets death in the passage merely as the natural term of life.

spiritual life and for the advance of his theological thought can scarcely be exaggerated. C. H. DODD has given us a fine sketch of Paul's advance in perfection as a result of this crisis [9]. Of more immediate interest to our present study is the fact that the episode forms the *point de départ* of Paul's conviction that he personally might well die before the second Coming of Christ. The *serious* possibility of such an eventuality does not appear to have occurred to him earlier, if we are to judge by the letters anterior to this period [10]. The value of such a realization is that henceforth Paul's attention focusses upon the Christian's present status and particularly upon the mystery of the Church, in which the Kingdom of Christ had become an earthly reality.

§ 2. - The Work of the Risen Christ through the Spirit. 2 Cor 3,18

From the beginning of chapter 3, Paul has been answering the charge of arrogance, on which his enemies have indicted him, with an encomium of the apostolic calling. He has shown (vv. 4-11) that the NT apostleship is a more glorious vocation than its OT type. In the present section (3,12-4,6), he justifies his frankness and assurance in preaching the Gospel. Paul felt strongly on this subject and the emotional nature of the passage has rendered its understanding rather difficult. One remark in particular, « the Lord is the Spirit » (v. 17a) remains a famous *crux interpretum*. Since space does not permit a detailed exegetical discussion of this verse [11],

---

[9] C. H. DODD, *The Mind of Paul : a Psychological Approach* in *BJRylL* 17 (1933) 103-105.

[10] That Paul already envisaged the mere possibility of dying and indeed longed for death as the means of being admitted to the company of the risen Christ is clear from Phil 1,23-24 (this letter, as we have attempted to show, antedates both Corinthian epistles) : « Now I am caught on the horns of a dilemma. On the one hand, I yearn to go off and be with Christ (that is by far the better thing). But, on the other hand, to go on living here below is more imperative so far as you are concerned ». While it must be admitted that the thought of his leaving his dear Philippians is certainly in Paul's mind here (and hence the possibility of his own death before the parousia). still the next verse shows that he did not entertain the thought seriously at this time. « Yet of this 1 am quite sure : 1 shall remain and shall continue to stand by all of you for your progress and consolation in Christian living ... ».

[11] KARL PRÜMM, *Die katholische Auslegung von 2 Kor. 3,17a in den letzten vier Jahrzehnten nach ihren Hauptrichtungen* in *Bib* 31 (1950) 316-345 ; 459-482 ; 32 (1951) 1-24.

we must content ourselves with stating that « the Lord » is Christ,
while « the Spirit » is most probably the Holy Ghost. While the patronage of CYRIL OF ALEXANDRIA vouches for the orthodoxy of such an interpretation [12], eminent Catholic authors have hesitated to adopt it on the
grounds that it necessarily implies a confusion between Christ's Person
and that of the Holy Spirit [13]. Still Paul has already (1 Cor 15,45) called
the risen Lord « a vivifying Spirit », and has stated that the Christian in
union with Christ becomes « one Spirit » with him (1 Cor 6,17). A writer,
who thus strongly insists upon the unity of operation between the risen
Christ and the Spirit in sanctifying the believer, and who invariably thinks
in Semitic rather than Greek categories of thought, would not experience
the difficulty felt by the occidental theologian [14] in stating that « the
Lord is the Spirit » [15].

Yet all of us, while with unveiled face we reflect, as in a mirror, the glory of
the Lord, are being transformed into the same image with ever-increasing glory,
as [one would expect] by the Lord [who is] Spirit.

[The Chester Beatty papyrus reads κατοπτριζόμεθα οἱ ... μεταμορφούμενοι].

All of us. Paul pauses to generalize (possibly in terms of his own Damascus experience) in the course of his defence of apostolic freedom of speech
(v. 12). He has stated emphatically that, unlike Moses, who veiled his
face before Israel, thereby obscuring the truth of the transitory nature of
OT religion, he, Paul, has nothing to hide (v. 13). What applies to Paul ,
applies to all Christians, since conversion, « turning » to the Lord, means
the removal of a veil of unbelief such as that which hides the truth from
the Jews (v. 16). As Moses only turned to Yahweh after removing the veil
(Ex 34,34), so conversion to Christ is necessary for the reception of the
« glory » of the risen Christ, which, mirror-like, the Christian reflects [16].
being transformed into the same image. The verb Paul employs is found in
the first two Synoptic accounts of Jesus' transfiguration (Mt 17,2 ; Mk
9,2). He will use it again (Rom 12,2) to describe the interior transformat-

---

[12] S. LYONNET, *S. Cyrille d' Alexandrie et 2 Cor.* 3,17 in *Bib* 32 (1951) 25-31.
[13] LYONNET, *art. cit.* 26, mentions PRAT. On the other hand, L. CERFAUX,
Le Christ dans la théologie de saint Paul 221 f. does adopt it.
[14] *Exemplo sit* C. SPICQ in his commentary, pp. 325-326.
[15] Paul's attitude is made very clear in a passage like Rom 8,9-10.
[16] This seems preferable to the translation which LIETZMANN gives « We behold
in a mirror ».

ion effected by the Eucharistic sacrifice in the Christian [17]. In this verse, he states that the communication of the risen Lord's glory changes the Christian into the « image » of Christ (cf. Rom 8,29), just as the divine « glory » bestowed on Christ transformed him into the image of God (2 Cor 4,4) [18]. Paul had in an earlier letter adumbrated the theme of the Christian as image of the « last Adam », but in an eschatological context (1 Cor 15,45-49) : through the glorious resurrection, « we shall bear the image of the heavenly man ». Christ is « image of God » because he possesses « equality with God » (Phil 2,6), « image » signifying « essence » or « form » [19]. As CERFAUX remarks, Christ is constituted « in his reality as a Person » due to his being God's image [20]. The Christian is « image of Christ » inasmuch as he possesses, through the risen Lord's gift of the Spirit, the adoptive sonship (Gal 4,6). This is the basis of Paul's contrast between the state of the Christian and that of the Jew, who by refusing to believe in Christ has rejected this divine filiation. The view of JACONO, adopted from ALLO, that it is the ability or inability to perceive « il senso profondo della S. Scrittura » which distinguishes the Jew and the Christian, is scarcely tenable.

Paul's expression of the image-theme in the present verse merits attention because it represents an advance over the eschatological formulation of 1 Cor, 15,45 ff. The apostle turns his mind to the *present* transfiguration of the believer into the image of Christ. Already in this life, the work of transformation is going forward in the Christian. It is not necessary to wait for the parousia to obtain a share in that δόξα of the risen Lord, but there is, here below, a constant advance *from glory to glory* [21].

The theme of « glory » is an important one in Pauline resurrection-

---

[17] We follow the interpretation of this passage of Rom given by A. FEUILLET, *Le plan salvifique de Dieu d'après l'Épître aux Romains* in *RB* 57 (1950) 511.

[18] CERFAUX, *op. cit.* 326.

[19] GERHARD KITTEL, εἰκών *TWNT II*, 394 : « Wenn Christus die εἰκών τοῦ Θεοῦ 2 K 4,4 ; Kol 1,15 gennant wird, so liegt gleichfalls aller Nachdruck auf der Ebenbürtigkeit der εἰκών mit dem Original ».

[20] CERFAUX, *op. cit.* 387 : « Nous pourrons dire que le fait d'être image constitue le Christ dans sa réalité de personne ».

[21] It may well be that Paul's expression here reflects the influence of contemporary apocalyptic writing : cf. PLUMMER in his commentary, p. 107.

theology [22], and one which Paul inherited from the OT as well as from rabbinic tradition [23]. Primarily a quality of the divine majesty of God (Rom 1,23 ; Eph, 1,17) [24], « glory » becomes one of the essential properties of the risen Christ, who has received it from the Father by being raised from death (Rom 6,4), and is henceforth « the Lord of glory » (1 Cor 2,8). This « glory » Christ communicates, in virtue of his glorified humanity, to the Christian (2 Thes 2,14 ; Phil 3,21 ; 1 Cor 2,7 ; Rom 2,7 ; 15,7) whilst the sinner remains deprived of it (Rom 3,23).

by the Lord who is Spirit. Paul states the cause of this transfiguration of the Christian : the risen Christ whose supernatural activity in sanctifying has already been identified with that of the Spirit (v. 17) [25].

It is to be noted that this verse contains the first clear statement of the Christian's possession of « glory » in the present life to be found in the Pauline letters. In his Thessalonian correspondence (cf. 1 Thes 2,12 ; 2 Thes 2,14 ; cf. also Phil 3,21 ; 4,19 ; 1 Cor 2,7 ; 15,43), the term is employed invariably in its primary (eschatological) sense and connected with the parousia and the future kingdom of God. Here however we have an indication that, probably as a result of his experiences in Ephesus, Paul has begun a re-evaluation of the Christian's present union with the risen Lord, and has as a result applied to it a term which *per se* is only applicable to the glorified body. The significance of this new trend in Pauline soteriology must not be lost sight of.

§ 3. - Paul's Apostleship A Participation in Christ's Death and Resurrection. 2 Cor 4,10-14

Having discussed the glorious nature of the Christian life and of the apostolic calling, Paul has, since 4,7, been considering his vocation under another angle, that of the sufferings and dangers inextricably interwoven with it. In reality, he is replying to an objection to what he

---

[22] BONSIRVEN, *op. cit.* 196, n. 3 : « Mot et idée de δόξα, gloire, tiennent une grande place chez S. Paul et caractérisent sa pensée. Inutile de citer les textes qui mentionnent cet attribut divin, — splendeur éblouissante, — de celui qu'aucune créature ne peut voir ».

[23] GERHARD KITTEL, δόξα, *TWNT II*, 251 f.

[24] MEINERTZ, *op. cit. II* 109.

[25] PLUMMER in his commentary gives various translations of this difficult phrase : cf. p. 108.

has earlier stated about the glorious nature of his vocation : how can such a high calling be consonant with the weak, precarious existence of those called to it ? WINDISCH has, in a happy phrase, entitled this section « Durch Tod zum Leben » [26]. The possession of supernatural favours [27] is contrasted with the danger of losing them, by means of metaphors (treasure contained in an earthenware jar, v. 7 ; illustrations from sport [28], vv. 8-9), which are finally abandoned for the mystical conception of dying and rising.

10 [We are] continually bearing the dying of Jesus in our body, in order that the life of Jesus also may be manifested in our body. 11 For always we the living are being handed over to death for Jesus' sake, in order that Jesus' life also be manifested in our mortal flesh. 12 And thus death is at work in us, but life in you. 13 Having the same spirit of faith as the Scripture [describes] : « I have faith, and so I spoke out », we also have faith, and hence we speak out, 14 because we know that he who raised Jesus will raise us with Jesus and place us with you.

[10a. τοῦ Κυρίου Ἰησοῦ is read by K, L, and the Harclean Syriac. It must be admitted that the use of the article with Ἰησοῦς, common in the Gospels, is rare in the epistles.

10b. τοῖς σώμασιν is preferred to the singular by 1739, the Vulgate, Peshitto versions, Origen.

12a. μὲν is inserted by some late mss. like K, L.

14a. Κύριον is not read by the Chester Beatty papyrus, Vat., 1739, the Vulgate, Armenian, Sahidic versions, Origen, Tertullian].

v. 10. *the dying of Jesus.* Paul's sufferings are identified with the sufferings of Jesus in his mortal life [29]. BONSIRVEN speaks of the « génitif mystique » in this connection [30]. The fact that such sufferings are borne *for Jesus' sake*

---

[26] Although one might object to much that WINDISCH has to say about these two terms, he has at least underscored the dying-and-rising doctrine which these verses contain.

[27] As PLUMMER, p. 125, points out, the frequency, with which verbs signifying *to possess* occur in this letter, shows how Paul loves to dwell upon the Christian's actual possession of these gifts.

[28] C. SPICQ, *L'image sportive de II Corinthiens, IV*, 7-9 in ETL 14 (1937) 209-229.

[29] Some mss. (D, F, G, among others) read Χριστοῦ for Ἰησοῦ . We might have expected Paul to use some title suggesting the influence of the risen Christ. It is probably his realism which dictated the use of « Jesus » : Paul is conscious that he participates in the passion of Jesus through grace. Cf. *Summa Theologica* III, 50, 6 ; also CERFAUX, *op. cit.* 375.

[30] BONSIRVEN, *op. cit.* 277.

(v. 11) gives them a special efficacy in carrying Christ's work of redemption to Paul's hearers. In Phil 3,10, Paul spoke of « a fellowship in his sufferings », while in Col 1,24 he will rejoice because « I am completing in my flesh what is wanting in the tribulations of Christ ». In this second citation, Paul thinks of his sufferings in an ecclesiastical context (« on behalf of his body which is the Church »), while in the first, he expresses himself in terms of the (more primitive) antithesis, present sufferings-future eschatological resurrection of the just. Here we have one of the earliest examples [31] of the later Pauline contrast between death and life. This new antithesis is, in all probability, the result of Paul's deliverance from death at Ephesus [32].

the life of Jesus. Paul does not appear to be thinking of the glorious resurrection here (vs. LIETZMANN) [33], although he clearly refers to it in v. 14. We are probably faced with one of those transitions in Pauline thought which will be more clearly expressed in subsequent letters (cf. Gal 2,19-20), or even in later paragraphs of this same epistle (cf. 2 Cor 5,15-17 ; 13,4b). Here *the life of Jesus* is the manifestation of the risen Christ's power in Paul's deliverance from death and in his serenity and courageous frankness in the face of persecution (SPICQ), as well as in the success of his ministry (ALLO, JACONO) [34].

v. 11. This parallels the preceding verse and clarifies its meaning. Like Jesus handed over to his enemies [35], the apostles continually face death in their missionary work, and yet they are snatched from such perils by the power of the risen Christ (SPICQ). The phrase *in our mortal flesh* seems to exclude the possibility that Paul thinks of the glorious resurrection. This manifestation of the life of the risen Lord occurs while the apos-

---

[31] Cf. 1 Cor 3,22 also.

[32] BONSIRVEN, *op. cit.* 304, gives another explanation of this.

[33] JACQUES DUPONT, *Gnosis* 107, is scarcely right in considering this text one which speaks of « la gloire du monde futur ».

[34] CERFAUX, *op. cit.* 245 : « Le processus dont parle saint Paul dans ce verset et le suivant n'a rien à voir directement avec une description de la vie chrétienne comme telle. Ce qui est en cause ... c'est l'activité apostolique. Cependant, il s'agit ontologiquement de la même ' vie ', vie en nous du Christ ressuscité. La vie apostolique n'est qu' une efflorescence, un développement de la vie communiquée par la résurrection du Christ ».

[35] The verb παραδίδωμι became a technical term very early in primitive Christian soteriology. Paul uses it very frequently.

tles are still subject to death. It is a kind of anticipation or pledge of the future resurrection [36].

These two verses illustrate the value of suffering in Paul's own life as a factor in the development of his theology of the resurrection. It is what HUBY has called « la loi du développement » [37], while WINDISCH calls suffering « das zweite Sakrament für Paulus » [38]. Actually, Paul realizes that it is the working-out of the sacrament of Baptism in the Christian life (cf. Rom 6,2-11).

v. 12. *death ... in us ... life in you.* WINDISCH finds the turn of thought here surprising [39]. In fact, the brief remark, which Paul does not develop further here (cf. 1 Cor 6,9 ; 13,4 ; Col 1,24), is simply a corollary from the principle laid down in the preceding verses. The sufferings of the apostolic preachers constitute a kind of treasure upon which the Church can draw (SPICQ) [40]. The use of the definite article would seem to indicate that Paul means *that death* and *life* of which he was just speaking (PLUMMER), which, as we have seen, is something more than mere physical death or suffering. This *death* possesses a redemptive efficacy, while the *life* is that communicated by the risen Lord. Hence the νέκρωσις of the apostle effects a supernatural result in his neophytes (ALLO).

v. 13. *the same spirit of faith.* Paul's faith is exercised about the same object, deliverance from death, as the psalmist's was when he wrote Ps. 115. In either case, escape from physical death is a type of future resurrection [41].

---

[36] This interpretation has the merit of continuing the line of thought expressed by the metaphors of the treasure in an earthenware jar and of Greek games.

[37] J. HUBY, *Mystiques Pauliniennes et Johanniques* (Paris, 1946) 39 : « La vie chrétienne est à la fois le prolongement et l'achèvement de la mort substantiellement accomplie au Baptême et la vivification croissante de la nature nouvelle que le baptisé a reçue de son union au Christ, de ' sa greffe en lui ' ».

[38] H. WINDISCH, *Paulus und Christus* (Leipzig, 1934) 234.

[39] *ibid.* 234.

[40] MEINERTZ, *op. cit. II* 164, expresses it better : « Mehr sagt 2 Kor 4, 10 ff., wo die apostolischen Leiden die ' Tötung Jesu ' genannt werden, die Paulus ständig an seinem Leibe herumtrage, und die in gleicher mystischer Verbundenheit auf das Offenbarwerden des ' Lebens Jesu an unserem Fleisch ' hinweisen. Aber darum wird hinzufügt, ' Also wirkt der Tod in uns, das Leben in euch'. Das kann nur heissen, dass das apostolisches mystisches ' Christussterben ' den mystisch verbundenen Christen ... übernatürliches Leben bringt ».

[41] As frequently in his citations from the Bible, Paul has the whole passage in mind (PLUMMER). Thus it makes little difference that the part cited after the LXX does not agree with the original Hebrew. Inspired by the same faith

v. 14. *he who raised Jesus will raise us with Jesus*. The object of faith is
extended to include the glorious resurrection, in which for Paul salvation
is definitively found. The verse is a repetition of the credal formula found
in 1 Thes 4,14 and has the same eschatological orientation [42]. Paul
however adds to the original credo the words *and place us with you*, a
recapitulation of the nexus between the « dying » of the apostle and the
« life » of his converts. It seems to imply that Paul's own resurrection
depends on his fidelity as an apostle. As he will state more explicitly at
the close of this letter, he finds his own salvation through his ministry
(2 Cor 13,4).

§ 4. - The Redemption as a New Creation. 2 Cor 5,14-21

In the section which begins at 5,10, Paul continues to discuss the
glories of the apostolic career in a more intimate and less polemical vein.
ALLO terms the paragraph « une philosophie de la rédemption ».

14 Indeed, Christ's love has put us under compulsion once we realized this truth:
one died for all; therefore all have died. 15 And he died for all in order that
the living may no longer live for themselves, but for him who died and was raised
for them. 16 As a result, from now on, we know no one in a merely human way.
Even if we knew Christ in a human way, we now no longer know him thus. 17
Accordingly, if a man be in union with Christ, there is a new creation. His old
life has disappeared. See, it is become new. 18 And all this comes from God,
who has reconciled us to himself through Christ and has given us the ministry of
reconciling [others]. 19 For the truth is that God was in Christ reconciling the
world to himself, instead of holding men's transgressions against them. And he has
confided to us the Gospel of reconciliation. 20 In Christ's name, therefore, we
come as ambassadors, since it is God who exhorts through us. We beg for the sake
of Christ: be reconciled with God. 21 He made him who knew no sin into sin for
our sakes, in order that we might in him become God's justice.

[14b. The overwhelming mss. authority attests the reading we follow. Sin. (3rd
corr.), Ephrem *rescr.*, with the Vulgate, Coptic and Armenian versions read ὅτι εἰ εἷς.
16b. With Merk, Nestle and most modern editors, we read εἰ καὶ (Sin., Vat., D)
rather than καὶ εἰ (F, G, the Latin versions and the Peshitto).
17b. καινά with Sin., Vat., Ephrem *rescr.*, D, the *vetus latina*, the Coptic versions,
is to be preferred to καινὰ τὰ πάντα (D 2nd, 3rd corr., K, L, P, and the Vulgate).

---

in God's help which the psalmist possessed, the Apostle does not hesitate to continue preaching the Gospel (SPICQ).
[42] CERFAUX, *op. cit.* 66.

21. γάρ should be omitted after τόν with Sin., Vat., Ephrem *rescr.*, D, F, G, and the Latin and Coptic versions].

v. 14. *Christ's love*. The phrase denotes Christ's love for men, as most commentators agree [43], rather than our love of Christ. At the beginning of this paragraph on the redemption, Paul states the unique motive for Christ's salutary work. The verb συνέχομαι probably means « restrains us from self-seeking » (PLUMMER) [44].

one died for all ; therefore all have died. This is one of the most mysterious statements in Paul's letters. One thing is clear however : Christ's atoning death did not release man from the obligation of death for his sins, it entailed it. Man somehow really died in Christ on the cross. The realism of Pauline baptismal theology (Rom 6,3 ff.) is based upon this principle. The difficulty of explaining the nature of this death in Christ need not deter us from admitting the fact [45].

v. 15. The purpose of the redemption is the orientation of the Christian life to the risen Christ. Death in Christ is a dying to the old, natural life of self which results in a new, supernatural life. The Christian existence springs both ontologically and in practice from the double act by which Christ redeemed us, his death and resurrection [46]. The phrase *he died for all* must be understood (as in v. 14) to involve the dying of every

---

[43] For a different view, cf. SPICQ's commentary ; also LIETZMANN in 1 Cor 13,13.

[44] The « urget » of the Vulgate, while giving literally the opposite sense, expresses a similar idea from the positive point of view. Cf. the long discussion of the meaning of this term by C. SPICQ, *Agapè dans le Nouveau Testament II* (Paris, 1959) 128-136. He concludes (pp. 135f) that, by his use of the word, Paul « suggère la force quasi incoercible de la charité du Christ sur la croix. Pour le chrétien qui contemple son Sauveur, il est moralement impossible de ne pas s'attacher à lui et de lui refuser le don de sa vie. Il est ' tenu serré ', comme enchaîné par son amour jailli de cette contemplation ».

[45] The parallel with Paul's thought in Rom 5,12 on Original sin is to be noted. Various authors give different interpretations : cf. CERFAUX, *op. cit.* 262, n. 4, who resumes the viewpoint of the Scandinavian school. E. HOCEDEZ gives a vague formulation : *Notre solidarité en Jésus-Christ et en Adam* in G 13 (1932) 389, n. 1 : « Sans doute nous ne sommes associés au Christ mourant que d'une façon idéale, en tant que *sa mort fut moralement la mort du genre humain dont il était le représentant* ».

[46] S. THOMAS AQUINAS, *In omnes S. Pauli Apostoli epistolas commentaria I* (Torino, 1924) 454 : « Nota autem, quod duo dicit, sc. quod mortuus est Christus, et quod resurrexit pro nobis ... ».

Christian [47]. LIETZMANN, who claims that the argument in v. 14 is « rein juristisch » in form, admits that here we have an « ausgesprochene mystische Gedankenreihe ».

v. 16. Christ's redemptive death and resurrection, proof of his love for man, has been stated as Paul's motive for his ministry. The new conditions of existence which result from this double act of the atonement are now declared the basis of his Gospel (PLUMMER). Paul draws two conclusions : the second (v. 17) providing the grounds for the first (v. 16).
we know no one in a merely human way. This *Zwischensatz* is undoubtedly polemical in scope (LIETZMANN) and is enunciated in characteristically Pauline fashion without benefit of those distinctions which our more precise mode of thinking requires. In the Christian world of supernatural reality, human standards have no place. Paul does not *will* to know anyone, even Christ himself, from a natural standpoint [48]. Paul's Corinthian opponents valued Cephas more than Paul because Cephas was an eye-witness of Jesus' mortal life. As Jewish Christians, they boasted of their connection with the apostolic community in Jerusalem. The Christian, Paul replies, must regard everything from the viewpoint of Christ's death and resurrection. Nothing else, not even the knowledge of Jesus « according to the flesh », matters. Thus the criticism that Paul never knew Christ personally is wide of the mark : even those who knew him thus, know him so no longer [49]. Paul's statement is not entirely free of exaggeration [50] ; and he would never have denied that the facts of Christ's earthy career must be preserved with care. He himself had followed the Jerusalem kerygma which included the ministry of Jesus. What interests us in this uncompromising statement, admittedly in need of a *distinguo*, is the basic position in Pauline soteriology of Christ's death and resurrection : there can be, on Paul's view, no proper Christian theology which does not take these twin events as its point of departure (cf. LIETZMANN).

v. 17. *there is a new creation.* For Paul, the Christian life must be defined

---

[47] The phrase ὑπὲρ αὐτῶν is to be construed with both participles (by no means « eine müssige Frage », as WINDISCH remarks) and means « on behalf of all », not « instead of all » (PLUMMER).
[48] The expression is similar to the remark of Christ as final judge (Mt 7,23 ; Lk 13, 7).
[49] PRAT, *op. cit. II*, 27 n. 1 calls it an unreal condition.
[50] CERFAUX, *op. cit.* 137f.

by its relation to Christ [51] : the Christian is a man *in union with Christ* [52].
As point of division between the old order and the new stands Christ's
death and resurrection, the new creative act of God the Father [53]. It is
not necessary to have recourse to the rabbinical expression *beriyyah ha-
dasah* (new creature [54]) to explain καινὴ κτίσις . It is far more likely
that Paul, following the example of the apostolic community (cf.
Ap 21,5) drew his inspiration from the Isaian « Book of Consolation »
(Is 43,18-19 ; also Is 65,17 ; 66,22). The entire purpose of God's revelation of salvation is contained in this *new creation*, inaugurated in
the risen Christ (SPICQ). The passage is the most powerful expression of
Christ's work ever written by Paul (WINDISCH) [55].
v. 18. *all this comes from God*. The ultimate source of man's redemption
is traced back, in Pauline soteriology, to God the Father (2 Cor 1,21 ;
2,14 ; 4,6 ; 5,5 ; Gal 4,4 ff ; 1 Cor 8,6 ; 11,12 ; Rom 3,25 ; 8,3f ; 11,36). It
is now described from the OT viewpoint rather than the Greek (PLUMMER)
as the reconciliation [56] of man with God [57]. The term, normally used of
the resumption of common life by husband and wife (cf. 1 Cor 7,11), is

[51] *ibid.* 220 ; also W. T. HAHN, *Das Mitsterben und Mitauferstehen mit Christus bei Paulus*, 97-100, who insists that the formula « cum Christo » cannot be
reversed. It is the *Christusgeschehen* which specifies the Christian's relation to
Christ.

[52] CERFAUX, *op. cit.* 242-253, criticizes the excesses of many theories regarding the meaning of our being « in » Christ.

[53] JOHANNES BEHM, καινός, *TWNT III*, 451-452.

[54] It is however interesting to note that the expression was used, according to the rabbis, in connection with the remission of sins by God on the day
of *Kippurim*. Cf. P. BILLERBECK, *Kommentar zum Neuen Testament aus Talmud
und Midrasch II*, 422.

[55] WINDISCH in his commentary, p. 184, states that this passage is « das
Gewaltigste was P. über das Werk Christi sagen kann ». Cf. also E. PERCY, *Die
Probleme der Kolosser- und Epheserbriefe* (Lund, 1946) 111 ; H. WEBER, « *Escha-
tologie* » und « *Mystik* » *im Neuen Testament* (Gütersloh, 1930) 89.

[56] FRIEDRICH BÜCHSEL, καταλλάσσω, καταλλαγή, *TWNT I*, 254-259.

[57] It is to be noted (with PLUMMER) that nowhere in the Pauline writings
is God said to be reconciled with men, nor is the verb ἱλάσκεσθαι ever used by
Paul. Indeed in Heb 2,17 where it is used, it does not have God as object. As
S. LYONNET has shown in *VD* 38 (1960) 68, the passive use of ἱλάσκεσθαι in Lk
18,13, is not to be translated « God, be reconciled with me ... », but rather, « God,
have mercy on me ». Moreover, it is not certain that the word ἱλασμός, which
Paul does not employ, connotes God's being reconciled (cf. I Jn 2,2 ; 4,10). As
for Paul's use of ἱλαστήριον in Rom 3, 25, we shall discuss its meaning in the
next chapter.

here for the first time in Paul's writings applied to the atonement. *who has reconciled us to himself through Christ.* This explains the *new creation* and gives the ultimate reason why *the living may no longer live for themselves. He has given us the ministry of reconciling others.* In this and the following verses, Paul has combined the conception of the redemption with that of his own apostolic calling to the point where the meaning of the first person plural pronoun is almost impossible to determine with certainty (cf. PLUMMER). This shows how clearly conditioned by the circumstances of his own conversion is Paul's theology of the redemption. It was a conversion in which the call to the Christian faith and to the apostleship were simultaneous.

v. 19. *God was in Christ reconciling the world to himself.* Paul now adds certain theological precisions to his statement in v. 18. LIETZMANN is scarcely right in regarding ἐν Χριστῷ as the equivalent of διὰ Χριστοῦ (v. 18) or in denying to Christ's resurrection any part in the redemption. JACONO, following ALLO, sees an implicit affirmation of the incarnation, which is nearer the truth. CERFAUX has caught Paul's meaning when he states that Christ's work through his death and resurrection was also God's work, not only because the divine will was thus carried out, but also because Christ formed a single principle of action with the Father [58]. That Paul speaks of the reconciliation of the κόσμος shows how un-Greek is the expression of his theological thought [59]. *instead of holding men's transgressions against them.* Paul borrows from the LXX the expression for a typically Semitic thought-form, which signifies that the fault has been pardoned [60]. This is what the reconciliation means in the concrete. *he has confided to us the Gospel of reconciliation.* This is what the atonement means to Paul personally : God has entrusted him with the continuance of his redemptive work [61].

v. 20. Paul stresses the dignity of the apostolic calling by employing an expression which was applied to the Emperor's legates [62]. Yet the super-

---

[58] CERFAUX, *op. cit.* 392.

[59] As understood by the Greeks, the cosmos, which was already arranged according to unalterable « natural laws », would not tolerate, much less *need*, any such reconciling interference from the divine sphere.

[60] Cf. the LXX rendering of Ps 32,2 which employs λογίζομαι

[61] By the expression, ὁ λόγος τῆς καταλλαγῆς, Paul means his preaching of the Gospel (cf. Acts 13,26 ; 1 Thes 1,8 ; Phil 2,16 ; 1 Cor 1,18 ; Col. 1,5 ; Eph 1,13).

[62] A. DEISSMANN, *Licht vom Osten*[1] (Tübingen, 1923) 320.

lative value of the apostolic ministry for Paul lies in the fact that *it is God who exhorts through us.* The passage provides a blueprint for a theology of the Christian ministry (SPICQ).

v. 21 At first sight, the statement appears to be concerned solely with Christ's passion and death as cause of man's reconciliation with God. Considered by itself, then, the verse might be interpreted as excluding any influx of Christ's resurrection as an essential co-cause, with his death, of the redemption. Actually however, it is a restatement, in terms of the antithesis sin-justice, of the thought exposed in the whole paragaph (from v. 14). Consequently, the verse can be adequately understood only in context of the dominant theme : the revelation of divine love through Christ's work for man's salvation (v. 14). Christ's love is revealed, as v. 15 makes clear, through his resurrection as well as through his death, since it is question there not merely of man's dying to self but also of receiving a communication of the new life by « him who died and was raised for them ».

He has made him who knew no sin into sin. In this first half of the verse, Paul is thinking of Jesus' earthly career as it culminates in the crucifixion. The idea is parallel to that found in Gal 3,13. SPICQ denies that Paul refers to the pre-existent Christ by *Him who knew no sin,* since that would imply that since his incarnation Christ has become a sinner [63]. CERFAUX [64] considers that Paul has Christ's death primarily in mind, although the idea of the incarnation is « à l' horizon ». He feels that Christ's pre-existence is involved here, since Paul means that Christ is exempt from all sin by right of his divine origin. This interpretation is consonant with the Pauline distinction between Christ « according to the flesh » and Christ « according to the Spirit » [65]. For a Christology which gives full value to the salvific aspects of the incarnation itself, we must await a St. John. Paul, on the other hand, habitually thinks of Christ's becoming man as an entry into the sinful solidarity of Adam (I Cor 15,46), which is dominated by the Law (Gal 4,4-5 ; Rom 8,3-4). The conception of the present verse is akin to the later notion of God's sending « his own Son in the likeness of sinful humanity » (Rom 8,3), a statement which,

---

[63] As we understand it, Paul's view is that Christ had to break with the sinful solidarity with Adam in which he (by his passibility and mortality), as well as the human race (by sin), was involved ; and then create a new supernatural solidarity as second Adam.

[64] CERFAUX, *op. cit.* 128f.

[65] *ibid.* 127.

thanks to the phrase « in the likeness » is more carefully nuanced. The term *sin* in the present statement, like its antithesis *God's justice*, is an abstraction representing the historical reality of fallen human nature, which Christ may be said to share inasmuch as he is capable, in his unglorified state, of suffering and dying.

that we might in him become God's justice. In his Thessalonian correspondence, Paul described the divine reality of the Christian life as holiness (ἁγιωσύνη). In the controversy with the Jews, referred to in the letter to the Philippians, he presented this same supernatural reality as « not any justice of my own making from the Law, but that which comes through faith in Christ, the justice from God based upon faith » (Phil 3,9). The turn of phrase « justice *from* God » indicates that Paul still thinks of it as descending from its divine source. In the present passage, it is called « *a* justice of God », — an indication that this supernatural gift is conceived as a sharing in God's own justice. Thus the verse is a statement, in terms of sin-justice, of the same reality which v. 15 depicted in terms of life, where the sinful life of selfishness is opposed to life for, or in relation with, Christ.

Paul's use of the term « justice of God » which appears here for the first time in his letters is of interest to our general study, not only because it exemplifies his proclivity to think in antitheses, but also because it represents a first attempt to express the divine communication of supernatural life to the Christian in the category of « justice ». Thus it provides a preview of a thought-pattern which, with the epistle to the Romans, will become characteristic of Pauline theology (cf. Rom 4,25). It is important to note that, at least by implication, the phrase *God's justice in him,* i. e. in the Christ who has been raised from death, connects the gift of sanctifying grace with Christ's resurrection as well as with his death for us.

§ 5. - A Further Pauline Expression of the Redemption. 2 Cor 8,9

A section of his letter is devoted by the apostle to a plea for Corinthian aid to the destitute church in Jerusalem (8,1-9,15). After proposing the example of generosity given by the Macedonian communities, Paul turns to the example of Christ himself.

For you know the liberality of our Lord Jesus Christ : how for your sakes he became poor, when he was rich, in order that you, through his poverty, might become rich.

[9a. Χριστοῦ is omitted by Vat. ; but it is most probably original].

The word χάρις here seems to demand some such translation as *liberality* (cf. LIETZMANN'S « Freigebigkeit ») [66]. *He became poor.* The verb refers, not to the moment of the incarnation of the Son, but to his whole earthly condition of redemptive suffering and mortality [67] (SPICQ). By the riches of Christ is meant all the divine prerogatives which are his by right as Son (Eph 3,8) and of which he voluntarily « emptied himself » (Phil 2,7) upon his entrance into the world. By the term poverty is meant the destitution of human nature dispossessed by sin of every supernatural blessing [68], and which Christ accepted as far as he could by assuming « the likeness of sinful humanity » (Rom 8,3). Paradoxically, Paul states that it was through the kenosis of his earthly life that Christ enriched mankind [69]. Implicit in such a statement is the thought of Christ's redemptive death by which « he abased himself still further » (Phil 2,8) to gain through his resurrection the riches with which he might endow mankind (LIETZMANN) [70]. *For you know.* This expression reminds us that the record of Jesus' earthly career formed part of the apostolic kerygma which Paul, like all the early Christian preachers, proclaimed (SPICQ) [71]. The conception expressed here is found nowhere else in Paul's letters (except for the hymn cited in Phil 2,6-11).

§ 6. - Paul's Ministry A Repetition of Christ's Dying and Rising. 2 Cor 13,4

The last verse of this letter which we have to consider forms part of Paul's warnings to the Corinthians in view of his imminent visit to them (12,19-13,10). Here we have a more explicit statement of the relation between himself and his neophytes which he touched upon in 4,12 : « death is at work in us, but life in you ».

---

[66] BONSIRVEN, *op. cit.* 146, remarks on the semantic development which this term underwent in Paul's theological thought.

[67] A. FEUILLET, *L' Homme-Dieu considéré dans sa condition terrestre de serviteur et de rédempteur* in *RB Vivre et Penser* (1942) 58-79.

[68] PRAT, *op. cit.* I, 179, n. 1.

[69] There is a similar paradox in Mk 12,44 (SPICQ).

[70] Paul does not, after the fashion of the later Greek theologians and Fathers, consider the incarnation *as such* to be an enrichment of human nature.

[71] CERFAUX, *op. cit.* 140f.

10. - D. M. STANLEY.

For indeed he was crucified out of weakness, but he lives by the power of God. Similarly we too are weak in him ; but we shall live with him by the power of God in your eyes.

[The majority of the better witnesses omit εἰ before ἐσταυρώθη which is the reading found in Alex., Sin. Beza (both 3rd corr.), E, L, the Vulgate and Syriac versions. After ἀσθενοῦμεν, ἐν is found in Vat., Beza, E, K, L, P, and the Vulgate, while σύν appears in Sin., Alex., F, G and the Coptic version. With Merk and Nestle, we follow the first group. Ζήσομεν is to be preferred, with Sin., Alex,. Vat., Beza first corr., to Ρήσωμεν (G) or Ρησόμεθα (Beza 3rd corr. E, K, L) ; εἰς ὑμᾶς is omitted by Vat., Beza 3rd corr., E, the Armenian version, and (twice) in Chrysostom].

The Corinthian adversaries have demanded proof of Paul's statement that « Christ speaks in me » (v. 3). They shall have it on his next visit, for Christ is he « who is not weak in your regard but is powerful in you ». The present verse explains these affirmations.
he was crucified out of weakness. The *weakness* of the mortal, passible Christ is contrasted with the divine power (PLUMMER) mentioned in the preceding verse. It is another way of describing Jesus « in the likeness of sinful humanity » (Rom 8,3). Since his resurrection however, *he lives by the power of God* : his new life is the result of the Father's communication of the divine δύναμις (Rom 1,4 ; 1 Cor 5,4 ; 6,14 ; Phil 3,10 ; Col 1,29 ; Eph 3,7.20). *We too are weak in him.* Paul sees his own sufferings as the *re-presentation* of the passibility of Christ the redeemer. *We shall live with him by the power of God in your eyes.* In 12,9 Paul mentioned the Lord's reply to his prayer for deliverance from the σκόλοψ τῇ σαρκί . « My grace is enough for you ; for [my] δύναμις triumphs in weakness ». And the apostle added : « Gladly then will I rather glory in my weaknesses in order that the δύναμις Χριστοῦ remain upon me » (cf. 2 Cor 1,5). Hitherto, the Corinthians have seen only the weakness of Christ in Paul. Soon they will experience his divine power [72] present also in the apostle, and so Paul's plenary apostolic powers will be demonstrated (LIETZMANN). Like his Master, the apostle participates in the passion and the risen power of Christ, a quasi-experimental verification of his union with him (SPICQ). The Corinthians will themselves feel the effects

---

[72] BONSIRVEN, *op. cit.* 198 : « Cette vie plénière est comprise dans la justification ... elle est le fruit précieux que poursuit la prédication ... et tout le labeur de l'évangélisation : l' Apôtre est vraiment père, enfantant pour la vraie vie, celle de Dieu dans le Christ ».

of Paul's participation in the dynamism of the risen Christ [73], and so come to appreciate the value of his apostolic calling.

§ 7. - The Exordium to Galatians. Gal 1,1-5

Like 2 Corinthians, the brief letter to the churches in Galatia was composed most probably while Paul was journeying towards Corinth. No Pauline epistle is so completely dominated by the exigencies of controversy. It is one of the most personal letters we have from Paul's pen [74]. It attests Paul's love for the Galatians whom he treats as his children [75] and to whom he sends this moving *appel au coeur*, abandoning any attempt at abstruse argumentation which would be beyond them [76]. Those who have been trying to destroy the Christian faith in Galatia are judaizing Christians who claim that the practice of the Law is necessary for salvation [77]. Paul's accusations against them are serious : they have changed the Gospel, or rather, destroyed it (1,6 f.) by contradicting the apostolic traditions (1,9) [78].

---

[73] CERFAUX, *op. cit.* 26.

[74] LAGRANGE, in his commentary, p. lix, remarks that Paul « n'a sans doute écrit aucune épître aussi dominée jusque dans le détail par le but pratique qu'il se proposait ... Il ne se propose pas seulement d'instruire, mais de convaincre ».

[75] Throughout the letter, Paul refers to the Galatians as children : their attitude to himself in the past was that of affectionate children and they would have given him the eyes out of their head (4,15) ; he calls them, « my little children » (4,19) ; like children, they have had a « pedagogue », the Law (3,24) during the time of their infancy (4,3) ; they are « children » of the Promise (4,29), sons of the free woman (4,31). Paul writes his postscript plainly, in large letters, as if to children (6,11).

[76] Paul calls the Galatians ἀνόητοι, a term which denotes not so much lack of intelligence as immaturity : they have not yet reached the « age of reason ». W. BAUER, *Griechisch-Deutsches Wörterbuch*⁴ (Berlin, 1952), gives as meaning of ἀνόητος « unverständig, unvernünftig » ; F. ZORELL, *Lexicon Graecum*² (Romae, 1931), translates it as « insipiens, vecors ». In modern Greek (MOULTON-MILLIGAN), the word means « unreasonable ».

[77] The nature of Abraham's promise contradicts this, since it was God's free gift and totally unmerited (3,18) by any « works ». Moreover, the Holy Spirit himself witnesses against the claims of the judaizing trouble-makers to the Galatian's adoptive sonship (4,6). The sons born under the Law's slavery are to be excluded from the inheritance (5,30). Hence, to accept circumcision now is to deny faith in Christ (5,3) and in the efficacy of the Cross (6,11).

[78] For Paul, any attempt at judaizing the Gentile converts is an attack upon the efficacious nature of the redemption (cf. 2,15f). The Judaizers are clearly op-

The letter contains few references, direct or indirect, to Christ's resurrection, or indeed to the act of man's redemption, a fact assumed as admitted by both parties to the dispute. Paul's point is simply that to insist on the necessity of circumcision or other Mosaic observances is to empty Christ's work of its meaning.

1 Paul, apostle, not by the favour of men nor through human intervention, but through Jesus Christ and God the Father who raised him from death, 2 and all the brethren with me, to the churches of Galatia : 3 grace be yours and peace from God our Father and Lord Jesus Christ, 4 who offered himself on account of our sins, to deliver us from the present wicked world according to the will of God our Father, 5 to whom be glory through all ages. Amen.

[3. ἡμῶν stands after Πατρὸς in Sin., Alex., P, and several cursive mss. It occurs after Κυρίου in Vat., Chester Beatty papyrus, 1739, and the Vulgate, Syriac, Armenian, and Gothic versions.
4a. περί is read by Sin., Alex., D, F, G, K, L, P and the Chester Beatty papyrus. ὑπέρ (adopted by Merk and Nestle) is attested by Vat., Sin. (first corr.), H, etc.].

v. 1. The unusual stress laid upon his apostolic vocation and upon its origin in this exordium is in keeping with the purpose of this letter (WILLIAMS). Of the two fundamental notions in the concept of apostleship (the commission to preach the Gospel and the divine mandate given through Christ), it is the second which is stressed in the remainder of the verse (SCHLIER) [79]. *God the Father who raised him from death.* Christ's resurrection is mentioned not merely because it constitutes « le premier témoignage » of an apostle (BUZY), but also because it was the risen Christ who called Paul to be an apostle (BONNARD). There is also another (polemical) motive involved. The fact that Paul had seen the risen Lord refutes any denial of his apostolic authority on the grounds that he had not known Jesus during his mortal life (BURTON). Over and above these reasons however, Paul has a special purpose in characterizing the Father as author of Christ's resurrection. The dominant theme of the letter is to be the

posed to the traditional teaching, since they persecute Paul (5,11) and display ulterior motives in urging circumcision on the Galatians (6,12f).

[79] The unusual use of διά with « God the Father » as well as with « Jesus Christ » is simply the result of Paul's emphasis upon the immediate, divine source of his office (BURTON) and of his intention to identify the action of Christ and the Father (LAGRANGE).

« Gospel of the promise » [80], a promise which, on Paul's view, the Father fulfilled to Abraham and to Jesus his Son by raising him from death (Gal 3,16 ; Acts 13,32-33).

vv. 3-4. In each of these verses, Paul refers to God as « our Father », since the Christian's adoptive sonship is a subsidiary *motif* in the promise-theme. *who offered himself on account of our sins*. This is Paul's answer to the judaizers, and he returns to it constantly in his letter. The « scandal of the cross » (Gal 5,11) is their refutation (Gal 2,19 ; 3,1.13 ; 5,24 ; 6,12. 14.17). Christ's offering of himself is *according to the will of God our Father*, a gratuitous gift of God through Christ (BONNARD). *to deliver us from the present wicked world*. Paul employs the categories of current Jewish theology in which « this world » is dominated by the « evil one », the « world to come », the messianic age or Kingdom of Christ which is opposed to the kingdom of Satan [81]. It is instructive to compare this passage with 1 Thes 1,10, where Christ is presented as God's Son « whom he has raised from death, Jesus our rescuer from the wrath to come ». There the emphasis is placed upon the redemptive resurrection and upon our deliverance from the divine judgment at the end of time. In reality, both statements express the same truth under different aspects. Christ, by his death and resurrection, has already freed us from the tyranny of sin, the Law, and Satan, while we await the full liberation of the glorious resurrection at his second Coming (LYONNET). In the Pauline kerygma, the thought of the risen Christ includes his redemptive death, just as the mention of the Cross includes his resurrection [82].

---

[80] D. M. STANLEY, *Theologia « Promissionis » apud S. Paulum* in *VD* 30 (1952) 129-142.

[81] The verb ἐξέληται, a *hapax* in Paul, connotes deliverance with violence and presupposes that the Christians were, before their conversion, under the devil's hostile domination (BONNARD). The aorist tense indicates that Paul is thinking of Christ's redemptive act on Calvary.

[82] Cf. GERHARD FRIEDRICH, κηρύσσω, *TWNT III*, 710 : « Ob man vom Gekreuzigten 1 K 1, 23 oder vom Auferstandenen 1 K 15, 12 redet, so meint man immer den ganzen Christus, der durch Tod und Auferstehung der Herr geworden ist und als solcher verkündet wird 2 K 4,5. Der Irdische und der Erhöhte lassen sich nicht scheiden. Man predigt nicht den Mythus vom sterbenden und auferstehenden Gott, auch nicht eine zeitlose Idee, sondern ein einmaliges, tatsächliches Ereignis, das Leben Jesu, seine geschichtliche Erscheinung Ag 9,20 ; 19,13 ». Thus DUNCAN is wrong, when, in his commentary, p. xli, he states that « from first to last, Galatians connects this redemptive work of Christ with His *death* ... In some of his later epistles, Paul represents believers as sharing in the resurrection-life of their Lord ... This is not so in Galatians ».

§ 8. - Christian Existence A Participation in Christ's Death and Life.
Gal 2,19-21

These verses form the conclusion of Paul's personal *apologia* (1,11-2,21). It is not clear whether they are to be included in Paul's protest to Peter (LYONNET), or whether Paul is now speaking in his own name and not that of the Jewish Christians (LAGRANGE), or whether the use of the first person singular is to be considered a literary conceit (BONNARD).

19 For through law I have died to law, in order that I may live for God. With Christ I remain co-crucified. 20 And thus I live no longer my own life, but in me Christ lives. As regards my present life in the flesh, it is a life of faith I live in the Son of God who loved me and handed himself over for my sake. 21 I do not nullify the gracious gift of God : for if justification comes through law, then Christ died uselessly.

[20b. The reading τοῦ Θεοῦ καὶ Χριστοῦ (Vat., D first corr., G) is less well attested than τοῦ Υἱοῦ τοῦ Θεοῦ (Sin., Alex., Ephrem *rescr.*, the Vulgate, Syriac versions, Marcion, Clement of Alex.). Marcion reads ἐξαγοράσαντος for ἀγαπήσαντος].

v. 19. *through law I have died to law.* The absence of the article makes Paul's statement valid with respect to any legal system (LIGHTFOOT), although in the concrete, he has the Mosaic code in mind. By death to law is meant the being withdrawn from its jurisdiction (BURTON). It is set in opposition here to the state of living *for God*. The difficulty is to understand what Paul means by death *through law*. LAGRANGE favours the interpretation of AMBROSIASTER : Paul speaks of the law of faith [83]. CHRYSOSTOM and THEODORET understand *law* as the prophetic character of the Mosaic law, which finds its fulfilment in Christ (Rom 10,4). Such a sense however is alien to the present discussion. Nor can this death

---

[83] Such an abrupt switch in the meaning of the term « law » appears, at first sight, to argue against such an interpretation, until we recall that such a procedure is not uncharacteristic of Paul's intuitive mind : cf. the rapidity of his transition from the « law of works » to the « law of faith » in Gal 2,16 as also in Rom 3,27 and Rom 8,2-4. Indeed, since as SCHLIER suggests (n.85 *infra*) the present · erse is parallel to Rom 6,4, it may be considered to express the same idea as Rom 8,4b which is an echo of Rom 6,4c with Rom 7,6c. Paul has perhaps been led to speak of the infused dynamism of the Christian life, imparted by the indwelling Spirit, as a « law » because of the prophetic description of « the New Covenant » found in Jer 31,31-33 and commented on in Ez 36, 26-27 (cf. 2 Cor 3,3 which contains an allusion to these passages).

through law denote the transgression of the Mosaic law [84], since that is precisely what Paul refuses to admit (v. 17 f.). SCHLIER is certainly right in seeking the key to the solution in the words which follow : *with Christ I remain co-crucified* [85]. Since the Christian was crucified with Christ and remains in that state in his new life, which he shares with the risen Christ, he is dead to the claims of the Mosaic code, and that, in virtue of the Law itself which disclaimed all relation with one crucified (LYON-NET) [86].

v. 20. *in me Christ lives.* As LYONNET has noted, this is one of the « formules hardies » found in this epistle, which will be restated with greater nicety of precision in Rom 8,11.15 [87]. It is remarkable that Paul makes no mention of the Holy Spirit in this description of the Christian life (BONNARD), but simply defines it in terms of the inhabitation of the risen Christ. This communicated life *for God* is the state of justification, as Paul will imply in v. 21. However, as CERFAUX has pointed out [88], the

---

[84] We find the interpretation of CERFAUX, *op. cit.* 118, unsatisfactory : « La Loi causait la mort de l'humanité en la précipitant dans le péché ... Cette mort, qui serait sans issue (elle est sans issue du côté de la Loi) prend un sens lorsque le Christ meurt sur la croix. La mort par la Loi était donc orientée vers ce moment décisif ; elle trouve son explication et sa justification profonde lorsque le Christ meurt, concentrant en lui toutes les malédictions partielles des péchés fomentés par la Loi. La Loi aboutit à la mort du Christ et se résout ainsi mystérieusement dans la vie qui naît. En ce moment se produit le grand revirement. La Loi meurt avec le Christ, nous mourons tous à la Loi, et nous vivons avec le Christ ».

[85] He refers to the moment of Baptism as the historical moment when the Christian dies to law ; thus, on SCHLIER's view, the passage is parallel to Rom 6,3-6.

[86] In the second edition of his commentary (1959), p. 29, LYONNET states : « Mais on peut aussi comprendre que le chrétien a renoncé à la loi pour obéir à l'A. T. ... ou mieux qu'il est mort à la loi mosaïque par une autre loi, celle de l'Esprit qui se substitue de fait à la première, comme Paul l'affirme explicitement en Rm 8,2-4 ». Another explanation (BONNARD) : this death of the Christian, which he shares with Christ, liberates him from the jurisdiction of the Law which first condemned Jesus to death. — In 2 Cor 5,15, Paul asserted that the purpose of Christ's death (and consequently, of the Christian's death in him) was « that the living may no longer live for themselves, but for him who died and was raised for them ». The present passage describes that death in terms of freedom from law.

[87] PRAT, *op. cit II*[7], 360, n. 2, compares this conception with the Johannine notion of « le Christ-Vie ».

[88] CERFAUX, *op. cit.* 240.

themes of « life » and « justification » will only be united into a complete synthesis in Romans. *my present life in the flesh.* The present state of the Christian is a life communicated and preserved by faith in Christ's redemptive work, considered as an act of his love [89].

v. 21. *I do not nullify the gracious gift of God.* The word resumes the whole work of redemption. The verb *nullify* implies that a return to the practice of the Law is a practical denial of the sovereign efficacy of the redemption and of the gratuity of salvation (LYONNET) [90]. *If justification comes through law.* In Phil 3,7-8 Paul considered his former practice of Judaism « loss » as compared with the « gain » he found in Christ. Now, as a result of the judaizing crisis in Galatia, he takes a much stronger stand against « justice through the Law ». Not only has the Law always been incapable of bestowing justification : to consider its observance necessary for salvation is to apostatize from Christianity.

§ 9. - Christ the Redeemer and the Promise to Abraham (1). Gal 3,13-14

The doctrinal section of this letter is contained in chs. 3-4. The exigencies of controversy force Paul to contrast the OT economy of the Mosaic Law with that of God's promise to Abraham, fulfilled in one only Son of Abraham, the Christ (Gal 3,16). Thus it is through union with Christ, not through the Law, that the Christian must seek the blessings promised to Abraham [91].

13 Christ has redeemed us from the curse of the Law by becoming for our sakes a curse (as Scripture says, « Cursed be he who hangs upon a gibbet ») 14 in order that Abraham's blessing be communicated to the Gentiles in Christ Jesus, in order that we receive the promise of the Spirit through faith.

---

[89] As we have remarked before, the verb παραδίδωμι belongs to primitive Christian soteriological vocabulary. It is borrowed from Is 53, and is, consequently, an interesting survival, in Pauline soteriology, of the Servant theology.

[90] The verb ἀθετεῖν is frequently employed in the LXX and in the NT in the sense of « render invalid », « account as nothing » (cf. SCHLIER).

[91] On the importance given to the Christian's connection with Abraham rather than with Moses (and the ensuing problem that arose for Gentile Christians), cf. PAUL DÉMANN, *La signification d' Abraham dans la perspective du Nouveau Testament* in *Cahiers Sioniens* 5 (1951) 136-159.

[14. ἐν Χριστῷ Ἰησοῦ is read by Alex., Ephrem *rescr.*, D, the Chester Beatty papyrus and almost all other mss. with the notable exception of Sin. and Vat., which read ἐν Ἰησοῦ Χριστῷ. Modern editors and commentators are divided. Von Soden and Merk follow the first reading, as do Lightfoot, Lyonnet, Cerfaux. Nestle adopts the second, which Burton insists is original. Lagrange, Bonnard, Schlier adopt the same reading.

εὐλογίαν is read instead of ἐπαγγελίαν by the Chester Beatty papyrus, D (first corr.), G, the Latin ms. tradition, Marcion, Ambrosiaster, Ephrem].

v. 13. The word ἐξαγοράζειν is employed metaphorically[92] : it expresses deliverance from the slavery of the Law by Christ. In this epistle, the notion is subordinated to the more fundamental idea of *liberation* (BONNARD). The curse of the Law is founded in man's inability to observe all its precepts and in the Law's impotency to justify anyone in God's sight. Christ, by « being born subject to law » (Gal 4,4), willed to appear to share its curse in the sense that he assumed the « likeness of sinful humanity » (Rom 8,3). He redeemed the Jews from the curse by his death on Calvary. In an attempt to make his point as vividly as possible, Paul makes free use of the LXX rendering of Dt 21,23 (cf. Dt 27,26)[93]. As LYONNET observes, the cadaver of the criminal hoisted, *after death*, upon a tree, presents only a *material* analogy with the crucified Christ. Paul's purpose, through such a bold image, is to underscore the utter incompatibility between the practice of Christianity and any Jewish observance, a truth which the Galatian controversy brought home to him, probably for the first time.

v. 14. Paul now states the purpose of the atonement, first with respect to pagans, then to the Jews. The reading *in Christ Jesus* which is to be preferred here on textual grounds, indicates that it is the risen Christ who, by liberating his own and our humanity from the yoke of the Law, has made possible the inclusion of the Gentiles in Abraham's blessing, thus fulfilling its promise of universality (Gal 3,8 ; Gn 18,18). This verse contains in embryo the thesis Paul will elaborate in Eph 2,14-18 (LAGRANGE). In the history of salvation, the Law placed an episodic limitation on the promise to Abraham (BONNARD). It was Christ's liberating death and his resurrection which removed this temporary restriction. *that we receive the promise of the Spirit*. The union of Jew and Gentile *in Christ Jesus* by the abrogation of the Law makes possible their receiving *through faith* the fulfilment of the promise, the Holy Spirit, gift of the risen Christ,

---

[92] FRIEDRICH BÜCHSEL, ἐξαγοράζω, *TWNT I*, 126-128.
[93] PRAT, *op. cit. II*, 247, notes Paul's omission of the phrase ὑπὸ Θεοῦ.

a fact of which the Galatians have had personal experience (Gal 3,3-5) [94]. It is efficacious faith in the accomplishment of the promise in Christ which distinguishes Christian faith from that of Abraham, which was the faithful adherence to a promise concerning the future (SCHLIER).

§ 10. - Christ the Redeemer and the Promise made to Abraham (2). Gal 3,26-29

One point remains to be elucidated : the exact relation of the Christian to Christ, to whom alone the fulfilment of Abraham's promise has been granted.

26 For you are all sons of God by faith in Christ Jesus. 27 All of you who have been baptized into Christ, have put on Christ. 28 There is neither Jew, nor Greek. There is neither slave nor free man. There is neither male nor female. For all of you are one in Christ Jesus. 29 Now if you are Christ's, then you are Abraham's seed, heirs according to the promise.

[28. Instead of οὐκ ἔνι, the Chester Beatty papyrus reads οὐκέτι ; εἷς ἐστέ ἐν Χριστῷ 'Ιησοῦ is attested by the majority of the best mss. (Vat., Ephrem *rescr.*, D, the Peshitto, Bohairic versions, Clement Alex., Athanasius, Theodoret), while F, G, the Latin ms. tradition, and the Vulgate read ἕν ἐστέ. Sin (first corr.), Alex., and the Chester Beatty papyrus have ἐστε Χριστοῦ 'Ιησοῦ.
29b. In place of Χριστοῦ, Beza reads εἷς ἐστέ ἐν Χριστῷ 'Ιησοῦ].

v. 26. *sons of God.* For the first time in his letters, Paul now develops the theme of the Christian's adoptive filiation, which illustrates the relation of the Christian to Christ. The conception of sonship arises quite naturally. Paul has compared the promise made to Abraham to a will (vv. 15-18) regulating an inheritance. Then the Law is compared to a pedagogue, the slave in Greek families who had charge of the child's discipline and led him to school. The Christian, come of age by faith and consequently freed from the Law (Paul is thinking of the Jewish Christian particularly), is heir to Abraham's promise and a son of God. *You are all sons of God.* The insertion of the word *all* shows that Gentile Christians are included as well. *Sons of God by faith in Christ Jesus.* The density of Paul's expression creates an ambiguity. Does the Christian become son

---

[94] This second purpose clause is co-ordinate with the first and, like it, dependent on ἐξηγόρασεν (Christ's act of liberation) (SCHLIER after LIETZMANN).

of God through his union with Christ (CORNELY, LOISY), or by faith in Christ (LAGRANGE, SCHLIER) ? Paul probably wished to insinuate both ideas. The adoptive sonship is the result of Christian faith (vv. 23,25) [95]. At the same time, it is because of the unity *in Christ Jesus* (v. 28) that the Christians may be said to be sons of God (SCHLIER). The experiential proof of this sonship, the gift of the Spirit, will be added in the next section we have to consider (Gal 4,6).

v. 27. *You have been baptized into Christ.* Baptism, the complement of faith and in no way opposed to it (LYONNET), is next mentioned as cause of this oneness in Christ [96], since it is the logical conclusion of the act of faith (LAGRANGE). By the external acceptance of the sacrament, the Christian gives tangible proof of his faith. *You have put on Christ,* that is, you have become one with him (LYONNET). As LAGRANGE points out, a reference to the assuming of a new baptismal robe is not likely here [97].

v. 28. *You are all one in Christ Jesus.* Union with Christ results in a « new creation » (2 Cor 5,17), removing all distinctions of race, class or sex. Since each has become one with Christ, all are one in him (LAGRANGE). Paul has in mind the reality he elsewhere calls « the Body of Christ » (SCHLIER), although he does not refer to it explicitly. While the notion of unity, especially between Jewish and Gentile Christians is Paul's whole purpose in writing this letter (BONNARD), still his immediate aim here is to identify all Christians with Christ who alone is « the seed » of Abraham and sole heir of the promise (v. 16).

v. 29. *If you are Christ's.* This is meant primarily, not in a moral, but in an historical and objective sense (BONNARD). Identified with Christ, the Christian is truly *Abraham's seed*, a beneficiary not only of Abraham's blessing but also of God's promised heritage since he is an adoptive son. Thus, as SCHLIER observes, the double thesis with which Paul began this paragraph (3,6 ff.) is reduced to one : Abraham's blessing belongs to faith, and Abraham's heritage belongs to Christ.

§ 11. - **The Redemption and the Adoptive Filiation. Gal 4,4-7**

In the last passage, Paul showed that the Christian is a son of God

---

[95] MEINERTZ, *op. cit.* II, 133.

[96] To be understood of the « personal Christ » : cf. CERFAUX, *op. cit.* 249 : « Les anciens sont bien unanimes. Aucun d'eux ne songerait à parler d' un Christ qui ne serait pas le Christ personnel ».

[97] MEINERTZ, *op. cit. II,* 136.

thanks to his identification with the risen Christ. Now he connects this
filiation more directly with the act of the redemption and defines it more
closely in terms of the Holy Spirit.

4 But when the fulness of time was come, God sent forth his Son, born of a woman, born subject to law, 5 in order that he might redeem those subject to law, in
order that we might receive the adoptive sonship. 6 The proof that you are sons :
God has sent the Spirit of his Son into our hearts, crying, « Abba », [that is] « Father ».
7 Thus you are no longer a slave but a son ; and if a son, then heir by God's
[grace].

[4b. In place of the commonly attested γενόμενον (ἐκ γυναικός), some few mss.
read γεννώμενον.
6. In the phrase τὸ πνεῦμα τοῦ Ὑιοῦ αὐτοῦ, the Chester Beatty papyrus omits τοῦ Ὑιοῦ.
7b. διὰ Θεοῦ, the more difficult reading, is attested by the best witnesses. There
are several variants].

v. 4. *the fulness of time.* This OT expression means that history has reached
its full complement of time and its consummation in Christ's death and
resurrection. As a result, the messianic age has begun (LYONNET). As
Paul has remarked (v. 2), it has occurred at the προθεσμία, the date
fixed by the Father. *God sent forth his Son.* The verb, used only
here and in v. 6 in Paul's writings, denotes in Acts a personal mission
from one place to another (BONNARD) (cf. Acts 7,12 ; 9,30 ; 11,22 ; 17,14 ;
22,21) [98]. In this verse it is used of the mission of the pre-existent Son,
while in v. 6, it denotes the mission of the Holy Spirit to the Christian.
The phrase *born* (lit. become) *of a woman* indicates a new mode of existence and not, as the proper verb, to be born, would imply, the beginning of existence (LAGRANGE) [99]. The expression *born subject to law* indicates the humiliation undergone by the Son in his sending forth (BURTON).
The fact that Christ's incarnation and mortal life are indicated by participles shows that Paul does not regard them as directly redemptive, but
rather a part of the (necessary) prelude to the act of the atonement [100].
v. 5. *that he might redeem those subject to law.* While the act of the redempt-

---

[98] In Acts 12,11 ; 13,26, it means a message from God to men.
[99] CERFAUX, *op. cit.* 140.
[100] BONSIRVEN, *op. cit.* 157, remarks in connection with this verse, « proposition générale qu' il ne faut pas rétrécir à une seule suite de l' Incarnation ». PRAT,
op. cit. II, 248 asserts that the meaning of the verse is an exact parallel with
Gal 3,13-14 : « Dans les deux cas ce n'est pas le *mode* de la rédemption qui est
indiqué, mais la *condition* ».

ion is not specified here, the unusual verb ἐξαγοράζειν recalls Gal. 3,13 where it was used with reference to Christ's death. By employing a more general phrase, *subject to law*, Paul wishes to include not only the Jews (LAGRANGE), who like Christ (v. 4) were born under the Mosaic code, but also the Gentiles, enslaved by τὰ στοιχεῖα τοῦ κόσμου (v. 3) [101]. *that we might receive the adoptive sonship.* Paul uses a juridical term to designate what he has already described at length in ch. 3. The conception does not however remain within juridical categories of thought. It comprises a new personal relation between God the Father and his sons, founded on love and faith, and sealed by the Spirit (BONNARD). Moreover it is the redemptive resurrection as well as death of God's Son which has enabled us to enter into this filial relationship [102]. All the gifts of supernatural life are given to the Christian in virtue of his participation in the Sonship of Christ [103], a point which is pivotal in Paul's theology of grace.

v. 6. The introductory ὅτι must be taken as declarative (LAGRANGE, LYONNET) [104]. The Spirit comes simultaneously with the gift of adoptive filiation (cf. Gal 3,14). Paul does not assert any relation of cause to effect between adoption and the gift of the Spirit (BONNARD). As in Gal 3,3 ff, Rom 8,14 ff, the fact of adoptive filiation is a datum of Christian experience. *the Spirit of his Son.* The Holy Ghost is, in Pauline theology (cf. Rom 8,9-11), the gift of the risen Christ. Here the Spirit is described in relation to Christ as Son of God since the Spirit witnesses to our adoptive sonship, which we possess by union with the risen Son. This witness of the Spirit is summed up in the prayer *Abba* !, ascribed by Mk 14,36 only to Christ himself [105]. The gift of the Son's prayer manifests experientially the full reality of our adoptive sonship (SCHLIER).

v. 7. *if a son, then heir.* The surprising use of the singular here adds to the personal nature of the relation (SCHLIER). Paul concludes his develop-

---

[101] That is, the stars and the spirits who rule them : cf. the excellent discussion by BONNARD in his commentary, pp. 84f.

[102] CERFAUX, *op. cit.* 333.

[103] Hence the importance assigned to the Father in the whole of Pauline soteriology, as will be pointed out later.

[104] S. ZEDDA, *L'adozione a figli di Dio e lo Spirito Santo* (Roma, 1952).

[105] S. LYONNET, *Notes au commentaire du Père Huby* in *Épître aux Romains²*, *VS* (Paris, 1957) 611 : « Aussi les chrétiens s'adressent-ils à Dieu en usant du terme même dont se servait le Christ, mais que jamais un Juif n'aurait osé employer dans sa prière ... ». Cf. JOACHIM JEREMIAS, *Kennzeichen der ipsissima vox Jesu* in *Synoptische Studien : Alfred Wikenhauser zum siebzigsten Geburtstag dargebracht ...* (München, 1953) 86-89.

ment of the inheritance theme : what he has described under the figure
of a heritage is identified as the reality of adoptive filiation (BONNARD).
The heritage comes to us by God's gracious favour, conferring on us the
dignity of sons (LAGRANGE).

§ 12. - The Redemption as the New Creation. Gal 6,14-15

In the postscript, Paul insists again upon the unique and universal
value of the redemptive work accomplished by the cross. He transposes
the idea in terms of the « new creation » (2 Cor 5,17).

14 As for me, may I never boast except in the cross of our Lord Jesus Christ,
through which the world has become a crucified cadaver to me, even as I am to
the world. 15 For neither circumcision nor the lack of it means anything. [What
counts is] a new creation.

[15. The οὐτὲ γὰρ read by Merk, Nestle here is supported by Vat., 1739, the Chester Beatty papyrus, the Peshitto and Harclean Syriac, while ἐν γὰρ Χριστῷ
Ἰησοῦ οὐτὲ is attested by Sin., Alex., Ephrem *rescr.*, D and the Vulgate].

v. 14. *may I never boast.* The term καυχᾶσθαι is characteristic of Paul in
the NT [106]. On the one hand, it signifies the Jews' self-satisfaction and
self-confidence in their own efforts before God. On the other, it has a
Christian sense, the confidence based on faith in God's power (Rom 3,27),
and as such, excludes all reliance upon self, the performance of salutary
actions being a gift of God (1 Cor 4,7). To the Galatians, Paul wishes to
make clear the issue between himself and the judaizers. For this reason,
he opposes to their natural viewpoint the doctrine of the cross. Their
boast is « in the flesh » (v. 13), his reposes in « the scandal of the cross »
(5,11). By the phrase *the cross of our Lord Jesus Christ* Paul means the
central act of man's salvation, the death and resurrection of Christ, or
better, the cross and its redemptive significance perceived in the light
of the resurrection. SCHLIER calls the cross here « Ideogramm für das
Erlösungsgeschehen ». The cross is the instrument *through which* [107].
Paul's crucifixion to the world and its crucifixion to him is accomplished
(LAGRANGE). By this crucifixion is meant, not an interior psychological

---

[106] R. BULTMANN, καυχάομαι, *TWNT III*, 648-653.
[107] The phrase δι οὗ, which might grammatically refer to « Jesus Christ »,
is probably better connected with the *nomen regens* σταυρῷ.

experience, but the historical event which accomplished man's salvation, and which forms the principal object of Christian faith (BONNARD) [108]. v. 15. *neither circumcision means anything.* In Gal 5,6 Paul stated in almost identical terms the contrast between the two religious systems : circumcision — or faith operating through charity. Here the opposition is between the old world of sin, of the Law, and a « new creation » in which the old differences have been abolished (LAGRANGE). Before God the creator of this new order, it is only Christ's death and resurrection which have inaugurated that order (2 Cor 5,17), which can have any significance.

This *new creation* might be termed « eschatological » (BONNARD), inasmuch as « it appertains, in this world, to the reality of the world to come », provided we understand Paul to speak of an objectively real supernatural state, which is the result of two objective events, viz. Christ's death and his resurrection. For it is a reality now present in the life of the Christian, although its full perfection will be attained only in the glorious resurrection of the just.

We are indebted to the Galatian crisis for the fact that Paul was thereby forced to express several themes hitherto latent in his mind : that of the Christian's adoptive sonship, that of the promise and heritage, as well as that of « Abraham's seed ». While some of these do not re-appear in subsequent epistles, that of adoptive filiation will receive a further development in Paul's letter to the Roman church, which we must now study.

---

[108] In order to recapture some of the horror which the word « crucify » suggested in Paul's time (forgotten by our long Christian association with the term), we have translated « become a crucified cadaver ».

Chapter VII

CHRIST'S RESURRECTION IN THE LETTER
TO THE ROMANS

Bibliography : H. Oltramare, *Commentaire sur l'Épître aux Romains* (Geneva-Paris, 1881-82). Frédéric Godet, *Commentaire sur l'Épître aux Romains*[2] (Paris, 1883-92). B. Weiss, *Der Brief an die Römer*[9], MK 4 (Göttingen, 1889). W. Sanday, A. C. Headlam, *The Epistle to the Romans*[1], ICC (Edinburgh, 1900). R. St John Parry, *Romans*, CGT (Cambridge, 1921). M. -J. Lagrange, *Épître aux Romains*[6], EB (Paris, 1950). Joseph Sickenberger, *An die Korinther und Römer*[4], BB (Bonn, 1932). C. H. Dodd, *The Epistle of Paul to the Romans*, MC (London, 1932). Hans Lietzmann, *An die Römer*[4], HNT 8 (Tübingen, 1933). P. Boylan, *St Paul's Epistle to the Romans* (Dublin, 1934). J. Huby, *Épître aux Romains*, VS 10 (Paris, 1940). Paul Althaus, *Der Brief an die Römer*[5], NTD (Tübingen, 1949). L. Cerfaux, *Une lecture de l'épître aux Romains* (Tournai-Paris, 1947). V. Jacono, *Le Epistole di S. Paolo ai Romani ...* (Torino-Roma, 1951). Joseph Kurzinger, *Der Brief an die Römer*, EBl (Würzburg, 1951). S. Lyonnet, *Les Épîtres de saint Paul aux Galates et aux Romains*[2], SB (Paris, 1959).

By comparison with Paul's writings to the Corinthian and Galatian churches, Romans is more in the nature of a theological treatise [1], a result, doubtless, of its scope, which is not polemical but aimed at introducing Paul as a preacher of the Gospel [2]. Accordingly, many points of doctrine,

---

[1] S. Lyonnet, in his commentary, p. 56, remarks that in Rom « la polémique passe au second plan et ... le thème positif de la vie chrétienne, ou plus exactement de l'espérance du salut ... devient le thème central ... » This epistle, he adds, «offre donc moins la synthèse de toute la pensée paulinienne qu'un certain nombre de thèses, — à la verité maîtresses, — centrées autour du problème de la justification ».

[2] Thus we find in this epistle allusions to credal formulae probably employed by Paul in his preaching (1,2-4 ; 4,25 ; 10,9 ; 14,7-9), reminiscences of his controversies with the Jews (3,3-9 ; 9,6-24), and Scriptural *catenae* composed with a view of convincing the synagogues of the Diaspora (3,10-18 ; 9,25-29 ; 10,18-21).

particularly those concerning the redemption, which have been touched on only briefly in other epistles, are here set forth a surety of touch and completeness, which makes Romans at once the most difficult and the most interesting of all the letters in the NT.

The theme of the epistle is that the Gospel is « God's power for salvation to the believer » (1,16). In his penetrating study of the letter's plan, S. LYONNET [3] has shown that the theme advances by two clearly-marked thought-patterns centering in two divine attributes, God's justice[4] and his love. As a manifestation of the divine justice, the Gospel is source of man's justification, which is the ontological foundation of Christian existence. As a revelation of God's love for man, the Gospel announces the unique hope of man's eschatological salvation, which is the created communication of that love (5,5).

Such being the epistle's general theme and its main motifs, it is of great importance to our present study to discover and evaluate the role which Christ's resurrection plays in the letter's presentation of Paul's soteriology. It will appear to be of no slight significance that Christ's resurrection occupies a place of honour in the opening lines [5] of Romans, and that the most explicit reference to the function of Christ's death and resurrection in the atonement occurs at the very heart of its doctrinal development (4,25).

§ 1. - The Resurrection's Function in the Christology of the Gospel. Rom 1,1-4

The relatively lengthy salutation (vv. 1-7) gives a preview of the epistle's major themes : the gratuitous nature of the divine election, faith's role in justification, the atonement effected by Christ's death and resurrection, the harmony of the two testaments (LYONNET).

---

[3] S. LYONNET, Note sur le plan de l'épître aux Romains in RSR 39 (1951) 301-316.

[4] This « justice of God » is a concept which is quite different from our modern ideas of vindictive or commutative justice. It is a biblical notion, found in Deutero-Isaias especially, and may be described as God's salvific activity in virtue of his promises of salvation. Cf. S. LYONNET, De « Justitia Dei » in Epistola ad Romanos in VD 25 (1947) 23-34 ; 118-121 ; 129-144 ; 193-203 ; 257-268 ; also Exegesis Epistolae ad Romanos I-IV[2] (Roma, 1960) 88 f.

[5] F. PRAT, La Théologie de Saint Paul II[7], 510 ff.

11. - D. M. STANLEY.

1 Paul, servant of Christ Jesus, apostle by vocation, set apart to [announce] God's good news 2 which he had previously promised through his prophets in the sacred books, 3 concerning his Son, born of David's line, as regards his human nature, 4 constituted Son of God in power, in accordance with his spirit of holiness, by resurrection of the dead : Jesus Christ, our Lord.

[1. Χριστοῦ Ἰησοῦ, preferred by Merk and Nestle, is attested by Vat., papyrus 10 which also belongs to the Hesychian recension, the Latin ms. tradition, Irenaeus, Origen, Ambrose, Augustine.

4. ὁρισθέντος is without a doubt the correct reading. The common rendering in the Latin versions, *praedestinatus* (cf. also the Syriac readings, Ephrem) appears to be unjustified.].

v. 1. *Paul, servant of Jesus Christ, apostle by vocation.* The two epithets Paul applies to himself recall two characteristic notes of his mission. He continues the redemptive work of Jesus as ' *Ebed Yahweh* [6], and he was called not only «to be a saint », as are all Christians, but « to be an apostle » (CERFAUX). *God's good news.* The kerygma is referred to God the Father as ultimate source of salvation, a common NT conception and one characteristic of Paul, as is also the term εὐαγγέλιον [7].

v. 2. *which he had previously promised.* This is a reminiscence of the original and extended treatment given the notion of God's promise in Galatians. It is a brief recapitulation of *the sacred books* of the OT, habitually employed by Paul in his preaching (Acts 17, 2 ; 26, 22-23 ; 28,23). The sentence explains the unusual phrase « the Gospel of God » (v. 1) and betrays « a pre-occupation of Paul's » (OLTRAMARE), his anxiety to point out that this *good news* is the fulfilment of a previous divine promise.

v. 3. *concerning his Son.* In this and the following verse, we have a *raccourci* of Paul's Christology. The title which Paul appears to have applied by preference to Christ from the beginning of his preaching (Acts 9,20) was « Son of God ». It belonged, as we have seen, to the data of his experience on the Damascus road [8]. As LAGRANGE observes, the phrase is employed in its full theological meaning. This is shown by the descrip-

------

[6] We have treated this interesting Pauline conception elsewhere : *The Theme of the Servant of Yahweh in Primitive Christian Soteriology, and its Transposition by St. Paul* in *CBQ* 16 (1954) 385-425.

[7] W. GROSSOUW, art. *Evangelium* in HAAG, *Bibel-Lexikon*, col. 456 : « Das Substantiv εὐαγγέλιον ist folgenderweise auf das NT verteilt : Mt 4 mal, Mk 8 mal, Paulusbriefe 60 mal, I Petr und Offb je 1 mal. Man kann somit sagen, dass das εὐαγγέλιον im NT vor allem ein paulinischer Begriff ist ».

[8] Cf. Ch. II, p. 49-50.

tion of Christ which follows it. At the same time, it is interesting to note that Paul has managed, in these lines, to sketch the process by which Jesus' disciples came to full faith in him as the Christ, then (after his resurrection) as Lord, that is, Son of God in the strict sense. Thus in the present verse, the mention of the title *his Son* in the context of the OT prophecies *might* mean no more than a reference to Jesus as the Messias [9]. The possibility of such an interpretation is enhanced by the allusion to Jesus' being *born of David's line*. « Son of David » had been traditionally applied to the Christ [10]. It is perhaps not too much to say that on Paul's view, Jesus revealed himself in his mortal life as the Messias.

v. 4. It is this verse which transforms the Pauline picture of Jesus Christ by its reference to his divinity, and so gives its full theological value to the title *his Son*. In Paul's Christology, it is the resurrection, understood as including the whole movement of Jesus' exaltation, which has provided the key to the mystery of his personality. *in accordance with his Spirit of holiness.* This phrase was understood by some of the Fathers of the Church (BOYLAN) as the Holy Ghost. In the opinion of many modern commentators, however, the expression connotes something intrinsic to Christ himself (like the words *as regards his human nature*) [11]. As LYONNET points out, it is the divine aspect of Christ as distinguished from his human aspect. It is perhaps typical of Paul's Semitic cast of thought that

---

[9] While the specific title « Son of God » (employed in Hellenism for the king or emperor as well as for men possessed of « divine » powers) was, so far as we now know, not given to the Messias in Judaism, it is employed in the OT to designate the messianic people and also the king (who at times was a type of the Messias). Cf. PAUL BILLERBECK, *Kommentar zum Neuen Testament aus Talmud und Midrasch III*, 15-22 ; also OSCAR CULLMANN, *Die Christologie des Neuen Testaments*, 276-281.

[10] W. BOUSSET, *Die Religion des Judentums im späthellenistischen Zeitalter*[3] (Tübingen, 1926) 226 ; M.-J. LAGRANGE, *Le judaisme avant Jésus-Christ* (Paris, 1931) 365.

[11] A. FEUILLET, *Le plan salvifique de Dieu d'après l'Épître aux Romains* in *RB* 57 (1950) 338, where he remarks that in Christ « l'Apôtre contemple, outre la nature humaine, une nature spirituelle très sainte ... en d'autres termes la divinité, à laquelle la résurrection a donné son plein rayonnement » ; also F. PRAT, *op. cit. II*[7], 513. — FEUILLET's remarks are substantially correct ; he does not however entirely escape the danger to which our modern, western mentality is prone, of making Paul say something in a way he would never have thought of. We believe that the phrase κατὰ πνεῦμα ἁγιωσύνης expresses something which, on Paul's view, is intrinsic to the *glorified* Christ, — and that, not in the order of essences or natures, but in the *existential* order (i. e. the order of activity).

he contemplates the Person of Jesus Christ from the viewpoint of *what he does rather than what he is*. He envisages him as Saviour of men in his risen state, that is, as bearer of the Spirit. As we have already seen, it is a Pauline theologoumenon that « the Lord is the Spirit » (2 Cor 3,17). The risen Christ constitutes with the Holy Ghost one operative principle in the sanctification of the Christian [12]. The Spirit is described here by a term which in the LXX always denotes one of the foremost OT divine attributes, ἀγιωσύνη [13].

It is because the mortal Jesus has been *constituted Son of God in power* that he is able to confer on men God's sanctifying Spirit. Just as, in the order of history, God's Son became man by being *born of David's line*, so in the realm of divine revelation he has been constituted as Lord [14]. The words *Son of God in power*, probably to be taken together (LAGRANGE ; cf. LIETZMANN), [14a] denote this newly-manifested universal

---

[12] We cannot insist too strongly that the phrase κατὰ πνεῦμα ἀγιωσύνης designates the risen Christ *in relation to the Christian*, the *quoad nos* of scholastic theology. Like other biblical writers, Paul does not contemplate the Word incarnate as he exists in himself but as he reveals himself to us through the operations of the supernatural order. Similarly, the expression κατὰ σάρκα of the preceding verse does not immediately denote the *natura humana Christi* in itself but as it affects the character of biblical Salvation-history. Accordingly, we cannot help but feel that there is something inexact about the following statement of L. CERFAUX, *Le Christ dans la théologie de saint Paul*, 222 : « L'Esprit, comme dans *Rom.*, 1, 4, définit la nature même du Christ ... » ; cf. also p. 236 : « Paul ne pouvait identifier le Christ avec l'Esprit-Saint. Et cependant, en envisageant l'oeuvre de sanctification, il est amené à concevoir le Christ sous des attributs qui le rapprochent de l'Esprit-Saint. Le Christ est 'esprit de sanctification' ». But this last remark is precisely what Paul did *not* say.

[13] The term appears in the LXX to designate the divine holiness in Ps 95 (96), 6 ; 96 (97), 12 ; 144 (145), 5 ; 29 (30), 12. *Once* only it is used of the Temple, 2 Mc 3,12, which derived its sanctity from the divine *shekinah*. Thus we have simply understood the phrase « Spirit of holiness » as « Holy Spirit » : for, on Paul's view, the « constitution » of Jesus Christ in his glorified state as « Son of God in power » necessarily includes the *operation* of the Holy Spirit.

[14] The use of ὁρίζω here corresponds exactly to the use of it in the primitive apostolic preaching : cf. examples of the usage in Peter's speech, Acts 10,42, and in Paul's discourse at Athens., Acts 17,31.

[14a] M.-E. BOISMARD, in his article, *Constitué Fils de Dieu (Rom 1 4)* in *RB* 60 (1953) 5-17, takes the phrase « in power » with « constituted ». We prefer, with S. LYONNET, *Notes au commentaire du Père Huby* in *Épître aux Romains*², 564-565, to understand it as a quality of the Son : « c'est en tant que le Père communique au Fils cette puissance, le rendant par là même capable de la communiquer à son tour à ses disciples ».

v. 21. *In the present dispensation.* By the temporal use of νυνὶ, which is put in the emphatic position, Paul wishes to oppose the age of salvation which is that of the Gospel (cf. v. 26 ἐν τῷ νῦν καιρῷ ; also 1,16), to the period when men were without Christ. By *God's justice*, Paul means not vindictive or commutative justice, nor the justice communicated to man (LAGRANGE), but that activity in God by which he proves himself faithful to his promises of salvation [22]. The definitive revelation of this divine characteristic has occurred, as Paul will presently explain, (the perfect tense of the verb is to be noted) in the redemption accomplished in Christ Jesus.

v. 22. *to all believers.* The manifestation of God's justice is made only to those who possess the eyes of faith. Granted the presence of that virtue, however, it is an absolutely universal revelation, and one made *without any distinction* between Jew and pagan. The whole purpose of the apostle in developing the theme of God's wrath (1,18-3,20) incurred by Jew no less than Gentile was precisely to demonstrate this universal need of being redeemed by Christ.

v. 23. *For all have sinned.* Paul states the reason for the universality of the redemption. All men are sinners, and as a result they *remain without the glory of God.* In the LXX, the term δόξα represents the *kabod* of Yahweh, the divine presence as manifested and communicated to man (Ex 24, 16-17 ; 40,34-38). It is unlikely that there is any reference here to the rabbinical tradition according to which Adam lost this divine « glory » through his sin [23]. While the *glory* is primarily one of the eschatological blessings connected with the resurrection from the dead [24] and remains an object of hope during the Christian's present existence (Rom 5,2 ; 8,18.21), yet, as Paul has already made clear (2 Cor 3,18), a share of it is even now imparted to the Christian who is justified (Rom 8,30).

v. 24. While the construction is awkward and impossible to determine with certainty (SANDAY-HEADLAM), the general meaning is clear. The

---

[22] Cf. the definition given by LYONNET in his commentary, p. 57 : « Par là l'Écriture désigne une activité salvifique où Dieu, agissant comme roi plus encore que comme juge, délivre son peuple de ses ennemis et le rétablit dans l'héritage promis à ses pères ».

[23] LIETZMANN gives references to this rabbinic speculation in his commentary. However in I Cor 15,46 Paul has already, it would seem, rejected this sort of interpretation of the story of Adam.

[24] Paul will describe Christ's resurrection as the result of the communication to him of the Father's « glory » : Rom 6,4.

revelation of God's divine activity in fulfilling his promise of saving his people is made to those *who are being justified*, since this communication is *gratuitous* and so a mark of God's χάρις. In this act by which God justifies the sinner, there is no question of a forensic declaration : the sinner who believes is made really « just » or holy (HUBY). The source of this justification is *the redemption in Christ Jesus*. The title *Christ Jesus* makes it clear that Paul is thinking of the risen Lord and provides a clue to the use of the word ἀπολύτρωσις , which, as Rom 8,23 shows, is eschatological in meaning. On Paul's view, there is no redemption in the full sense without the glorification of man's material nature. Consequently, at the present period, only in the risen Christ is the redemption fully realized. As LYONNET remarks, the use of ἀπολύτρωσις shows that Paul is thinking of the messianic « liberation » wrought by God through a new covenant sealed with the blood of his Son. The conception is elaborated after the analogy with Israel's redemption out of Egypt (PARRY), when Yahweh acquired a people for himself (Ex 19,5-6). Paul states that it is through the glorified humanity of Jesus Christ (SANDAY-HEADLAM) that the grace of justification, man's first step towards the ultimate supernatural goal, comes to the believer. Paul does not refer again, in the remainder of the paragraph, to this aspect of the atonement, however, since he wishes to discuss Christ's redemptive act in terms of the divine forgiveness of man's sinfulness.

v. 25. *whom God publicly exposed* [a kind of new] *mercy-seat*. The verb used here could mean « proposed to himself *ab aeterno* » (LAGRANGE), but the suggested translation fits the context more aptly where so much insistence is placed upon the revelation of God's justice (SANDAY-HEADLAM, HUBY). The historical moment of which Paul is thinking is that of Christ's death upon the cross, rather than that of his resurrection and ascension, as PARRY suggests. The meaning of ἱλαστήριον, used substantively by the LXX to translate *kapporeth*, the « mercy-seat », is very much disputed [25]. It would appear that Paul is seeking to establish an analogy between the *religious significance* of the OT instrument of forgiveness of Israel's collective sins and the infinitely efficacious means provided in the NT (LYONNET). Christ, publicly exposed by the Father upon

---

[25] FRIEDRICH BÜCHSEL, JOHANNES HERMANN, ἵλεως, ἱλάσκομαι, ἱλασμός, ἱλαστήριον *TWNT III*, 300-324 ; L. MORALDI, *Sensus vocis* ἱλαστήριον *in Rom* 3,25 in *VD* 26 (1948) 257-276 ; T. W. MANSON, Ἱλαστήριον in *JTS* 46 (1945) 1-10 ; V. TAYLOR, *Great Texts Reconsidered* in *ExpT* 50 (1938-39) 295-300 ; L. MORRIS, *The Meaning of* ἱλαστήριον *in Romans* 3,25 in *NTS* 2 (1955-56) 33-43.

the cross *in his blood*, signifies *personally* the forgiving presence of God, who is thus revealed as faithful to his promises of redeeming mankind. Christ's blood shed on Calvary is to be considered the means by which the new covenant between the Father and the Christian people has been effected [26]. *to show his justice at work.* The variation in the prepositions εἰς and (v. 26) πρὸς has been explained as denoting the ultimate and more immediate purpose of God respectively (SANDAY-HEADLAM). It seems more probable however that Paul has employed two different prepositions because, as LYONNET has pointed out [27], he wishes to show the working of God's saving activity first with respect to the Chosen people, then with respect to the Gentiles. By the phrase, *those sins committed in the past*, Paul refers to the offenses of Israel against the covenant made with God and forgiven by him, particularly through the rite of the Day of Atonement. Paul says equivalently that the Jew must not think he has no need of Christ's redemptive death because his sins have already been forgiven by this OT ritual, for by its very nature this divine forgiveness was imparted beforehand only in anticipation and because of Christ's dying for the sins of all. Thus this initial pardon was, of its very nature, a relative, not an absolute thing, and consequently is not called an ἄφεσις but a πάρεσις, [27a] which does not replace but rather presupposes the definitive and unique manifestation of God's justice upon Calvary [28]. This is the first aspect of this ἔνδειξις [28a], for Paul has been endeavouring to prove to the Jew in the preceding section that he, no less than the Gentile, has an imperative need of being saved through Christ's

---

[26] It will be remembered that the Day of Atonement among the Jews was a kind of renewal of the Covenant Yahweh had made with his people which they had violated by sin. J. BONSIRVEN, *op. cit.* 164 : « Rédemption que Dieu opère par la fonction qu' il assigne à Jésus-Christ. Elle accomplit le dessein divin figuré dans la fête de l'Expiation (*Kippour*) ».

[27] LYONNET, in his commentary, p. 83, n. *e.*, says : « Ce demi-pardon, une sorte de non-imputation ... plutôt que de sursis, n'avait de sens qu'en vue du pardon définitif, destruction totale du péché par la justification de l'homme ». He explains his position most convincingly in *Notes sur l'exégèse de l'Épître aux Romains* in *Bib* 38 (1957) 40-61 ; and we have followed his interpretation here as faithfully as possible.

[27a]. LYONNET, *art. cit.* 57-59.

[28] It must be recalled that throughout this passage there is no question of God's « vindictive » justice, which Paul describes by the term « God's anger » : cf. LYONNET, *art. cit.* 48-49.

[28a]. LYONNET, *art. cit.* 44, n. 2.

death. Even if, as BULTMANN believes [29], vv. 24-25 are a citation from some traditional Christian credal formula, this explanation seems by far the most satisfactory solution to a difficult passage.

v. 26. *in God's patience*. The phrase, as LYONNET has shown [29a], is to be taken in close connection with the divine, anticipated *pardon* of the preceding verse (and for this reason it appears there in our translation). The words describe God's attitude towards the sins of his covenanted people in the period when the Mosaic ritual and code remained in force. In this era, God showed himself « patient » by deploying his salvific activity to condemn and forgive his people's sins only in relation to an event that he knew was to come in the future. God « contented himself », so to speak, by anticipating the benefits of Christ's death, the central act of salvation-history.

to show his justice at work in the present era. The word which Paul uses here to designate the Christian dispensation, καῖρος, means the time determined by divine providence. This display of God's justice now includes all, even the Gentiles ; for Paul's thesis is the absolutely universal redemptive character of Christ's saving death. Its effects are extended, not only to the past sins of Israel, but to the sins of all mankind. The result is the definitive revelation of God's justice : *he is just and the one who justifies*. Once God's justice is understood in the biblical sense in which Paul has been using it throughout this first section of his letter, there is no need to consider that any opposition exists between these two ideas. God is faithful to his promises of salvation, given in the OT, because of his saving activity in imparting forgiveness to all men through Christ's death and conferring justification or sanctity upon the sinner [30]. Man's only response in this divine dialogue between himself and the just God is *faith in Jesus*, i. e. faith which unites the Christian to Jesus, who having by his death unleashed the dynamic of God's saving activity is now, in his risen state, the very embodiment of « the redemption found in Christ Jesus » (v. 24). In this whole passage, the thought of Christ's resurrection as part of the Christian salvation-event is only remotely implied, since Paul is preoccupied with the divine forgiveness of sin (and particularly

[29] R. BULTMANN, *Theologie des Neuen Testaments*, 47 : « Es liegt also offenbar ein Satz der Tradition vor, der vielleicht auf die Urgemeinde zurückgeführt werden darf ». Cf. the critique of this position by LYONNET, *art. cit.* 56.

[29a]. LYONNET, *art. cit.* 59.

[30] CERFAUX, *op. cit.* 239.

of Israel's past sins). This aspect of Christ's work the Apostle connects with the redemptive death, while relating the new life of grace to the resurrection : « he was handed over for our sins, and raised for our justification » (Rom 4,25).

§ 3. - The Function of Christ's Death and Resurrection in Man's Redemption. Rom 4,25

Having completed his development on the divine justice, Paul illustrates and confirms it from the history of Abraham : 4,1-25 (LYONNET). Abraham, « father of us all », Gentile as well as Jewish Christians, attests that justification comes by nothing man can do but only through faith in God's promises and by his free gift (v. 16). The accent is on the reliability and the gratuity of the divine promise. The object of Abraham's faith is « the God who brings the dead to life, and calls into being what is non-existent » (v. 17). Equivalently, Paul declares, the object of Christian and of Abrahamitic faith is the same, since we believe in « him who raised Jesus our Lord from the dead » (vv. 23-24). In the verse we have to consider, Paul adds a further specification to the object of Christian faith. It is salvific precisely because it comprehends the total act of man's redemption by Christ.

(Jesus Christ our Lord) 15 who was handed over for our sins, and raised for our justification.
[Instead of δικαίωσιν, δικαιοσύνην is read by D (corr.) and several Greek minuscule mss.].

The history of the exegesis of this text reveals some very interesting interpretations, which in turn reflect various theological trends in soteriological thought [31]. Even in recent years, the verse has been understood in a number of ways, which vary according to the exegete's conception of Paulinism [32].

---

[31] D. M. STANLEY, *Ad Historiam Exegeseos Rom* 4,25 in *VD* 29 (1951) 257-274.

[32] D. VÖLTER, *Die Verse Röm 3,22b-26 und ihre Stellung innerhalb des ersten Kapitels des Römerbriefes* in *ZNW* 10 (1909) 180-183. This author finds these verses, viz. Rom 3,22b-26, contain a theory of justifying faith based on Christ's atoning death, which contradicts the viewpoint presented in Rom 4,24-25, viz. justi-

Who was handed over for our sins. This first half of the verse describes Christ's death by means of an allusion to the fourth Servant Song (cf. Is. 53,12). For this reason, BULTMANN considers the verse as a borrowing from some primitive Christian formula of the redemption familiar to Paul [33]. Whether or not this hypothesis be correct, the statement is admirably suited to serve as a point of departure for Paul's more characteristic view of the redemption. In Deutero-Isaias, prominence is given to the vicarious satisfaction [34] effected by the Servant's death (Is 53,4-6,8, 11-12). His free acquiescence in the divine plan of salvation is underscored by his exaltation (Is 52,13-15 ; 53,10-12) by Yahweh as his reward for obedience, a quality of his work implied by his characterization as a lamb (Is 53,7). The antithesis sin-justification found in this Servant Song is admirably adapted to the context of Paul's development [35] in this first section of his letter to Rome.

At the same time, it is to be noted that certain values which we are accustomed to find in Paul's view of Christ's redemptive death are not expressed in the formula he here employs. The Apostle contents himself with the Deutero-Isaian expression in which the love-motif remains latent. Moreover, Christ's « handing over » is still (cf. Is 53,12) expressed passively. Finally, there is little insistence upon the solidarity of all men with Christ the Suffering Servant (present only by implication in Deutero-Isaias). In order to highlight this important aspect of Christian soteriology, Paul will combine the Servant theme with that of the Second Adam (cf. Rom 5,12-21).

Christ's death is here related to the forgiveness of man's sin, while his resurrection is connected with man's justification. The preposition διά with the accusative denotes a cause as operative in the mind of the agent. Here it is the intention which the Father had in « handing Christ over » and in raising him from death (the Father is undoubtedly implied as the agent responsible for both actions, since Paul habitually attrib-

---

fication by the Life-Spirit of the risen Christ in the believer. S. LYONNET (*La valeur sotériologique de la résurrection du Christ selon saint Paul* in G 39 (1958) 295-318) has shown how Rom 4,25 presents Christ's death and resurrection as the two essential aspects of the redemption as the mystery of God's love, considered in terms of efficient, not meritorious causality.

[33] BULTMANN, *op. cit.* 47.

[34] Cf. the nuanced description of this vicarious satisfaction given by C. CHARLIER, *Le Serviteur glorifié* in *BiViChr* 1 (1953) 56-77.

[35] CERFAUX, *op. cit.* 26.

utes Christ's resurrection to the Father's work). Paul has already discussed the function of Christ's death in the remission of man's sins (Rom 3,
24-25). In the next section of this epistle, he will correlate the new life
conferred in Baptism with the Father's act of raising Christ (6,4). He will
also discuss the relation between this new life and man's justification
(8,10). Accordingly the present verse is a *trait d' union* between the two
major dogmatic portions of Paul's epistle, and as such, recapitulates his
doctrine concerning the function of Christ's death and resurrection in
man's redemption.

he was raised for our justification. The term δικαίωσις is probably
employed as a simple synonym for δικαιοσύνη without any apprecia-
ble change of meaning [36]. What does Paul mean by stating that Jesus was
raised for our justification ? The parallel form of the sentence is dictated by something more than the canons of rhetorical elegance (vs OLTRA-
MARE). It is based upon Paul's insight into the meaning of the atonement.
Just as the Father revealed his justice in forgiving sins by means of Christ's
death, so too his raising of Christ manifests his fidelity to his promises
of salvation because this resurrection has resulted in our justification [37].
It is true to say that Christ's resurrection effects man's justification by
constituting the object of justifying faith (LIETZMANN). Yet the omission
of the phrase διὰ πίστεως here (cf. Rom 3,21,25) indicates that Paul
has in mind a more direct connection between Christ's rising to a new
life « with God » (Rom 6,10) and the Christian life which he here calls « our
justification ». As LAGRANGE notes, Paul's statement proves the existence,
in the Pauline conception of justification, of « un élément intérieur de vie »,
which is caused by Christ's resurrection. If the verse means anything,
it witnesses to a theological conception of the atonement in which
Christ's resurrection plays a role, with respect to man's justification, that
is in the same category of causality as his death, with respect to man's
forgiveness [37a].

---

[36] Generally speaking, Greek nouns like δικαίωσις are *nomina actionis*, while
those with a desinence like δικαίωμα denote the result of an action. It is doubtful
whether the distinction was preserved in NT Greek. In Rom 5,18b, δικαίωσις is
in contrast with κατάκριμα (which in Rom 5,16 is opposed to δικαίωμα).

[37] GODET, in his commentary, is certainly wrong in considering that our
justification is the moral cause of Christ's resurrection.

[37a]. S. LYONNET, *La valeur sotériologique de la résurrection du Christ selon
Saint Paul* in G 39 (1958) 295-318, provides a magnificent exposition of St Thomas' thought concerning the nature of this causality.

§ 4. - **Redemption as a Manifestation of Divine Love. Rom 5,8-11**

This passage belongs to the transitional paragraph between the theme of divine justice and man's justification, and that of divine love and man's eschatological salvation (LYONNET). The apostle transposes the doctrine of the reconciliation (cf. 2 Cor 5,18-21) in terms of God's (and Christ's) love for men. These verses are an expansion of the statement that « the love of God is poured forth in our hearts through the gift of the Holy Spirit to us » (5,5b). This outpouring of divine love is the result of Christ's death which has destroyed our sinfulness and of his resurrection which has effected that union with the risen Lord, which is the normal condition of the Christian (HUBY). This divine love guarantees our ultimate salvation, the eschatological « redemption of our bodies » (Rom 8,23).

8 For God demonstrates his own love for us by the fact that, whilst we were still sinners, Christ died on our behalf. 9 How much more then, now that we are justified by his blood, shall we be saved by him from wrath. 10 For if, though we were enemies, we were reconciled with God through the death of his Son, how much more, since we have been reconciled, shall we be saved by his life. 11 And moreover, our ground for boasting [is] in God through our Lord Jesus Christ, through whom we have obtained our reconciliation.

[8a. The reading τὴν ἑαυτοῦ ἀγάπην εἰς ἡμᾶς ὁ Θεός which we follow with Merk and Nestle is attested by Sin., Alex., Ephrem *rescr.*, etc. D. with E, F, G, L, read simply ὁ Θεός εἰς ἡμᾶς.

11. There is some slight ms. authority for καυχώμεθα instead of the participle. It is also found in the *vet. lat.* and the Peshitto versions].

v. 8. *God proves his own love for us.* As in 2 Cor 5,18 ff., Paul ascribes the redemptive work of Christ to the Father as principal source. In this passage however, which is a more developed formulation of 1 Thes 4,14 [38], he dwells explicitly upon the motive of divine love. God has « put together a proof of his love » [39]. The first part of the proof lies in the fact that *whilst we were still sinners, Christ died on our behalf.* The second part, implicitly stated in v. 10b, is the communication of Christ's risen life to us in order to complete the work of reconciliation. The third part, v. 9b,

---

[38] CERFAUX, *op. cit.* 86.
[39] συνίστημι means literally « to construct a whole of various parts » (PARRY).

consists in our eschatological salvation, stated negatively as a deliverance *from wrath*, then positively, v. 10b, as a being saved *by his life*.

Christ died on our behalf. These words imply the very close union existing between Christ's love for men and that of the Father (GODET) [40]. The phrase *on our behalf* is taken directly from the apostolic kerygma (cf. 1 Cor 15,3).

v. 9. *we are justified by his blood.* The phrase *by his blood* is not exactly the equivalent of *through the death of his Son* in v. 10 (LIETZMANN) [41], although it does indicate that, on Paul's view, the Christian's justification is a real quality (LAGRANGE). Just as Paul has already (Rom 4,25) referred man's justification to Christ's resurrection [42], so now he refers it to his death, — a fact which proves that in Pauline soteriology both death and resurrection are conceived as two movements of the single redemptive act. *We shall be saved by him from wrath.* The eschatological ὀργὴ Θεοῦ will be definitively manifested at the final judgment (Rom 2,5), and it is of that moment Paul is thinking primarily. However, as is clear from Rom 1,18-3,20, God's wrath manifests itself in the course of history also. Justification does not free the Christian from the conflict with evil (PARRY).

v. 10. The *a fortiori* argument of v. 9 is now repeated in more general (JACONO), or perhaps rather, more positive (LAGRANGE) terms : *enemies* instead of *sinners, reconciled* instead of *justified*, deliverance *by his life* instead of *from wrath*. The conception of the atonement as a reconciliation of man with God is expressed, in the entire NT, only in Paul's letters [43]. The passive form of the verb used here shows that the change is

---

[40] CERFAUX, *op. cit.* 100 : « L'amour du Christ fait penser à l'amour de Dieu. Saint Paul confond volontairement les deux. Il passe de l'un à l'autre dans la même phrase ».

[41] S. LYONNET has shown that the function of Christ's blood in the *NT* is already typified in *OT* ritual (blood of the paschal lamb, of the Sinaitic covenant, of the sacrifice on the Day of Atonement) and is, in consequence, to be understood in a similar, if infinitely more perfect, manner : cf. the section on *Le rôle du sang* in *Introduction à la Bible II*, 869-874. For the Hebrews, the function of the blood of the victim was essentially to symbolize the people's consecration to Yahweh and their purification. It *did not represent* the penalty of death due to sin, inflicted, by divine consent, upon a substitute victim.

[42] Paul normally thinks of man's justification positively, i. e. in terms of the new life communicated by the Spirit of the risen Christ : cf. 8,1 ff.

[43] In addition to Paul's Corinthian and Roman epistles, the idea is found in Col 1,20-22 and Eph 2,16.

effected entirely in man and that it is principally God's work [44], though
man's cooperation is stated elsewhere (2 Cor 5,18.20).

While it is clear from the parallelism between vv. 9-10 that justification
and reconciliation are synonyms, [45], still this metaphor of reconciliation
will provide Paul with a new application of the theme in the Roman
Captivity epistles : the *entente* between Jews and Gentiles in the Christian
Church. *through the death of his Son.* The phrase sets in relief the love of
God for men. His love has gone to the lengths of sacrificing his only Son
for us, a fact which hints that the divine love for man is *paternal*, and so
underscores the reality of man's adoptive filiation (Gal 4,4 ff. ; Rom 8,15).
we shall be saved by his life. The salvation meant is the glorious resurrection (Rom 8,23). The *life* is that of the risen Christ communicated to us
already by his gift of the Spirit, mentioned explicitly in v. 5. It is this
participated life, mentioned in 2 Cor 4,10-11 and described here as our
justification or reconciliation, which, on Paul's view, constitutes the internal principle of our future resurrection. This verse belongs to that series
of texts (1 Cor 6,14 ; 15,20-22) which assert an intrinsic relation between
Christ's resurrection and that of the just, and which are in contrast with
Paul's earlier view (1 Thes 4,14 ; 2 Cor 4,14), where the connection is
affirmed purely in terms of God's will.

v. 11. *our Lord Jesus Christ.* This formula, with slight variations [46], is
used as a finale in each of the chapters of this section on the love of God
(Rom 5,21 ; 6,23 ; 7,25 ; 8,39). It commemorates Jesus who is the Christ
and who, through his resurrection, became the Lord of the universe, whom
the Christian awaits in his parousia [47]. By communicating his life to the
justified Christian, the risen Christ constitutes the « boast » in God [48],
previously described as based on « the hope of the glory of God » (v. 2),
the eschatological blessings accompanying the resurrection of the just.

§ 5. - The Risen Christ as Second Adam. Rom 5,19

The remainder of ch. 5 is devoted to a sketch of Christ as the second

---

[44] FRIEDRICH BÜCHSEL, καταλλάσσω, ἀποκαταλλάσσω, καταλλαγή, *TWNT I*,
254-259.

[45] CERFAUX, *op. cit.* 111.

[46] LYONNET, *art. cit., Note sur le plan ...* 303, n. 8.

[47] It corresponds to the phrase in the Ap 1,4.8 ; 4,8.

[48] Can there be a reference to the primitive Christian liturgy ? Cf. LIETZ-
MANN's remarks in his commentary.

Adam, the fullest development of this theme found in Paul's epistles. The doctrine appears as a conclusion [49] from the fact of Christian experience, that the believer has been reconciled with God by the vivifying union with the risen Christ [50]. By employing the principle of the Christian's solidarity with Christ, Paul sketches another, sinful solidarity opposed to it, the solidarity with Adam [51].

However, it is rather the Pauline doctrine of the second Adam and not the theology of Original Sin which interests us in this passage. As PRAT has remarked, the pericope provides the most complete and original picture of Christ as redeemer which Paul has left us [52]. Its originality may be gauged by the fact that it represents a new synthesis in which there appear combined the theological values inherent in the earlier, Palestinian presentation of Christ as the 'Ebed Yahweh together with certain advantages found in the Adam symbolism of the OT creation story. The great contribution of this new image of Christ as the second Adam is its essentially representational character [53]. We have seen that the mysterious identification of the Christian community with Christ was a quality of the mystical experience which effected Paul's conversion [54]. Moreover, the principal point of contrast between Adam and Christ (disobedience — obedience) made this second Adam theme a particularly apt vehicle to express, more explicitly perhaps than in the Servant-*motif*, the basic idea underlying the view of Christ's death as vicarious atonement, viz. its voluntareity and complete liberty.

In the preliminary draft of the second Adam theme (I Cor 15,21-22 45-49), Paul insisted upon the solidarity of all Christians with Christ. His purpose in that passage was to set forth the radical opposition between the risen Christ as agent of the glorious resurrection of the just and Adam as author of natural life and of death (understood in the full, biblical sense). Less attention was drawn to the parallelism existing between

---

[49] The expression in v. 12, διὰ τοῦτο, is not to be overlooked.

[50] As LYONNET in his commentary p. 88 n. *b* observes, « la justice est, en effet, une première participation à la vie du Christ ressuscité ».

[51] It is of paramount importance for the understanding of this passage to remember that it is from the idea of our solidarity with Christ that Paul comes to express the doctrine of Original Sin. Cf. the pertinent remarks of BONSIRVEN, *op. cit.* 114 f.

[52] .PRAT, *op. cit. II*[7], 203.

[53] *ibid.* 208 f.

[54] Ch. II, p. 42.

12. - D. M. STANLEY.

Adam and Christ as type and antitype [55]. In this first exploitation of the theme, Paul does not appear to have considered Christ's role as second Adam except from the moment, at his own resurrection from death, when he assumed the « spiritual body », which enabled him to perform his office as bearer of the Spirit to men. It is only in the present paragraph that Paul begins to push Christ's role as second Adam back beyond his resurrection and to assert expressly that, already in undergoing death for the redemption of mankind, Jesus was acting as the new Adam.

That the Apostle never seems to have pursued the parallel further and developed its implications for the public life of Jesus [56] is perhaps an indication of the unfinished nature of Pauline soteriology on this point. More probably, however, this is due to a principle which is frequently seen to function in Paul's thought on the redemption, viz. that the Christ « in the flesh » was not, properly speaking, a redeemer. While in no sense a sinner himself, he did, in his unglorified state, belong to the sinful solidarity of the first Adam (cf. especially Rom 6,10 b ; Rom 8,3 ; Gal 4,4-6).

As we have remarked above, the earlier Servant soteriology appears in Paul's description of Christ as second Adam [56a]. The Deutero-Isaian phrase, « the many », which describes the rest of mankind in relation to the Servant, reappears throughout the present pericope (cf. vv. 15.19, where the expression is used twice).

The note of obedience, which appears here, as it did also in the hymn cited to the Philippians (Phil 2,8), is conceived in opposition to Adam's disobedience. Thus Paul makes explicit a conception which rightly belonged to the character of the 'Ebed Yahweh, but which was never actually expressed in the Fourth Servant Song.

This passage in Romans is of great interest to our study because it illustrates admirably the manner in which Pauline soteriology developed by making use of the theological values and biblical symbolism discovered and employed by previous apostolic tradition, and, at the same time, by imparting his own personal *cachet* to these data. The result was a new synthesis which we may rightly call Pauline in the proper sense of the term.

By means of a series of comparisons and contrasts [57], Paul passes

---

[55] PRAT, *op. cit. II*, 209.

[56] BONSIRVEN, *op. cit.* 90.

[56a]. L. BOUYER, 'ΑΡΠΑΓΜΟΣ in *RSR* 39 (1951-1952) 281-288 (*Mélanges Lebreton I*).

[57] PRAT, *op. cit. II*, 209 f.

quickly in review the whole period of sacred history from Eden to the coming of Christ [58], in order to work out the conception of Adam and Christ, each head of a solidarity which includes the whole of humanity. The verse we are considering expresses in its final form the Pauline analogy between the first and the second Adam.

For just as, through the disobedience of one man, the rest were constituted sinners, so too, through the obedience of one man, the rest will be constituted just.

[The Chester Beatty papyrus reads κατέστησαν for κατεστάθησαν].

This verse forms the climax of the contrast between Adam and Christ instituted with v. 15. Here the comparison beween the two is expressed in perfect parallel. The respective influence of each upon the human race is considered, not, as in v. 18, in its effects, but in its cause (LAGRANGE). Moreover, Adam's act is here finally designated as specifically one of disobedience in opposition to Christ's redemptive act, proclaimed in the apostolic kerygma as one of obedience (Phil 2,8). In v. 15, we have a general designation : Adam's is « an act of sin » παράπτωμα, Christ's, « an act of grace » (χάρισμα). The development which follows assumes the form of the Semitic *concatenatio* [59], and displays the activity of the first and second Adam first in its results, then in itself. Adam's παράπτωμα causes death, spiritual as well as physical, in his descendants (15a). The χάρισμα is described first as an act of the Father's benevolence (ἡ χάρις τοῦ Θεοῦ), then as « a gift of benevolence » (ἡ δωρεὰ ἐν χάριτι) of Christ (15c). The gift of the redemption however surpasses the sinful act of Adam. The judgment which he incurred resulted in the universal condemnation (κατάκριμα) of humanity, while Christ's gracious act caused justification in all believers, despite their many sins (16). Adam's sin brought the reign of death, his descendants with himself being reduced to a state of slavery. Those who accept Christ's superabundant and gratuitous gift of justification are snatched from that slavery and given a share in his Kingdom by the divine life communicated to them by the risen Lord (17). In verse 18, we have the reca-

---

[58] As LYONNET has pointed out in his commentary, there are four periods of sacred history sketched here : in Eden, before the giving of the Mosaic Law, after the Law, the coming of Christ.

[59] In which the relation of the thought-patterns is marked by the repetition of keywords or similar phrases.

pitulation of the whole movement of Paul's thought. Adam's παράπτωμα resulted in humanity's condemnation (κατάκριμα), while Christ's act of justice (δικαίωμα) produced « the justification that leads to life » (δικαίωσις ζωῆς).

through the disobedience of one man. Adam's sin was a transgression of God's command (v. 14). It entailed, because of the principle of solidarity, the constitution of a sinful progeny, both because of the transmission of Original Sin and the resultant actual sins of humanity. *through the obedience of one man.* To undo the disobedience of Adam, Christ freely performed the act whereby mankind was redeemed. It is remarkable that all through this passage there is nowhere any express reference either to his death or his resurrection, Paul's intention being to consider the atonement as primarily an internal act of will. The designation of Christ's work as an act of obedience, however, is, given the Servant theme of the apostolic preaching, an implicit reference to his death. The repeated mention of « life », which must be understood in its fullest, biblical sense (supernatural, eternal life), denotes the effects of his resurrection (vv. 17.18.21). *the rest will be constituted just.* The state of justification already obtained by all believers (cf. 5,1 ; the future tense merely allows for the continuance through history of Christ's justifying activity) results from Christ's redemptive obedience and provides the grounds for the solidarity of all Christians with their Lord.

This sketch of the redemption as the work of the second Adam adds considerably to its adumbration in 1 Cor 15,21-22 ; 45-49. In these earlier passages, the second Adam's activity is depicted in terms of the glorious resurrection of the just. Accordingly, the solidarity of all Christians with Christ « as vivifying Spirit » is there conceived as something only to be realized at his parousia, when « we shall bear the image of the heavenly man » (v. 49). In the paragraph we have been considering here, the theme of the second Adam has been transposed in terms of justification, grace, eternal life. If then Christ fulfils this function during the present Christian existence as well as at his second coming, he is presented as second Adam by his act of obedience to the Father, viz. in that double act by which « he was handed over for our sins and raised for our justification ». Paul sums up this new conception of the role of the second Adam at the end of the pericope by stating that « grace will hold dominion by means of justification leading to eternal life through Jesus Christ our Lord » (v. 21), that is through him who has attained universal dominion through his death and resurrection.

§ 6. - Baptismal Symbolism derives from Christ's Redemptive Work. Rom 6,3-11

The tradition of the primitive Church guarded the memory of a command given her by the glorified Christ in regard to Baptism (Mt 28,18 f ; Acts 2,38 ; 8,12 ; 10,48). By his will, it was designated as the ordinary means of obtaining the remission of sins, the gift of the Holy Spirit. It was the necessary mode of aggregation to the Christian community, even in the case of those whose conversion had been marked by extraordinary charisms (Acts 9,17-18 ; 10,48 ; 11,16-17). Paul had received the practice of Baptism from apostolic tradition. It was left to him however to develop the theology of its symbolism. It is instructive to observe that this development, in his epistles, appears to go hand in hand with the elaboration of his thought on « the body of Christ ». Before the Corinthian letters, references to Baptism are rare and somewhat vague (2 Thes 2,13 ; Phil 2,1). In 1 Cor 1,13, Paul first states the relation of Baptism to the death of Christ [60] : « Surely Paul was not crucified for you, nor were you baptized in the name of Paul ? » Later, the sacrament is explained as a rite of initiation into the community of the new Israel (10,1-2) [61]. This conception had already appeared in the theology of the primitive community (cf. Acts 2,47). More characteristically Pauline is the statement connected with the first sketch of « the Body of Christ » (1 Cor 12,4-31) : « Indeed in one Spirit all of us have been baptized into one Body whether Jews or Greeks, slaves or freemen » (v. 13 ; cf. also 6,17). As CERFAUX has conclusively shown [62], Paul asserts that it is the physical, risen Body which constitutes the community's unifying principle, the term « Christ » (v. 12) signifying not the « mystical « Christ, in the sense of a « tertium quid », distinct from Christ and the Christians united with him, but the glorified Lord himself with whom each Christian is mystically identified. In the passage we now wish to consider, Paul gives a completely evolved formulation of his baptismal doctrine.

3 You are surely aware that we, who were baptized into Christ Jesus, were baptized into his death. 4 We were then buried together with him by this baptism into his death that, just as Christ was raised from death by the glory of the Father, so

---

[60] D. M. STANLEY, *The New Testament Doctrine of Baptism* in *TS* 18 (1957) 205-206.

[61] D. M. STANLEY, *Baptism in the New Testament* in *Scr* 8 (1956) 52.

[62] CERFAUX, *La Théologie de l'Église suivant saint Paul*[2] (Paris, 1948) 205 ff.

also we may live by a new kind of life. 5 If we have grown together with him into
the likeness of his death, so also shall we grow with him into the likeness of his
resurrection. 6 For this we know : our old self has been crucified together with him,
in order that our sinful body be reduced to impotence, so that we are no longer
slaves to sin. 7 A dead man is in a state of freedom from sin. 8 Now, if we died
with Christ, we believe that we shall also share his life. 9 Indeed we know that Christ,
once raised from death, dies no more. Death no longer plays master over him.
10 The death he died was a death to sin once for all : the life he lives, he lives
to God. 11 So you likewise must consider yourselves dead with reference to sin,
but alive with respect to God in Christ Jesus.

[3. Ἰησοῦν is omitted by Vat. and some minuscule mss.
4. γάρ is read instead of οὖν by Origen, the Vulgate, and other Latin mss., while
the Peshitto and Armenian versions have no connective.
5. ἅμα is substituted for ἀλλά in G and the Latin mss. tradition.
8. γάρ is read for δέ by the Chester Beatty papyrus and G. The words τῷ Χριστῷ
are added to αὐτῷ in D (first corr.), the Vulgate and Peshitto versions, and
Ephrem.
11. εἶναι is omitted by Alex., D, E, F, G, the Chester Beatty papyrus, the Peshitto, Bohairic, Armenian and Ethiopic versions. The majority of better mss.
(Chester Beatty, Vat., Alex., Beza, G, 1739) omit τῷ Κυρίῳ ἡμῶν after Ἰησοῦ,
which is read by Sin., Ephrem rescr., the Vulgate, etc.].

v. 3. Paul's reply to the cynical objection of the libertine (v. 1 : we ought
to continue sinning that God's gift of grace may be increased) is to invoke
the authority of the *depositum fidei*. The phrase, *You are surely aware,*
shows that he is appealing to a tenet of the faith admitted by all (PAR-
RY) [63]. *we who were baptized into Christ Jesus.* HUBY, following PRAT [64],
considers the word *baptize* to have its primitive sense of « plunge » in
this sentence. It is sufficient to realize that, in the Christian technical
term, this original meaning is still operative in the sacramental symbolism
(LAGRANGE). This seems clear from the unusual form of the expression,
used only here and in Gal 3,27. Baptism is an act of incorporation into
Christ (SANDAY-HEADLAM) [64 bis]. *were baptized into his death.* Christ's
redemptive death is, on Paul's view, the point of departure of the Christian life. As CORNELY points out [65], Paul never says that we were born
with Christ, circumcized with Christ, baptized in the Jordan with Christ.

---

[63] Thus, it might be translated, « Of course, you believe ... ».

[64] PRAT, *op. cit. I,* 265.

[64 bis] GÜNTHER BORNKAMM, *Taufe und neues Leben bei Paulus* in *TB* 18
(1939) 235.

[65] R. CORNELY, *Commentarius in S. Pauli Apostoli Epistolas, I, Epistola
ad Romanos* (Paris, 1896) 316, n. 1.

He only employs these expressions to signify « those things which Christ performed after his exaltation on the cross » [66]. The reason for this is Paul's characteristic conception of Christ as redeemer, a role which begins only with his passion and death. For him, the « Christ according to the flesh » does not appear to exercise any salvific activity in Paulinism. Consequently, to be justified and (eventually) saved, the Christian must be united with Christ's act of being « handed over » to death for his sins and « raised for his justification ».

This verse recalls the history of Israel in the deliverance from Egyptian bondage, when, as a people, she was « baptized into Moses » (1 Cor 10,2). The result of Baptism, for Paul, is union with Christ in those acts specifically performed for man's salvation. Jesus had, during his mortal life, spoken of his own death as a baptism (Mk 10,38 ; Lk 12,50). It was left to Paul's genius to incorporate this idea into Christian baptismal theology [67].

How did Paul understand this union with the death of Christ which he asserts was accomplished for the individual Christian in Baptism ? Dom ODO CASEL has claimed that in the Christian's reception of this sacrament Christ undergoes a mystical death (and resurrection) [68]. W. T. HAHN has pointed out that, in the expression « we died with Christ in Baptism », it is the death of Christ which specifies the relation, not vice-versa [69]. J. COOLS has denied in his critique of CASEL's theory that there can be any question, in Pauline doctrine, of Christ's dying and rising at the moment of our Baptism [70]. He insists upon the ἐφάπαξ in v. 10, and asks, with reference to 2 Cor 5,14, how Paul could say we died and rose with Christ at a time when we did not exist. His solution is that we died « idéalement » with Christ on Calvary [70 bis]. One has the feeling that such a distinction does not advance the solution of the problem very far.

To find a satisfactory answer to this question, it will help to note

[66] ibid. 315. « de iis, quae Christus post suam exaltationem in crucem gessit ».
[67] OSCAR CULLMANN, Le baptême des enfants et la doctrine biblique du baptême (Neuchâtel-Paris, 1948) 13 ff.
[68] O. CASEL, Mysteriengegenwart in JL 8 (1928) 145-224 (cf. 157).
[69] W. T. HAHN, Das Mitsterben und Mitauferstehen mit Christus bei Paulus, 99.
[70] J. COOLS, La présence mystique du Christ dans le baptême in Mémorial Lagrange (Paris, 1940) 295-305.
[70 bis] ibid. 305 : « Il s'agit donc de la mort mystique de tous les hommes, qui eut lieu idéalement au Calvaire par la mort physique du Christ, leur représentant commun, et qui eut lieu réellement pour chacun d'eux au baptême, dans l'acte de leur incorporation au Christ ».

that Paul habitually uses the passive in expressing this baptismal dying and rising with Christ (Gal 2,20 ; Rom 6,4.5.6 ; Col 2,12 ; 3,1), the exceptions to this rule being 1 Thes 5,10 ; Rom 6,8 ; 8,17 ; Col 2,20. Moreover, it is clear from certain texts (Col 2,13 ; Eph 2,6 ; even Rom 8, 29) that the Father is the agent here as he is in Christ's own death and resurrection (Rom 5,8 ; 8,32), and as he will be in our own eschatological resurrection (1 Thes 4,14 ; 2 Cor 4,14). Paul's use of verbs compounded with the preposition σύν would indicate that the Father's activity transcends time, terminating both in Christ's dying and rising and in the Christian's dying and rising with Christ in Baptism.

v. 4. *We were buried together with him by this baptism into his death*. Paul now expresses this union with Christ's death in terms of sacramental symbolism, as he will later in Col 2,12. The burial of Christ was an important item in the apostolic kerygma inherited by Paul (1 Cor 15,4 ; Acts 13,29), who insisted on it not merely for its evidential value (PARRY) but also because Christ has been first revealed to him as one risen from death (cf. Acts 25,19) [71]. In the present discussion of Baptism, Paul sees the neophyte's « burial » in the sacramental waters as a symbol of his union with Christ's death.

Christ was raised from death by the glory of the Father. In the OT [72], the miracles of the Exodus out of Egypt are attributed to the *kabod* of Yahweh (Ex 15,7.11 ; 16,7.10 ; Ps 113,9). Here Paul attributes to this same *glory* Christ's resurrection. He has made it clear in earlier letters that this *glory* is communicated to Christ's sacred humanity (2 Thes 2,14 ; 2 Cor 3,18 ; 4,6), thereby establishing him as « Son of God in power » (Rom 1,4), for our salvation (1 Cor 6,14). The Father's *glory* is synonymous with his power (Col. 1,11 ; 2 Thes 1,10). It is this *glory* communicated to Christ's humanity which causes in the baptized *a new kind of life*, that « justification leading to eternal life » (Rom 5,21). Paul's teaching on Baptism is a corollary of his second Adam doctrine in ch. 5 (DODD) [73].

v. 5. The expression is involved because of a mixed metaphor [74]. We have

---

[71] J. VENNE, *St Paul's Three Chapters on Holiness* (London 1877) 11.

[72] M. -E. BOISMARD, *Le Prologue de Saint Jean* (Paris, 1953) 71.

[73] The conception of Baptism as a sacrament of initiation into the Christian community belongs to the primitive apostolic teaching : Paul's theology specifies this character of the sacrament further by pointing out that it is our incorporation into Christ as Second Adam.

[74] PAUL GAECHTER, *Zur Exegese von Röm. VI*, 5 in *ZKT* 54 (1930) 88-92.

« grown into Christ » : we have been « fashioned after the pattern of his death and resurrection » [75] ». Since Paul clearly considers our participation in Christ's double redemptive act as something very real (LIETZMANN), he may have fused these two figures together in order to insist upon the reality of what happens in Baptism. It does not depend upon any effort of the human imagination, nor even entirely upon man's will : it is something wrought by grace in the baptismal experience [76]. We are not « to act as if » we were dead to the old life : *we are dead, we have been raised to an entirely new existence* [77]. The second half of this chapter will sketch the consequences of this truth for the practice of Christianity [78].

So also shall we grow into the likeness of his resurrection. Paul's thought is not entirely clear here, perhaps because we are dealing with another transitional stage in his theology. It is to be noted that nowhere in this paragraph does Paul state explicitly that we have been raised with Christ in Baptism (as he will in Col 2,12), although he implies it. The future tense of the verb here may be taken as logical, or perhaps better, in view of the following verses, as envisaging our participation in Christ's resurrection less as something already accomplished in Baptism, and rather as the practice of a risen life imposed upon the Christian (LAGRANGE). The thought is akin to that expressed in Phil 3,10-12 ; 2 Cor 3,18 ; 4,10 ; 5,15.

v. 6. *our old self has been crucified together with him.* The expression, ὁ παλαιὸς ἄνθρωπος, likely an invention of Paul's, designates the human nature with which each man is born. The results of this co-crucifixion have been positively described in Gal 2,19-20. Here it is depicted as the reduction to impotence of man's sinful nature, as the liberation from slavery. This was the work accomplished by the second Adam, which benefits all who enter into solidarity with him through Baptism (VIARD).
v. 7. The general principle enunciated by this verse is applied primarily to Christ as second Adam (cf. Rom 5, 16b ; 1 Cor 15,55-57). By his death; he has broken the sinful solidarity which bound him through birth « under the Law » (Gal 4,4) to Adam. United to Christ's death in Baptism,

---

[75] R. SCHNACKENBURG, *Das Heilsgeschehen bei der Taufe nach dem Apostel Paulus* (München, 1950) 39-48.

[76] F.-J. LEENHARDT, *Le Baptême chrétien, son origine, sa signification* (Neuchâtel-Paris 1946) 51.

[77] E. PERCY, *Die Probleme der Kolosser- und Epheserbriefe*, 110.

[78] Cf. the excursus by LIETZMANN in his commentary : *Todestaufe und christliche Ethik*, 65-68.

the Christian also *is in a state of freedom from sin*. Such an explanation is to be preferred to that which regards the verse as a general juridical principle [79].

v. 8. *we believe that we shall also share his life*. Paul now considers the positive effect of our baptismal death with Christ as an entry into new life (PARRY). This new life which is inaugurated in this world can only be perceived by faith (LYONNET). For Paul, the Christian already participates in this new life [80]. Still it is instructive to note that he expresses it as something future (as he did in v. 4). Both moments are essential to the conception of the supernatural state of the Christian as life. In the Captivity epistles, Paul will dwell more upon this aspect of life as a present possession.

vv. 9-10. Paul underscores here the definitive character of Christ's death because he wishes to insist that the Christian's baptismal dying to sin must be « once for all. » It is Christ's death which broke sin's dominion over him, a dominion exercised insofar as he appeared, in his mortal life, « in the likeness of sinful flesh » (Rom 8,3). The construction of vv. 8-10 is modeled on vv. 5-7 (VIARD). Paul intends to show that it is being united through Baptism to Christ's death and resurrection that enables the Christian really to die to his selfish, sinful life and rise to the life of grace. The Christian existence is specified by Christ's twofold redemptive act, which inaugurates his function as the second Adam.

v. 11. This verse forms the conclusion of the paragraph and also the principle on which the exhortation, contained in the rest of the chapter, is based [81]. Just as Christ's sacred humanity has been withdrawn from the ambit of sin and belongs henceforth only to « the sphere of the divine », so the Christian, existing provisorily in the flesh, lives already in heaven (LYONNET). *in Christ Jesus*. The phrase, which appears here for only the second time in Romans (cf. 3,24), resumes the Pauline doctrine of the second Adam.

§ 7. - The Christian's Liberation from the Law. Rom 7,4-6

In ch. 5,12 ff, Paul dealt with Christ's work as second Adam inasmuch

---

[79] Cf. LAGRANGE in his commentary, who admits that it is surprising that Paul should give such « a rather trivial reason » for his statement in v. 6.

[80] CERFAUX, *Le Christ dans la théologie de saint Paul*, 87, considers that Paul is here thinking both of the eschatological resurrection of the just *and* of the present Christian life.

[81] *ibid.* 248.

as he freed us from sin and its consequence, total death [82]. In ch. 6,1-11, the second Adam is described as liberating the Christian from his selfish ego. In ch. 7,1-6, a third aspect of his work is presented : the liberation of the Christian from the Mosaic Law. PIERRE BENOIT [83] has pointed out the double perspective in Paul's attitude to the Law. It was « holy » (Rom 7,12.14.22 ; 8,7), instituted « for life » (Rom 7,10), although incapable of giving life (Gal 3,21). Paul could not share the naive view of his Jewish contemporaries that the works of the Law had the power to justify the sinner, or that the Law had produced the definitive economy of salvation (Gal 3,24). He was too much aware that, as it had functioned concretely in Israel's history, the Law had, by the perverse will of men, been an instrument of death (Gal 3,19 ; Rom 7,13). In the present paragraph, Paul begins by enunciating the principle, illustrated by marriage, that death terminates the Law's power over its subjects (vv. 1-3).

4 And so, my brothers, you also were made to die to the Law through Christ's body, so as to belong to another, to him who was raised from death that we might produce fruit for God. 5 When we depended on our weak sinful selves, our desires for sinful things [made possible by] the Law, misused our [natural] powers to produce fruit for death. 6 But now we have broken with the Law, since we have died to that which held us enslaved, so as to offer a new kind of service through the Spirit and not the old, outmoded servitude according to the letter.

[6. Instead of ἀποθανόντες, τοῦ θανάτου is read by D, the Vulgate, Ambrosiaster, Augustine, Pelagius. Ἡμᾶς is omitted by Vat., G.].

The example drawn from the dissolution of the marriage-bond which Paul uses at the beginning of this section has greatly embarrassed the commentators : for apparently, it is the wrong person who dies. V. 4 makes it clear that the widow represents the Christian Church ; but what does the dead husband stand for ? Is it the permanent ego in the state prior to Christian conversion (SANDAY-HEADLAM, PARRY), or Christ who was subject to the Law during his mortal life (KÜHL, CERFAUX), or « the old self » who enslaved the ego (PRAT), or the Mosaic Law (LIETZMANN) ? Actually this would seem to be a false problem, which has been raised due

---

[82] THOMAS BARROSSE, *Death and Sin in St. Paul's Epistle to the Romans* in *CBQ* 15 (1953) 438-459.

[83] PIERRE BENOIT, *La Loi et la Croix d'après saint Paul* (Rom. VII, 7-VIII, 4) -n *RB* 47 (1938) 481-509.

to a tendency natural to our western mentality of allegorizing an important detail in this parable.

v. 4. *You also were made to die to the Law through Christ's body*. What does the expression *Christ's body* mean ? Is it the crucified body of Christ (SANDAY-HEADLAM) ? Is it the « pre-resurrection body of Christ » (PARRY) ? Is it his « mystical » Body [84] ? It is the sacred humanity of the second Adam who « was handed over for our sins and raised for our justification » (Rom 4,25). By virtue of their baptismal solidarity with the second Adam, the Christians participate in Christ's dying and rising by which he rid himself of his « body of flesh » and acquired a « spiritual » body (1 Cor 15,44b-46) (LYONNET). When the second Adam died in this body which was « in the likeness of sinful flesh » (Rom 8,3), then « all died » (2 Cor 5,14).

so as to belong to another. Nowhere perhaps is Paul so conscious of the difference between the state of the mortal Christ and his risen state, as he is here. The Christian is united to Christ in his death, and so *made to die through Christ's body*. But the purpose of that union is *to belong to another*, to the second Adam, the glorified Lord. Union with Christ's death is necessary if the Christian is to die to the Law. More important, it is necessary if he is, with Christ risen, *to live to God in Christ Jesus* (Rom 6,11). The result of this « new marriage » is wholly supernatural, *that we might produce fruit for God*.

vv. 5-6. Here we have a further explanation of v. 4. V. 5 summarizes the history of humanity's solidarity with the first Adam (cf. 5,12-21 ; 7,7-24). As in chapters 2-3, Paul equivalates man's state under the Law with the absence of Christ's grace [85]. This is *the servitude according to the letter*, which is now outmoded, thanks to Christ's death and resurrrection. Opposed to it is *a new kind of service through the Spirit*, to be described fully in ch. 8. The source of the Christian life, according to Paul, is the indwelling of the Spirit in the believer (2 Cor 2,3), which makes him aware of his divine adoption (Gal 4,6), bestows on him the Father's love (Rom 5,5), unites him so closely to the risen Christ (Rom 8,9-11), to the point where the Spirit's dynamic presence coalesces with that of the glorified Christ (2 Cor 3,16-18).

---

[84] H. SEESEMANN, *Der Begriff KOINONIA im Neuen Testament* in *BZNW* 14 (Berlin, 1933) 36.

[85] Thus Sin (here personified) is the tyrannical power enslaving man (not the Law as HUBY maintains in his commentary).

§ 8. - The Atonement as a Work proper to God as Father, to Christ as Son. Rom 8,3-4

Having reviewed Christ's liberation of the Christian from sin-death, self, the Law, Paul now describes the Christian's assurance of eschatological salvation as a work proper to the Father and the Son. In connection with his first theme, Paul sketched the atonement as the definitive manifestation of God's fidelity : his activation of his promises of salvation (3,21-26). He now begins to construct a new thesis which will conclude (cf. 8,31-39) that man's redemption is the effect of divine love incarnate « in Christ Jesus our Lord » (8,39). In the earlier picture, Christ's death was uppermost in Paul's mind, the risen Christ being referred to only once (3,24). Now attention is directed to the glorified Christ : « Christ Jesus is he who died, or rather, he who was raised » (8,34).

Since the development in 7,7-24 must be considered a digression, the opening remarks of ch. 8, which are stated as a conclusion of an argument [86], should be connected with the verses we considered in the last section (7,4-6). In sharp contrast with the previous state of condemnation [87], the present union of the Christian with Christ Jesus (8,1), the work of the Holy Spirit, « the Spirit of life », frees him from total death [88].

3 Now God, by sending his own Son in the likeness of sinful humanity and on account of sin, condemned sin in that humanity (a task impossible for the Law, seeing it was reduced to utter helplessness by sinful human nature), 4 in order that the justice of the Law might be fulfilled in us, whose conduct is governed not by sinful human nature but by the Spirit.

[3. καὶ περὶ ἁμαρτίας is omitted, probably through haplography, in a few minuscule mss.].

---

[86] The connective ἄρα appears to indicate here (as usually) the introduction of the conclusion of an argument.

[87] The term κατάκριμα expresses the state of condemnation resulting from sin, not an act of condemnation : cf. CORNELY, op. cit. 297 where the word is explained as « condemnatio executioni mandata ». Apart from this text, the expression occurs only in Rom 5,16b and 5,18. Note that in the latter verse, it is contrasted with δικαίωσις ζωῆς which is the *state* of justification. The effects of the divine condemnation, which constitute the state of the human race since Adam, are graphically described in 7,13-24.

[88] A. HULSBOSCH, *Passibilitas et mors Christi in doctrina soteriologica S. Pauli* in *DThomasP* 47-49 (1944-46) 216 : « Necesse est notemus liberationem a damnatione oriri ex interna hominis renovatione, qua ex carnali spiritualis efficitur ».

v. 3. An anacoluthon makes the work of translating the verse awkward, although the meaning is clear. Paul refers to the event in the Salvation-history which effected the Christian's existence « in Christ Jesus » and freed him from « condemnation » or « the law of sin and death »[88a]. By an act of paternal solicitude towards his sons amongst men, God did what the Law failed to do : he bestowed eternal life through his Son by the gift of the Holy Spirit (8,11,14). *by sending his own Son.* The emphatic possessive pronoun underscores the community of the divine nature between the Father and the Son (SANDAY-HEADLAM). Paul is thinking of the sacrifice of Isaac (Gn 22,16), a type of God's love of us (cf. 5,8-10 ; 8,32). This divine gift to man contains all other gifts (v. 31). Paul includes Christ's incarnation and mortal life in the participle πέμψας : they are preparatory to the condemnation of sin[89]. On Paul's view, it is only with Jesus' passion and death that his properly redemptive role begins. *in the likeness of sinful humanity.* There is no hint of suggestion that Christ's human nature was not real : it was like ours, except for sin (2 Cor 5,21 ; cf. Heb 4,15), insofar as Christ, « born under the Law », entered the solidarity headed by the first Adam by becoming passible and mortal (LYONNET). In the LXX version of Is. 53,10 the phrase περὶ ἁμαρτίας translates the term *ašam*, a sin-offering, a figure which formed part of the Deutero-Isaian Suffering Servant's picture (Is 53,3). Accordingly, it is thought by some that Paul represents Christ as an offering for sin here (SANDAY-HEADLAM, PARRY), although some modern commentators prefer to keep the reference more general (LAGRANGE, LIETZMANN, LYONNET). Hence we have translated the expression *on account of sin.*

God condemned sin in that humanity. What was the nature of this condemnation in Paul's eyes ? LAGRANGE'S view that « God condemned sin by the incarnation of his Son » is unacceptable, since Paul only regards Christ's redemptive work as effected by his death and resurrection. Nor, as PIERRE BENOIT maintains, can Christ's mortal life be included[90]. BE-

---

[88a]. The Greek aorist participle normally, as here, expresses an act anterior to the tense of the main verb : M. ZERWICK, *Graecitas Biblica*[2] § 195.

[89] For a helpful discussion of the reality expressed by means of the juridical terminology in this passage, cf. the remarks of S. LYONNET, *Mort du Christ et victoire sur Satan (La sotériologie paulinienne)* in *Introduction à la Bible II*, 885-887.

[90] P. BENOIT, *art. cit.* 496 : « il serait étrange que, cette seule fois, Paul insiste sur la conduite du Christ parmi nous, comme il ne le fait nulle part ailleurs ».

NOIT considers the condemnation of sin to consist in Jesus' death as a penalty paid to the Mosaic Law [91]. To this it may be objected that, for Paul, the death-penalty imposed by the Law for sin included eternal death (Rom 6,23), which cannot in any sense be applied to Christ. WEISS, whose view is shared by HOLTZMANN [92], considers that Christ's victory over temptation is what is meant here. Such a view is singularly un-Pauline. For SANDAY-HEADLAM, « the key to this difficult clause is supplied by ch. VI. 7-10 ». That passage shows that Christ's victory over sin occurs, not in the incarnation, nor in his sinlessness during his mortal life, but in his death and resurrection. LIETZMANN remarks that the power of sin which made itself felt in Jesus' σάρξ was overcome by the πνεῦμα, so that he remained sinless.

It would appear from the whole context of ch. 8 that Paul included Christ's resurrection as well his death in this condemnation of sin in the flesh. This divine act brought it about that « there is no condemnation for those in union with Christ Jesus », i. e. with the glorified Christ (v. 1), since the Christian now obeys « the law of the Spirit of life in Christ Jesus » (v. 2). In the paragraph immediately following (vv. 5-13), the Christian life is called « spiritual » (v. 5) because of the inhabitation of « the Spirit of God », or « of Christ » (v. 9), or of Christ himself (v. 10). Accordingly, as LYONNET observes, it was « by his death, inseparable from his resurrection, that Christ has destroyed sin's domination precisely there where sin had reigned, 'in the flesh' » [93]. By the phrase, ἐν τῇ σαρκί, Paul means primarily the sacred humanity of Christ, which by its glorification was freed from the only vestige of sin's power over it, passibility and mortality. This was however, for Paul, not an isolated instance, but an event of cosmic significance, which is re-enacted in the flesh of every Christian (LIETZMANN).

v. 4. *in order that the justice of the Law might be fulfilled in us.* The purpose of the redemption is stated in terms of δικαίωμα, a term which here means « that which is laid down as right » (SANDAY-HEADLAM), or all the commandments of the Law taken collectively. Paul is hinting here

---

[91] *ibid.* 505 f, 509.

[92] H. J. HOLTZMANN, *Lehrbuch der Neutestamentlichen Theologie II* [2], 82.

[93] S. LYONNET, in his commentary, p. 100 n. *c* : « Seul le Christ par sa mort victorieuse « a condamné le péché » ... là précisément où le péché régnait, « dans la chair », passant le premier de la condition charnelle à la condition spirituelle, devenant « esprit vivifiant » ... et par là capable de nous communiquer l'Esprit ... ».

at something he will state more clearly later in this epistle (13,8-10) :
« Love is the fulfilment of the Law ». A new dynamism has been infused
into the Christian through Christ's death and resurrection, enabling him
to carry out to perfection the full scope of the Law. « God's love has been
poured into our hearts through the Holy Spirit who has been given to
us » (Rom 5,5). God's divine purpose will only be finally achieved with
the « redemption of our bodies » (v. 23), when the God « who raised Christ
Jesus from death » will complete the work he has begun in us by imparting « the Spirit of him who raised Jesus » and will cause us to rise
« through the Spirit who dwells within us » (v. 11).

These verses which speak of Christ's redemptive death and resurrection as a work proper to God as Father and to Christ as the Son imply
without asserting it explicitly that man's redemption was above all a
work of divine love. For in this gift of his Son, the Father has bestowed all
grace upon men (8,32). This love is manifested uniquely, in the mind of
Paul, by the risen Lord, « Christ Jesus who died, or rather who was raised »
(8,34). No one can deprive us of this salvation, « the love of Christ » for us
(8,35), or, to state it fully, « the love of God in Christ Jesus our Lord »
(8,39).

§ 9. - The Cosmic Effects of the Christian's Adoptive Sonship. Rom 8,19-23

In the course of ch. 8, Paul returns to the question of the Christian's
adoptive filiation (vv. 14 ff.). He had considered this theme in Gal 3,23-
4,7. He now gives us a sketch of its cosmic proportions.

19 Creation, with utmost eagerness, awaits on tip-toe the revelation of the sons of
God. 20 The created world has been doomed to disappointment, not of its own
accord, but on account of him who frustrated it, 21 [And so it waits] in hopeful
expectation, because creation itself will also be liberated from the enslavement of
corruption [in order to enjoy] the freedom of the glory of the sons of God. 22
We know indeed that the whole created universe groans and travails with the pangs
of childbirth until the present time. 23 And moreover, we ourselves, who possess
the firstfruits of the Spirit, are also groaning in our hearts, as we eagerly await
the redemption of our body.

[This whole pericope (19-22) is missing in Marcion.
20. For οὐχ ἑκοῦσα, οὐ θέλουσα is read by G, perhaps under the influence of the
Latin tradition. It is also found in the Vulgate, Irenaeus, and Hilary.
21 διότι is read by Sin., D (first corr.), G : ὅτι (adopted by Merk) is the reading

of the Hesychian and Byzantine recensions, as well as of the Chester Beatty papyrus.

22. For συστενάζει, several Greek minuscules read στενάζει together with the Peshitto, Armenian versions, Origen and Ambrosiaster. Instead of συνωδίνει, G reads ὀδύνει.

23. The term υἱοθεσίαν is omitted by the Chester Beatty papyrus, by 1739, D, G., Ambrose, Ephrem, Pelagius, etc.]

v. 19. As LAGRANGE remarks, this passage was a source of great embarrassment to the Fathers [94]. In recent years, it has again become a focal point of attention by the theologians who discuss the theology of work and the meaning of human civilization [95]. As the ancient commentators held, the word *creation* here denotes the irrational universe (LIETZMANN) which was cursed by Adam's fall (Gn 3,17-18). The highly expressive Hellenistic word ἀποκαραδοκία implies a « straining forward », lit. « an awaiting with outstretched head » (SANDAY-HEADLAM) ; hence our « on tip-toe ». The compound verb ἀποδέχεσθαι implies a concentrated waiting. *the revelation of the sons of God.* The Christian's adoptive filiation is always a present possession in the NT (cf. remarks on v. 23 *infra*), but its full manifestation must await Christ's second Coming, which Paul also has called an ἀποκάλυψις (2 Thes 1,7 ; 1 Cor 1,7). Paul here implies that the liberation of irrational creaturedom is bound up with this eschatological revelation of the adoptive sonship of the Christian. In adopting this view, Paul seems to be heir of the theological current of Jewish thought which held a kind of *harmonia praestabilita* to exist between the physical and moral worlds [96]. The difficulty of interpreting the passage is mainly due to the apocalyptic turn of expression which has been taken over from contemporary Judaism.

---

[94] Both LAGRANGE and CORNELY in their commentaries give the various patristic opinions.

[95] L. MALEVEZ, *La philosophie chrétienne du progrès* in NRT 64 (1937) 377-385 ; H.-M. FÉRET, *Apocalypse, histoire et eschatologie chrétienne* in *Dieu Vivant* § 2 (1945) 117-134 ; L. CERFAUX, *Le Royaume de Dieu* in VieSp 75 (1946) 645-656 ; J. HUBY, *Autour de l'Apocalypse* in *Dieu Vivant* § 5 (1946) 119-130 ; J. DANIÉLOU, *Saint Irénée et les origines de la théologie de l'histoire* in RSR 34 (1947) 227-231 ; *idem, La pensée chrétienne* in NRT 69 (1947) 930-940 ; G. FESSARD, *Théologie et Histoire* in *Dieu Vivant* § 8 (1947) 37-65 ; R. AUBERT, *Discussions récentes autour de la théologie de l'histoire* in ColMech 18 (1948) 129-149 ; G. THILS, *Théologie des réalités terrestres II. Théologie de l'histoire* (Bruges, 1949) ; R. AUBERT, *La théologie catholique au milieu du XXe siècle.* (Louvain, 1954).

[96] A. FEUILLET, *art. Isaie, VDBS IV*, 708, 720.

13. - D. M. STANLEY.

v. 20. Paul sums up the repercussions of Adam's fall in irrational nature
by saying that it has been made subject to ματαιότης, « ineffective-
ness », the disappointing emptiness of a promise unfulfilled. It is allied
to the Pauline conception of φθορά, « corruption », which he opposed
to ἀφθαρσία (1 Cor 15,42), and to ζωὴ αἰώνιος (Gal 6,8). The terms
have an essentially supernatural content, both « corruption » and « vanity »
being connected with sin. The material world, on Paul's view, shares
man's destiny, since it was created for him and is, as a result of Adam's
sin, found at present in a violent state of frustration or corruption
(LYONNET). Thus it seems likely that by, *him who frustrated it,* Paul designates Adam (CHRYSOSTOM), or man in general (LYONNET), rather than
God (LAGRANGE, LIETZMANN).

v. 21. *creation itself will also be liberated.* Since man's redemption necessarily affects his material as well as his spiritual nature (v. 23), then the
material universe will somehow, through man's participation in the
« glory » proper to his adoptive filiation, come to share the freedom of
redeemed humanity. As LYONNET remarks, it is characteristic of Paul's
soteriology that the Christian does not sacrifice his body for his soul,
nor the material world for that of the spirit. In opposition to the basic
tenets of Hellenistic philosophy, Paul asserts that nothing in the material universe is excluded from the redemption. In this optimistic view
of creation, it is the resurrection of the body which is the operative factor. Thus, in God's raising of Christ, Paul finds the divine answer to the
problems of Jewish apocalyptic.

v. 22. *the whole created universe groans and travails.* The verb more probably means « groans in concert » (THEODORE of Mopsuestia says », στενάζει
συμφώνως »), as modern commentators agree (LIETZMANN, HUBY, LA-
GRANGE). It does not mean « groans with us ». *We know.* The Christian
knows that the irrational creatures cannot attain their end in the context of human sins, without Christ's redemptive work. He knows it by
faith through divine revelation (Gn 3,17), not by experience or scientific
observation. The whole creation is suffering the pangs of childbirth, as
Jesus had himself remarked (Mt 24,8 ; Mk 13,8), in order to bring forth
the new world, « the new heavens and the new earth » mentioned so frequently in Jewish apocalyptic tradition (Is 65,17 ; 66,12 ; Acts 3,21 ;
Ap 21,1 ; Mt 19,28 ; 5,18). This element of continuity in the historical
process is of paramount importance in any Christian theology of history[97].

---

[97] THILS, *op. cit. II,* 25.

v. 23. *we ourselves who possess the firstfruits of the Spirit*. This expectation of the « universal restoration » (Acts 3,21) is heightened in the Christian because of the Spirit who « comes to the aid of our weakness » (v. 26) and « intercedes for us with ineffable groanings » (v. 27). The Christian, already an adoptive son of God, possesses the ἀπαρχή of the Holy Spirit, a term which, like ἀρραβών (2 Cor 5,5), is a « first instalment » (SANDAY-HEADLAM, LIETZMANN, LAGRANGE). Paul is thinking primarily of the witness of the Spirit to our adoptive sonship (cf. v. 15 ; Gal 3,3 ff ; 4,6), and also, probably, of the charismatic gifts so abundantly bestowed upon the early Church. In the opinion of P. BENOIT [98], the term υἱοθεσία is interpolated into the text. The messianic notion of « adoptive sonship » (like that of « redemption » or « acquisition ») is ambivalent. Accordingly, it may be said to be at once an object of Chistian hope, and a present possession of the Christian. *the redemption of our bodies*. The lively expectation of the justified Christian is summed up in the Pauline eschatological σωτηρία (Rom 5,9-10 ; 8,24), which is described here as the deliverance of man's complete, material personality. For Paul, salvation reaches the whole man, not merely his soul ; and hence will be attained only with the glorious resurrection of the body. This Pauline conception must be kept in mind in order to grasp Paul's view of Christ's redemptive work. A lack of appreciation of this essentially eschatological character of Pauline soteriology has resulted in the modern, truncated theologies of the redemption, which are concerned only with Jesus' death, and neglect the function of his resurrection.

§ 10. - The Christian Profession of Faith and Christ's Resurrection. Rom. 10,9

After elaborating his second theorem, that God's love for man, revealed in Christ's death and resurrection, is our surest pledge of salvation (chs. 5-8), Paul anticipates an objection to his position : how explain the collective refusal of Israel to accept the Gospel ? In answering it, he manages to turn it into a Scriptural illustration of his theme (chs. 9-11). The present paragraph suggests that in rejecting the Christ, in whom the Law is fulfilled (v. 4), the Jews have refused to submit to God's justice, « attested

---

[98] P. BENOIT, « *Nous gémissons, attendant la délivrance de notre corps* » in *RSR* 39 (1951-1952) 267-280. We follow the practice of S. LYONNET in his translation of Romans in *BJ*, and omit the phrase here.

by the Law and the prophets » (Rom 3,21). Thus Judaism has come to refuse justification by faith, although Moses had, « in one of the least legalistic chapters of the Pentateuch » (LYONNET), already hinted at the new law of faith, Dt 30,12 ff. By employing a characteristically rabbinic argument [99], Paul demonstrates that justification by faith does not so much demand that man do something, but rather that he accept with faith what has already been done for him by God the Father : viz., Christ's descent into this world by the incarnation (v. 6), and his resurrection (v. 7). This is the symbol of Christian faith preached by Paul (v. 8), which demands public profession as well as internal assent.

If you confess with your mouth, « Jesus is Lord, » and you believe with your heart that God has raised him from death, you will be saved.

['Ιησοῦν Χριστὸν is read by the Chester Beatty papyrus and Alex. — Vat. reads ὁμολογήσῃς τὸ ῥῆμα ἐν τῷ στόματί σου ὅτι Κύριος 'Ιησοῦς, which is also found in the Sahidic version and in Clement of Alexandria.]

The text mentions the profession of faith before referring to the internal act which it presupposes, because of the text of Dt 30, 14 cited in v. 8. As CERFAUX remarks [100], Paul employs a credal formula which he has inherited from the Palestinian community : Jesus is *Kyrios* [101]. The object of this profession of faith is the present reign of the glorified Christ which unites his resurrection with his second Coming [102]. This in turn is based upon the essential act of faith in the Father's accomplishing of the redemption through Jesus' death and resurrection. Hence the passage shows that Pauline faith, although containing an element of confidence, is essentially an intellectual act. Even a Protestant critic like C. H. DODD, for whom Pauline faith is « fundamentally a trustful attitude towards God, not intellectual belief », is forced to admit that here at least Paul « seems to equate saving faith with belief in a certain proposition » [103].

---

[99] J. BONSIRVEN, *Exégèse rabbinique et exégèse paulinienne* (Paris, 1939) 306, 328, 331. Cf. also the remarks of S. LYONNET in his revision of J. HUBY, *Épître aux Romains*, 625-627, and his article in *Mélanges bibliques rédigés en l'honneur d'André Robert* (Paris, 1957) 494-506 : *Saint Paul et l'exégèse juive de son temps. A propos de Rom.*, 10,6-8.

[100] CERFAUX, *Le Christ* ... 350.

[101] R. BULTMANN, *Theologie des Neuen Testaments* 81, 124.

[102] CERFAUX, *op. cit.* 20.

[103] Cf. BULTMANN, *op. cit.* 313.

The verse provides us with evidence that the early Christian community's profession of faith in Christ's divinity reposes primarily on belief in his death and resurrection.

§ 11. - The Application of Soteriological Formulae to the Problem of Israel's Salvation. Rom 11,15

In the third section of his discussion of Israel's destiny (11,1-36), Paul insists that her infidelity is only partial and provisory (LYONNET). At this stage of the development of Paul's theology of history, he has come to the realization that before the collectivity of Israel can accept faith in Jesus as the Christ, « the full number of the pagans » must enter the Christian Church (11,25-26). What repercussion such a view had upon the early Church's expectations of a proximate parousia, we have discussed elsewhere [104]. What interests us here is how Paul's conception of Israel's rejection and conversion is based on his soteriology.

Indeed, if their rejection [signified] the reconciliation of the world, what will their admission [mean] but life from death ?

[κόσμῳ is read instead of κόσμου by the Peshitto and a few Greek mss. πρόληψις is attested by Ephr. rescr. and a few other mss.].

Paul has spoken of God's saving activity as a *reconciliation* earlier (5,10 ; 2 Cor 5,18-20) where it was effected « by the death of his Son ». Here it is expressed in terms of Israel's *rejection*. However, as Paul firmly believes and hopes, the *admission* of the Chosen people into Christian salvation is a certainty, reserved for some future date. He thinks of it as a « resurrection », *life from death*. Thus we catch a glimpse of the applicability of Paul's conception of the Christian life as a dying and rising with Christ to the status of the Jews. The Salvation-history as it has affected and will affect them is here translated by the Apostle in terms of Christ's death and resurrection. On Paul's view, history is not evolutionary : it consists of a series of crises, like Israel's *rejection* and *admission*. The reason for this theology of history is, of course, the events from which all history ultimately derives its meaning, the death and resurrection of Christ.

---

[104] *Kingdom to Church : The Structural Development of Apostolic Christianity in the New Testament* in *TS* 16 (1955) 19 f.

§ 12. - The Finality of Christ's Death and Resurrection. Rom 14,7-9

The last reference to Christ's redemptive activity in Romans is found in the section devoted to the duties of charity incumbent upon « the strong » with respect to « the weak ». In such a context, it is natural that Paul should remind his addressees of the repercussions of the Christian's actions upon his neighbour, and that he should give the basic reason for the essentially social character of the Christian vocation : our solidarity in Christ [105]. He has already alluded to this doctrine in 2 Cor 5,15 : the Christian's daily living is consecrated to him who died and rose to give Christian life a new orientation. Now the conception is widened to include even the Christian's death as an act of service of the risen Christ. Consequently, we may say that Romans ends where it began (Rom 1,4) with the Kingship of the risen Lord.

7 Indeed none of us lives for himself and none dies for himself. 8 While we live, we live for the Lord ; and when we die, we die for the Lord. And so, whether we live or whether we die, we are the Lord's. 9 For to this purpose Christ died and came to life : that he should be Lord both of the dead and of the living.

[8b. In place of ἀποθνήσκωμεν, some mss. read ἀποθάνωμεν, while for ἀποθνήσκομεν Sin. Ephr. *rescr.* and others read ἀποθνήσκωμεν. 9. The reading here adopted, ἀπέθανεν καὶ ἔζησεν, is the best attested : Sin., Alex., Vat., Ephr. *rescr.*, the Bohairic and Sahidic versions, Cyril. In G, the Vulgate, Ambrose, Pelagius, Origen, we find ἀπέθανεν καὶ ἀνέστη. D, Irenaeus read ἔζησε καὶ ἀπέθανε καὶ ἀνέστη while the Peshitto has ἀπέθανε καὶ ἔζησεν καὶ ἀνέστη].

v. 7. Even the paganism of antiquity realized that the individual cannot live his own life. However, the ancient civilizations tended to place man's finality in the city-state (cf. LAGRANGE). For the Christian who

---

[105] This doctrine we find reflected in the Fathers of the Church : e. g. St. Cyril, *In Joannis Evangelium*, lib. XI, *PG* 74,565 : Christ « came back to life, having broken the power of death, effecting the resurrection, not for his own benefit, inasmuch as he is Logos and God, but through himself and in himself granting this (grace) to us. For the whole of human nature triumphed in Christ over the bonds of death. » ; cf. also St. Ambrose, *De Fide Resurrectionis*, cited in *Breviarium Romanum*, Dom. V post Pascha, 2 noct., lect. vi : « For if he did not rise for us, then he did not rise, since he had no personal reason for rising ... For himself, the resurrection was not necessary, since the bonds of death did not hold him captive ; because, though as man he was dead, still in the city of death he was free ».

has died to the « old self » sacramentally in Baptism (Rom 6,6) and must continue to do so through the practice of Christianity (Gal 5,24), a selfish life is inconceivable.

v. 8. *whether we live or whether we die, we are the Lord's.* Not only must the Christian life be lived in union with Christ, and hence in direct dependence on him ; but in death also, the Christian must remain united to the risen Lord, since he, by dying, has changed the nature of death. Christian death, no less than Christian life, is revealed to Paul as « a new creation ». This view is novel indeed compared with the view of death taken by centuries of Jewish tradition, where, as we remarked earlier, it was regarded as a separation from the God of the living [106]. The present verse recalls 1 Thes 5,10, where Christ is pictured as he « who died for us, in order that whether we wake or whether we sleep, we may live together with him ». From the general context of that early epistle (cf. 1 Thes 4,14), we may say that the conception there was governed by the eschatological view which seeks in God's will the link between the glorious resurrection of the Christian and that of Christ. Now, in virtue of a deepening of his theological thought (cf. 1 Cor 6,17 ; Rom 8,9-11), Paul takes a more intrinsic view of this same truth.

v. 9. *that he should be Lord both of the dead and of the living.* In this statement of the purpose of the redemption, Paul returns to the notion of the Kingdom, of Christ's sovereignty, stressing his power even over the world of death. The emphasis appears in the word-order which is less natural than « the living and the dead » would be. It is to be noted that Christ's universal domination, a theme which will be taken up *ex professo* in the Roman Captivity letters, is the result of his resurrection as well as of his death. It is also interesting that the present statement contains the antithesis, death-life, rather than that of death-resurrection. It is characteristic of Paul's thought at this stage of his development that he conceives the Christian in this world as participating rather in Christ's new *life* than in his resurrection (cf. Rom 6,4-11). Only in his later letters, Colossians and Ephesians, will he state that the Christian has already been raised with Christ in this present state of existence.

---

[106] Ch. V, p. 123.

CHAPTER VIII

PAUL'S LETTERS TO THE COLOSSIANS AND TO THE EPHESIANS

Bibliography : J. B. LIGHTFOOT, *St. Paul's Epistles to the Colossians and to Philemon*[2] (London, 1876). H. OLTRAMARE, *Commentaire sur les épîtres de saint Paul aux Colossiens, aux Ephésiens et à Philémon* (Paris, 1891). J. ARMITAGE ROBINSON, *St Paul's Epistle to the Ephesians* (London, 1903). B. F. WESTCOTT, *Saint Paul's Epistle to the Ephesians* (London, 1906). T. K. ABBOTT, *Epistles to the Ephesians and to the Colossians, ICC* (Edinburgh, n. d.). MARTIN DIBELIUS, *An die Kolosser, Epheser, an Philemon*[2], *HNT* 12 (Tübingen, 1927). E. F. SCOTT, *The Epistles of Paul to the Colossians, to Philemon, and to the Ephesians, MC* (London, 1930). A. MÉDEBIELLE, *Épîtres de la Captivité, SBP* XII (Paris, 1938). J. HUBY, *Les Épîtres de la Captivité*[14], *VS* 8 (Paris, 1947). P. BENOIT, *Les Épîtres de Saint Paul aux Philippiens, à Philémon, aux Colossiens, aux Ephésiens, BJ* (Paris, 1949). H. RENDTORFF, *Die Kleineren Briefe des Apostels Paulus, NTD* 8 (Göttingen, 1949). CHARLES MASSON, *L'Épître de saint Paul aux Colossiens, CNT* X (Neuchâtel-Paris, 1950) ; *L'Épître de saint Paul aux Ephésiens, CNT* IX (Neuchâtel-Paris, 1953). E. LOHMEYER, *Die Briefe an die Kolosser und an Philemon*[10], (ed. W. Schmauch) *MK* 92 (Göttingen, 1954). C. F. D. MOULE, *The Epistles of Paul the Apostle to the Colossians and to Philemon, CGTC* (Cambridge, 1957) H. SCHLIER, *Der Brief an die Epheser* (Düsseldorf, 1957).

Of the three letters written from his first Roman Captivity, that to the Colossians and that to the Ephesians are of particular interest for our theme. The brief note written to Philemon, which is from the same period, does not concern us here. We shall assume the authenticity of these epistles here without reviewing the arguments for it, which have been convincingly presented by E. PERCY and J. SCHMID [1]. The present

---

[1] J. SCHMID, *Zeit und Ort der paulinischen Gefangenschaftsbriefe* (Freiburg, 1931). E. PERCY, *Die Probleme der Kolosser- und Epheserbriefe* (Lund, 1946).

tendency on the part of the critics is to accept Colossians as Pauline ; and if the same cannot be said as yet of Ephesians, its acceptance as genuinely Pauline by H. SCHLIER in his recent commentary [2] is a strong argument in favour of the traditional position which has always considered it as written by Paul.

The most recent Catholic studies of our two epistles have all taken cognizance of the theological advance in Pauline thought which they represent regarding the redemption, the Church, and the liturgy [3]. The most obvious cause of this re-orientation of Pauline soteriology lies in the threat to Christianity in Asia Minor from a kind of pre-Gnostic movement usually known as the Colossian error or « heresy ». Since its character can only be deduced from Paul's obscure references to it in these letters, it necessarily remains somewhat of an enigma. L. CERFAUX distinguishes three different aspects of this Asiatic syncretism : one pagan, one Jewish, and one Christian [4]. The pagan element would consist of a « Mystery-cult » of the cosmic forces with certain ascetical practices, purification-rites and a kind of « philosophy », which was the forerunner of second-century Gnosticism. An adaptation of the movement by certain Jewish groups of Asia Minor would have identified the cosmic powers with angels,

---

[2] HEINRICH SCHLIER, *Der Brief an die Epheser* : *ein Kommentar* (Düsseldorf, 1957). The question of the Pauline authenticity of this letter is to be distinguished from the problem of its title, or rather, of its addressees. The words ἐν Ἐφέσῳ in 1,1 are missing in 3rd cent. mss (Vat., Sin., the Chester Beatty papyrus) as well as in the important witness 1739. The opinion of Msgr. CERFAUX inclines towards accepting this early testimony : « il sera prudent de se fier plutôt à la plus ancienne tradition manuscrite ... Les vrais destinataires restent donc objet de litige » (*Introduction à la Bible II*, 497). On the other hand, S. LYONNET hesitates to regard the phrase as an interpolation. The internal evidence provided by the epistle inclines us to regard the community to which Paul writes as evangelized by another (and consequently as probably not that of Ephesus where Paul worked for almost three years). If 1,15 is admittedly a weak argument for the fact that the addressess are unknown to Paul, the passage in 3,2-4 appears to indicate that the community is learning of Paul's version of the kerygma for the first time in this letter ; and 4,21 would favour such an hypothesis even more. Further corroboration of this position may be seen in the fact that Paul (5,1) urges these Christians to imitate, not himself, as he habitually does with communities of his own founding (I Thes 1,6 ; 2 Thes 3,9 ; Phil 3,17 ; 1 Cor 4,16), but God the Father (Eph 5,1).

[3] Cf. the introductions of BENOIT and SCHLIER in their commentaries ; also L. CERFAUX in *Introduction à la Bible II* (Tournai, 1959) 494-495 ; 503-513.

[4] *ibid.* 495 f ; cf. also S. LYONNET, *L' Étude du milieu littéraire et l' exégèse du Nouveau Testament* in *Bib* 37 (1956) 27-38.

while the solar and lunar feasts, as well as the dietary regulations, would
have fitted into the general pattern of contemporary Judaism. As to
whether, or how far, these erroneous doctrines had perverted Colossian
Christianity, it is impossible to say. PIERRE BENOIT has wisely pointed
out the fallacy of considering Paul's statements in his letter to Colossae
as a kind of « photographic negative », outlining the teaching of heretical
Colossian Christians ; and he has rightly insisted that more credit be
given to the creative genius of Paul's mind [5].

Apart from its polemic against the threat to Christian doctrine from
this oriental syncretism, the letter to the Colossian Church displays a
marked interest in the Christian liturgy. This seems clear from the use
made by Paul throughout the epistle of a hymn, probably familiar to his
addressees from their own liturgical reunions, which has much the same
function here as the Prologue in the Fourth Gospel. In the course of the
letter, the Apostle refers to the doctrinal function of such hymns which
were sung by the community during the celebration of the liturgy (3,16-17) [6].
Perhaps also one may discern a certain intention to oppose the erroneous
doctrines endangering Christian life in Colossae by a deeper understanding
of the Christian liturgy in the Apostle's use of a number of metaphors
drawn from cultic terminology (1,12.22.25.27 f ; 2,7 ; 3,17 ; 4,2). Finally,
we have an explicit indication of Paul's intention to compose this epistle
for reading at a liturgical function (4,16), the clearest statement of this
kind in the whole Pauline *corpus* (cf. 1 Thes 5,27 ; 2 Cor 1,1).

§ 1. - A Hymn from the Early Christian Liturgy. Col 1,13-20

Immediately after the thanksgiving (1, 3 ff) and a brief prayer (1,9 ff),
Paul cites this hymn which sums up the Christian doctrine of salvation in
Christ.

> 13 Who rescued us from the power of darkness,
>   set us instead beneath the dominion of the Son of his love,
> 14 in whom we possess redemption,
>   the remission of our sins.
>
> 15 Who is the image of the unseen God,
>   first-born before all creatures ;

---

[5] Cf. BENOIT's commentary, p. 49.
[6] D. M. STANLEY, « *Carmenque Christo quasi Deo dicere* ... » in *CBQ* 20 (1958)
173-175.

16 since in him all things have been created,
   things of heaven, things of earth,
   things seen and things unseen,
   Thrones and Dominions,
   Principalities and Powers.

   All things have been created by him, for him.
17 Yes, he it is who stands before all else.
   All things in him keep their coherence.
18 Yes, he it is who stands Head of his Body, the Church.

   Who is the Beginning,
   first-born from among the dead,
   so that he might in every order take precedence,
19 since God was pleased to make all the fulness dwell in him
20 and through him reconcile all things to himself,
   things of earth and things of heaven,
   making peace through the blood of his cross.

[14. Vat. reads ἔσχομεν, where almost all other mss. have ἔχομεν. The addition of δια̇ τοῦ αἵματος αὐτοῦ after ἀπολύτρωσις in many minuscule mss. is probably inter-polated from Eph 1,7.
16. τὰ preceding ἐν οὐρανοῖς and ἐπὶ τῆς γῆς is omitted by the Chester Beatty papyrus, Vat., Sin., 1739, and others.
20. δἰ αὐτοῦ is omitted by Vat., 1739, D, etc., but appears in Sin., Alex., C, K, P].

Most modern commentators agree that vv. 15-20 originally formed part of a liturgical hymn, although they divide the strophes in various ways [7]. We have included vv. 13-14 with their reference to the part of the Father in effecting man's salvation (it is possible that the hymn may have had a trinitarian structure) [8], since they introduce the theme of the « first-born » Son, a motif characteristic of Pauline soteriology. Moreover, they would seem to provide an indication that this liturgical composit-ion was written in honour of the Son *qua* incarnate, as BONSIRVEN has rightly seen [9].

---

[7] C. MASSON, who considers the passage a hymn, mentions in his commentary, p. 104, the names of J. WEISS, A. DEISSMANN, E. NORDEN, M. DIBELIUS, E. LOH-MEYER, E. STAUFFER, E. PERCY, J. HÉRING, as authors who recognize the litur-gical style of the passage or call it a Christological hymn. To these names may be added those of P. BENOIT, L. CERFAUX, E. KÄSEMANN.
[8] E. KÄSEMANN, *Eine urchristliche Taufliturgie* in *Festschrift Rudolf Bultmann* (Stuttgart-Köln, 1949). The author maintains that v. 13 belongs to the hymn in its present form.
[9] J. BONSIRVEN, *L'Évangile de Paul* 86-88. This view is not a common one amongst Catholic exegetes.

v. 13. *who rescued us*. The work of the redemption, described here first negatively, then positively (MASSON), is presented as originating with the Father, whose redeeming power transcends the sinful dominion of Satan indicated by the phrase *the power of darkness* (Lk 22,53) [10]. The words *the dominion of the Son of his love* refer to the Church as the earthly phase in the realization of the Kingdom of God (1 Cor 15,23-28). More important, the Church is described here as the dominion or Kingdom of Christ inasmuch as he is *the Son* and insofar as he is object of the Father's love. The phrase implies that the very existence of the Church, as the dominion of Christ, is a concrete symbol of the Father's love for his Son. Thus, as the realization of Christ's kingdom on earth, acquired by his death and resurrection (cf. vv. 13-14.18-20), the Church, born of the divine love of Father and Son, provides, so to say, a new « motive » for the Father's love of the Son. Christian salvation is seen as the proper work of God as Father and of Christ as Son, the expression of their mutual love. v. 14. It is in Jesus Christ, as *the Son* of God's paternal *love*, that *we possess redemption*. The risen Christ, in his glorified humanity, possesses the fulness of the redemption ; and we, by our supernatural union with Christ, may be said to possess it by anticipation, although it will only be completed in us by the glorious resurrection of the body. The reality of our Christian salvation is presented under a positive aspect as *redemption*, a familiar Pauline metaphor drawn from Israel's liberation from Egypt, and under a negative aspect as *the remission of our sins*, which may, as LIGHTFOOT suggests, have assumed a new importance because of the Colossian error.

In the verses which follow, the incarnate and glorified Son is praised on account of the twofold relation which he bears to God's new Chosen people, the Christian Church. As creator, he holds the primacy over the whole community of creatures (vv. 15-17) : as redeemer, he is Head of the Christian community of the Church (vv. 18-20). It is to be recalled that, on the biblical view, these are not regarded as two distinct orders — the « natural » as opposed to the « supernatural » — but rather as two ways in which man is related to God [11]. The OT authors habitually thought of God's creation of the world as the first of the *magnalia Dei*, wrought in favour of his people.

---

[10] Cf. S. LYONNET, *Theologia Biblica Novi Testamenti* (1) : *de Peccato et Redemptione* (Rome, 1956) 63.

[11] The view of L. CERFAUX, *Le Christ dans la théologie de saint Paul*, 299, s inaccurate on this point.

v. 15. The incarnate Son is first called the *image of the unseen God.* The
notion of image involves that of resemblance (MÉDEBIELLE). Christ's
divine filiation constitutes primarily his resemblance to the Father. There
is also a resemblance which he displays through his sacred humanity in
his role as revealer to men of the « God no man has ever seen » (Jn 1,18).
The title *first-born before all creatures* also expresses a twofold relationship of Christ : he is *first-born* with reference to the Father's eternal act
of generation, and also, in his humanity, with reference to all the rest
of creation over which he holds precedence. These titles belong to the
vocabulary of the theme of the new or second Adam (cf. 1 Cor 15,49 ;
Rom 8,29), as does that in v. 18, *first-born from among the dead* (cf. 1 Cor
15,20-22).

Vv. 16-17 explain in greater detail how Christ as incarnate Son constitutes the perfection of the universe. *All things* have been created *in him*
as the centre of creation's harmony and unity, *by him* inasmuch as his
mediation is total and embraces all causality [12], *for him* as crown of the
the commonwealth of creatures. This primacy includes precedence over
all angelic creatures, specified by their various names in order to empha-
size Christ's superiority over any rivals suggested by false teaching (MOULE).
With v. 18, the supremacy of Christ over the Church is expressed through
three titles : *Head, Beginning, first-born from among the dead.* Here we
are introduced to a conception which is new in Pauline soteriology, viz.
the idea that Christ, through the twofold act of his death and resurrection
by which he effected man's salvation, has attained primacy over the
Church [13]. The title *first-born from among the dead* means that Christ's
resurrection involves the resurrection of all believers (MASSON). He is
accordingly a new *Beginning*, surpassing that of the divine act of creation. The exact sense of this title is hard to define, since it can mean
either « beginning » or « source ». Possibly both notions are suggested here,
and Christ is thought of as « the originating power » (LIGHTFOOT) with
respect to the Church.

The way in which Christ as *Head* is distinguished from the Church

---

[12] Cf. BONSIRVEN, *op. cit.* 88 : « ' Créées par lui ', on peut l'entendre au sens,
soit de cause efficiente, soit de cause instrumentale : l' un et l'autre se rapportent
difficilement à Jésus-Christ, en tant que tel. Peut-on le lui appliquer par communication des idiomes ? Ou bien, voulant marquer que la médiation du Christ dans
la création est totale, l' Apôtre épuise-t-il à son sujet toutes les prépositions indi-
quant une participation ... ? ».

[13] E. PERCY, *op. cit.* 75 f.

as *his Body* represents a new development in a celebrated Pauline theme
(I Cor 10,17 ; 12,12 ; Rom 12,5), and possesses certain advantages over
the early use of the Body metaphor, which included Christ with the
Church. It enables Paul to express the close union between Christ
and the Church without occasioning any misconception as to how he is
identified with the Church [14]. The repeated use which Paul makes of this
new comparison in the letters from this period (cf. Col 2,19 ; Eph 1,22.23 ;
4,15 ; 5,23) is a sign of his own satisfaction with it. In fact, the introduction of the notion of love in connection with two of the above named passages (cf. Eph 4,15 ; 5,23) suggests what is perhaps the most basic reason
for Paul's use of the antithesis, Head-Body. It permits him to express
that altereity which is essential to the relation of love which exists between Christ and the Church. In his earlier conception of the Body of
Christ, it is significant that, while his purpose in employing it is to teach
the necessity of unity (I Cor 12,12-31 ; Rom 12,4-8), Paul speaks of the
fundamental duty of fraternal love as a consequence (I Cor 13, I ff ;
Rom 12,9 ff). While he constantly refers in all his epistles to the *reality*
of divine love (both the Father's and Christ's for Christians, notably in
Rom 5,5 ; 8,34-39) it is only when Paul has hit upon the expression,
Head-Body, that he can find room in the Body-metaphor for the mutual
relationship of love between Christ and the Church.

v. 19. *all the fulness*. Here we meet with a celebrated *crux interpretum* :
the meaning of παν τό πλήρωμα [14 bis]. There is a secondary difficulty
with regard to the subject of the main verb. It appears to be more satisfactory to assume that the Father is the subject (BENOIT), since the
work of reconciliation is usually described as originating with him [15].
In 2,9, the phrase *all the fulness* is expanded to *all the fulness of the
divinity*, which is said to *dwell* in Christ. In view of the fact that this hymn
contains the chief themes developed in this letter, we may safely assume
that Paul understood παν τό πλήρωμα in our verse to contain the same
meaning as he gives it in 2,9. Moreover, since in 2,9 b Paul adds the
words *and you have been filled in union with him*, it would seem that παν
τό πλήρωμα signifies Christ's divinity in the existential, rather than the
essential order, i. e. that participation in the divine nature which God

---

[14] V. TAYLOR, *The Names of Jesus* (London, 1953) 101f.

[14 bis] P. BENOIT, *Corps, tête et plérôme dans les épîtres de la captivité* in *RB*
63 (1956) 5-44.

[15] Moreover, the participial form ειρηνοποιήσας presupposes a masculine ante-
cedent.

grants to the Christian through his union with the risen Christ. In short, πλήρωμα is employed in the same sense as it has in the Johannine Prologue (cf. Jn 1,16).

v. 20. *through him reconcile all things*. This verse refers to the historical event through which this communication to man of Christ's divine fulness was made possible : his redemptive death on Calvary. It is here presented by means of two characteristically Pauline metaphors : as a reconciliation of the whole universe with the Father[16] (cf. 2 Cor 5,19), and as a peace-making (cf. Rom 5,1 ; Eph 2,14-15) through the Son's voluntary offering of his life for the world's salvation (MASSON)[17]. These metaphors cast new light upon the meaning of *first-born from among the dead* in v. 18. It is as risen from a death which brought men peace through their reconciliation with the Father, that Christ now appears as *first-born* of the Father's adoptive sons (cf. Rom 8,29). Christ's death forms a close unity with his resurrection. As CERFAUX remarks[18], « the efficiency of the death is naturally linked to that of the resurrection, and forms a unity with it ».

As we have stated, exegetes agree that this hymn is cited by Paul from the early Christian liturgy, whether that of Baptism, as KÄSEMANN believes[19], or that of the Eucharist, as DAHL has proposed[20]. It would appear to be a passage familiar enough to the Christians of Asia Minor so that Paul can employ it as the theme of this whole epistle. Moreover, Paul himself must have been acquainted with it for a long time, given the fact that so many of its expressions and conceptions recall passages in his earlier letters. Yet the spirit of the passage considered as a whole is, I venture to suggest, more reminiscent of the Johannine than of the Pauline writings. The general scheme of the hymn, with its description of Christ's work first in creation and then in the redemption, follows the movement of the Johannine Prologue. The conception of the Son as the incarnate revelation of the invisible Father (cf. Jn 1,18), of his divine fulness which he communicates to men (Jn 1,16), of the reconciliation and peace he brings through his Blood (cf. the Johannine image of God's Lamb,

---

[16] In Col 1,22 ; Eph 2,16, there is a variation in the form (ἀποκαταλλάσσειν), while in 2 Cor 5,18.19 ; Rom 5,10 καταλλάσσειν is employed. It is doubtful if there is any change in the meaning of these terms.

[17] S. LYONNET, *La sotériologie paulinienne* in *Introduction à la Bible II*, 875-877 ; 880-882.

[18] L. CERFAUX, *op. cit.* 300.

[19] E. KÄSEMANN, *art. cit. supra*, p. 203, n. 8.

[20] N. A. DAHL, *Anamnesis* in *ST* 1 (1947) 69-95.

Jn 1,29) would appear to support the hypothesis that the hymn took its origin from the school of John [21]. Such a contact with the powerful Christian theological thought of Asia Minor would explain the distinctively new orientation of Pauline soteriology exhibited by these last two letters of his to the churches of Asia Minor much more satisfactorily than any mere polemic against the so-called Colossian « heresy ».

§ 2. - The Mystery of Christ's Presence in the Community. Col 1,21-28

This passage, which follows immediately on the citation of the hymn, develops the theme of reconciliation in terms of the conversion of the Colossians from paganism. Since Paul personally had no part in this conversion, which was brought about by Epaphras as « minister of Christ » (1,7), and he had never visited Colossae (2,1) or its neighbourhood, he is led to express another relationship between himself as « minister of the Church » (1,25) and these Christians of Asia Minor in terms of his present sufferings.

21 You also were once estranged and hostile in your attitude because of your evil deeds. 22 But now he has reconciled you by his mortal body through his death to present you as holy and spotless and blameless in his presence, 23 provided only you cling to the faith, firmly grounded and solid, without being shaken from your hope in the Good News you have listened to. (It has been preached to every creature under heaven ; and I, Paul, have been made its minister). 24 At present, I am rejoicing in my sufferings for you. Yes, I am completing in my own person what is wanting in Christ's tribulations for his Body, which is the Church. 25 I indeed have been made her minister according to the divine programme entrusted to me in your regard to complete God's word, 26 that Mystery hidden for centuries and for generations which has now been revealed to his saints, 27 to whom God has willed to make known the glorious riches of this Mystery among the pagans : I mean, Christ in you, the hope of glory. 28 Him we proclaim, exhorting every man and teaching every man with all wisdom, that we may present every man as mature in Christ.

[22. ἀποκατηλλάγητε is read by the Chester Beatty papyrus and Vat., while ἀποκαταλλαγέντες is found in D, G, and some Latin mss.
24. μου is added after παθήμασιν by Sin. *corr*, and a number of minuscule mss.
27. ὅ ἐστιν is read by Alex., Vat., and other mss. including the Chester Beatty papyrus].

---

[21] The terms τὸ σκότος, ἀρχή, πλήρωμα are also to be found in the Johannine writings.

vv. 21-22. *Estranged* and *hostile* as pagans and as sinners both to God and to God's people, the Colossians were in need of reconciliation and of Christ's peace-making. This was accomplished by Christ's death *by his mortal body*, or literally « in the body of his flesh », which can be considered to have shared in the sinful solidarity (of the first Adam) with these pagans, inasmuch as it was capable of suffering and dying (cf. Rom 7,4 ; 8,3). The keywords here σῶμα and σάρξ will occur again in v. 24. *to present you as holy and spotless*. The purpose of the reconciliation is here presented by means of what are probably liturgical metaphors (cf. 1 Cor 8,8 ; Rom 12,1), which also recur at the end of the paragraph (v. 28). The unusual phrase *in his presence*, found only in Eph 1,4 and Jude 24, seems also to have a liturgical significance. Paul is probably thinking of the presentation of the Colossian church in the Eucharistic liturgy.

v. 23. *provided only you cling to the faith.* Faith is the necessary Christian response in the dialogue of salvation to the revelation found in the kerygma. Its object, God's reconciliation, is the firm foundation of the Church (1 Cor 3,11) erected upon Christ (MASSON). The *Good News* of Christ's redemptive death and resurrection is the basis of Christian *hope* in the eschatological salvation. In a parenthesis, Paul describes the universality of the Gospel and his own role as *minister* in the « liturgy » of the pagan's conversion.

v. 24. *my sufferings for you.* Paul rejoices that through his imprisonment (2,1) he exercises another kind of διακονία towards the Colossian community. *what is wanting in Christ's tribulations.* To grasp this difficult notion, it is necessary to recall that θλῖψις is nowhere applied to Christ's own passion in the NT, and that, in this letter (cf. 2,11-12) as always, Paul regards Christ's passion and death as possessing a unique propitiatory value which is fully efficacious and complete. However the Church must grow into the image of Christ (3,10) by sharing in the messianic *tribulations* or eschatological sufferings which began with Christ's passion and continue until his parousia (cf. Phil 1,29 ; 3,10 ; 2 Cor 1,5-7)[22]. Paul here expresses his own personal share in this suffering as part of his continuing the vocation of Christ as the Suffering Servant of God[23]. The risen Christ's humanity, freed from the condition of σάρξ, the passibility

[22] H. SCHLIER, θλῖψις, *TWNT III*, 143-148.
[23] For a different view, cf. L. CERFAUX, *Saint Paul et le « serviteur de Dieu » d' Isaïe* in *Recueil Lucien Cerfaux II* (Gembloux, 1954) 453.

14. - D. M. STANLEY.

it had during his earthly life, is now capable of suffering through the
Apostle's σάρξ *for his Body, which is the Church.*

v. 25. *her minister.* By sharing *Christ's tribulations* which bear a relation
to *his Body,* Paul becomes a *minister* of the Church in a new sense, since
his sufferings are the means to the realization of God's economy for the
Gentiles' Salvation. *to complete God's word.* In itself, the Gospel is of course
complete, just as Christ's sufferings were complete (cf. Gal 1,6-9). Yet
it can be said to be completed by becoming incarnate, so to say, in the
faith of the Christian Church (cf. 1 Thes 1,8).

v. 26. *that Mystery.* The divine « liturgy » of the reconciliation of the Gentiles within the Church is now designated by a term which, to his readers,
probably suggested a rite. Paul does not use the word in this sense : for
him, it signifies the divine economy of salvation particularly as revealed
by the call of pagans as well as Jews to the Church [24].

v. 27. *Christ in you.* The phrase constitutes a kind of definition of *the
Mystery.* It seems clear that Paul means a presence of Christ in the
Colossian Christians, not as individuals (cf. Rom 8,10), but as a community which forms part of the Body of Christ, his Church. It constitutes
their *hope of glory* because it is the presence of the risen Christ (LOH-
MEYER). How is the risen Christ present to the Colossian community *as a
community* and as their *hope of glory* ? Paul is probably thinking of the
Eucharistic offering, the most properly community-action of any Christian group (Rom 12,1-2), which for him possesses a particularly eschatological orientation (cf. 1 Cor 11,26). This liturgical presence of Christ
(which would account for the liturgical metaphors in v. 22, repeated in
v. 28, as well as Paul's choice of the term *Mystery* here and in v. 27, with
its liturgical overtones) is, we suggest, also present in Paul's thought
as exposed in the following verse.

v. 28. *Him we proclaim.* Here it is not his function as *minister* of the Gospel,
i. e. as preacher to non-believers, but his role as *minister* of the Church,

---

[24] Cf. the various studies of the term *Mystery* : D. DEDEN, *Le « Mystère »
paulinien* in *ETL* 13 (1936) 403-442 ; S. LYONNET, *Hellénisme et Christianisme* in
Bib 26 (1945) 117-120 ; K. PRÜMM, « *Mysterion » von Paulus bis Origenes* in *ZKT*
61 (1937) 391-425 ; *Zur Phänomenologie des paulinischen Mysterion und dessen
seelischer Aufnahme* in *Bib* 37 (1956) 135-161 ; art. *Mystères, VDBS VI,* 10-225 ;
E. VOGT, « *Mysteria » in textibus Qumran* in *Bib* 37 (1956) 247-257 ; RAYMOND E.
BROWN, *The Semitic Background of the New Testament Mysterion* in *Bib* 39 (1958)
426-448 ; 40 (1959) 70-87 ; *The Pre-Christian Semitic Concept of « Mystery »* in
CBQ 20 (1958) 417-443.

i. e. within the community, that Paul describes. The term νουθετεῖν is always used in Paul's letters to signify a specifically Christian and community act (cf. 1 Thes 5,12 ; 2 Thes 3,15 ; 1 Cor 4,14 ; Rom 15,14). The same may be said of διδάσκειν (cf. 1 Cor 4,17 ; Rom 12,7 ; Eph 4,21). Moreover, it is a question here of *wisdom*, which Paul only imparts to *mature* Christians (1 Cor 2,6 ff) [25]. The purpose of this instruction of the Christian community is to *present every man as mature in Christ*. Paul's use of the liturgical word παριστάναι is again significant. As A. BEA has pointed out, the combining of instruction with sacrifice was from the beginning a unique feature of the Christian Eucharistic liturgy [26]. Accordingly, it would seem probable that Paul is thinking of it in these verses and that the presence of the risen Christ in the Colossian community, assembled for worship at the Eucharist, constitutes for the Apostle a concrete example of that *Mystery among the pagans* of which he speaks in vv. 26-27.

§ 3. - Christian Salvation and the Baptismal Liturgy. Col 2,9-15

After expressing his concern for the faith of the communities of Asia Minor (2,1-3), Paul warns against the dangers of false doctrine (2,4). The communities are to base their whole life upon Christ (2,6-7) not upon any false « philosophy » (2,8). This leads him to restate the doctrine of Christ's saving work by means of the liturgy of Baptism.

9 In him dwells incarnate all the fulness of the divinity. Indeed, you have been filled in union with him, 10 who is Head of every Principality and Power. 11 In him also you were circumcised with a circumcision not performed by [human] hand at the putting off of your sinful selves by Christ's circumcision. 12 Buried together with him at Baptism, you were thereby also raised together with him through faith in the force of God who raised him from death. 13 Yes, you who were dead, thanks to your transgressions and the uncircumcised state of your sinful nature, he brought to life together with him. He has graciously pardoned us all our transgressions : 14 he wiped out our debtor's account with its terms, which was outstanding against us ; and he wrote it off by nailing it to the cross. 15 Having despoiled the Principalities and Powers, he made them a spectacle before the world, leading them captive in his triumph.

---

[25] The word τέλειος is not used by Paul in the sense it had in the Hellenistic Mystery cults (MASSON vs DIBELIUS).

[26] A. BEA, *Valeur pastorale de la parole de Dieu dans la liturgie* in *La Maison-Dieu* 47-48 (1956) 131f.

[12. βαπτισμῷ is read in place of βαπτίσματι by Vat., Sin. *corr.*, 1739, as also by the Chester Beatty papyrus and other mss.

13. In place of (συνεζωοποίησεν) ὑμᾶς, ἡμᾶς is read by the Chester Beatty papyrus, Vat., and other mss. A few mss. read ὑμῖν for ἡμῖν].

v. 9. Paul gives a solemn affirmation of Christ's divinity as it operates in the existential order of Christian salvation : to πᾶν τὸ πλήρωμα τῆς θεότητος corresponds ἐστὲ πεπληρωμένοι, indicating that *the fulness of the divinity* of Christ is to be understood in its salvific relationship to the Church. The difficult σωματικῶς probably refers to the glorified humanity of the risen Christ, which has become the perfect instrument of grace for the Church as the Body of her exalted Head. Paul's use of the present tense, *dwells*, is a further indication that it is not the incarnation as such that is meant, but rather that constitution of Christ as « Son of God in power » (Rom 1,4), which is the result of his passion and resurrection.

v. 10. The fact that Christ's Headship includes dominion over all the angels is a hint to the Colossians that these angelic creatures must not be given the worship due to Christ alone.

v. 11. The metaphor of circumcision to describe Baptism is quite Pauline (Rom 2, 29), hence there is no need to suppose (MASSON) that the Colossian heretics were practising circumcision [27]. The phrase ἀπέκδυσις τοῦ σώματος τῆς σαρκὸς, which defines this baptismal « circumcision », is reminiscent of the earlier statement that Christ's work of reconciliation was effected ἐν τῷ σώματι τῆς σαρκὸς αὐτοῦ. Consequently, Baptism is here called *Christ's circumcision*, not merely because he is author of this sacrament which draws its efficacy from him (MÉDEBIELLE), but principally to point out that the Christian experiences sacramentally what Christ underwent in his death and resurrection.

v. 12. Here, as in Rom 6,4, Baptism is described as the Christian's participation in Christ's burial (i. e. his death) and resurrection, or in Christ's absolute obedience to the Father, which his death and resurrection signified (MOULE). In the present passage, Paul brings the expression of his baptismal teaching to perfection. MASSON is scarcely right in considering this verse a mere repetition of Rom 6,3 ff, where the meaning of the Chris-

---

[27] More probably this figure appealed to Paul as an illustration of the relation between justifying faith and the sacrament of Baptism : cf. Rom 4,9-12, where Abraham's circumcision is called a σημεῖον and a σφραγὶς of his justification by faith.

tian's participation in Christ's resurrection was left ambiguous (cf. Rom 6,5). That Paul now understands it as an *actual*, not merely an eschatological, participation is clear from 3,1. All that is needed is a *manifestation* of the Christian's new risen state, like that of the risen Christ at his parousia (3,4). *the force of God who raised him from death* constitutes the object of justifying faith which operates in Baptism. Just as, for Israel, Yahweh was the God who brought his people out of Egypt, so, for the Christian Church, the Father is he who raised Christ (MASSON).

v. 13. *you who were dead ... he brought to life together with him.* Here we have a recapitulation of the preceding with the antithesis, death-life. God the Father is clearly indicated as author of this vivifying act in Christian Baptism. Indeed, it is the same act by which the Father raised Christ from death.

The section which follows (13b-15) seems to be an echo of some early baptismal hymn, if it is not an actual citation from one. *He has graciously pardoned us all our transgressions.* Stress is laid on the fact that God's universal forgiveness is essentially an act of divine benevolence and loving kindness [28]. This aspect of the divine act of the redemption must be considered as governing the thought of the following verse.

v. 14. By means of a metaphor drawn from the cancellation of a debt, Paul probably wishes to stress the completeness of God's forgiveness [29] and its historical reality as expressed in Christ's death. The baffling expression τοῖς δόγμασιν probably indicates the terms of an acknowledgement of debt [30]. In any event, it does not seem there is any parallel with Eph 2,15 where there is question of the Mosaic Law [31].

v. 15. It is possible, as LOHMEYER suggests, that this verse describes Christ's exaltation through his death, resurrection, and ascension, in terms of the three steps involved in the coronation of an Oriental monarch : *elevation* to the divine dignity (here by the despoiling of the angels) ;

---

[28] This is the first time in Paul's letters that the verb χαρίζεσθαι is employed in the sense of « to forgive » : cf. also 3,13 ; Eph 4,32.

[29] The vigorous metaphors contained in ἐξαλείψας and ἦρκεν ἐκ τοῦ μέσου would seem to suggest this.

[30] Cf. J. A. T. ROBINSON, *The Body* (London, 1952) 43, n. 1.

[31] Hence BENOIT does not seem to be right in considering the expression to refer to the sentence of death prescribed by the Mosaic (or human moral) law against sin. Moreover, it does not appear to be consonant with what we know of Paul's soteriological viewpoint to assert, as BENOIT does in his commentary, p. 61, *n.* b, that God « suppressed this sentence by carrying it out upon the person of his Son ».

presentation to the gods of the national pantheon (Christ's public proclamation by the Father as King) ; and the *enthonement* or accession to
supreme power (expressed here under the figure of a royal triumph over
the angels). What is of interest to us in these lines is the clear assertion of the cosmic effects of Christ's death and, particularly, of his resurrection.

§ 4. - A New Variation upon the Theme of the Second Adam. Col. 3,9b-11

Paul asserts (3,1) as the principle of the Christian life the fact that
the members of the Colossian community, like all Christians who have
received Baptism, are actually risen with Christ. This truth forms the
basis of Christian morality (3,2-9). In the lines which follow, Paul rephrases this same truth in terms of the second Adam theme.

9b You have put off your old man with his habits, 10 and you have put on that
new man, constantly being renewed in view of perfect knowledge in the image
of his Creator, 11 where there is no « Greek and Jew », « circumcised and uncircumcised », « barbarian, Scythian », « slave, freeman », but Christ, all in all.

[11. ἄρσεν καὶ θῆλυ occurs after ἔνι (an interpolation from Gal 3,28) in D,
as well as in Ambrose, Augustine, Pelagius].

v. 9 b. *your old man.* It is by Baptism that the Christian has *put off* his
sinful state, described in 2,10 as τὸ σῶμα τῆς σαρκὸς, here as ὁ πάλαιος
ἄνθρωπος. The expression (cf. Rom 6,6 ; Eph 4,22) does not indicate merely
the character of an individual, but carries a deeper, corporate significance
(MOULE). Paul is thinking of the contrast between the first and the
second Adam (1 Cor 15,21-22.45-47 ; Rom 5,12 ff), and describes Baptism
here as the breaking of the old, sinful solidarity with the first parent and
the entering of the new solidarity of grace with Christ. The passage is a
restatement of Gal 3,27-28, where however there was question of the
Christian's (especially the Gentile Christian's) relation to Abraham.
v. 10. The positive aspect of Baptism is described as a putting on of the
new self, the supernatural union with Christ as the new Adam. *constantly renewed in view of perfect knowledge.* Here we have a new development
of the second Adam theme : if our entrance into the solidarity with Christ
is *initially* effected by Baptism, this union with the second Adam is
dependent for its growth upon the faithful practice of the Christian life.

That this *perfect knowledge* of which Paul speaks is « true moral knowledge » can be seen from Paul's evident allusion to Gn 3,1-22 where the
first man attempts to « be like God » by eating the fruit that gives knowledge of « good and evil ». Although created « in the image of God » (Gn
1,27), the first man by his disobedience did not become « like God »
but through his « knowledge of good and evil » found only death (Gn
2,17 ; 3,22-23). The Christian, on the contrary, through his advance
towards *perfect knowledge* grows *in the image of his Creator*, i. e. in
likeness to Christ who is God's image (2 Cor 3,18).

v. 11. *Christ, all in all*. This summary statement is of paramount interest for a proper understanding of the function of Christ's resurrection
in Christian salvation. It is something more than merely a vigorous way
of stating that Christ is « absolutely everything » (MOULE), or that he is
the « new Man » found in every Christian (LOHMEYER), or that all men
are equal (DIBELIUS). In the glorified humanity of the risen Christ, *the
Image of his Creator* has, in one sense, been perfectly realized. He is
« first-born before all creatures » (Col 1,15), « first-born from among the
dead » (Col 1,18), as « Image of the unseen God » (Col 1,15). In another
sense, however, the complete glorification of Christ's humanity includes
the perfect assimilation of all Christians, who must pass through
death and resurrection before they can be said to be fully one with Christ.

It is the working-out of this process which gives its true significance to
the period of Salvation-history between Christ's resurrection and his
parousia (which will effect the glorious resurrection of the just). If, as
Paul has done in 1 Cor 15,25-28, the process be considered in the course
of its execution, attention is given to the struggle to be waged until « the
last enemy », death, is overcome. From this viewpoint, Christ's reign is
not fully established, the Father is not yet « all in all », the Son has not
reached the state of perfect « subjection » to the Father which demands
the glorification of the Christian people. The ultimate goal of Salvation-
history in such a consideration is reached when God the Father is « all
in all » (1 Cor 15,28).

In the present passage, Paul underscores another aspect of this
same Christian reality. Since Baptism has already united the Christian
to the risen Christ by making the neophyte share in the death and resurrection of his Lord (Rom 6,3 ff.), the victory is basically (though only
initially) won, and in a real sense, « Christ is *all in all*.» This implies, as
Paul has already stated at the beginning of this chapter, that the parousia
is thought of, not as effecting but merely manifesting, the « glory » with
which the Christian is already « filled » (3,1-3). Indeed, when the Christian

life is looked at in this manner, Paul can assert that God the Father is actually now « in all » (Eph 4,6), even though he is perfectly aware that the struggle is still going forward (Eph 6,12). The fact that Paul can describe the present life of the Christian, either by saying that Christ is *all in all*, as here, or that the Father « is in all » (Eph 4,6), is a valuable indication that 1 Cor 15,28 is not to be understood in any subordinationist sense.

§ 5. - The Definitive Formulation of Pauline Soteriology. Eph 1,3-14

The soteriological doctrine which we have seen adumbrated in Colossians under various new aspects is presented in Ephesians incorporated into a complete and final synthesis of Pauline thought. SCHLIER calls this letter a « Mysterienrede », or meditation on Wisdom as found in the Mystery of Christ [32]. Paul here expresses his conception of the Christian Salvation-history as a unified whole. This unity of the divine « economy » is symbolized principally in the unity displayed by the Church, where Jews and pagans are called to live in peace and harmony. Expressed as « the Mystery », this unity is nothing less than the « recapitulation » in Christ of the entire creation, inanimate as well as human and angelic (1,10).

The novelty of this conception, we believe, lies in Paul's realization that the « keystone » (Eph 2,20) in the whole divinely ordained order of salvation is to be found in *the Person of Jesus Christ*. In no other passage of Paul's letters does the refrain « in Him » appear so frequently and with such profound depth of meaning as it does in the passage we are about to examine (1,3-14). In the earlier epistles, the Apostle's attention was concentrated on the nature of salvation as divine *activity* : originating with the Father, carried out with loving obedience by Christ in his death and resurrection, terminating, by means of Baptism, in the individual Christian and his response of justifying faith [33]. Now, however, Paul

---

[32] Cf. his illuminating discussion of the theological development represented by this letter, in his commentary, pp. 20-22. Cf. also HEINRICH SCHLIER, VIKTOR WARNACH, *Die Kirche im Epheserbrief* (Münster, 1949).

[33] Salvation as the Father's activity : 1 Thes 4,14 ; 1 Cor 6,14 ; 15,20 ; 2 Cor 5, 18-19 ; Gal 4,4-5 ; Rom 1,4 ; 3,21-26 ; 4,25 ; 8,3-4.32 ; as Christ's activity, 1 Thes 5,10 ; 1 Cor 15,3-4 ; 2 Cor 5,14-15 ; 8,9 ; Gal 1,4 ; 3,13 ; Rom 5,10-11.19. The only text which is close to the conception found in Ephesians is perhaps Gal 2,20.

contemplates the harmoniously unified order of salvation in the risen Christ, divine revelation incarnate or *the Mystery*, who by his presence in the Church (and especially in her liturgy) provides that wisdom and true knowledge which is the blueprint for her Christian life.

Accordingly, for the first time in all his letters, Paul can present salvation as a reality already acquired in the present existence of the Christian (Eph2, 5.8). When Paul calls the Gospel « the Good News of your salvation » (1,13), he does not appear to be using the term, salvation, in the purely eschatological sense it had in Rom 1,16.

The *Sitz im Leben* for this Christian contemplation of the Mystery of our salvation lies within the Church, more specifically in the Church's liturgy, the august Eucharistic action which forms the centre of the Church's community life and through which, in the presence of her risen Head, she renews that κοινωνία, of which the Eucharist is the efficacious symbol (1 Cor 10,17). It is through the Eucharistic liturgy that the Church is « filled with the Spirit, by reciting songs, hymns, inspired canticles, by singing to the Lord and chanting his praises …. giving thanks always for everything in the Person of our Lord Jesus Christ to God the Father » (Eph 5,18-20).

Finally, Paul has set forth in this epistle more clearly than anywhere else his most characteristic and basic view of Christian salvation as accomplished by the Father's action *as Father* through his Son, his « well-beloved », towards men whom he makes adoptive sons in the Holy Spirit, « the pledge of our inheritance ».

In the passage which we have now to consider, we are not dealing with Paul's usual epistolary thanksgiving (cf. 1,15 ff) but with a solemn act of thanks, much more elevated in tone and modeled on those liturgical recitals of the « magnalia Dei » which from the apostolic age were associated with the central act of Christian worship, the Eucharist [34]. In one lengthy sentence (vv.3-14), Paul has summed up the various moments in God's loving plan of salvation in favour of « the people of his acquiring ».

---

[34] L. CERFAUX, *Le Christ dans la théologie de saint Paul*, 306 : « Les actions de grâces épistolaires, dans les épîtres de la captivité, s'étirent et prennent un galbe liturgique. Il est assez vraisemblable qu'elles conservent des échos des actions de grâces eucharistiques. Le plus bel exemple nous est fourni par le début de l'épître aux Ephésiens, 1, 3-14 ».

3 Blessed be God the Father of our Lord Jesus Christ, who has blessed us with every sort of spiritual blessing in the heavenly realm in Christ, 4 inasmuch as he has chosen us in him from before the world's creation to be holy and blameless in his presence. Out of love, 5 he predestined us for adoptive sonship through Jesus Christ for himself, according to the good pleasure of his will, 6 to the praise of the glory of his grace which he has graciously bestowed on us in his well-beloved. 7 It is in him that we possess the redemption through his blood, the remission of transgressions, according to the riches of his grace, 8 which he has bountifully given us in every sort of wisdom and understanding, 9 by making known to us, according to his good pleasure, the Mystery of his will which he determined beforehand in him 10 for the realization of the fulness of time : to sum up all things under one Head in Christ, those in the heavenly realm and those on earth, in him. 11 It is in him moreover that we have received our portion, being predestined according to the pre-established plan of him who brings everything about according to the counsel of his will, 12 that we, as those who were first to hope, might be in Christ to the praise of his glory. 13 It is in him that you also have heeded the word of truth, the Gospel of your salvation : in him too, once you were Christians, you have been sealed by the promised Holy Spirit, 14 who is the pledge of our inheritance to ready the redemption of the people of God's acquiring, to the praise of his glory.

[5. διά is omitted by the Chester Beatty papyrus.
6. υἱῷ αὐτοῦ is added after ἠγαπημένῳ in D and G, as well as in Origen, Ambrosiaster, Jerome, and Pelagius.
7. ἔσχομεν is read for ἔχομεν by D and a few other mss. χρηστότητος is read in place of χάριτος by Alex. and a number of minuscule mss.
10. τά ἐν τοῖς οὐρανοῖς is read by Alex., G, K, and most minuscule mss.
11. In place of the ἐκληρώθημεν found in Sin., Vat., and most minuscule mss., Alex., D, and G read ἐκλήθημεν].

v. 3 *God the Father* : literally « God and Father » which however is practically one concept : « the fatherly God and divine Father of Christ in whom we recognize God as our God and Father » (SCHLIER). *who has blessed us*, at our entrance into the Church (ABBOTT). *Spiritual blessing* : these will be enumerated in the following verses (BENOIT). *in Christ* — the dominant theme throughout. It means through our union with him as members of his Body.

v. 4 *inasmuch as*. The Greek term καθώς indicates source as well as comparison here. *He has chosen us* : to exist for the Christian is to be chosen by God (SCHLIER). The phrase *in his presence*, as in Col 1,22, has a liturgical signification like the words *holy and blameless*.

v. 5. *Out of love* is more probably to be construed with *he predestined* (ORIGEN and CHRYSOSTOM). *for adoptive sonship* indicates the end or purpose of our predestination. This conception is capital in Pauline soteriology : of this sonship, Christ is source and model (BENOIT) : cf. Rom 8,29 ; Gal 4,5. The word εὐδοκία here expresses God's efficacious salvific Will.

v. 6 The refrain, *to the praise of the glory of his grace,* is repeated with some slight variation in vv. 12,14. It is an indication of the liturgical style which Paul uses here. *his grace* is a more comprehensive term than our « sanctifying grace » (BENOIT), and means God's favour or undeserved bounty (ABBOTT). Our eternal choice is already an act of the divine condescension. God does this *in his well-beloved* Son, i. e. we experience the divine love in him who is sole object of the Father's love. On Paul's view, it is by acting formally as Father that God accomplishes our salvation : cf. Col 1,13-14.

v. 7 *We possess the redemption* in the glorified humanity of the risen Christ. This is an act of God's *grace* or favour like his gracious act of forgiveness of our sins. Both have been accomplished historically through the death of Christ in which he acted as God's well-beloved Son (Rom 8,32). The phrase *in his blood* probably suggests the sacrificial aspect of Christ's redemptive death (ABBOTT).

v. 8 *every sort of wisdom and understanding.* The Church is blessed by sharing in the divine Mystery of God's eternal plan, the source of all Christian wisdom and true morality.

v. 9. *the Mystery* : the divine plan manifested in Christ and also in the Church, in which Jews and Gentiles are united in Christian charity. Paul's conception of the Mystery *par excellence,* germinally present in his earlier letters (1 Cor 2,1 ; Rom 16,25), is one of the most important developments in his last two epistles (Col 1,26-27 ; 2,2 ; 4,3 ; Eph 3,3-4 : 6,19). Concretely, the Mystery is Christ in the dimension of his Body, the Church (SCHLIER).

v. 10. *to sum up under one Head* : the Greek term means literally « to recapitulate », « to sum up » (ARMITAGE ROBINSON). However Paul probably uses it in the context of his conception of Christ as Head (Col 1,18 ; 2,10 ; Eph 1,22 ; 4,15). The idea of extending Christ's salvific work to heaven is new and may be the result of the difficulties at Colossae (ABBOTT).

v. 11. Here and in the following verse, *we* designates the Jewish Christians who find their « Erbland » (SCHLIER) in the Church. Paul remains always conscious of his solidarity with the Chosen people of God.

v. 12. Following the apostolic tradition (Acts 3,19-21), Paul habitually preached first to the Jews to whom the divine « oracles » were confided

(Rom 3,2). To the Jewish Christians remains the inalienable glory of being the first to hope in Jesus as the Messias.

v. 13. Paul now speaks to the recipients of his letter as Gentile Christians. *the Gospel of your salvation* probably means the Gospel which has saved you (SCHLIER), given the new viewpoint displayed only in this letter by Paul as regards the Christian's actual possession of salvation (cf. 2,5.8). Hence Paul's meaning is different here from his celebrated definition of the Gospel as « God's power unto salvation », i. e. eschatological salvation (Rom 1,16). *Once you were Christians* : the participle πιστεύσαντες, indicating the Christian's initial act of baptismal faith, is equivalent to « having joined the Church ». *You have been sealed* indicates the purpose of this whole long period which began in v. 3 (SCHLIER). *by the promised Holy Spirit*. It is the presence of the Holy Ghost in the Gentile Christians (an *experienced* presence, cf. Gal 3,3 ff ; 4,6 ; Rom 8,14 ff), which assures them of their divine election and salvation [35]. The Spirit is the object of the promise made by God in the OT (Gal 3,14 ff).

v. 14. The presence of the Spirit within the individual Christian and in the Church is the reality which enables Paul to state that « you have been saved » already in this life (2,5. 8). The *inheritance* comes to us in virtue of our adoption as sons of God ; it is reserved for heaven. Meanwhile, the Spirit effects the redemption of the Church as God's *segullah* (cf. Mal 3,17 in LXX). The Christians constitute God's new Chosen people, acquired through the redemptive death of Christ and his resurrection with the consequent gift of the Spirit.

§ 6. - The Christian's Comprehension of Christ's Resurrection. Eph 1,19b-23

Once his great thanksgiving is ended, Paul begins a prayer for his addressees that they may acquire true Christian wisdom (1,15 ff.). We shall quote only the part which refers to Christ's resurrection.

19b ... to judge by the force of his mighty strength, 20 which he has exerted in Christ by raising him from death and seating him at his right hand in heaven 21 above every Principality and Power and Force and Dominion and every title that is invoked, not only in this world but also in the world to come. 22 And he has put all things beneath his feet and has given him as Head over everything to the Church.

---

[35] J. BONSIRVEN, *op. cit.* 102.

[20. Sin., D, G, K, L, P, with the Chester Beatty papyrus read the aorist ἐνήργησεν instead of the perfect].

v. 19 b. *his mighty strength* or, literally, the strength of his might. The word κράτος is employed almost invariably (cf. Heb 2,14) for God's might. Christ's resurrection is attributed to the Father as an act most properly his. In the following verses, Paul contemplates Christ's resurrection under five aspects : his being raised from death, his heavenly enthronement, his exaltation over all angelic creatures, the subjection of the universe to his dominion, and his headship over the Church.

v. 20. *he has exerted in Christ.* The use of the perfect tense is to be remarked : the effects of the Father's exercise of power through Christ's resurrection continue into the present era, the « last times ». This power is now effective *in Christ* : it is the risen Christ whom Paul chiefly contemplates in this epistle. Consequently, mention must be made also of his exaltation to the Father's right hand (Ps 110,1) which signifies the universal dominion, a uniquely divine prerogative, which Christ now exercises. Paul is here employing doctrine which was from the first traditional in the apostolic kerygma (Acts 2,32-33), but he has incorporated it into his own soteriological synthesis.

v. 21. Paul explains the *sessio ad dexteram Patris* in terms of Christ's primacy over the entire angelic creation. The term ὄνομα signifies a title of rank here (ARMITAGE ROBINSON).

v. 22. By a citation from Ps 8,7, Paul emphasizes the subjection of the entire universe to the risen Christ. This is necessary here in order to define more exactly the meaning of Christ's headship of the Church : it is precisely *as Head over everything* that Christ's primacy in the Church has been acquired (cf. Mt 28,18-20) [36]. This doctrine is implied in Col 1,17-18 : here it becomes explicit. Thus Christ's relationship to the Church as Head of his Body is contained in the mystery of his resurrection.

---

[36] V. WARNACH, *op. cit.* 11 : « Indessen ist die Kirche nicht irgendeine Erscheinungsweise der Christuswirklichkeit neben etwa möglichen anderen : sie ist d e r Leib Christi ... in einer ganz r e a l e n und k o n k r e t e n Bedeutung : sie ist der durch das Kreuzesleiden und die Auferstehung pneumatisch verklärte Leib Christi, der eben wegen seiner pneumatischen, über Raum und Zeit erhabenen Seinsweise die Weite und Fülle erlangt hat, alle Gläubigen als Glieder in sich einzubeziehen, damit sie so an der personalen Lebensgemeinschaft mit Christus teilhaben können ».

§ 7. - **Salvation the Act of God's Merciful Love. Eph 2,4-8**

Paul begins, with chapter 2, a description of the greatness of God's redemptive work in Christ. After a brief allusion to the Gentile Christians' former unredeemed condition as pagans (2,1-3), Paul presents the, accomplishment of man's salvation as an expression of God's love for all pagans as well as Jews. The specifically new aspect of Paul's soteriological doctrine found here for the first time, at least in its definitive formulation, is the view that Christian salvation is already a reality in the believer's possession.

4 But God, being rich in mercy, through the great love he had for us, 5 even while we were dead because of our transgressions, quickened us together with Christ (it is by his favour you have been saved), 6 and raised us up together with him and made us sit together with him in the heavenly realm, in Christ Jesus : 7 that he might show, in ages to come, the surpassing riches of his love by his kindliness towards us in Christ Jesus. 8 It is by his favour you have been saved through faith, and that, not thanks to yourselves : it is God's gift.

[5. ἐν is added after συνεζωοποίησεν by Vat. and the Chester Beatty papyrus with other mss].

v. 4. The only motive which is given here for God's redemptive work in Christ is his love for men. God's love is described here as merciful, copious, gratuitous, kind, benevolent, tender (MÉDEBIELLE). The first person plural in this paragraph includes both Jewish and Gentile Christians.

v. 5. *you have been saved*. This view of salvation as already acquired by the Christian (Paul's use of the perfect tense here and in v. 8 is without parallel in his letters) is peculiar to the Captivity epistles (cf. Col. 3,1-4). At the same time, this new attitude, an emphasis upon the values of the Christian's present life, is quite consistent with Paul's earlier conception of salvation as the supreme, eschatological reality (1 Thes 5,9 ; 2 Thes 2,13 ; Phil 1,19.28 ; 2,12 ; 1 Cor 5,5 ; 9,22 ; 10,33 ; Rom 5,9-10 ; 9,27 ; 10,9 ; 11,14.26 ; 13,11), the term of a process already inaugurated during this life (1 Cor 1,18 ; 15,2 ; 2 Cor 2,15) and consummated, thanks to the return of the parousiac Christ (Phil 3,20), by the glorious resurrection of the body (Rom 8,23). The first step in the Christian salvation-process is the experience of baptism which Paul has once described by saying that « we were saved in hope » (Rom 8,24), i. e. at baptism, the Christian was given a title to salvation by the virtue of hope. Paul's use of the aorist tense in this passage, in contrast with his use of the perfect in the present verse, would seem to indicate a shift in viewpoint. Paul's increased awareness of the sense in which salvation may be said to be the Christian's present possession may be seen in v. 8, where he tells his addressees that « you have been saved through faith » (the verb is again in the perfect tense). Faith assures the acquisition, in a very real sense, of the eschatological blessing of salvation even in this life.

quickened us together with Christ. The compound verb employed here (the term appears only in the Captivity epistles : cf. Col 2,13) in the aorist tense, which indicates that it refers to the Christian baptismal experience, provides the justification for the assertion *you have been saved.* It is by virtue of his sharing in the new, supernatural life of the risen Christ that the Christian may be said to have acquired salvation in his present existence. Elsewhere in Paul, the simple verb ζωοποιεῖν is not used to denote the effecting of the Christian's present supernatural status, but only in connection with Christ's resurrection or the final resurrection of the just (1 Cor 15,22.36.45 ; Rom 4,17 ; 8,11).

v. 6. *raised us up ... made us sit together with him in heaven.* As a Semite, Paul cannot conceive of salvation except as affecting man in his total, corporate personality (cf. Rom 8,23) ; hence for him, salvation involves the resurrection of the body. Accordingly, in order to express his new insight that, as life, salvation is already possessed by the Christian, he must postulate a glorious resurrection already in this life, modeled on that of Christ, i. e. followed by the sessio *ad dexteram Patris.* We have another example of this same Semitic conception in Ap 20,4-5, where the author calls it « the first resurrection » : the same two ideas of life and participation in Christ's dominion are present (« they came to life and ruled with Christ a thousand years »). It is in Col 3,1-4 that Paul first begins to formulate this new notion of salvation as participated in by the Christian through Baptism, although he has not yet worked it out so completely as in the present passage : « If therefore you were raised together with Christ, seek the things above, where Christ is seated at God's right hand ... your life has been hidden with Christ in God. When Christ will be revealed, who is our life, then also you will be revealed with him in glory ». This life which is given through Baptism is already possessed by the Christian, and needs only the final revelation of the parousia to be seen in its full reality. The union of the Christian with Christ raised from death is so real and intimate that it includes participation in Christ's heavenly triumph, at least in the order of grace (BENOIT).

v. 7. *his kindliness towards us.* The term χρηστότης, which Paul uses elsewhere of God (cf. Rom 2,4 ; 11,22), denotes that kindness which is tender

and considerate (WESTCOTT). It is predicated of men also (2 Cor 6,6 ; Gal
5,22 ; Rom 3,12 ; Col 3,12) where it signifies a supernatural virtue.
v. 8. Here and in the two verses which follow, we have a résumé of Paul's
characteristic doctrine on the gratuitous nature of salvation (BENOIT),
which constitutes a striking proof of this letter's authenticity.

§ 8. - Christ our Peace: New Variation on Reconciliation Theme : Eph 2,14-18

As an illustration of his remarks on the gratuitous nature of Christian
salvation (2,8-10), Paul reminds the Gentile Christians of their former
status « without Christ » and without any share through Israel in God's
promise (2,11-12). Through the saving effects of Christ's blood, they have
now « drawn near » to the new Chosen people, and to God « in Christ Jesus » (2,13).

14 He personally is our Peace, since he brought the two together by tearing
down the wall of the enclosure, 15 by doing away with the hatred, by means
of his own mortal humanity, i. e. by abolishing the Law of the commandments
with its decrees, in order that he might in himself create the two into one new
man, thus making peace ; 16 and so reconcile both in one body to God through
the cross, having by it killed the hatred. 17 And coming, he proclaimed the Good
News of peace to you who were far off, peace also to those who were near, 18
since through him we both have access, in one Spirit, to the Father.

[15. ἐν δόγμασιν is omitted by the Chester Beatty papyrus, which also reads
κοινόν for καινόν. ἐν ἑαυτῷ is read for ἐν αὐτῷ by Sin *corr.*, D, G, K, L, and
most minuscule mss.
16. The reading ἐν ἑαυτῷ appears in G as well as in some minuscule and Latin
mss].

v. 14. *personally* : αὐτὸς means « he in his own person » (ARMITAGE
ROBINSON). *our Peace.* Is 57,19, alluded to in the preceding verse, spoke
of the peace of the Messianic age : it is fulfilled in Christ, Paul tells us,
as he will explain at once. This whole pericope, composed in praise of
Christ our Peace, has a certain hymn-like quality (SCHLIER). *brought the two
together.* Paul first refers in very general terms (hence the neuter) to
the two systems, the Jewish and the pagan, which were opposed to one
another in the world which Christ entered. Their unity in the Church,
as a result of Christ's redemptive death, is here described symbolically as
the consequence of the destruction of a protective wall or hedge. Prob-

ably, Paul alludes to the wall of separation in the Temple. The meaning of the metaphor is analogous to the rending of the Temple veil in Mt 27,51.

v. 15. *the hatred* immediately meant is probably that between Jews and Gentiles, which is however an expression of that more fundamental hatred (v. 16) displayed by humanity to God. *his own mortal humanity*. The word σάρξ recalls the similar expression in Col 1,22: it signifies Christ's human nature, inasmuch as it had become one with the sinful solidarity of the first Adam through its passibility and mortality (cf. Gal 4,4; Rom 8,3). This condition was « done away with » by the cross and the resurrection : this meant, Paul explains, that Jewish-Gentile enmity was «done away with», as well as the Law, which was a « hedge », protecting the Chosen people from pagan influence, and so an occasion of *the hatred* which existed between Jew and Gentile.

In Romans 3,31, Paul insisted that his teaching about the primacy of « the law of faith » does not « do away with » law : on the contrary, it « provides a basis » for it. By this statement he anticipates his doctrine in Romans 8,1 ff concerning the «law of the Spirit», i. e. the dynamic indwelling of the Holy Spirit in the Christian which provides the power to « fulfil the injunction of the Law » (Rom 8,4). Thus the « new Law » whose interior, supernatural character was foretold by the prophets (cf. Jer 31,33) is not opposed to the old Law as a higher moral code to a less perfect one, but as « the Spirit » to « the letter » (Rom 7,6 ; 2 Cor 3,6), which gives the Christian the power to realize fully the goal at which the Law was aiming, the fulfilment of God's will by love. Hence, Paul can assert (Rom 13,8-10) that the Law is summed up in the command of brotherly love given by Christ (Jn 13,34), for the presence of the indwelling Spirit who gives the power to love is identified as « God's love poured forth in our hearts » (Rom 5,5). This doctrine accords perfectly with what Paul states in our present verse, and explains why he states so precisely, that what was abolished by Christ's death was *the Law of the commandments with its decrees*. It has been abrogated as a code of specific precepts and ordinances (ARMITAGE ROBINSON).

The purpose of this breaking down of barriers between the Chosen people and the pagans is the creation of the new Adam, already mentioned in 2,10 ; (cf. 4,24). This is simply one aspect of the work of the risen Christ in *making peace* : the union of all humanity in the new Adam, i. e. himself in his risen and glorified condition.

v. 16. *reconcile both ... to God*. This is the more basic aspect of the reconciliation which Christ effected : the whole verse is in close parallel with

Col 1,22. Here, as there, the *one body* is Christ's mortal humanity which underwent death on the cross. The use of the phrase ἐν ἑνὶ σώματι however suggests that Paul is also thinking of that Body, the Church [37], which resulted from Christ's death and resurrection, and which, with its glorified Head, forms the *one new man* (v. 15). *killed the hatred*. Paul refers again to the enmity existing between Jew and Gentile (v. 15), but considers it in its wider context as the hostility towards God which unredeemed man displayed. By employing the word *killed* here, Paul gives a deeply theological insight into the real meaning of Christ's redemptive death. From the merely human point of view, Christ was *killed* : more truly however, it was Christ who *killed* sin, or *hatred* by his cross and resurrection (WESTCOTT).

v. 17. Allusions to Is 52,7 and 57,19 underly the conception here. The meaning of the phrase *and coming* is difficult. More probably, it does not refer to Christ's earthly career, but to his return to his Church through the operation of the Holy Spirit after his own glorification. This return, of which the post-resurrection appearances constitute a tangible sign (Jn 14,13) was a theme in the apostolic preaching (Acts 3,26 ; 26,23). Paul will himslf develop this theme more fully in 4,7-13. *the Good News of peace*. It is by the apostolic kerygma, called in this epistle, « the Gospel of your salvation »(1,13) and « the Gospel of peace » (6,15), that the union of Jewish and Gentile Christians has been inaugurated in the Church.

v. 18. *through him, we both have access, in one Spirit, to the Father*. This verse is a summary of this whole passage, and may be considered one of the most complete and summary statements of Pauline soteriology and of the function of Christ's resurrection in effecting man's salvation. Salvation is described as an *access*, a liturgical metaphor which anticipates the principal conception of Christ's redemptive work presented by the author of Hebrews (cf. Heb 9,11-12.24-28 ; 10,19-22). The figure also recapitulates Paul's own usage of sacrificial terminology in speaking of Christ's death (cf. 5,2) as the Christian paschal sacrifice (1 Cor 5,7), as the prophet-

---

[37] H. SCHLIER, *Die Kirche im Epheserbriefe* 85 : « Wie man die Einzelheiten der Stelle von 2,14-16 aber auch auslegen mag, das ist deutlich : der Ursprung der Kirche in Zeit und Welt liegt in dem Leibe Christi Jesu am Kreuz, sofern in diesem Leibe Juden und Heiden aufgenommen, in gleicher Weise neubegründet und Gott hingegeben wurden. Dieser Leib Christi am Kreuz, dieser konkrete, fleischliche Leib des am Kreuz sich zum Himmel aufrichtenden Erlösers, der da in sich den Menschen die Versöhnung mit Gott gewährt, ist schon potentiell oder auch virtuell der Leib der Kirche aus Juden und Heiden ».

ic fulfilment of the sacrifice of the Day of Atonement (Rom 3,25), or of Abraham's sacrifice of Isaac (Rom 8,32), as Christ's « offering of himself » (Gal 1,4), or « handing himself over » for our sins (Gal 2,20).

Paul has already employed this symbolism of *access* in Rom 5,1-2, where he equates it with our *peace* with God, a biblical image representing the totality of the messianic blessings, which implies the redemptive resurrection, since « we shall be saved through his life » (Rom 5,10b), as well as the efficacy of « the Blood of his Cross » (Col 1,20). The risen Christ is simply « our peace » which he has effected by his work of the « new creation », (2 Cor 5,17 ; Gal 6,15), creating out of Jew and Gentile « one new Man » (Eph 2,15) ; for by his death and resurrection, God has « summed up all things under one Head in Christ » (Eph 1,10).

This liturgical metaphor of *access* has the advantage of resuming the various other symbols used in Paul's writing to describe man's redemption. It presupposes our liberation from the old Law (Gal 4,5 ; Rom 7,4 ; Gal 2,19 ; Rom 8,2-4) which, as is stated in the present passage, formed a wall of division between pagans and the Chosen People (2,14). It presupposes our *reconciliation* (2 Cor 5,19-20 ; Rom 5,10-11 ; Col 1,20.22) with God, or our *rescue* from sin (2 Cor 1,10 ; Gal 1,4), or our *pardon* (Col 2,13b-14), the *remission of our sins* (Col 1,14 ; 1,7). It expresses admirably the positive aspects of our *redemption* « in Christ Jesus » (Rom 3,24), or « through his blood » (1,7) which is our union with God. It implies the rejection of the old self and the assumption of the new Adam, the risen Christ (Col 3, 1b-11). Finally, it evokes all the values contained in the notion of *the Mystery* which Paul has exploited particularly in the Captivity epistles (Rom 16,25-26 ; Col 1,26-27 ; Eph 1,9-10 ; 3,3-10).

This access has been made possible *through him*, i. e. Christ, (Col 1,13.20) as the second Adam (Col 3,9b-11 ; Rom 5,19), who by his resurrection is become the « Life-giving Spirit » (1 Cor 15,45), and who is also the ' *Ebed Yahweh* (Phil 2,6-11). The Christian's new status has been effected by participation in the death, resurrection, and glorification of Christ (Col 2,12-13 ; Phil 3,10-11 ; Rom 6,4-6) through baptism, « Christ's circumcision » (Col 3,11). Moreover, it is *through him* as *Son* that we are given this access to *the Father*, since Christ « was constituted Son of God in power by resurrection of the dead » (Rom 1,4), and thus capable of transmitting to us our adoptive sonship (Eph 1,5 ; Gal 4,5).

It is an access to God *as Father*, the result of his paternal love and mercy (Eph, 2,4-7 ; Rom 5,8) or of « the exercise of his mighty strength » displayed in the raising of his Son (Eph, 1,19b-22 ; 1 Thes 4,14). It calls forth the imitation of God as Father « like beloved children » (Eph 5,1), or the living « a life of love » (Eph 5,2), or the living « for God » (Gal 2,17), or for him « who died and was raised for us » (2 Cor 5,15 ; Rom 14,7-9).

It is an access *in one Spirit*, the source of union within the Christian community (Eph 4,3-4 ; 1 Cor 12,4 ; 2 Cor 13,13), of union with the risen Christ (1 Cor 6,17), whose Spirit he is (Rom 8,9b) as well as « the Spirit of him who raised Jesus from death » (Rom 8,11). He is the sanctifier (2 Thes 2,13), the « Spirit of adoptive sonship » (Rom 8,15) since his indwelling is the prophetic fulfilment of the Father's promise to Abraham (Gal 3,14). His operation in the hearts of Christians is identified with that of the risen Christ (2 Cor 3,17 ; 1 Cor 15,45).

§ 9. - Christ's Lesson of Love. Eph 4,32-5,2

This passage, which occurs in the course of Paul's exhortation to the Gentile Christians, to whom he writes (4,1-6,22), is a brief summary of the whole spirit of Pauline morality. They must endeavour to preserve the unity of the Body of Christ (4,1-16) by putting off their old pagan habits to enter more completely into that Body (4,17-31).

4,32 But be kind to one another, merciful : forgive one another just as God has forgiven us in Christ. 5,1 Therefore, become imitators of God like beloved children. 2 Live a life of love, just as Christ loved you and handed himself over for our sake as a sweet-smelling offering and sacrifice to God.

[2. ἡμᾶς is read for ὑμᾶς by the Chester Beatty papyrus and several other mss. The reading followed here is most commonly adopted by modern editors.]

v. 32. The passage is parallel to Col 3,12-13 : here however Paul mentions the forgiveness of the Father *in Christ*, an idea expressed in 2 Cor 5,19. *just as.* The word denotes not merely comparison but also the source of this Christian forgiveness (SCHLIER). The motive given here is similar to that in the parable of the unforgiving Servant (cf. Mt 18,33).
v. 1. *become imitators of God.* This conception is not found elsewhere in Paul's letters : he habitually proposes himself for imitation (1 Thes 1,6 ; 2 Thes 3,7 ; Phil 3,17 ; 1 Cor 4,16 ; 11,1 ; Gal 4,12) [38]. Since this letter is written to a community which the Apostle did not found and which he appears not to have known personally, he simply proposes the traditional

---

[38] D. M. STANLEY, « *Become Imitators of me* » : *The Pauline conception of Apostolic Tradition* in *Bib* 40 (1959) 275-293.

Christian doctrine to them, which derives from Jesus' own teaching (cf. Mt 5,44-48). This throws considerable light on Paul's conception of the Father's forgiveness of men *in Christ* (v. 32). Since our imitation of the Father in freely forgiving one another is based upon his work of reconciliation accomplished by his Son's death and resurrection, we have here « a decisive proof that St. Paul did not view the Atonement in the light of payment of a debt or endurance of penalty demanded by divine justice » (ABBOTT) [38a]. *like beloved children.* In forgiving one another, we are living as adoptive sons of the Father by imitating him in his supreme self-revelation through Christ's redemptive death.

v. 2. *Live a life of love.* The Christian life is essentially one of love, since Christian salvation is the result of Christ's infinite act of love. *handed himself over.* Once (Rom 8,32) or possibly twice (Rom 4,25), Paul speaks of the Father handing over his Son for us. More commonly, as here, it is Christ who handed himself over (Gal 1,4 ; 2,20 ; Eph 5,2 ; cf. 1 Tim 2,6 ; Ti 2,14). The description of Christ's death here as a sacrifice is intended to show how pleasing to God Christ's act of self-immolation was (DIBELIUS). It is the voluntareity and love in Christ's redemptive death which is brought into clear relief here (MÉDEBIELLE). This portrayal of Christ's death as a sacrifice, which is so prominent in the soteriological conception of Hebrews, is not absent from Paul's own writings (cf. 1 Cor 5,7 ; Rom 3,25). Indeed, it may be said that the notion of sacrifice is expressed by the « handing over » of himself by Christ referred to above, especially since the Father's « handing over » of « his own Son » (Rom 8,32) is an allusion to Abraham's sacrifice of Isaac.

§ 10. - Christ's Redemptive Death as an Act of Love for the Church. Eph 5,25-26

This passage appears in a series of remarks which concern the various relationships which exist within the family (5,21-6,9).

25 You husbands, love your wives just as Christ also loved the Church and handed himself over for her sake, 26 in order that he might cleanse and sanctify her by the bath of water, [which is accompanied] by a word.

[25. ἑαυτῶν is read after γυναῖκας in D, K, L, and several of the versions. It is however omitted by Sin., Vat., Alex. ; G reads ὑμῶν].

[38a] This view is already found in the *Summa Theologica*, III, q. 46 a. 2 ad 3.

v. 25. The love of husband for wife in Christianity is based upon Christ's love of the Church. Here for the only time in Paul's letters, his redemptive death is represented explicitly as an act of love towards the Church [39]. In v. 23, Christ was called « the Saviour of his Body », i. e. the Church. This characterization of Christ is also quite singular in the NT (SCHLIER). v. 26. Here the Apostle carries still further his conception that Christ died out of love for the Church, by asserting that that purpose is realized in Christian Baptism, the sacrament of initiation, by which Christ chose to *cleanse and sanctify* the Church. The figure of marriage was used in the OT to depict the Covenant as an act of Yahweh's love for his people (Os 2,14 ff; Jer 2,1-3,22; Is 51,4-8; 61,10). In fact, Ezekiel's magnificent allegory based on this theme may well have inspired the present conception in Paul (Ez 16,8-9). *accompanied by a word*. The term ῥῆμα here, as in Rom 10,8-9; Heb 6,5, more probably refers to the baptismal confession of faith made by the proselyte at his reception of the sacrament of Baptism.

This brief passage is significant for the development of Paul's soteriological doctrine at this period of his life. Throughout these two letters from the Apostle's Roman Captivity, he has constantly been thinking of Christ's work of salvation in terms of the Church and of her sacraments and liturgy (cf. Col. 1,13-28; 2,11-13; 3,1-4; Eph 1,3-14; 2,1-21; 4,4-13). It is the present pericope however which shows, more clearly perhaps than any other, how Paul's attention has come to be concentrated upon the action of the risen Christ in the Church, and particularly in her liturgy.

---

[39] H. SCHLIER, *Die Kirche im Epheserbriefe* 104 : « So kann man nach dem Epheserbriefe die ' Geschichte ' des Werdens der Kirche auch als ' Geschichte ' der Liebe begreifen. Die Kirche ruht in der ewigen Bewegung der Liebe Gottes in Christus (1,4f). Sie entsteht in derselben Liebe. Denn in ihr hat uns Gott in Christus geliebt und ihn für uns hingegeben (2,5 ; 5,2.25) ».

CHAPTER IX

THE PASTORALS AND CHRIST'S RESURRECTION

Bibliography : BERNHARD WEISS, Die Briefe Pauli an Timotheus und Titus⁶, MK (Göttingen, 1902). J. N. BERNARD, The Pastoral Epistles, CGT (Cambridge, 1906). MARTIN DIBELIUS, Die Pastoralbriefe², HNT 13 (Tübingen, 1931). MAX MEINERTZ, Die Pastoralbriefe des heiligen Paulus⁴, BB (Bonn, 1931). WALTER LOCK, The Pastoral Epistles, ICC (Edinburgh, 1936). G. BARDY, Épîtres Pastorales, SB 12 (Paris, 1946). C. SPICQ, Les Épîtres Pastorales, EB (Paris, 1947). JOACHIM JEREMIAS, Die Briefe an Timotheus und Titus⁴, NTD 9 (Göttingen, 1947). ADRIEN BOUDOU, Les Épîtres Pastorales, VS 15 (Paris, 1950). PIERRE DORNIER, Les Épîtres de saint Paul à Timothée et à Tite², BJ (Paris, 1958).

The style of these letters is very informal and somewhat personal. They consequently exhibit little evidence of any well-knit plan, which might prove of assistance in grasping their dogmatic content. Doctrinal assertions alternate with exhortation and personal recommendations.

Great emphasis is laid upon the concept of salvation. Through Baptism it is already a present possession of the Christian (Ti 3,5) ; yet, in its final phase, it is connected with ultimate incorporation into the « heavenly Kingdom », which is here considered as belonging to the risen Christ (2 Tm 4,1.18) and bears an essential relation to « eternal glory » (2 Tm 2,10). It is as bestowing salvation that God's gracious gesture towards men through Jesus Christ is chiefly characterized (Ti 2,11). Indeed, the most proper title for God is that of « Saviour » (1 Tm 1,1 ; 2,3 ; 4,10 ; Ti 1,3 ; 2,10 ; 3,4), as it is also for Jesus Christ (Ti 1,4 ; 2,13 ; 3,6 ; 2 Tm 1,10). It has rightly been said that the doctrine of the Trinity, of the Christian Mystery, and of the Church in these epistles is viewed under the soteriological aspect (SPICQ). While this is not peculiar to the Pastorals, still it may be said that these letters display a special awareness that Christian salvation can become a reality for the individual only in the Church, through her teaching and the efficacious working of her sacraments.

§ 1. - Paul's Personal Experience of Christian Salvation. 1 Tm 1,15-16

This passage occurs in the course of the thanksgiving section, in which Paul encourages Timothy by enumerating the graces which he himself has received through his vocation (LOCK), which is to preach « the Good News of the glory of the blessed God » (1,11). This Gospel is identified with the risen Christ, who, in his glorified state, as God's image, is the perfect expression of the divinity (2 Cor 4,4). Paul now illustrates the theorem concerning salvation, found earlier in Rom 3,21-26 (DORNIER), from his own experience.

15 This saying merits confidence and is worthy of special acceptance : « Christ Jesus came into the world to save sinners », among whom I rank first. 16 Now the reason I have been accorded mercy is this : that in me, first of all, Jesus Christ might show the full measure of his long-suffering, in order to provide a preliminary sketch for those who will assuredly believe in him to [the acquiring of] eternal life.

[15a. The reading ἀνθρώπινος for πιστὸς in some old Latin mss. is probably not original. Jerome referred to it as « latinorum codicum vitiositas » (PL XXII 431). 16b. Χριστὸς Ἰησοῦς is read by Alex., D, and the Vulgate, Gothic, and Sahidic versions ; Ἰησοῦς Χριστὸς by Sin., K, L, P, and the Syriac, Coptic, Armenian, Ethiopic versions].

In this section, which begins with v. 12, Paul is probably recalling his own conversion on the Damascus road. His personal experience of divine grace is the most potent motive-force in his preaching (SPICQ). Hence he has the glorified Christ in mind, the Christ of whom he had first-hand knowledge through the meeting which gave him his vocation as an apostle.

v. 15. *This saying merits confidence.* The expression, peculiar to the Pastorals, serves, in the opinion of all commentators, to introduce a citation of great importance. It would appear to be connected, not with the kerygma (DIBELIUS), but, as Ti 1,9 indicates, with the « teaching » of the Christian community. The Johannine quality of this axiom (cf. also v. 16, *believe in him to eternal life*) would indicate that it emanates from the school of that apostle. It will be recalled that Paul writes to Timothy at Ephesus, the traditional centre of Johannine theology.

Christ Jesus is the most common title given to the God-Man in the Pastorals, *Jesus Christ* being used less frequently. The simple name, Jesus, common in Paul's earlier letters, where it usually indicates a Palestinian source, is never used in these last epistles ; nor, with the exception of 1 Tm 5,11, does the single title, Christ, appear. One reason for this is that the Christology of the Pastorals is very frequently expressed in formulae already traditional in the Church (SPICQ). Another, that the double name, in Hellenistic Christianity, has come to be regarded as *nomen* and *cognomen*[1]. The most important reason is theological : it was to the *risen* Lord and his impact upon contemporary events that the early Church directed her attention, her worship, her petitions. The phrase *came into the world* is characteristically Johannine (Jn 1,9 ; 6,14 ; 11,27), while the whole sentence is reminiscent of Lk 19,10. Paul himself had expressed the same idea (Gal 4,4 ff ; Rom 8,3-4). As elsewhere in Paul, it is not the idea of the incarnation as such which is prominent (vs. SPICQ) in effecting man's salvation (cf. Ti 3,4-7 ; 2 Tm 1,10), nor is there probably any reference to Christ's pre-existence (LOCK). Christ's coming is a prelude to the redemption, *to save sinners, among whom I rank first*. The theme of salvation is very much to the fore in the Pastorals. While it is still regarded, in a sense, as eschatological (2 Tm 2,10 ; 4,18 ; Ti 2,13), it is rather thought of as already communicated to the Christian by means of the sacraments (Ti 3,5 ; 2 Tm 1,9). As all the commentators point out, Paul still regards himself as a sinner, and a great one, without making any comparisons with other men (SPICQ). He thinks of himself as the first of sinners, partly from humility, but also because he considers himself the first of the saved (BARDY), as a sketch, preliminary to the finished work of the divine Artist, which will be completed through eschatological salvation.

v. 16. Just as in Rom 3,25 God is pictured as having « publicly exposed Christ as a kind of new mercy-seat ... in his blood, with the ultimate purpose of manifesting his justice », so here Christ is represented as giving proof of *the full measure of his long-suffering, in order to provide a preliminary sketch for those who will assuredly believe*. However, it is to be observed that, since Paul is speaking of the effects of grace in his own life (whether at his conversion or in the course of his apostolate), he thinks of the contemporary activity of the exalted Christ. « the power of his resurrection » (Phil 3,10) in human history. BONSIRVEN says that the Christian life is defined in terms of the Christian's relations with Christ and the Spirit[2]. Paul knows from what has happened to himself that these relations transcend the merely moral order : he has experience of the

---

[1] L. CERFAUX, *Le Christ dans la théologie de saint Paul* 376-379.
[2] J. BONSIRVEN, *L'Évangile de Paul* 197-198.

risen Christ as a vital principle of the new life within him (Phil 1,21 ;
Gal 2,20-21 ; Col 3,4). Hence the Christian life can properly be termed
eternal life.

§ 2. - The Gospel Message of Salvation. 1 Tm 2,3-7

The whole of ch. 2 is concerned with the Christian liturgical cult :
the first half is devoted to liturgical prayer (vv. 1-8), while the second half
defines the position of woman in the Church's life (vv. 9-15). Paul urges
that prayer be offered for the whole of humanity, and especially for
those who, like Nero and his government, are « in authority »[3]. He
appears to have accepted the Roman state in its political and social aspects,
and does not pose the problem of the opposition between the Church
and the self-deifying Empire, so keenly felt by the author of the Apocalypse[4].

3 This is something beautiful and acceptable in the eyes of our Saviour-God,
4 who desires that all men be saved and come to a realization of truth.
5   « God is one.
         One also is God's Mediator, and man's,
         Christ Jesus, man himself,
6   Who gave himself as ransom on behalf of all men ».
Such was, in God's good time, his testimony. 7 Of this message I have been constituted herald and apostle (I am not lying, but telling the truth), as instructor of
pagans in the truth of the faith.

[3a. γὰρ is inserted after τοῦτο by many mss. of secondary quality.
6b. οὗ τὸ μαρτύριον ... ἐδόθη, read by D (first corr.), Ambrosiaster, is an attempt
at clarifying an obscure passage.
7a. Alex. reads ἐπιστεύθην for ἐτέθην ; ἐν ᾧ is read by F, the Vulgate, Ambrosiaster instead of εἰς ὅν.
7b. Χριστῷ is added after λέγω by Sin. (first corr.), D (2nd corr.), etc.
7c. in place of πίστει, Alex. reads πνεύματι, Sin. reads γνώσει].

v. 3 *This is something beautiful.* The salvation-doctrine of the Pastorals
is described frequently in terms of the Greek ideal of beauty[5]. Paul

---

³ E. STAUFFER, *Die Theologie des Neuen Testaments*, § 49. *Kirche und Staat*,
175-178.
        ⁴ H. M. FÉRET, *L'Apocalypse de saint Jean : vision chrétienne de l'histoire*
(Paris, 1946) 84-95.
        ⁵ C. SPICQ, *op. cit.* CXCVI ff.

appears to be making it appealing for the Hellenistic peoples. Thus he attempts to present the Gospel in terms they can appreciate. Once he realized that the pagans of the Greek world were to be called ahead of the Jews to Christianity (cf. Rom 11,25-26), the truly universalist character of the Church became impressed upon him. This explanation of the remarkable frequency with which the word καλός occurs in the Pastorals is, I believe, a more fundamental one than that given by W. GRUNDMANN, who attributes it to the preoccupation of second generation Christianity with questions of « the external appearance and perseverance of Christian conduct » [6]. It is to be recalled however that this notion of « beauty » has become a religious concept. Here it derives its meaning from the universal salvific Will of God, *who desires that all men be saved*. Man's salvation is described in terms of its ultimate basis, the acceptance of Christian doctrine. It is a *realization of truth*, the result of supernatural faith in the kerygma. While the expression is found only in the Pastorals, the conception is Johannine (Jn 17,3).

v. 5. The ultimate reason for the universality of God's plan of salvation is the fact that *God is one*. In vv. 5-6, we have quoted a *Bekenntnisformel*, part of a very early statement of Christian faith, in which Christ appears as the Deutero-Isaian Suffering servant and is also Son of Man (JEREMIAS), or, perhaps more exactly, as the second Adam (a fact which explains the insistence upon Christ's humanity). Polytheism is essentially nationalistic or racialist in outlook : the gods of a particular state or city are only interested in the welfare of the local inhabitants. Christianity, like Judaism, opposes such religious chauvinism. In contradistinction to Israel's religion however, which postulated a plurality of mediators (the angels, Moses) between God and his people, Christianity asserts the unicity of Christ's mediation. This office springs from his humanity : because Christ is *man himself*, he can mediate between God and men.

v. 6. Yet this quotation does not contemplate the incarnation in itself. The mediation, of which there is question here, is thought of as beginning with Christ's death, *who gave himself as ransom on behalf of all men*. It is of course as risen from death (cf. the use of the title *Christ Jesus* ; also Rom 8,34) that Christ carries out this work of mediation. SPICQ draws attention to the novelty of the expression ἀντίλυτρον ὑπὲρ πάντων. The biblical hapax ἀντίλυτρον has been composed on the basis of traditional data (cf. Mk 10,45 ; Mt 20,28). As such, it expresses the idea of substi-

---

[6] W. GRUNDMANN, καλός, *TWNT III*, 552.

tution, while ὑπέρ simply states that Christ's act of redemption was
a benefit to all men. The force of the substitution-idea is modified by
the insistence on Christ's human nature (v. 5), which makes him *solidaire*
with the whole human family. He takes the place of men only insofar
as he is God. We might add that, for Paul, it was through the conception
of the risen Christ as second Adam that the question of substition-
solidarity was fundamentally solved. By taking man's place in dying and
rising, Christ has actually involved all humanity in his redemptive action
(2 Cor 5,14-15) by founding in his own glorified humanity a new solidarity
of grace. This act of salvation was Christ's *testimony* to, or proof of, the
Father's universal salvific will.

v. 7. It is this fact of God's desire to save, not merely the Chosen people,
but all mankind, which has given Paul's vocation as *instructor of pagans* its reality : his preaching of the Gospel is merely a continuation of
this *testimony* rendered by Christ to his Father (SPICQ).

§ 3. - The « Mystery » Identified with the Glorified Christ. 1 Tm 3,16

The review of the duties of deacons, in the paragraph immediately
preceding this quotation (1 Tm 3,9), alluded to a favourite Pauline
theme : « the Mystery », or divine plan of salvation (cf. Rom 16,25-26 ;
1 Cor 2,7-8 ; Col 1,26-27 ; 2,2-3 ; Eph 1,9-10 ; 3,8-12 ; 6,19) as revealed
through the teaching of the Church. In a striking transition between
the first part of his letter, describing Timothy as champion of Christian
truth, organizer of divine worship, and pastor (DORNIER), and the second
half, largely concerned with practical issues, Paul recalls the Christian
reality which is the Church. This thought leads to that of the glorified
Christ, who incarnates « the Mystery », a conception which is admirably
expressed in a hymn, probably in use in the Ephesian church's baptismal liturgy [7]. SPICQ is probably right in connecting the strophes cited
here with those quoted in Eph 5,14.

> Wake up, you sleeper,
> and arise from death,
> and Christ will shine his light upon you ...

---

[7] J. SCHMITT, *Jésus ressuscité dans la prédication apostolique* 100.

Profound is the Mystery of our religion,
« [He] who was revealed by flesh
was justified by spirit
was beheld by angels
was proclaimed amongst nations
was believed in throughout the world
was assumed in glory ».

[the reading ὅς , attested by Sin, Alex., Ephr. *rescr.* (all first corr.) and by the
Sahidic, Coptic, Ethiopic versions, many Fathers and all modern editors, is to
be preferred to the neuter ὅ , read by Beza (first corr.), the Vulgate and some
Latin Fathers. Some less reliable mss. read Θεός].

The hymn naturally falls into three parts, each section consisting
of two lines. It has been suggested that this triple structure is based upon
the ancient Near Eastern coronation-rite (JEREMIAS, SPICQ), a literary
form found elsewhere in the NT [8] : the monarch's *elevation* to the divine
dignity, his *presentation* to the gods of the national pantheon, his
enthronement, or accession to supreme power. In each of the three sections
there is a pair of antitheses : flesh-spirit, angels-nations, world-glory.
revealed by flesh. This line has been thought to refer to the incarnation
(SPICQ). While this view cannot be excluded *a priori*, it appears difficult to accept because of the meaning most commonly given to σάρξ in
the NT. The term signifies human nature in its weakness, creatureliness,
sinfulness by which it is contrasted with the divine. The contrast with
spirit in the following line would indicate that such is its meaning here.
In the Pauline letters, Christ's σάρξ and its significance are described
constantly in function of his redemptive death (Rom 8,3 ; Col 1,22 ;
Eph 2,14). The Pastoral epistles refer to the two comings of Christ, in a
way peculiar to them, as two « epiphanies » or manifestations : the first,
a manifestation of God's « saving favour » (Ti 2,11), of his « kindliness »
(Ti 3,4) ; the second, a manifestation of « glory » (Ti 2,13). The first
« epiphany of our Saviour Christ Jesus » is said to have occurred by his
« having reduced death to impotence » (2 Tm 1,10), a clear reference to
Christ's saving death. In view of all this, it seems more probable that our
verse ought to be understood as an allusion to Christ's death in its
redemptive character.
was justified by spirit. From its obvious antithetic parallelism with the
preceding verse, this line may be expected to contain a reference to

---

[8] Cf. Heb 1,5-13 ; also Col 2,15.

Christ's resurrection. The term spirit, like flesh, signifies something intrinsic to Christ, the result of the operation, in his sacred humanity, of the Holy Spirit : cf. « according to the Spirit of holiness » (Rom 1,4). The main problem here is to determine the meaning of the operative word *justified*. It is not impossible that the term is a borrowing from the vocabulary of the Greek Mystery religions, where it signified « to divinize » [9]. The meaning of the verse would then provide a parallel to Rom 1,4, where Christ is said to « have been constituted Son of God in power by resurrection from death ». A. DESCAMPS [10] understands the word *justified* as synonymous with « glorified », because of the affinity existing in the Bible between justice and glory. L. CERFAUX [11] remarks that the archaic title, « the Just One », given to Christ in the primitive preaching, has a meaning analogous to « the Holy One », the other early epithet used of Christ. Accordingly, it seems most probable that, however we explain the meaning of *justified*, there is question of Christ's resurrection here, as both B. WEISS and J. JEREMIAS insist [12].

was seen by angels ... proclaimed amongst nations. These two lines describe the glorified Christ's « presentation », first to the angels for their adoration (cf. Phil 2,10), then to the nations of the world through the promulgation of the Gospel (JEREMIAS). CERFAUX [13] finds a parallel to this conception in the *Ascension of Isaias*, and considers that these strophes describe Christ's triumph in the two realms where Judaism had failed : the world of the Gentiles and that of the celestial powers. The author may well be thinking of Pentecost, which connected Christ's exaltation to God's right hand (hence above all angelic beings) with the inauguration of the apostolic preaching to « men of every nation under heaven » (cf. Acts 2,5-36).

was believed in throughout the world ... assumed in glory. Here again we have *the Mystery* described in terms of its earthly and celestial effects (JEREMIAS). If we consider that the second strophe contains a reference to the

---

[9] Cf. WALTER BAUER, *Griechisch-Deutsches Wörterbuch zu den Schriften des Neuen Testaments und der übrigen urchristlichen Literatur*[4] (Berlin, 1952) *sub voce*.

[10] A. DESCAMPS, *Les justes et la justice dans le christianisme primitif* (Louvain, 1950) 88.

[11] L. CERFAUX, *op. cit.* 282.

[12] WEISS is most emphatic : cf. his commentary, p. 157 : « Gemeint ist ohne Frage die Auferweckung Christi ». Cf. also JEREMIAS' commentary, pp. 21-22 : « In beiden Fällen ist sachlich mit der Rechtfertigung die Auferstehung gemeint ».

[13] CERFAUX, *op. cit* 282.

ascension, then we must admit that the chronological order has been abandoned, the ascension being anterior to the Pentecostal events mentioned in the preceding strophe (SPICQ). However, it is important to recall that, according to a very primitive soteriological conception, Christ's ascension was considered as initiating upon earth, through the presence of the Holy Spirit, an age of faith and messianic blessing. « By raising his Servant, God has sent him to you, first of all, to bless you, by turning each of you from your iniquity » (Acts 3,26) [14]. Paul has himself expressed the same idea in Eph 4,8 ff.

Thus this hymn, sung during the baptismal liturgy, commemorates the principal events of the Christian salvation-history which concurred in creating the symbolism of Christian Baptism : Christ's death, resurrection, ascension, and the episode of the first Pentecost [15]. It was this last event which gave the disciples their first insight into the meaning of Christ's ascension, and which led, as the Cornelius episode in Acts shows [16], to the evangelization of the Gentile world.

§ 4. - The Hellenized Version of the Gospel. Ti 2,11-14

In the first part of the second chapter of this epistle, Paul has given detailed instructions about the duties of the aged, the young, and of slaves. These verses are appended as a doctrinal foundation for the practice of these duties by the Christians of Crete (DORNIER). The passage has been called « a hymn to God's grace » and « a résumé of Pauline theology » (SPICQ). The section is of interest to us, since it gives a transposition in Hellenistic terms of the apostolic preaching, regarding as specifically Christian, virtues cultivated by Hellenism. The word ἐπιφάνεια employed, here to denote Christ's second Coming, also betrays « an influence of the Hellenistic idiom upon Pauline vocabulary » [17].

11 God's gracious gift appeared, a source of salvation for all men, 12 teaching us that by rejecting once for all impiety and the ideals of the world, we are to live a life of self-control and justice and piety in the present age, 13 while we wait

---

[14] D. M. STANLEY, *The Conception of Salvation in Primitive Christian Preaching* in *CBQ* 18 (1956) 244-245.

[15] D. M. STANLEY, *The New Testament Doctrine of Baptism* in *TS* 18 (1957) 203-207.

[16] *ibid.* 208.

[17] CERFAUX, *op. cit.* 31.

for the blessed hope, the manifestation of our great God and Saviour, Jesus Christ,
14 who gave himself on our behalf to ransom us from all irreligiousness, and to
purify for himself a people of his own, anxious to do good.

[11. Instead of σωτήριος, Sin. (first corr.) reads σωτῆρος, while G and some Latin
mss. have τοῦ σωτῆρος ἡμῶν. Merk prefers ἡ σωτήριος (rejected by Spicq as a
correction) with von Soden and Vogels.
13. Ἰησοῦ Χριστοῦ, found in Merk and Spicq, is attested by Alex., Ephr. rescr.,
K, L, and Beza, while Χριστοῦ Ἰησοῦ, favoured by Nestle, is read by Sin. (first
corr.), F, G].

v. 11. The aorist tense of the verb which is placed in the emphatic position emphasizes the unique and unexpected (SPICQ) character of God's
gracious act of salvation. There is clearly question of some single event
in the salvation-history. In order to identify this event, it is of the
utmost importance to observe that it is designated as an « epiphany ». We
are dealing here with the conception, already seen to be proper to the
Pastorals, of the two « manifestations » of Christ. The whole period which
the NT calls « the last times » has the two « epiphanies » of Christ as its
frame of reference. While the second of these is the parousia (v. 13), the
first, as we have seen already, is more probably Christ's death (and
resurrection). The Pastorals constantly connect the conception of the Father or Christ as Saviour with the latter's redemptive death (cf. 1 Tm
2,4-5 ; 2 Tm 1,10) or with the work of the risen Christ (Ti 3,4-6). This
use of the word « epiphany » probably reveals a consciously antipolemic
attitude against the cult of the Roman emperor (DIBELIUS).
v. 12. The pedagogical purpose of Christ's redemptive work is expressed
here, both positively and negatively, in terms borrowed from Hellenism [18].
It is at Baptism that the Christian has definitively broken with *impiety
and the ideals of the world* (JEREMIAS), the aorist participle signifying a
complete rupture with the past (SPICQ). The early apostolic kerygma had
asserted this same truth in other terms (Acts 2,38). The Christian life is
presented in terms of the Greek ethical ideal : *self-control*, which regu-
lates one's attitude towards oneself ; *justice*, which governs relations with
the neighbour ; *piety*, which determines the Christian's dealings with
God (JEREMIAS, SPICQ).
v. 13. The object of Christian hope is the parousiac Christ, whose divinity

---

[18] Thus the use of παιδεύειν here is Hellenistic, not biblical, as it is in 1 Cor
11,32 ; 2 Cor 6,9.

is strikingly asserted [19]. It may be that the second Coming of Christ is thought of as a *manifestation* because of an increased awareness of, or attention to, the invisible presence of Christ in his Church and especially in the Christian liturgy. It will not be so much a parousia, as a *manifestation* of the risen Lord which will occur at the end of time.

v. 14. *who gave himself on our behalf to ransom us.* The verse explains the function of Jesus' first « epiphany ». The redemptive death, recalled in terms current in the apostolic kerygma, is the first essential element of this *manifestation.* As we have remarked earlier, the phrase, *he gave himself,* is used throughout the *NT* to describe the voluntareity of Jesus' redemptive death : in the Synoptic tradition (Mk 10,45 ; Mt 20,28 ; Lk 22,19), in the Johannine tradition (Jn 6,51), in Pauline soteriology (Gal 1,4 ; 2,20 ; Rom 4,25 ; Eph 5,2.25 ; 1 Tm 2,6). The verb recalls the primary OT type of Christian salvation, Israel's exodus out of Egypt (Lk 24,21). It is a close parallel to the first half of Rom 4,25 : « who was handed over for our sins ».

To purify for himself a people of his own. These words express the more positive aspect of Christ's redemptive work : the union with the risen Christ which is effected through the communication of the Holy Spirit (and hence implies the salvific causality of Christ's resurrection). The idea is presented by borrowing anther OT conception, which formed an important aspect of the theological interpretation of Israel's liberation from Egypt : divine choice and acquisition of Israel as the Chosen People, Yahweh's *segullah* (Ex 19,5 ; Dt 7,6). Luke applies the term to the Church (Acts 20,28), the new Israel. Paul has used it in his earliest letters to define the relationship between the Christian community and Christ. In God's designs, the Christian people is « *an acquisition* of salvation through our Lord Jesus Christ », which implies, in addition to Jesus' death (« who died for us »), the efficiency of his salutary resurrection (« that ... we may live together with him ») (1 Thes 5,9-10). The term appears in a second text which also involves the causality of Christ's resurrection, since this *acquisition* is described as a participation in Christ's glorification (« for an acquisition of the glory of our Lord Jesus Christ ») which is effected « through the sanctification by the Spirit » (2 Thes 2,13-14), communicated by the risen Christ through the instrumentality of his glorified humanity. In Eph 1,13-14, the Christians' union with the risen Christ is explained as a « sealing by the promised Holy

---

[19] Cf. SPICQ's remarks in his commentary, pp. 365 f.

16. - D. M. STANLEY.

Spirit », « the pledge of our inheritance », whose operation within those
chosen by the Father is described by the phrase, « to ready the redemption
of the People of God's acquiring », or *acquisition*.

Later, in this same letter, Paul describes this aspect of Christian salvation in function of Baptism, which confers « the utter newness of
the Holy Spirit » (Ti 3,5). This gift of the Spirit is the work of the risen
Christ, (« whom he poured out over us prodigally through Jesus Christ
our Saviour »), which brings about our justification and our inheritance
as God's *segullah* (Ti 3,6-7). Thus the words *to purify for himself a people
of his own* are parallel in meaning to the second half of Rom 4,25, « he
was raised for our justification », and they express, in terms of the
segullah-motif, the redemptive causality of Christ's resurrection. Paul has
asserted that this « justification » produces « life » in us : indeed this is
the meaning of the indwelling of the risen Christ (Rom 8,10), or of « the
Spirit of Christ », the essential condition of « belonging to him » (Rom 8,
9), of being, in other words, *a people of his own*, Christ's *acquisition*.

§ 5. - The Quintessence of the Christian Gospel. Ti 3,4-7

This passage, which is in some respects parallel to the one we have
just considered (Ti 2,11-14), provides the dogmatic basis for the general
duties of the Christian which have just been outlined (Ti 3,1-3). Like the
preceding passage, it may be described as « the heart of the epistle »
(SPICQ). It is distinguished from the former passage, however, in one
notable respect : Christian salvation is not connected with Christ's death
and resurrection, but with the Christian sacrament of Baptism, which
confers the Holy Spirit.

4 « But when our Saviour-God's goodness and love for men made its appearance,
5   « it was not through any justifying acts we had ourselves performed,
        but by his mercy,
        that he saved us by means of a bath [effecting] a rebirth
        and the utter newness of the Holy Spirit,
6   whom he poured out over us prodigally,
        through Jesus Christ our Saviour,
7   in order that once justified by his loving graciousness,
        we might actually become heirs according to a hope of eternal life ».

[5a. ὧν is read for ἅ after δικαιοσύνη by K, L, P, E ; διά is read before
πνεύματος ἁγίου by D (first corr.), F, G.
7b. Instead of γενηθῶμεν, K, L read γενώμεθα with the majority of cursive
mss].

v. 4. The preceding verse had described the universal sinful state of humanity, including in it even the Chosen people, « even us ». The present verse refers to the saving events which constitute the historical « epiphany » of Christ, but in the sacramental context of Baptism. In this respect, the passage is a more explicit statement of the beginning of the Christian life than Eph 2,3-10, to which it forms a sort of parallel. The two terms which are used to describe the revelation of God's redemptive activity in Christ, χρηστότης (merciful tenderness) and φιλανθρωπία (benevolence towards inferiors), are found in the more solemn formulae of Hellenistic *Hofstil* (JEREMIAS), and were often associated in Greek philosophical writing (SPICQ).

v. 5. The rest of the present passage is a citation of a hymn, probably from the baptismal liturgy. God's act of salvation is described as it is operative in Christian Baptism, and not, as in Col 1,20, « through the blood of his cross ». Baptism is *a bath* effecting *rebirth*. This figure was used in 1 Cor 6,11 and Eph 5,26. What is new here is the word παλιγγενεσία, which occurs only once elsewhere in the NT (Mt 19,28), where it has an eschatological and cosmic sense. Its use here reminds us that for the early Church this sacrament always possessed an eschatological orientation [20]. It is to be noted that the term, borrowed from Pythagorean or Stoic vocabulary, has evidently acquired a new Christian meaning, familiar to Titus, since Paul does not stop to explain it further. In fact, it may be regarded as self-evident, since Baptism is « the fundamental experience of all Christians » (DIBELIUS).

This baptismal *bath* also confers *the utter newness of the Holy Spirit*. The term ἀνακαίνωσις, employed only here in connection with Baptism and in Rom 12,2 in connection with the Eucharistic sacrifice [21], suggests the sense of something « surprising, wonderful, unheard of », always connoted by the word καινός in the NT [22]. The word here appears to add to the notion of rebirth, the idea of a gradual, moral transformation of the Christian (SPICQ). What is most extraordinary however about the whole phrase used here to describe Baptism is the fact that, for the first time in Christian literature, its two principal elements, water

---

[20] D. M. STANLEY, *Baptism in the New Testament* in *Scr* 8 (1956) 46.

[21] I believe that Rom 12,1-2 contains a reference to the Eucharistic liturgy, the offering by the faithful of themselves, as well as of the risen Christ truly present under the sacred species.

[22] J. BEHM, καινός , *TWNT III*, 450-452.

and the Spirit, appear side by side [23]. Somewhat later, the definition of Baptism will receive its definitive formulation in the Fourth Gospel (Jn 3,5), a sentence which represents the term of a protracted evolution of theological thought regarding this sacrament [24].

vv. 6-7. It is by the mediation of the risen Christ, bearer of the Spirit according to Pauline theology [25], that this sacramental *bath* effects what it signifies. It is a constant theorem with Paul that the sacramental efficacy of Baptism derives from Christ's death and resurrection (cf. Rom 6,3-11). The Trinitarian orientation of Baptism is asserted here (MEINERTZ) : the Father pours out the Spirit through Jesus Christ. Paul also asserts that the purpose of the baptismal rebirth is the Christian's adoptive filiation, which here, as in Gal 4,7 ; Rom 8,17, is regarded as a present possession of the baptized (B. WEISS). Yet the entry into full possession of this heritage is reserved for the future *eternal life* (SPICQ).

§ 6. - The Conception of the First « Manifestation ». 2 Tm 1,8-11

With the second letter to Timothy, we arrive at what purports to be the last extant epistle from Paul's pen. He writes to urge his disciple to perseverance and fidelity in the execution of his apostolic office. Hence he is led to dwell upon the graces which Timothy received through his ordination as very personal motives for courageous action (DORNIER). He also bases his exhortation upon a profound dogmatic formula, which appears in the passage we now wish to discuss (SPICQ).

8 Never be ashamed of the testimony [to be rendered] to our Lord, nor of that to myself, his prisoner, but take your share [with me] in suffering for the Good News in proportion to the power of God,
9   « who saved us
         and called us by a holy vocation,
         not for what we have done
         but by his own gracious design,
         granted us in Christ Jesus from eternity,

---

[23] R. BULTMANN, *Theologie des Neuen Testaments* 137.

[24] Cf. *art. cit. The New Testament Doctrine of Baptism* 210 f.

[25] 2 Thes 2,13-14 ; 1 Cor 6,17 ; 15,45 ; 2 Cor 3,3 ; 3,17 ; Rom 1,4 ; 8,10. The Holy Spirit is called the Spirit of Christ (Phil 1,19 ; Rom 8,9) or Spirit of the Son (Gal 4,6).

10   but only revealed at the present time through
              the manifestation of our Saviour Christ Jesus,
          who reduced death to impotence
          and made the light of life and immortality shine out
              by means of the Good News »,
11   of which I have been constituted herald and apostle and instructor.

[10a. Ἰησοῦ Χριστοῦ is read by Ephr. *rescr.*, K, L, P.
11. ἔθνων is omitted after διδάσκαλος by Sin., Alex. Its insertion by the Vulgate
and the other witnesses is probably due to 1 Tm 2,7].

v. 8. The notion of the *martyrion*, or witness, is closely allied in the NT
to that of apostle [26]. Humanly speaking, the crucified Christ, like the
condemned Paul himself, would be cause for shame before the persecuting
power of Rome and the Hellenistic culture of a city like Ephesus. It is
the power of God which enables Timothy to overcome such cowardice. In
reality, Paul's sufferings are a participation in Christ's own passion (Col
1,24). He is Christ's prisoner, not Caesar's (JEREMIAS). Timothy has
been given, through the sacrament of Orders, the divine power to share
this same passion of Christ.
v. 9. This *power of God* is revealed in the salvation-history, which Paul
now recalls, probably in the form of a citation from the liturgy (JERE-
MIAS). PRAT considers vv. 9-10 an irrefragable argument, from the termi-
nological and theological viewpoints, for the Pauline authenticity of this
letter [27], and it may be a composition of the Apostle himself. As JERE-
MIAS points out, the hymn refers to three fundamental Christian dogmas :
(1) God has declared his salvific will by saving us and giving us a Christian
vocation ; (2) this grace is given solely in Jesus Christ ; (3) Christ's work
as Saviour consists in his conquest of death and his gift of life. The gratuity of God's gift of salvation is underscored by representing it as an
act, which like our predestination is *from eternity*. This supreme act of
divine graciousness is moreover given to us *in Christ Jesus*. How that
grace was communicated in time is explained in the following verse.
    v. 10. Mention is made here of the first *manifestation* of Christ, a
term which, like the title *Saviour*, was employed in the language of the
Mystery religions and the cult of the Caesars. This latter term, which
never appears in the archaic, Palestinian sources used in the NT, becomes

[26] L. CERFAUX, *Témoins du Christ d'après de Livre des Actes* in *Ang* 20
(1943) 166-183.
[27] F. PRAT, *La Théologie de Saint Paul* I[8] 397.

more frequent in the inspired literature connected with Greek-speaking Christian centres (JEREMIAS). It is applied to Christ sixteen times in the NT, of which four occur in the Pastorals, where it is still applied primarily to the Father (Acts 5,31 ; 10,23 ; Phil 3,20 ; Eph 5,23 ; Ti 1,4 ; 2,13 ; 3,6 ; 2 Tm 1,10 ; Lk 2,11 ; Jn 4,42 ; 1 Jn 4,14 ; 2 Pt 1, 1.11 ; 2,20 ; 3,2.18). The Aramaic-speaking communities had no need to use such a title, since they were conscious of the etymology of the name « Jesus », « Yah(weh) saves » (cf. Mt 1,21). — The term *manifestation*, to which we have referred earlier, was employed to designate the birthday of the divinized ruler, his accession to the throne, some specially remarkable event in his life, or his return from abroad (DIBELIUS). In the rest of the sentence, Paul makes clear what he understands by this first *manifestation* of God's gracious love in Christ.

Who reduced death to impotence. Paul's constant teaching is that, by dying himself, Christ has changed the nature, or at least nullified the baleful power, of death (1 Cor 15,26 ; cf. Heb 2,14 ; 1 Thes 5,10 ; 1 Cor 15,22 ; 2 Cor 4,10 ; Rom 6,6.10 ; 14,8-9). By *death*, as opposed to *life and immortality*, Paul signifies the total concept of death, viz. sin together with final separation from God, of which physical death is a symbol. This triumph of Christ over death clearly involves his resurrection (1 Cor 15,20 ; Col 1,18).

made the light of life and immortality shine out by means of the Good News. Elsewhere Paul has referred to the Gospel as « the Good News of the glory of Christ, who is the image of God » (2 Cor 4,4), and as « the Good News of the glory of the blessed God » (1 Tm 1,11). The term « glory » here retains its biblical sense of a theophany, which has occurred in the person of the glorified Christ (DORNIER). Paul connects this « glory » with the Gospel because it proclaims the glorified Christ [28]. As is now clear to us, the *written* Gospels reveal the importance of Christ's resurrection in the understanding of his divinity attained by the first disciples [29]. The important place held by the resurrection of Christ in the *oral* kerygma is abundantly demonstrated by the evidence given in the NT. Accordingly, the phrase we are considering is intended by Paul to refer to Christ's resurrection, which is the source of *life and immortality*. These last words are to be understood in the full biblical sense of super-

---

[28] J. SCHMITT, *op. cit.* 183.
[29] D. M. STANLEY, *Didache as a Constitutive Element of the Gospel Form* in *CBQ* 17 (1955) 228.

natural and eternal life which affect man in his entire material personality (SPICQ). The theme of incorruption or *immortality*, recalled here, belongs to the early kerygma which applied Ps 15,10 to Christ's resurrection as one of the most important OT *testimonia* (Acts 2,27-31 ; 13,31-37). Paul himself made use of this same motif in his teaching on the resurrection-body (1 Cor 15,42.50.53-54 ; cf. 1 Cor 9,25 ; Rom 2,7). *Immortality* is a property of God Himself (1 Tm 1,17) and of the risen Christ (Eph 6,24).

The value of this verse is the explanation it offers for an understanding of what Paul means by the first *manifestation* of Christ, viz. his death and resurrection, not his incarnation.

§ 7. - Two Citations Taken from Paul's Gospel. 2 Tm 2,8-13

Ch. 2 of this letter continues Paul's exhortation to Timothy. He borrows motives first from human experience (military life, sport, and farming, vv. 3-7), then from the Gospel (vv. 8-10), itself « a power to salvation » (Rom 1,16). He concludes by citing a liturgical hymn which was probably part of the baptismal liturgy familiar to Timothy (vv. 11-13).

8 Keep vivid the memory of
      « Jesus Christ
      now raised from death,
      of David's line ... »,
as my version of the Good News puts it. 9 That is why I endure suffering, even chains, like a criminal. Yet God's word has not been chained up. 10 My reason for putting up with it all is for the Chosen people's sake, that they may themselves also share the salvation found in Christ Jesus with eternal glory. 11 This statement merits confidence.

      « If we have died with him, we shall also live with him :
12   if we keep enduring, we shall reign with him ;
      if we deny him, he too will deny us :
13   if we are unfaithful, he is still to be trusted »,
      since he cannot deny his own nature.

[10. The present, ἀρνούμεθα , is read by some mss].

v. 8 JEREMIAS thinks this is a citation of an early credal formula of Palestinian origin, similar to Rom 1,3-4 [30]. However, it would seem

---

[30] This is also the opinion of R. BULTMANN : cf. *op. cit.* 50 n. 1 ; cf. H. WINDISCH, *Zur Christologie der Pastoralbriefe* in *ZNT* 34 (1935) 213-216.

to be one which the Apostle himself created and used in his instructions. It expresses the fundamental Christian truth, expressed more fully by the hymn in Phil 2,5-11, that Jesus has attained his glory as risen Lord by way of the cross. The idea is particularly apt here, where Paul endeavours to persuade Timothy that suffering, even death, is part of the apostle's vocation. It is to be noted that the strophe stresses Christ's resurrection, as being of paramount importance in Paul's Gospel. The risen Christ, on the view of Paul, who saw him by the Damascus road in glory, is the primary object of Christian faith and Christian hope. The reference to Christ's human nature is also intended as a motive to strengthen Timothy for the fight. There is question here of Jesus, not so much as true Jewish Messias (BERNARD), as of his capacity for compassionating « his brothers in humanity » (SPICQ), which springs from his own human nature.

vv. 9-10. These two verses belong together and express Paul's theology of suffering in the apostolate. He has himself had personal experience of the cross by which Christ won salvation for his followers. Accordingly, in his turn, the Apostle finds his principal motive for suffering in offering it *for the Chosen people's sake*, the new Israel, the Christian Church. Such is the divinely revealed way to that *salvation found in Christ Jesus with eternal glory*. For Paul, his own suffering and martyrdom are all part of his vocation as a preacher of the Gospel (JEREMIAS). Here as elsewhere in Paul, the picture of the risen Christ is associated with *glory*. For Paul, Christian salvation is exhibited best and primarily in the glorified humanity of Christ (2 Thes 1,9-10 ; 2,13-14 ; Phil 3,21; 4,19 ; 2 Cor 3,18 ; Rom 5,2 ; Col 1,27 ; Eph 1,6).

vv. 11-13. As the solemn introductory formula indicates, we have here a quotation (possibly the continuation of the formula in v. 8) which consists of four verses set in parallel, the conclusion at the end being possibly added by the author (SPICQ). It may be a song composed in time of persecution (LOCK). It appears to be of Semitic, rather than Hellenistic origin, as its style and turn of phrase would indicate (JEREMIAS). It may well have been composed by Paul himself.

v. 11. *If we have died with Him, we shall also live with Him.* The sentence is an application to martyrdom of a theorem which appears in various forms in Paul's letters. It is applied to Christian death generally in 1 Thes 4,14. It derives from Paul's conviction that Jesus' own death has created a completely new thing, Christian death (1 Thes 5,10). It is applied to Paul's own apostolate (Phil 3,10-11 ; 2 Cor 4,10-11), as well as to Christian existence (2 Cor 5,14-15 ; Gal 2,19-20 ; Rom 8,17 ; 14,7-9).

It is worked out most thoroughly in Pauline baptismal theology (Rom 6,3-11).

v. 12. *If we keep enduring, we shall share his sovereignty.* In the last strophe, the thought moved from past to future. The present one looks from present suffering to future triumph. The ideas suggested by the citation in v. 8 recur here in these two verses : *we shall live* continues the thought of *raised from death*, while *we shall reign* recalls *of David's line* (LOCK). — The present strophe recalls a saying of Jesus recorded in the Synoptic tradition (Mk 13,13; Mt 10,22) : « It is the man who bears things patiently until the end, who will be saved ». Paul has repeatedly dwelt on this theme (Rom 2,7 ; 8,24-25 ; 2 Cor 1,6-8), its closest parallel being 2 Thes 1,4-5 : « ... we take pride ... in your constancy and faith through all the persecutions and tribulations you are bearing, a proof of God's just judgment that you will be found worthy of God's Kingdom for the sake of which you also are suffering ... ».

If we deny him, he too will deny us. This recalls another saying of Jesus (Mt 10,33) : « the man disowning me in front of his fellow human beings I will disown in front of my heavenly Father ».

v. 13. *If we are unfaithful, he is still to be trusted.* Paul has expressed this thought in Rom 3,3-4 ; 11,30-32. In fact, the whole first section of that letter (1,17-4,25) is a demonstration of God's faithfulness to his promises of salvation (LYONNET). Consistent with what he had written there, Paul now adds a gloss of his own to the hymn : *since he cannot deny his own nature.* The thought is found in Nm 23,19 and also in Rom 3,4. Faithfulness is used constantly to characterize the activity of God the Father and of Christ in Paul's writing (1 Thes 5, 24 ; 2 Thes 3,3 ; 1 Cor 1,9 ; 10,13 ; 2 Cor 1,18).

This last summary of the Gospel Paul has been preaching during his whole apostolic career highlights the same doctrinal truths which we have seen stressed in all his letters. At the heart of Paul's version of the Good News is the resurrection of Christ.

CHAPTER X

CHRIST'S RESURRECTION IN PAULINE SOTERIOLOGY

We have reviewed the texts in Paul's letters which indicate either by express assertion or by implication, that Christ's resurrection is involved in the Apostle's conception of Christian salvation. It remains now to answer the question which inspired this investigation : what is the function of Christ's resurrection in Pauline soteriology ?

As we have seen, Paul's initiation into the meaning of the Christian Mystery at the moment of his conversion stands in striking contrast with the formative event of the first Pentecost through which the first disciples had been created into the Christian Church. Theirs was essentially an experience of the Spirit, distinct from Jesus Christ exalted as Son of God, who had sent the Spirit upon the community, and distinct from the Father, from whom the glorified Lord Jesus had received him as object of the divine promise (Acts 2,32-33). Thus it was through the presence of the Holy Spirit that the apostles had been given the revelation of Christ's divinity and of the salvific nature of his death and resurrection « according to the Scriptures » [1]. On the other hand, Paul's momentous meeting with the Christ of glory on the Damascus road revealed to him first and foremost that the One raised from death was the Son of God. Paul's experience was primarily that of Christ as God's Son, and of God who had raised him as Father. It was only after being received into the Church by Baptism that Paul had experience of the Holy Spirit (Acts 9,17) [2].

---

[1] Pp. 23-26.

[2] Obviously, the Holy Spirit was already at work in Paul through his meeting with the risen Christ, bearer of the Spirit, on the Damascus road. However, the words of Ananias (« that you may be filled with a Holy Spirit ») would appear

Each of these experiences was genuinely Christian, a means of revelation of Christianity's most fundamental truths. Yet the distinctive character of each naturally tended to produce certain variations in the conception of Christian salvation. The profound impression made upon Paul's mind by the disclosure of the identity of the One raised from death as God's Son with the crucified Jesus of Nazareth led Paul to realize that Christ had, as God's Son, undergone the ignominious death on Calvary. Thus from the very beginning of his apostolic career, Paul's preaching of the Good News of salvation through Christ's death and resurrection can be summarized by saying, « he proclaimed that Jesus is the Son of God » (Acts 9,30). From this brief remark, we get a hint of the way in which Paul will, in his later theological writing, co-ordinate Christ's death and resurrection as two aspects of the redemptive work of the Father and the Son.

From another résumé of Paul's kerygma in Acts, we obtain an intimation of the very close connection which always existed in the Apostle's thought between Christ's resurrection and his divine Sonship.

« We also proclaim to you the Good News that God has accomplished the promise, made to the patriarchs, for us their descendants by raising Jesus, as moreover it has been written in Psalm 2, ' You are my Son : this day have I begotten you' » (Acts 13,32 f).

This conception, peculiar to Paul, is found nowhere in the apostolic preaching which emanated from Jerusalem. It provides an indication of how profoundly Paul's first experience of the risen Christ as Son of God influenced his more mature soteriological thinking.

Accordingly, we propose to present a synthesis of Pauline soteriology by means of three theorems which we believe to be basic in its structure. (1) Christian salvation originates from God as the Father both of Christ and of the Christian. (2) It has been completely realized by Jesus Christ as God's Son in his own sacred humanity, and through that humanity, now glorified, it is in process of being realized in the Christian. (3) Its present reality and its future realization in the Christian depend upon the indwelling Holy Spirit as principle of the Christian's adoptive filiation.

---

to indicate that Paul's first *conscious* experience of the Spirit came, after he was baptized, with « the imposition of hands ». It will be recalled that, while Paul is said to have received Christian Baptism, there is no NT evidence to the effect that the other apostles were baptized sacramentally. They appear to have received only the Pentecostal « Baptism with a Holy Spirit » : cf. *The New Testament Doctrine of Baptism : an essay in Biblical Theology* in *TS* 18 (1957) 207.

§ 1. - Hebrews' Development of the Earlier Palestinian Soteriology

Before we discuss this threefold structure of Pauline soteriology, it may be helpful to summarize the soteriological viewpoint of the epistle to the Hebrews, which forms a contrast with that of Paul inasmuch as its lines of development appear to have been determined by one prominent element in the data of the Pentecostal experience of the Jerusalem community, viz. the celestial exaltation of Christ [3]. Accordingly, it may be taken to exemplify that Palestinian soteriology which contemplated Christ as the glorified Servant of Yahweh, exalted in divine majesty at God's right hand until the time of his parousia (Acts 3,19-21).

« The capital point » for the author of Hebrews is not Christ's death or his resurrection, but the fact that « we have a highpriest who has taken his seat at the right of the throne of God's majesty in heaven » (Heb 8,1). Thus, in the epistle to the Hebrews, Christian salvation appears as the fruit of the exalted Christ's heavenly sacrifice and his sacerdotal intercession [4].

Now, while such liturgically inspired themes are undoubtedly present in many soteriological texts found in the Pauline epistles, as we have seen [5] (indeed, the influence of the Christian liturgy upon Paul's literary expression is continually perceptible from his earliest letters and becomes increasingly prominent in Colossians and Ephesians), they appear to occupy no more than a secondary place of interest in his most characteristic formulation of the conception of Christian salvation, as compared, for instance, with those themes which he borrowed from the Genesis Creation-stories [6]. To be sure, Paul presents Christ's death as a sacrifice not infrequently [7]. He refers explicitly, at least once, to Christ's heavenly intercession (Rom 8,34). However, he nowhere gives Christ the title of highpriest ; and it is only in the Pastorals that Jesus is called « mediator » (1 Tm 2,5).

---

[3] Pp. 25-26.

[4] C. Spicq, *L' Épître aux Hébreux I* (Paris, 1952) 311-316.

[5] Pp. 112, 169, 226-7.

[6] P. 78, n. 60.

[7] Paul describes Christ's death as the fulfilment of the Passover sacrifice (1 Cor 5, 7), or of the sacrifice of the Day of Atonement (Rom 3,25). He also expresses the sacrificial character of Christ's death by repeated references to his « handing himself over » (cf. Gal 1,4 ; 2,20 ; Eph 5,2).

The author of Hebrews, on the other hand, makes Christ's death and resurrection only the point of departure of a soteriogical conception centred upon the ascension and the heavenly sacrifice. Only once at the very end of his epistle (13,20), does he refer to Christ's resurrection explicitly. Jesus' sufferings and his death for all men (2,9) are thought of primarily as a necessary preparation for his celestial sacerdotal functions, inasmuch as they « perfected » Christ, making him the Christian's guide to heavenly salvation (2,10). His experience of suffering is principally of interest to our author insofar as it made him a « merciful and reliable highpriest » (2,17 ; 4,15), by providing him with an experimental knowledge of obedience (5,8). It thus constituted him « principle of eternal salvation » (5,9). By his unique sacrifice (9,26 ; 10,12) of himself as victim (7,27), Jesus won man's redemption (9,11-12) and was made *pontifex* by God (6,20 ; 5,5 ff). Since Christ is called highpriest « in virtue of the power of imperishable life » (7,16), it would seem (although the author never makes the point explicitly) that his sacerdotal consecration involved also his resurrection when he received this new « life » in order to communicate it to men. Since, however, it is clear that Christ is already constituted highpriest before his heavenly exaltation (4,14 ; 6,20 ; 7,26 ; 10,12), his death and resurrection are considered rather as *sine qua non* prerequisites for his principal salvific activity, effected not on this earth but in heaven.

The great originality of this soteriological conception consists in its highlighting of the heavenly sacrifice offered by the exalted Christ to God. Christ has entered the celestial sanctuary, armed with his own Blood, and has « offered himself spotless to God through an eternal Spirit » (9, 11-14). It is this act of self-oblation, of which Christ's sacrificial death on Calvary was but the external expression (10,5-9) and with which it forms an inseparable unity, that determines Hebrews' notion of Christian salvation : « it is in virtue of this will that we are sanctified by the oblation of the body of Jesus Christ once for all » (10,10). The various titles which the author gives to Christ derive their signification from this heavenly offering and intercessory function of the exalted Christ : ἀρχηγός (2,10 ; 12,2), πρόδρομος (6,20), guarantor of the new Covenant (7,22 ; 8,6-13 ; 9,15 ; 10,15-18), μεσίτης (8,6 ; 9,15 ; 12,24), and τελειωτής (12,2).

Indeed, this sacrificial and liturgical orientation of the soteriology of Hebrews has left its influence upon the conception of the Fatherhood of God and upon the divine Sonship of Jesus Christ as exhibited by the epistle. The Father « perfected » Jesus « by sufferings as the [liturgical] leader towards salvation » because of his divine plan « to lead a great number of sons to glory » (2,10). The sacred writer places his exhortation to the *imitatio Christi* under the same liturgical symbolism : it is « by fixing our eyes upon Jesus, the leader of our faith ... seated at God's right hand henceforth » (12,2) that we must accept the Father's paternal correction (12,5-9) by which « he treats us as sons ». The implied purpose in this divine παιδεῖα is our preparation to share in the celestial liturgy of which Christ is protagonist. The Sonship of Christ is described in function of his highpriestly character. If God has now definitively spoken (ἐλάλησεν) to us « in one who is Son » (1,2), it is because his « cleansing Blood more eloquent (κρεῖττον λαλοῦντι) than that of Abel » (12,4) still makes itself heard. As Son, Christ is head of the Church, God's « house » (3,6), and is « our sovereign highpriest » (4,14). By his sacred passion (described by figures borrowed from the liturgy as « petitions and supplications ») [8], Jesus Christ, « Son though he was, learned obedience from what he suffered ; and after being made perfect, he has become for all who obey him the principle of eternal salvation, since he was endowed by God with the title of highpriest ... » (5,7-10). Where Paul presents Christ, who, as he is well aware was « his Son » *simpliciter* in his pre-existence (Rom 1,3), as « having been constituted Son of God in power by resurrection of the dead » (Rom 1,4), the author of Hebrews thinks of Christ, eternally « one who is Son » (1,2), as having been appointed by God's oath to make him « highpriest forever according to the order of Melchisedech » (7,17), as « Son made perfect for eternity » (7,28).

Thus the soteriological thought of the epistle to the Hebrews dwells upon the one aspect of Christ's glorified life which became a focal point in the early Jerusalem kerygma : the *sessio ad dexteram Patris*. It was this moment in the exaltation of the risen Christ which provided the apostolic community with the key to the Mystery of Jesus. It likewise provided the author of Hebrews with his basic insight into the meaning of Christian salvation, viz. the priestly nature of Christ's heavenly intercession. In contrast with this restricted viewpoint, Pauline soteriology moves within a wider frame of reference, which includes Christ's coming amongst men, his passion, death, resurrection, ascension and parousia. It envisages Christian salvation as mankind's return to the Father as his adoptive sons through the redemptive activity of Jesus Christ as Son, in

---

[8] C. Spicq, *L' Épître aux Hébreux II* (Paris, 1953) 112.

the Holy Spirit, whose indwelling in men's hearts realizes the presence of the risen Christ in them and constitutes their divine adoption as sons of the Father [9].

§ 2. - God as Father is Author of Christian Salvation

It is axiomatic in Pauline soteriology that the work of Christian salvation originates with God the Father. In this, Paul shows himself faithful to the primitive apostolic tradition. In the primitive preaching, not only was the resurrection of Christ expressly attributed to God (Acts 2,24 ; 3,15 ; 4,10 ; 5,30 ; 10,40 ; 13,30.37 ; 17,31) but also Christ's death was thought of as God's work (a conception inspired principally by Isaias 53). If Jesus' death was frequently presented as the criminal work of the Jews and pagans (Acts 2,23.36 ; 3,15 ; 4,10 ; 10,39 ; 13,28), nonetheless its redemptive significance was clearly indicated (Acts 2,23 ; 3,18 ; 17,3 ; 1 Cor 15,3). It was left to Paul's genius to advance the Christian understanding of Christ's death by *explaining how it was properly* the Father's work, and thus co-ordinating it with Christ's resurrection.

THE PAULINE CONCEPTION OF GOD AS FATHER

The concept of God as Father, which occurs but once in the examples of the primitive kerygma which have come down to us (Acts 2,23), may be said to be particularly dear to Paul. It was Paul undoubtedly who instituted the ancient Christian custom of giving God this title in the epistolary salutation. Here in the Pauline epistles, God is called « the Father » (1 Thes 1,1) or, more commonly, « our Father » (2 Thes 1,1). Paul's characteristic wish for « grace and peace », the summation of all the blessings of Christian salvation, is « from God our Father » (Phil 1,2 ; 1 Cor 1,3 ; 2 Cor 1,2 ; Gal 1,3 ; Rom 1,7 ; Col 1,2 ; Eph 1,2). Even

---

[9] That Christ's resurrection plays a much more dominant role in Pauline soteriology than in that sketched by the author of Hebrews (where it remains merely a prelude to Christ's entry into the heavenly Temple) will become clear in the synthesis of Paul's doctrine presented in the following sections. For Paul, Christ's constitution as « Son of God in power » (Rom 1,4) is the immediate effect of his resurrection. Likewise, the resurrection of the just, through which they attain to « the freedom of the glory of the children of God » (Rom 8,21), will be caused by the risen Christ (cf. *inter alia* Phil 3,20-21).

in the Pastoral epistles, where the name Father is nowhere else applied
to God (it is replaced by the epithet, Saviour), the salutation still retains
the formula, « grace, mercy, peace from God the Father » (1 Tm 1,2 ;
2 Tm 1,2 ; Ti 1,4).

This Pauline habit of thinking of God as Father may be traced back to
Paul's conversion, which he regarded as the Father's revelation of « his
Son in me » (Gal 1,16) [10]. His recognition of the risen Christ as Son of
God was simultaneously a new consciousness of the nature of God as
Father. This revelation of God's Fatherhood surpassed anything Paul may
have learned from the OT. Accordingly, God appears constantly in the
Apostle's letters as « the Father of our Lord Jesus Christ » (2 Cor 1,3 :
11,31 ; Rom 15,6 ; Col 1,3 ; Eph 1,3).

Moreover, Paul can find no better term to describe the Christians'
relationship to God than that of « our Father ». The individual Christian
community, like that of Thessalonica, may be thought of in this way :
« the church of the Thessalonians in God the Father » (1 Thes 1,1). Their
existence as a community is to be lived « in the presence of God our Father » (1 Thes 1,3), since they hope, at Christ's parousia, to appear
« blameless in holiness in the presence of God our Father » (1 Thes 3,13).
More frequently, perhaps, Paul uses the phrase to denote the relation of
the whole Christian Church to God. It is as « God our Father » that he
« has loved us and given us eternal consolation ... » (2 Thes 2,17). It is as
« our Father » that God will bring Paul back to his Thessalonians (1
Thes 3,11). The spiritual ambition of the Philippians is to become
« blameless children of God » (Phil 2,15) ; and the doxology with which
Paul ends his letter to them praises God as « our Father » (Phil 4,20). The
Corinthians are reminded that God's OT promise was made to them,
« I shall be to you a Father, and you will be to me as sons and daughters »
(2 Cor 6,7).

It is the Fatherhood of God which underscores the all-important doctrine of the divine unicity. In opposition to the numberless deities of
the pagan pantheon, there is « for us one God the Father » (1 Cor 8,6).
God's unicity, in its turn, illustrates the universality of God's Fatherhood,
« one God and Father of all » (Eph 4,6).

In his relations with the individual Christian, God is regarded as
« the Father of mercy and God of every sort of consolation » (2 Cor 1, 3).

---

[10] P. 46.

In his relation to the risen Christ, « the God of our Lord Jesus Christ » may be called « the Father of glory » (Eph 1,17).

It is a commonplace that throughout his letters Paul's prayers are always addressed to God. The specifically Christian character of this prayer is to be found in the fact that it is directed to God as Father. It is in prayer that the Christian, aided by the Spirit, experiences his filial relationship to the Father (Gal 4,6 ; Rom 8,15). The distinctively Christian quality of prayer is gratitude for the benefits of salvation, an act of thanksgiving expressed to « God the Father who made us worthy to share the destiny of the saints in light » (Col 1,12). Gratefulness « to God the Father » is the characteristically Christian attitude, both in the liturgical worship of the community and in the lives of each member of the community (Col 3,16-17).

Before we discuss the specific moments in the Christian salvation-history which, in Pauline soteriology, involve the Fatherhood of God, it will be useful to recall that Paul thinks of the whole present order of creation, the object of God's salvific plan, as bearing a transcendental relation to God as Father. It is as Father that God is to be considered the source of the created order, as well as its final end (1 Cor 8,6 ; Rom 11,36). It is God's Fatherhood which has determined the character of the various forms of human society within the created order (Eph 3,14). Man's return to God through Christ's redemptive work is fundamentally, for Paul, « an access in one Spirit to the Father » (Eph 2,18). The consummation of the present order of salvation will be attained when Christ « hands over the Kingdom to God the Father » (1 Cor 15,24), when as Father, « God will be all in all » (1 Cor 15,28) [11].

RELATION OF CHRIST'S DEATH TO GOD THE FATHER

In the early preaching, as we have already observed, Christ's death was habitually ascribed to human malice or ignorance [12]. Hence it is not surprising that the conception of Christ's death as the work of God

---

[11] The passage presents the coming-to-be of the Kingdom *first* as Christ's *domination* of all creatures (vv. 25-27), *then* as the *subjection* of all, even « the Son himself », to the Father (v. 28). Thus the Apostle (who is no « subordinationist ») thinks of salvation, in its final consummation, as *the perfection of filiation* : all, *pro modo suo*, in the Son, share his filial relationship to the Father.

[12] Pp. 28-30.

17. - D. M. STANLEY.

the Father becomes clearly expressed in Paul's letters only gradually
and with a certain hesitation.

In the first epistles, we find Christ's death attributed once to the
Jews, « who killed the Lord Jesus and the prophets » (1 Thes 2,15), once
to certain mysterious « powers of this world », who « crucified the Lord
of glory » (1 Cor 2,8). Paul can also consider Christ's death in terms of
his passible and mortal condition, which he assumed by coming « in the
likeness of sinful humanity » (Rom 8,3) :

> « For indeed he was crucified out of weakness, but he lives by the power
> of God » (2 Cor 13,4).

From the first, Paul does relate Christ's death to the divine will.
This is at least implicit in a text which describes God's predestination of
the Christian people [13].

> « God has not destined us for wrath, but for an acquisition of salvation
> through our Lord Jesus Christ who died for us » (1 Thes 5,9-10).

It is implied also, together with Christ's resurrection, when Paul describes
the Christian life as originating from God the Father.

> « Now from him comes your existence in Christ Jesus, who became for
> us Wisdom from God, that is, Justice and Sanctification and Redemp-
> tion » (1 Cor 1,30).

This « becoming » of the glorified « Christ Jesus » involves his atoning
death, as the explanatory word « Redemption » indicates [14].

Paul can present the Father's part in Christ's redemptive death (and
also his resurrection through which he was « justified », 1 Tm 3,16) by
means of the antithesis Sin-Justice.

> « He has made him who knew no sin into sin for our sakes, in order that
> we might in him become God's justice » (2 Cor 5,21) [15].

In the epistle to the Galatian community, Paul expressly connects
Christ's death with the divine will. Here it is significant that God is presented as willing that death inasmuch as he is « our Father ».

---

[13] P. 79.
[14] P. 109.
[15] Pp. 143-144.

« Grace and peace be yours from God our Father and our Lord Jesus Christ, who offered himself on account of our sins, to deliver us from the present wicked world according to the will of God our Father » (Gal 1,3-4) [16].

There is a series of texts in the Pauline epistles which depict the work of salvation as the « reconciliation » of man with God. While this exclusively Pauline conception implies also God's work in raising Christ from death, it is primarily through Christ's redemptive death that God is thought to « reconcile » mankind to himself.

« And all this comes from God, who has reconciled us to himself through Christ and has given us the ministry of reconciling [others]. For the truth is that God was in Christ reconciling the world to himself, instead of holding men's transgressions against them » (2 Cor 5,18-19)[17].

This « reconciliation » is more explicitly connected with Christ's death in the letter to the Roman church.

« For if, though we were enemies, we were reconciled with God through the death of his Son, how much more, since we have been reconciled, shall we be saved by his life ? » (Rom 5,10) [18].

This « reconciliation » is again connected closely with Christ's death in the closing lines of the hymn cited in the epistle to the Colossians, which described God as Father in the opening stanza (Col 1,13).

« God was pleased to make all the fulness dwell in him and through him reconcile all things to himself... making peace through the blood of his cross » (Col 1,19-20) [19].

In this connection, we wish to mention also a passage in Ephesians, where however the technical term « reconciliation » does not occur. Paul speaks of God's forgiveness of us as that of a father towards his children.

« Forgive one another, just as God has forgiven us in Christ. Therefore, become imitators of God like beloved children » (Eph 4,32 f) [20].

---

[16] P. 149.
[17] P. 142.
[18] Pp. 175-176.
[19] Pp. 206-208.
[20] P. 229.

The most extended description of Christ's atoning death to be found
in the *corpus Paulinum* is the difficult passage in Romans where Christ
upon the cross appears as the very incarnation of God's justice, i. e. his
fidelity to his promises of salvation. The primitive kerygma always proclaimed Christ's redemptive death as being « according to the Scriptures » (1 Cor 15,3). Paul has his own individual way of expressing this
truth in terms of God's promise made to Abraham. This conception, it
is to be noted, involves that of the Fatherhood of God. This promise,
realized by the Father's sending of his own Son (Gal 4,4) is appropriated
by the Christian people « through faith in Jesus Christ » (Gal 3,22) by which
we are « all sons of God » (Gal 3,25). In Romans, Paul exposes the Gospel
which he preaches as the fulfilment of God's divine promise (Rom 1,2-3)
« concerning his. Son ». This is the context in which the famous lines describing Christ's atoning death are to be understood [21].

> « In the present dispensation, however, without benefit of law, God's justice,
> attested by the Law and the prophets, has been definitively revealed ...to
> all believers ... who are being justified gratuitously by his loving favour
> through the redemption found in Christ Jesus, whom God publicly exposed,
> [a kind of new] mercy-seat, through faith, in his blood ... » (Rom 3,21-25).

As we have pointed out, there is no question here of our modern concept
of justice, either vindictive or commutative, but of God's fatherly fidelity
to his own « word of salvation », of which Christ's redemptive death is
the concrete symbol.

The most striking and poignant expression of the Father's part in
Christ's death is perhaps the passage in which Paul employs the story of
Abraham's sacrifice of Isaac (Gn 22,1-12) to underscore the meaning of
Christ's atoning death as a deliberate act by God as Father :

> « who did not even spare his own Son, but handed him over for us all ... »
> (Rom 8,32).

This statement represents the perfect expression of Paul's soteriological
thought, in which Christ's death comes to figure as the formal work of
the Father as Father. Here the word, which in the Gospel tradition
(cf. 1 Cor 11,23) had become a *terminus technicus* for Judas' treacherous

---

[21] The passage describes Christ on the cross as the incarnation of the Father's
« justice », his activity by which he makes good his OT promises of salvation. Paul
makes the point even more explicitly in Rom 5,8-11.

act of betrayal and which in Acts 3,13 is used to stigmatize the Jewish betrayal of Jesus, παραδιδόναι, is applied to the Father's action in the death of Christ. It is easy to understand how Paul prefers to use it of Christ's own act of self-surrender through his voluntary acceptance of his death (Gal 2,20 ; Eph, 5,2.25). That Paul did arrive at this almost startling insight into the Father's role as Father in Christ's death is of paramount importance in his soteriology. It enabled him to unite Christ's death with his resurrection in a more profound synthesis than had been achieved by any other writer of the apostolic age, as may be seen by another passage in Romans, where the Father is implicitly thought of as the primary agent in effecting Christian salvation [22] :

« he was handed over for our sins and raised for our justification » (Rom 4,25).

CHRIST'S RESURRECTION, FUNCTION OF GOD AS FATHER

If the explicit expression of the Father's role in Christ's death appears only gradually in Paul's writings, the Father's activity in Christ's resurrection is prominent from the beginning. Only once does Paul say « Christ rose » (1 Thes 4,14), a passage which appears to be a citation from an ancient credal formula [23]. Elsewhere, he invariably employs the expression Christ « was raised », a term which implies the Father's agency even where it is not formally expressed (1 Cor 15,4.12.20 ; 2 Cor 5,15 ; Rom 4,25 ; 7,4 ; 2 Tm 2,8). In one sense, Paul is merely repeating a datum found in the apostolic preaching which attributed Christ's resurrection to God. Paul's originality however lies in his attribution of Christ's resurrection to God as Father, both of Christ and of the Christians.

We find this conception in the very first reference made to this mystery in his letters. He characterizes the Thessalonians' practice of Christianity by saying that they

« await his Son from heaven, whom he has raised from death, Jesus our rescuer from the wrath to come » (1 Thes 1,10) [24].

It is as « his Son » that God raised Jesus from death ; or, conversely, as he remarks to the Galatians, it is « God the Father who raised him

---

[22] Pp. 171-173.
[23] Pp. 77-79.
[24] Pp. 75-77.

from death » (Gal 1,1). Indeed, of all the characterizations of God found in the Pauline epistles, the most common and most basic is that God is he who raised Christ from death (1 Cor 6,14 ; 15,15 ; 2 Cor 1,9 ; 4,14 Rom 4,24 ; 8,11 ; 10,9 ; Col 2,12 ; Eph 1,20). A variation on this idea is found in the statement that « Christ was raised from death by the glory of the Father » (Rom 6,4). The divine prerogative of « glory », which has been communicated to Christ at his resurrection, is closely associated in Paul's mind with the Father, so that he can refer to him simply as « the Father of glory » (Eph 1,17).

The text, which perhaps best represents Paul's awareness of how deeply God *as* Father is involved in the resurrection of Christ, is found in the preamble to Romans [25]. Christ, who has already been described as « his Son » (Rom 1,3), is declared to have been « constituted Son of God in power as regards the Holy Spirit by resurrection of the dead » (Rom 1,4). Psychologically, the conception stems from Paul's initial Christian experience on the Damascus road. Theologically, it expresses Paul's conviction that God's raising of Christ from death has somehow enhanced the Father-Son relationship (which, of course, Paul knows to have existed *ab aeterno*). It is « as regards the Spirit of holiness » that Christ is « Son of God in power », i. e. in his risen state, Christ is able to give to Christians the « Spirit of the Son » (Gal 4,6), which makes us adoptive sons of the Father (Rom 8,14). This is simply the carrying out of God's eternal plan for man's redemption through his Son : to imprint upon the Christian « the character of the image of his Son, that he should be firstborn of many brothers » (Rom 8,29). Thus, it is not only as Father of Christ but as « our Father » that God works the resurrection of his Son.

That Paul is deeply aware that the work of salvation is properly God's work as Father may be seen in three texts where Christ's death, as well as his resurrection, are involved. The first of these occurs in Galatians, where it sums up the Pauline doctrine of the fulfilment of the divine promise, made to Abraham, in favour of his true descendants, the Christian people [26].

> « But when the fulness of time was come, God sent forth his Son, born of a woman, born subject to law, in order that he might redeem those subject to law : in order that we might receive the adoptive sonship » (Gal 4,4-5).

[25] Pp. 162-166.
[26] Pp. 156-157.

Here a twofold aspect of God's activity as the source of man's redemption is considered. It is as Father of Christ that he sent him to redeem mankind ; it is as our Father that he decreed the form of our redemption, viz. « that we might receive the adoptive sonship ». The mission of the Son « to redeem » is accomplished, as Paul has stated in Gal 3,13, by Christ's death, through which he willed to appear as « a curse » by « hanging upon a gibbet ». Christ's resurrection is the divine act by which the divine adoptive filiation was communicated, since it is by faith in « Christ Jesus », i. e. the risen Christ, that « you are all sons of God » (Gal 3,26).

The second text, which presents God's act of salvation as proceeding from him formally as Father, is found in Romans, where Paul describes the Christian life as liberty from condemnation, because it is governed by « the law of the Spirit who gives life in Christ Jesus » (Rom 8,1-2). With his characteristic fondness for antithesis, Paul sees this state of non-condemnation as the result of a condemnation of sin, carried out by God as Father in the sacred humanity of his incarnate Son through his death and resurrection.

> « Now God, by sending his own Son in the likeness of [our] sinful flesh and on account of sin, condemned sin in that humanity (a task impossible for the Law, seeing it was reduced to utter helplessness by sinful human nature), in order that the justice of the Law might be fulfilled in us whose conduct is governed not by sinful human nature, but by the Spirit » (Rom 8,3-4) [27].

This divine condemnation of sin took place in Jesus' passible and mortal human nature by his death (cf. Gal 3,13 ; 2 Cor 5,21 ; Rom 5,10). But it was not merely a negative act, since it resulted in man's fulfilling the aim of the Mosaic Law with the aid of the Spirit, communicated to him by the risen Christ. Consequently, this condemnation by the Father is realized by Christ as man's redeemer, « handed over for our sins, and raised for our justification » (Rom 4,25).

The third text occurs in the hymn-like prologue to Ephesians which Paul composed in praise of « God the Father of our Lord Jesus Christ » (Eph 1,3). The Apostle describes the divine plan for man's redemption, the « Mystery » of the recapitulation of « all things under one Head in Christ » [28].

---

[27] Pp. 189-192.
[28] Pp. 218-220.

« By love, he predestined us for adoptive sonship through Jesus Christ ...
his beloved Son, in whom we possess the redemption through his blood,
the remission of transgressions, according to the riches of his grace »
(Eph 1,5-7).

Here again it is the Father who, out of his paternal love for us, has
willed to save us by forgiving our sins through the redemptive death of
Christ and to confer adoptive filiation on us through Christ's resurrection.

SALVATION AS THE MANIFESTATION OF THE FATHER'S LOVE

The love of God as the operative force in the Father's salvific plan
is a constant theme in the Pauline letters. « God our Father » is best known
as « he who loved us » (2 Thes 2,16 ; 1 Thes 1,4 ; 2 Cor 13,13 ; Rom 8,37 ;
Col 3,12). He is « the God of love » (2 Cor 13,11), or simply « Love » (Phil
2,1). By his gift to man of the Spirit, the Father's « love has been poured
out in our hearts » (Rom 5,5) : it is incarnate « in Christ Jesus » (Rom
8,39 ; Eph 1,6). Accordingly, it is as author of our salvation that God
reveals his love for us [29].

« God demonstrates his love for us by the fact that, whilst we were still
sinners, Christ died on our behalf. How much more then, now that we
are justified by his blood, shall we be saved by him from wrath ? » (Rom
5,8-9).

This same love was already operative in our predestination as adoptive
sons (Eph 1,5), since this eternal divine activity issues from God as
Father of Christ and of ourselves (Rom 8,29).

Perhaps this theme of the Father's love is most strikingly expressed
in a passage in Ephesians, where Paul asserts that this love has effected
the impossible, by associating us with his Son made man as object of those
very divine acts of his through which he accomplished our redemption [30].

« But God, being rich in mercy, through the great love he had for us, even
while we were dead because of our transgressions, quickened us together
with Christ ... raised us up together with him, and made us sit together
with him in the heavenly realm, in Christ Jesus : that he might show,
in ages to come, the surpassing riches of his love by his kindliness towards
us in Christ Jesus » (Eph 2,4-7).

[29] Pp. 174-176.
[30] Pp. 222-224.

THE CHRISTIAN AS OBJECT OF THE FATHER'S SALVIFIC ACTIVITY

The text we have just cited introduces us to a view of man's salvation that is exclusively Pauline. By a series of verbs which he has coined, all compounds beginning with the preposition σύν, the Apostle declares that, in Baptism, God associates us with Christ in the principal moments of Christ's redemptive activity. Perhaps no other NT author has managed to present such a graphic picture of the way in which salvation comes to man, or of the way in which the Father's activity in Christ's death and resurrection actually terminates in the individual Christian. Indeed, the difference between this Pauline conception and the modern theological distinction between « objective » and « subjective » redemption (Christ's work as distinguished from its application to the Christian) must be noted, if we are to appreciate the realistic character of Pauline soteriology. From Paul's point of view, the Father's action in the Christian's baptismal experience is simply the extension of his action in « handing over » his Son and in raising him from death. In the one instance, as in the other, God acts « objectively » as the author of man's salvation.

The first of this series of Pauline neologisms appears in the letter to the Galatians, where Paul gives a striking picture of his own supernatural Christian life. « I have been crucified together with Christ » (Gal 2,19). That this co-crucifixion occurs sacramentally in Baptism is clear from a famous passage in Romans [31].

> « We were then buried together with him by this baptism into his death ...
> our old self has been crucified together with him » (Rom 6,4-6).

This association of us by the Father with Christ's death and burial is the basis for Christian hope in our future association with Christ in glory :

> « Now, if we died with Christ, we believe that we shall also share his life »
> (Rom 6,8).

If this passage does not make it clear whether the Christian is actually associated with Christ's resurrection in this life, the parallel texts in Colossians and Ephesians leave the reader no longer in doubt. Christian salvation can be said, in a certain sense, to be completely in the Chris-

---

[31] Pp. 182-184.

tian's possession already here below. Through God's activity in the sacrament of Baptism, we have not only been buried with Christ, we have been
« raised together with him », or « brought to life together with him »
(Col 2,12-13 ; 3,1). Indeed, all that remains to be accomplished is the
revelation of this state ; and this manifestation will occur at Christ's
own epiphany at his parousia (Col 3,4). The letter to the Ephesians carries the conception through to its final conclusion : through Baptism God
has « quickened us together with Christ », « raised us up with him »,
« made us sit together with him in the heavenly realm » (Eph 2,4-6).
And this saving activity of God belongs to him properly as Father, since
it reaches us through the sacred humanity of his Son.

§ 3. - Christian Salvation Effected by Jesus Christ as God's Son

If, as we have just seen, Christian salvation has its origins in God's
eternal will and in his initiative as Father, in the soteriology presented
by Paul's epistles, it is equally true that the carrying out of the divine
plan for man's definitive salvation is attributed to Jesus Christ as
God's incarnate Son. The prominence given to Christ's divine Sonship,
as we have observed, is to be traced back to the data of Paul's first experience of the risen Christ near Damascus, which were found to characterize Paul's first attempts at preaching the Christian Gospel (Acts 9,20).
The paramount importance of Christ's resurrection in such a soteriological viewpoint will appear evident from a study of the texts in Paul's
writings which deal with the saving activity of Christ as Son of God.

Paul's Concept of Christ as Son of God

The early Pauline letters describe Christ's divine Sonship in its relations with the eschatological idea of salvation. It is as God's Son that Jesus
will return at his parousia, « our rescuer from the wrath to come »
(1 Thes 1,10). The Christian vocation, essentially a « call » by God the
Father, is orientated to that « fellowship with his Son » which will become
a reality at the end of time « on the day of our Lord Jesus Christ » (1
Cor 1,8-9). Human history is to reach its consummation when, as Son,
the risen Christ « will hand over the Kingdom to God the Father » (1
Cor 15,24), and « the Son himself will be subject to him who subjected
the universe, in order that God be all in all » (1 Cor 15,28) [32].

---

[32] Cf. n. 11 *supra*.

It is with the epistle to the Galatians that Paul begins to under-score, by means of his own supernatural experiences, the intimate and per-sonal nature of the Christian's present relationship to the risen Christ as Son of God. He refers to his own conversion as the Father's revela-tion « of his Son in me » (Gal 1,16). He perceives that the pattern of his own Christian life is determined by its relation to Christ as Son : « By faith I live in the Son of God » (Gal 2,20) [33]. The same verse recalls that it was as God's Son that Christ gave the supreme proof of his love by dying for men. For Paul, he is pre-eminently « the Son of God, who loved me and handed himself over for my sake ». This redemption, effected by the Father's sending of his Son, had as its purpose man's adoptive filia-tion, revealed by the indwelling « Spirit of his Son » (Gal 4,4-6) [34].

The summary of Paul's Gospel which he addressed to the Roman church is aptly called « the Gospel of God concerning his Son » (Rom 1,1-3), or simply, « the Gospel of his Son » (Rom 1,9). It was as Son of God that « Christ died on our behalf » : « we were reconciled with God through the death of his Son » ; it is by his life as « Son of God in power » that « we shall be saved » (Rom 5,8-10). It was in the sacred humanity of the incar-nate Son that the Father effectively condemned sin through Christ's death and resurrection (Rom 8,3). The principal significance of Christ's death for Paul lies in his dying as Son of God : « God did not spare his own Son » (Rom 8,32). It is Christ's resurrection as Son of God that has determined the pattern of the Christian's predestination : « Those whom he foreknew, he also predestined to share the character of the image of his Son, that he should be first-born of many brothers » (Rom 8,29).

In the letter to the Colossians, Paul first introduces the notion of Christ as Head of his Body, the Church (Col 1,18-20) [35]. He calls the Church « the Kingdom of the Son of his love » (Col 1,13). It is, consequently, as God's beloved Son that Christ holds the primacy in the earthly phase of « the Kingdom », the Church. In Ephesians, Paul describes the goal of the Church's growth as « Body of Christ » (cf. Col 3,10) as « the perfect knowledge of the Son of God » (Eph 4,13). It is thus as God's Son that Christ constitutes what Paul repeatedly calls « the Mystery » in these two letters of the Roman Captivity (Col 2,2-3 ; 1,27 ; Eph 1,10) [36].

---

[33] P. 151.
[34] Pp. 156-157.
[35] P. 205.
[36] P. 210.

CHRIST'S DEATH AS CAUSE OF CHRISTIAN SALVATION

While, as we have seen, Paul considers that Christ's redemptive death is to be attributed primarily to the initiative of God as Father, he also thinks of it very frequently as the work of Christ as Son. If the Father is said to have « handed over » his Son (Rom 8,32 ; 4,25), Christ is also said to have « handed himself over » to death for us (Gal 2,20 ; Eph 5,2.25). If the Father has « reconciled » man to himself through his Son's death (2 Cor 5,18 ; Col 1,20.22), Christ has accomplished this reconciliation through his death (Rom 5, 10 ; Eph 2,16). The unity of the work of Father and Son in effecting this redemptive reconciliation is expressed in Paul's statement that « God was in Christ reconciling the world to himself, instead of holding men's transgressions against them » (2 Cor 5,19) [37]. At the same time, Paul is aware that Christ was not merely a passive instrument in undergoing death, as may be seen by his use of terms used to describe Christ's act, which are not employed with reference to the Father's work. By his death, Christ « delivered » us (Gal 1,4) and « redeemed » us (Gal 3,13 ; 4,5).

The saving character of Christ's death appears clearly in Paul's conception of it as an act of obedience to the Father's Will, by which the freedom and voluntareity of Christ's acceptance of it is underscored [38]. In the hymn which Paul cites in Phil 2,6-11, the picture of Christ as the Suffering Servant of God includes his « becoming obedient unto death, even the death of the Cross ». In the sequel, Christ's exaltation appears as the reward of this meritorious action [39]. Paul's own idea of the redemptive nature of this obedience is seen in his sketch of Christ as the second Adam. Obedience to God in opposition to Adam's disobedience is the principal element in the contrast drawn between Christ and the first man.

« For just as through the disobedience of one man, the rest were constituted sinners, so too through the obedience of one man, the rest will be constituted just » (Rom 5,19).

Paul considers that Christ's obedience as the new Adam is cause of man's justification and eternal life in the same way in which the first Adam's disobedience was cause of sin and death in humanity (Rom 5,18.21) [40].

---

[37] P. 142.

[38] Cf. S. LYONNET, *La sotériologie paulinienne* in *Introduction à la Bible II* 880-882.

[39] P. 99.

[40] Pp. 179-180.

Christ's death is first and foremost an expression of his love for men, as well as the revelation of the Father's love (Rom 5,8 ; Eph 5,1). This truth appears to have impressed itself upon Paul's mind as a result of his reflection upon the completely universal scope of Christ's death [41].

« Indeed, Christ's love has put us under compulsion, once we realized this truth : one died for all ; therefore all have died » (2 Cor 5,14).

However, it is principally as a symbol of the efficacious nature of Christ's love for us that Paul thinks of Christ's death ; and then he necessarily associates Christ's resurrection with his death, since it has resulted in man's union with the risen Christ.

« I live in the Son of God, who loved me and handed himself over for my sake » (Gal 2,20).
« Live a life of love, just as Christ loved you and handed himself over for our sake ... » (Eph 5,2).
« ... as Christ also loved the Church and handed himself over for her sake, in order that he might cleanse and sanctify her ... to present the Church to himself ... » (Eph 5,25-27).

Finally, it remains to mention a view of Christ's death which is peculiarly Pauline : Christ has through his own death changed the meaning of death for the Christian. It is now a falling asleep through Jesus (1 Thes 4,14) [42] : it is the means of our being « with Christ » in a fuller sense than is possible in this life (Phil 1,21-23), for death now causes us « to dwell near the Lord » (2 Cor 5,8). Death has become a step in the process of salvation, which will culminate in the « redemption of our bodies » (Rom 8,23) [43] : we must be « handed over to death through Jesus », if we are to share his new risen existence (2 Cor 4,10-12). What has given the Christian this victory over death, to which he is still subject, is Christ's resurrection. God gives us the victory through the risen Christ (1 Cor 15,57). For that reason, Paul may be said never to think of Christ's redemptive death without somehow thinking of Christ's salutary resurrection.

---

[41] P. 139.
[42] P. 78.
[43] P. 195.

CHRIST'S RESURRECTION AS AN INTEGRAL PART OF HIS WORK OF SALVATION

The primitive apostolic preaching appears, from the evidence of Acts, to have given greater prominence to Christ's resurrection than to his death. Paul, on the other hand, because of his experience with the judaizing Christian Pharisees for whom the Cross was a « scandal » and with the pagans of Greek culture for whom it was « foolishness », made « Christ crucified » the centre of his kerygma (1 Cor 1,23). He asserts that he came to Corinth knowing nothing « but Jesus Christ and him crucified » (1 Cor 2,2). He describes his evangelization of the Galatians as a « placarding » of « Jesus Christ as crucified » (Gal 3,1). Yet, even in these emphatic assertions, the thought of the resurrection is not entirely lacking, as Paul's use of the perfect participle ἐσταυρωμένος implies. We find in Romans an expression which more adequately represents the central theme of Pauline soteriological thought : « Jesus Christ who died, — or rather, who was raised » (Rom 8,34) [44]. So closely does Paul associate Christ's resurrection with his death as cause of Christian salvation that he habitually thinks of the redeemer of men as « him who died and was raised for them » (2 Cor 5,15) [45].

Paul's use of the term « redemption » (ἀπολύτρωσις) may serve to illustrate how Christ's resurrection essentially appertains to the Pauline conception of salvation. In one sense, redemption will become the possession of the Christian only at Christ's parousia, « the day of redemption » (Eph 4,30), through the glorious resurrection of the just, « the redemption of our bodies » (Rom 8,23). This is because, from the Semitic point of view which is also Paul's, salvation in the full sense must affect man in his entire personality, its material no less than its spiritual components.

There is however a sense in which, for Paul, redemption already exists as an accomplished fact. It is found in its total reality in the glorified humanity of the risen Christ, and through that humanity it exerts an influence upon the contemporary Christian life of grace. Indeed, this supernatural existence springs from the Christian's union with the

---

[44] M. MEINERTZ, *Theologie des Neuen Testaments II* 93 : « Der Tod Christi ist nicht das Ende, er wirkt auch nicht für sich allein, sondern er erhält seinen vollen Wert erst durch die Auferstehung ... Triumphierend antwortet Paulus Röm 8,34 auf die Frage, wer urteilen könne : ' Christus Jesus ist da, der gestorben, mehr noch, der auferweckt ist ' ».

[45] P. 139.

risen Christ ; and to this extent, the Christian may be said to possess redemption. Hence Paul calls it

> « your existence in Christ Jesus, who became for us Wisdom from God, that is, Justice and Sanctification and Redemption » (1 Cor 1,30) [46].

In other words, it is his by death *and* resurrection that Christ has become redemption incarnate. The Pauline view of the effects of Christ's redemptive work exploits a somewhat different set of values from those which appear in our modern, more juridical notion, which concentrates attention almost exclusively upon Christ's death in its satisfactory and meritorious aspects. For Paul, the redemption has resulted in the glorification of Christ's humanity, which has thus become the perfect instrument of our justification, and, ultimately, of our eschatological salvation. Accordingly, Paul describes those who accept the Christian faith

> « as being justified gratuitously by his loving favour through the redemption in Christ Jesus » (Rom 3,24).

The hymn in Colossians characterizes the risen Christ as him « in whom we possess redemption » (Col 1,14). Ephesians echoes the same thought : « It is in him that we possess the redemption through his blood » (Eph 1,7). In the same passage, Paul explains that it is through the risen Christ's gift of the Spirit that the Christians are given a greater and greater share in this reality.

> « In him too, once you were Christians, you have been sealed with the promised Holy Spirit, who is the pledge of our inheritance, to ready the redemption of the people of God's acquiring, to the praise of his glory » (Eph 1,14) [46a].

That Christ's resurrection is, for Paul, an intrinsic cause of Christian salvation may also be seen from the fact that it is somehow involved in the forgiveness of man's sins (1 Cor 15,17) and in man's justification (Rom 4,25). This last text draws a close parallel between the causality exerted by Christ's death upon our sins and that exercised by his resurrection upon our state of justice. If Christ's death has made us « dead to sin » (Rom 6,11), his resurrection has made us « alive to God ». Paul

---

[46] Pp. 108-110.
[46a] P. 220.

can even consider this twofold state as the effect of Christ's resurrection, inasmuch as it is the result of the risen Christ's presence within us :

> « If Christ is in you, the body is dead with respect to sin, but the spirit is life with respect to justification » (Rom 8,10).

Christ's resurrection is also a cause of the Christian's final resurrection to eternal life. Christ was raised « as firstfruits of those who have fallen asleep » (1 Cor 15,20) [47], or as « first-born from among the dead » (Col 1,18), since it is through that « power », communicated to Christ's humanity at his own resurrection, that God will raise us (1 Cor 6,14).

Christ's Saving Work Fully Completed in his own Human Nature

We have already referred in passing to the Pauline view that Christ's redemptive activity has been carried to completion at least in his own sacred humanity. However, since the conception is basic to Paul's soteriology, it requires some further amplification.

To begin with, it is to be observed that Paul nowhere adopts the viewpoint so characteristic of the Fourth Gospel, that the assumption of man's nature by the Word, the Son of God, is the primary determining factor in Christian salvation.

> « The Word became a mortal man ;
> he pitched his tent among us.
> And we have beheld his glory ...
> of his abundance we have all received our share,
> grace instead of grace ... » (Jn 1,14-16).

For Paul, salvation takes its origin from Christ's death and resurrection. The resurrection remains the moment when Christ was « constituted Son of God in power » (Rom 1,4) [48], as his death is the moment when he died « to sin once for all » (Rom 6,10) [49].

What view does Paul take of Jesus' earthly life and its significance in salvation-history ? The hymn Paul cites in Philippians gives a hint of his attitude.

---

[47] Pp. 120-124.
[48] Pp. 163-166.
[49] P. 186.

« He despoiled himself,
accepted the role of the Servant,
and adopted the likeness of men » (Phil 2,7) [50].

In the light of his divine prerogatives, revealed by his resurrection, the Son's becoming man was an impoverishment. This same point of view is manifested in another passage from Paul's letters.

« For you know the liberality of our Lord Jesus Christ : how for your sake he became poor, when he was rich, in order that you, through his poverty, might become rich » (2 Cor 8,9).

The Son of God entered the human family « born of a woman, born subject to law » (Gal 4,4). He was sent by the Father « in the likeness of sinful humanity » (Rom 8,3). This attitude of Paul towards the earthly condition of Jesus, which he assumed in order to share the universal sentence condemning all men to undergo suffering and death, may be faithfully represented in modern theological terms by saying that the mortal Christ, for Paul, appeared as man-to-be-redeemed. It must be remembered that Paul's concept of Jesus in his earthly state was derived from his knowledge of the risen Christ. If the possession and exercise of divine power is an essential attribute of the risen Son of God (1 Cor 6,14 ; Rom 1,4), then his previous condition was one of « weakness » (2 Cor 13,4). Since Christ « was raised by the glory of the Father » (Rom 6,4), he was anteriorly somehow without that glory, i. e. he resembled sinful mankind, « deprived of the glory of God » (Rom 3, 23). Because, in his risen state, he is the very embodiment of the divine « justice », he can be said to have been made « into sin » prior to his glorification (2 Cor 5,21). If he now represents the perfect fulfilment of « Abraham's blessing », it is possible to say that once he appeared in men's eyes to « have become a curse » (Gal 3,13).

One of the most striking features of this whole soteriological conception is the nicety with which Paul defines Christ's relation to sin. By his assumption of man's nature, which had been radically effected by Adam's sin (Rom 5,12 ff), God's Son appeared « in the likeness of sinful humanity » (Rom 8,3). This means that Christ made himself as like other men, all of whom were sinners, as was possible for one « who knew no sin » (2 Cor 5,21). This likeness can be called « weakness » (2 Cor 13,4),

---

[50] Pp. 97-98.

18. - D. M. STANLEY.

humanity's return to the natural condition of suffering and dying which
is the effect of the divine condemnation of Adam's sin [51]. For Paul, this
status of the incarnate Son provided the possibility of his redemptive
work on man's behalf. It also explains why that redemptive activity
consisted of resurrection as well as death, since it was by being raised to
a new life, not less than by dying to this old existence, that Christ now
presents the picture of man-redeemed, or, as Paul states it, « the redemption in Christ Jesus » (Rom 3,24).

CHRIST AS THE SECOND OR LAST ADAM

The earliest Christological or soteriological conception, which was
developed in Palestinian Christianity, appears to have been that of Christ
as the suffering and glorified Servant of Yahweh (Phil 2,6-11). This view
of Christ's redemptive work was marked by two chief characteristics : a
certain emphasis upon the vicarious [52] nature of Jesus' death and the
presentation of his resurrection as a reward for his meritorious obedience
to the divine will. By contrast, Paul seems to have thought of the death
and resurrection of Christ primarily in terms of man's solidarity [53] with
him. « One died for all : therefore all have died » (2 Cor 5,14). « You also
were made to die to the Law through Christ's Body» (Rom 7,4). «All of you
are one Christ Jesus » (Gal 3,28). Christ was raised from death as « firstfruits of those who have fallen asleep » (1 Cor 15,20), as « first-born
from among the dead » (Col 1,18). In his risen state, Christ has a new
relation to the Christian, even in the material side of his personality
(« The Lord is for the body »), since the future resurrection of the just

---

[51] S. LYONNET, La sotériologie paulinienne 882 : « Dieu envoie donc son
propre Fils se faire l' un d'entre nous et, par solidarité avec nous, prendre sur
lui ... la condition ... d'hommes réduits par le péché d' Adam à leur condition natu-
relle, non seulement capables de mourir, mais condamnés à mourir ».

[52] The orthodox understanding of vicarious satisfaction stresses the fact
that Christ's death was salutary insofar as it was an act of Christ's liberty, the
manifestation of his obedience and his love. Paul expresses this conception, for
example, in Rom 5,19.

[53] The view of Christ's death as vicarious satisfaction, of course, also includes
(without highlighting) this idea of solidarity : cf. S. LYONNET, La Sotériologie paulinienne 876 f : « D'ailleurs le Christ n'est évidemment pas retourné à son Père pour
nous éviter d'y retourner à notre tour et en ce sens il n'est pas mort ' à notre
place ' ».

will be effected through the « power » possessed by Christ's glorified humanity (1 Cor 6,13-14). As a result of this viewpoint, Christ's resurrection is considered more as a benefit to men, « for our justification » (Rom 4,25) than as a personal reward for Christ. He can be said to have been « constituted Son of God in power » because his resurrection has inaugurated the « resurrection of the dead » (Rom 1,4).

The vehicle which Paul chose to express this soteriological conception is the theme of Christ as the new Adam. It is significant that it first makes its appearance in Paul's apology for the Christian belief in the resurrection of the just, where the basis of his whole argument is the principle that Christ's resurrection is simply the first stage of the glorious resurrection of the Christian people (1 Cor 15,14 ff).

In this first enucleation of his theme [54], Paul underscores the solidarity of all with Christ in the eschatological resurrection of the just.

> « Since through a man [came] death :
> so also through a man [will come] resurrection of the dead ;
> because just as in Adam all die,
> so also in Christ all will be brought to life » (1 Cor 15,21-22).

Here it is clear that Paul thinks of Christ as the new Adam in his risen state. Later in the same chapter, when he draws a contrast between the character of the first and the second Adam, Paul leaves no doubt that Christ assumed the role of the second Adam at the moment of his resurrection [55].

> « the first man, Adam, became a living being :
> the last Adam became a life-giving Spirit » (1 Cor 15,45).

When Paul returns to the theme in Romans, we discover an interesting new development [56].

> « Just as through the disobedience of one man
> the rest were constituted sinners,
> so too through the obedience of one man,
> the rest will be constituted just » (Rom 5,19).

---

[54] Pp. 123-124.
[55] Pp. 125-126.
[56] Pp. 176-180.

Already through his voluntary acceptance of death as God's will, Christ was acting as the new Adam : his salutary act of obedience repaired the damage inflicted upon humanity by the first Adam's disobedience.

« Just as sin was king in death,
so also grace will be king through justification leading
to eternal life through Jesus Christ our Lord » (Rom 5,21).

The epistles of the Roman Captivity return to this theme of the new Adam as an illustration of the unity of all Christians in Christ [57].

« You have put off your old man with his habits, and you have put on that new man, constantly being renewed in view of perfect knowledge in the Image of his Creator, where there is no 'Greek and Jew', 'circumcised and uncircumcised', 'barbarian' 'Scythian', 'slave', 'freeman', but Christ, all in all » (Col 3,9b-11).

Here Paul has simply re-expressed the relationship of the individual Christian to Christ (cf. Gal 3,28) as the second Adam.

Similarly, the epistle to the Ephesians rephrases the reconciliation-motif which was prominent in the soteriology of the so-called « great » epistles [58].

« He personally is our Peace, since he brought the two sides together ... in order that he might in himself create the two into one new man, thus making peace ; and so reconcile both in one body to God through the cross, having by it killed the hatred » (Eph 2,14-16).

In this same letter, Paul also resumes his celebrated conception of the Church as Christ's Body under the second Adam theme.

« And he gave some as apostles, others as prophets, others as preachers, others as shepherds and teachers ... for the building-up of the Body of Christ, until we all attain the oneness of faith and perfect knowledge of the Son of God, the perfect man ... » (Eph 4,11-13).

These instances of the subordination of other soteriological themes to that of the new Adam would appear to indicate how fundamental it became to Paul's theology in the final phase of his creative activity. The

[57] Pp. 214-216.
[58] Pp. 224-226.

place of paramount importance which Christ's resurrection holds in the new Adam conception, both for its genesis and its mature expression, indicates how essential Christ's resurrection is to Pauline soteriology.

SIGNIFICANCE OF CHRIST'S DEATH AND RESURRECTION IN SALVATION-HISTORY

Our analysis of certain key-texts in Paul's letters indicated that his soteriology evolved gradually under the impact of the varied experiences of his apostolic career. This development of Paul's thought appears to have been due, in large measure, to a deeper insight into the significance of Christ's death and resurrection for the whole history of salvation. This can, we believe, be illustrated to some extent by means of three texts, possessing a certain literary parallelism, which occur at different periods of Paul's literary activity.

The first of these is found in the first extant Pauline epistle. Here [59] the purpose of Christ's redemptive death (and that of his resurrection, which is clearly implied) is expressed in terms of his eschatological office as Saviour. No mention is made of the influence of Christ's death and resurrection upon present Christian existence. « Our Lord Jesus Christ » is presented as he

> « who died for us, in order that, whether we wake or whether we sleep, we may live together with him » (1 Thes 5,10).

Since at this period of his career, Paul concentrates his attention almost entirely (cf. however Phil 3,10-11) upon the work of Christ at the parousia (Phil 3,20-21), the finality of Christ's death and resurrection is stated here in function of the transformation (1 Cor 15,51 ; 1 Thes 4,17) of those still alive and the glorious resurrection of those already dead (1 Thes 4,14) at Christ's second Coming.

The second text, which in its form closely resembles the first, displays a markedly different orientation. Paul now considers Christ's death and resurrection in their effect upon the life of the Christian in this world [60].

---

[59] P. 80.
[60] P. 139.

> « And he died, in order that the living may no longer live for themselves,
> but for him who died and was raised for them » (2 Cor 5,15).

During the years between the writing of his earlier letters and the composition of 2 Corinthians, Paul had faced several crises which forced him to
rethink his soteriology : the serious difficulty which the dogma of the resurrection of the just presented to the Greek mind (1 Cor 15, 1 ff) ; opposition
to his own apostolic authority in the Corinthian community (2 Cor 10,10) ;
his own experience at Ephesus of coming face to face with death (2 Cor
1,8). As a consequence, Paul's attention (cf. 2 Cor 1,9-10) becomes concentrated upon the meaning of the Christian life in function of its present supernatural values rather than in its relation to the parousia. He
now begins to construct a theology of history, whose pattern has been
determined by Christ's death and resurrection. While he first expresses
this insight in terms of his own experience, it can be applied to the
life of every Christian, and explains what the Apostle means by living
« for him who died and was raised » [61].

> « [We are] continually bearing the dying of Jesus in our body, in order that
> the life of Jesus also may be manifested in our body. For always we
> the living are being handed over to death for Jesus' sake, in order that
> Jesus' life also be manifested in our mortal flesh » (2 Cor 4,10-11).

This form, imposed upon Christian existence by Christ's death and resurrection, is initially communicated through the sacrament of Baptism
(Rom 6,3-6).

The third parallel passage is found near the end of Paul's letter to
the Romans [62].

> « For this purpose Christ died and came to life, that he should be Lord
> both of the dead and of the living » (Rom 14,9).

Certain significant modifications in this expression of the purpose of
Christ's salvific activity reflect Paul's mature soteriological thought. He
now explicitly associates the causality of Christ's resurrection with that of
his death. At this stage, the Apostle considers these two events as com-
plementary phases of Christ's work of salvation (Rom 4,25). Moreover,
he now states the scope of this twofold *Heilsereignis* in a more compre-

---

[61] Pp. 135-137.
[62] P. 199.

hensive manner. In 2 Cor 5,15, Christian existence in this world was related to Christ's death. In 1 Thes 5,10, the change in Christian existence
at the parousia was connected with Christ's death. Now Christ's universal sovereignty, the result of his constitution as « Son of God in power »
(Rom 1,4), is thought of as something already realized both in this world
and the next. Christ's death and resurrection have issued in the new life
par excellence, which he communicates to the Christian through Baptism
(Rom 6,4), as the basis of eschatological salvation (Rom 5,10).

Not only the life of the individual Christian, but the whole movement of salvation-history is governed by the dynamic of Christ's death
and resurrection. Israel's rejection and future re-admission to Christ's
Kingdom is a kind of dying and rising (Rom 11,15). The present, violent state of the material creation is like death, « the enslavement of
corruption », while its future participation in « the freedom of the glory
of the sons of God » is comparable to resurrection (Rom 8,19-22). Thus,
for Paul, the dialectic of human history consists in a series of crises, of
dyings and risings, involving the individual, the nation, the universe,
because such was the form in which the salvation of all men has been
accomplished by him « who died and was raised for them » (2 Cor 5,15).

§ 4. - Christian Salvation and the Spirit of our Adoptive Filiation

If, as we have endeavoured to show in the preceding sections of
this chapter, Paul tended to think of salvation primarily as the work of
God as Father and of Christ as Son of God, it will not be surprising to
find that the function of the Holy Spirit in Pauline soteriology is referred chiefly to the adoptive sonship of the Christian. In fact, Paul, who
regards the giving of the Spirit as the characteristic activity of the risen
Christ (1 Cor 15,45), identifies the Spirit's operation within the Christian
with that of the risen Christ (Rom 8,9-10). The origin of such a distinctive viewpoint probably lies in the character of Paul's conversion as
an experience of the risen Christ as Son of God, to which his experience
of the Spirit, after his Baptism, was subordinated.

It is significant that, in the customary wish for « grace and peace »
with which Paul always begins his letters, there is never any reference
to the Holy Spirit. Similarly, in the concluding doxologies and prayers,
the Spirit is almost never named. In this respect, the final verse of 2
Corinthians is practically unique.

« May the grace of the Lord Jesus Christ and the love of God [the Father] and the fellowship of the Holy Spirit [remain] with you all » (2 Cor 13,13).

To this isolated instance, we may add a verse from Romans which may possibly have formed the conclusion of an earlier redaction of the epistle.

« Now I exhort you, brothers, through our Lord Jesus Christ and through the love of the Spirit, to unite your efforts to mine in your prayers on my behalf to God ... » (Rom 15,30).

THE WORK OF THE SPIRIT WITHIN THE CHRISTIAN CHURCH

In both the texts just cited, the work of the Spirit is concerned with the Church as a community. « Fellowship », κοινωνία, is the result of that fraternal love which the Spirit's presence produces in the Christian people. This same doctrine appears in Paul's enumeration of motives for union in the Philippian church. The Trinitarian structure of the passage is not difficult to perceive.

« If there be any motivation in Christ, if there be any persuasion from Love, if there be any fellowship of the Spirit ... fill up my joy by adopting the same attitude of mind, displaying the same love ... » (Phil 2,1-2).

The thought here is governed by the role characteristic of each of the divine Persons in the work of salvation : the selfless obedience of the Son, which Paul will presently describe (Phil 2,6-11), the love of the Father as author of our redemption, the fellowship which the presence of the Spirit produces in the Church.

Paul has already told the Philippians that « to live as a citizen » of the Kingdom in a way « worthy of the Gospel of Christ » they must « stand fast in one Spirit » (Phil 1,27). The only genuine Christian love is that which is specified « by the Spirit » (Col 1,8). Christian unity is produced and preserved, amid the greatest diversity of charismatic gifts, because, as Paul tells the Corinthians, these graces all emanate from « the same Spirit » (1 Cor 12,4). In fact, Christian unity is properly called « the unity of the Spirit » (Eph 4,3) : the oneness of the Body of Christ, the Church, corresponds to the « one Spirit » (Eph 4,4).

The form of the Christian approach to God is determined from its very inception by the Holy Spirit. It is he who gives that inner message which makes Paul's preaching « forceful » and not « mere words » (1 Thes

1,5), so that it can be called a « demonstration of the Spirit and of power » (I Cor 2,4). This same activity makes the conversion of the pagans an « offering of the Gentiles ... sanctified by the Holy Spirit » (Rom 15,16). When Paul calls the Gospel « God's power for salvation to every man with faith » (Rom 1,16), he means that « Christ has worked through me [to effect] the obedience of pagans ... by the power of God's Spirit » (Rom 15,19).

It is the Spirit who reveals the Father's divine plan of predestination, since he alone knows God's secrets (I Cor 2,10-11). The Spirit is likewise the source of Christian faith in the divinity of Christ (I Cor 12,3). He has revealed the Mystery of Christian salvation « to the holy apostles and prophets » (Eph 3,5), Hence it is « through the Holy Spirit who dwells in you » that Timothy must « guard the deposit » (2 Tm 1,14). The « Kingdom of God », the object of the Gospel-message, may be defined as « peace and joy in the Holy Spirit » (Rom 14,17).

The Spirit's activity is prominent in the initiation of the neophyte into the Church by Baptism. « You have been washed, you have been sanctified, you have been justified, by the Name of the Lord Jesus Christ and by the Spirit of our God » (I Cor 6, 11). Baptism can be called « Christ's circumcision » (Col 2,11) or « circumcision of the heart by the Spirit » (Rom 2,29). The « rebirth » which it effects is a « renovation by the Holy Spirit » (Ti 3,5).

Christian liturgical worship, the cult offered to God by the community as such, is distinguished from the outmoded worship of Judaism, precisely because it is « according to the Spirit » (Phil 3,3). The spiritual nature of Christian cult derives from the fact that the Christian « access to the Father » is « in one Spirit » (Eph 2,18) [63].

THE INDWELLING SPIRIT

The follower of Christ, who has received from his Lord the injunction to « pray always » (Lk 18,1) is able to do so « in the Spirit » (Eph 6,15). For Paul, the assistance of the Spirit in the Christian prayer-life is of paramount importance. He assumes that through prayer the Christian enjoys a true, experimental knowledge of the Spirit. « Do not quench the Spirit », he warns the Thessalonians (I Thes 5,19). This experience

[63] Pp. 224-226.

of the Spirit is something that is almost tangible in Paul's eyes : he can contrast it with the undergoing of circumcision (Gal 3,3), the observance of the Mosaic Law (Gal 3,5), or the « getting drunk on wine » (Eph 5,18).

It is this conviction of the perceptible character of the activity of the Spirit within the Christian, which enabled Paul to determine the place of law in the Christian dispensation. Since the Christian is « led by the Spirit », there is no necessity for law, at least ideally speaking, in the Christian Church (Gal 5,18). The principal contrast between the religion of Moses and that of Christ is, in Paul's mind, the opposition between « the letter » and « the Spirit » (2 Cor 3,6 ; Rom 7,6). The superiority of Christianity does not consist merely in the possession of a higher religious ideal or of a more exacting code of conduct. It derives principally from the interior, dynamic quality of « the law of the Spirit of life », in contrast with which the Mosaic Law appears as « the law of sin and of death » (Rom 8,2) [64].

This characteristically Pauline viewpoint discloses the importance, for Paul, of the indwelling of the Spirit within the Christian. Because of this divine inhabitation, the Christian becomes « God's sanctuary » (1 Cor 3,16), « the sanctuary of the living God » (2 Cor 6,16), replacing the OT Holy of Holies, where God had once dwelt with his people. The risen Christ is the « keystone » in this « holy sanctuary in the Lord », which is « God's dwelling by the Spirit » (Eph 2,21-22). This is the source of the dignity of the Christian, since, thanks to this indwelling of the Spirit, he belongs only to God (1 Cor 6,19). Indeed, without this presence of the Holy Spirit, no one can be said to belong to Christ (Rom 8,9). The closeness and intimacy of the union of the Christian with his risen Lord can be seen from Paul's statement that the two form « one Spirit » (1 Cor 6,17).

Paul thinks of this inhabitation of the Spirit as the concrete realization of the Father's love for the Christian : « The love of God has been

---

[64] St. Thomas, *Summa Theologica*, 1-2, 106, 2 : « ad legem Evangelii duo pertinent. Unum quidem principaliter : scilicet ipsa gratia Spiritus Sancti interius data. Et quantum ad hoc, nova lex iustificat ... Aliud pertinet ad legem Evangelii secundario : scilicet documenta fidei, et praecepta ordinantia affectum humanum et humanos actus. Et quantum ad hoc, lex nova non iustificat. Unde Apostolus dicit ... *Littera occidit, spiritus autem vivificat*. Et Augustinus exponit ... quod per litteram intelligitur quaelibet scriptura extra homines existens, etiam moralium praeceptorum qualia continentur in Evangelio. Unde etiam littera Evangelii occideret, nisi adesset interius gratia fidei sanans».

poured out in our hearts through the gift of the Holy Spirit to us »
(Rom 5, 5). The indwelling Spirit will also play an essential role in the
Father's eschatological raising of the Christian in glory.

> « If the Spirit of him who raised Jesus from death dwells in you, he who
> raised Christ from death will also vivify your mortal bodies through his
> Spirit who dwells in you » (Rom 8,11).

Paul calls this inhabitation of the Spirit « the firstfruits of the Spirit »,
since it arouses in the Christian a deep yearning for « the redemption of
our bodies », the glorious resurrection through which salvation will
finally become a complete reality (Rom 8, 23).

THE RELATION OF THE SPIRIT TO THE RISEN CHRIST

We have already remarked upon the close relation which Paul considers
to exist between the Holy Spirit and the risen Christ. The Spirit is no
less « Christ's Spirit » (Phil 1,19 ; Rom 8,9), « the Spirit of his Son »
(Gal 4,6) than « God's Spirit » (1 Thes 4,8 ; Phil 3,3 ; 1 Cor 3,16). Indeed,
in several passages in the Pauline epistles, the operation of the Spirit
with that of the risen Christ is insisted upon by means of arresting phrases.
So intimately is the Spirit associated with the work of the new Adam,
in Paul's mind, that he can simply state that « the last Adam became
lifegiving Spirit » (1 Cor 15,45). With somewhat disconcerting brevity,
Paul can assert that « The Lord is the Spirit » (2 Cor 3,17). It is a fundamental principle of Pauline soteriology that « the Spirit of holiness »,
the Holy Spirit, is an intrinsic element in the risen Christ's constitution as « Son of God in power » (Rom 1,4). Thus Paul can speak of the
Spirit's indwelling as the presence of the risen Christ in the Christian.

> « He who does not possess Christ's Spirit does not belong to him. But if
> Christ be in you ... » (Rom 8,9-10).

We catch an echo of this same viewpoint in the primitive Christian hymn
which is cited in 1 Tm 3,16, where the glorified Christ is said to have
been « justified by spirit », where the glorification of Christ's sacred
humanity is described at the effect of the indwelling of the Holy Spirit [65].

---

[65] P. 238.

The Spirit of the Christian's Adoptive Filiation

The term υἱοθεσία occurs in the NT only in Paul's letters (Gal 4,5 ; Rom 8,15 ; 9,4 ; Eph 1,5). Consequently it may said that the most characteristically Pauline view of the work of the Spirit is that which presents him as the Spirit of our adoptive filiation.

From his earliest letters, Paul's concept of salvation involved the activity of the Holy Spirit [66].

> « God has chosen you as firstfruits for salvation through the sanctification by the Spirit... to which he has called you ... for an acquisition of the glory of our Lord Jesus Christ » (2 Thes 2,13-14).

If salvation has been acquired for us through the death and resurrection of Christ (1 Thes 5,9-10), it is also the result of « sanctification by the Spirit ».

In his letter to the Galatians, Paul ascribes the Christian's adoptive sonship to the work both of the Son and of the Spirit. « You are all sons of God through faith in Christ Jesus » (Gal 3,26), i.e. by believing in his death and resurrection, through which God released those « fenced about by law » (Gal 3,26) to make them his sons [67].

> « But when the fulness of time was come, God sent forth his Son, born of a woman, born subject to law, in order that he might redeem those subject to law, in order that we might receive the adoptive sonship » (Gal 4,4-5).

The Spirit too plays an essential role in our adoptive sonship. In the first place, he reveals to us the reality of our adoption as sons of God. Only through the Spirit does the Christian recognize God as his Father. In the second place, the assistance of the Spirit is essential in order that the Christian can address God by the intimate name of Father.

> « The proof that you are sons : God has sent the Spirit of his Son into our hearts, crying 'Abba', that is, 'Father' ' (Gal 4,6).

Paul returns to this idea in Romans in order to develop it more fully :

---

[66] Pp. 91-93.
[67] Pp. 156-157.

the indwelling Spirit is in fact the new life-principle by which the Christian exists as a son of God.

« Indeed, whoever are moved by God's Spirit are God's sons. Thus you have not received a spirit of slavery ... you have received the Spirit of adoptive sonship, in whom we cry ' Abba ', that is, ' Father '. The Spirit himself testifies to our spirit that we are God's children » (Rom 8, 14-16).

In the same chapter of Romans, Paul explains how the Spirit instructs us to pray as God's adoptive sons, in accordance with the Father's designs for our salvation. Indeed, the Spirit himself intercedes for us with the Father, who from eternity has decreed our assimilation to his only Son.

« Likewise, the Spirit also comes to the aid of our weakness, since we do not know what we should pray for. But the Spirit intercedes with inexpressible longing. He who searches hearts knows the Spirit's intention, namely, that he intercedes for the saints according to God's designs » (Rom 8,26-27).

Paul immediately states what these divine designs are :

« Those he knew beforehand he also predestined to take on the character of the image of his Son, so that he might be the first-born of many brothers » (Rom 8,29).

Paul returns to the conception of the Christian's adoptive filiation in the epistle to the Ephesians, where he speaks of the Father's plan of Salvation to be effected by Christ's death and resurrection [68].

« Out of love he predestined us for adoptive sonship through Jesus Christ for himself ... » (Eph 1,5).

Again the Spirit has his part to play :

« You have been sealed by the promised Holy Spirit, who is the pledge of our inheritance ... » (Eph 1,14).

It is the Spirit's presence within the Christian that constitutes his guarantee that he will inherit what is his by right of adoptive sonship, since it is this very presence which enables the Christian to act as a son of the Father.

In the letters to the Colossians and Ephesians, Paul once more iden-

---

[68] Pp. 218-219.

tifies the presence of the glorified Christ in the Christian with the indwelling of the Spirit. In the course of his development of the notion
of the Mystery, God's universal plan of salvation, Paul finds this Mystery concretely realized by « Christ in you, the hope of glory » (Col 1,27).
This presence of Christ, the new supernatural life-principle of Christian
existence (Col 3,4) is the result of the activity of the Holy Spirit.

> « May he [the Father] grant you the grace to be strengthened by power
> through his Spirit with respect to the inner man, that Christ may dwell
> through faith in your hearts ... » (Eph 3,16-17).

If it is necessary to point to a single sentence in all Paul's letters
which adequately sums up his soteriological thought and represents its
most mature expression, we venture to suggest that such a sentence is
to be found in the epistle to the Ephesians, where Paul speaks of Christ's
mediation in producing union between Christians of pagan and Jewish
origin [69].

> « through him, we both have access in one Spirit to the Father »
> (Eph 2,18).

The return of man to God has been effected by the death and resurrection
of Christ. Since, on Paul's view, it is an « access » to God as « the Father »,
it has been accomplished by Christ through those two acts which mark
him most properly as Son of God : his death, which revealed his filial
obedience and proved his Father's love for men, and his resurrection,
which revealed his constitution as « Son of God in power ». Paul has
already given a hint of this whole conception in Rom 5,1 ff, where he
employed the figure of « access » (a typically Jewish notion) [70] to describe
the process of Christian salvation. At the same time, this « access » through
the work of the Son to « the Father » is « in one Spirit ». The inhabitation of the Holy Spirit, which is also the presence of the risen Son of
God, makes man God's adoptive son. One day, through this indwelling
Spirit, the Father « who raised Jesus from death » will give man the
fulness of salvation, by imparting Life to mortal man in the glorious
resurrection of the just.

---

[69] Pp. 224-228.

[70] JOSEPH BONSIRVEN, *Textes rabbiniques des deux premiers siècles chrétiens
pour servir à l' intelligence du Nouveau Testament* (Rome, 1954) 1 (where he cites
the Shema) : « C'est nous que tu a choisis de toute nation et langue ; et tu nous
a faits proches de ton grand nom, à jamais, en vérité ... ».

SCRIPTURAL CITATIONS

Gn

1,3 : 48, 78.
1,11 : 78.
1,26 : 126.
1,26-27 : 78.
1,27 : 78, 215.
1,29 : 78.
1,31 : 78.
2,7 : 78, 125, 126.
2,17 : 78, 215.
2,18 : 78.
2,22-23 : 78.
2,24 : 78.
3,1-22 : 215.
3,4 : 78.
3,5 : 78.
3,7 : 78.
3,8 : 78.
3,13 : 78.
3,16 : 78.
3,17 : 194.
3,17-18 : 193.
3,17-19 : 78.
3,19 : 78, 126.
3,22-23 : 215.
5,3 : 78.
6,5 : 78.
18,18 : 153.
22,1-12 : 260.
22,16 : 190.

Ex

12,15-16 : 111.
13,7 : 111.

13,21 : 116.
14,19-20 : 116.
14,22 : 116.
15,7 : 184.
15,11 : 184.
16,7 : 184.
16,10 : 184.
16,14 : 116.
17,6 : 116.
19,5 : 23, 241.
19,5-6 : 167.
24,16-17 : 167.
34,34 : 132.
40,34-38 : 166.

Lv

23,10-14 : 122.

Nm

15,18-21 : 122.
20,11 : 116.
23,11 : 249.

Dt

7,6 : 241.
16,5 : 111.
21,23 : 153.
26,18 : 91.
27,26 : 153.

30,12 ff : 196.
30,14 : 196.

Ps

2,7 : 32, 51, 52.
8,7 : 221.
15,10 : 247.
16,8-11 : 28.
77,24 : 116.
104,39 : 116.
110,1 : 28, 221.
113,9 : 184.
115 : 137.
118,22 : 30.

Wis

2,23-24 : 12.
16,20 : 116.

Is

2,3 : 71.
42,7 : 45.
42,16 : 45.
43,18-19 : 141.
45,23 : 99.
49,1 : 46.
51,4-8 : 230.
52,7 : 226.
52,13-15 : 172.
53 : 90, 98, 255.
53,2-3 : 98.
55,3 : 190.
53,4-6 : 172.
53,7 : 172.
53,7-8 : 35.
53,8 : 172.
53,10 : 190.
53,10-12 : 172.
53,11-12 : 172.
53,12 : 172.
55,3 : 52.
57,19 : 224, 226.

61,1 ff : 45.
61,10 : 230.
65,17 : 141, 194.
66,12 : 194.
66,22 : 141.

Jer

1,7 : 45.
2,1-3,22 : 230.
23,7-8 : 83.
31,33 : 23, 225.

Ez

2,1 ff : 45.
16,8-9 : 230.

Os

2,14 f : 230.

Jl

2,32 b.c : 25.

So

1,12 : 111.

Mal

3,17 : 89, 220.

Mt

1,21 : 246.
5,18 : 194.
5,44-48 : 229.
9,24 : 87.
10,22 : 249.

10,33 : 249.
12,18 ff : 45.
13,33 : 111.
17,2 : 132.
18,33 : 228.
19,28 : 194, 243.
20,28 : 235, 241.
24,8 : 194.
27,51 : 225.
28,18 f : 181.
28,18-20 : 221.

Mk

9,2 : 132.
10,38 : 183.
10,45 : 235, 241.
13,8 : 194.
13,13 : 249.
14,36 : 157.

Lk

2,11 : 246.
4,1 : 87.
4,18 f : 45.
12,50 : 183.
13,20-21 : 111.
18,1 : 281.
19,10 : 233.
22,19 : 241.
22,53 : 204.
24,12 : 241.
24,29 : 23.
24,44-49 : 24.

Jn

1,14-16 : 271.
1,16 : 207.
1,18, : 205, 207.
1,19 : 233.
1,29 : 111, 208.
1,36 : 111.
3,5 : 244.

3,14 : 50.
4,42 : 246.
5,22 : 37.
6,14 : 233.
6,51 : 241.
7,38 : 48.
7,39 : 23.
8,28 : 50.
11,11 : 87.
11,27 : 233.
12,32 : 50.
12,34 : 50.
13,34 : 225.
14,13 : 226.
16,13 : 23.
17,3 : 235.
18,33-19,16 : 54.
19,36 : 111.

Acts

1,3 : 24.
1,4 : 23.
1,5 : 24.
1,6 : 24.
1,8 : 24, 32, 71.
1,11 : 24.
1,15 : 24.
1,25-26 : 24.
2,1-13 : 24.
2,5-36 : 238.
2,14-21 : 28.
2,14-36 : 28 ff.
2,14-36 : 25.
2,17-21 : 34.
2,20 : 31, 74.
2,21 : 32.
2,22 : 28, 32.
2,23 : 28, 32, 255.
2,24 : 28, 255.
2,24-31 : 119.
2,25-28 : 28, 34.
2,27-31 : 247.
2,29-31 : 28.
2,31 : 34.
2,32 : 28, 32.
2,32-33 : 221, 250.
2,33 : 25, 32, 33, 34, 50.

19. - D. M. STANLEY.

2,33-34 : 44.
2,33-35 : 28.
2,34-35 : 34.
2,36 : 28, 32, 33, 34, 255.
2,38 : 181, 240.
2,38-39 : 28.
2,47 : 181.
3,12-26 : 29.
3,12-26 : 28.
3,13 : 32, 261.
3,13-15 : 33, 34.
3,14 : 32.
3,14-15 : 29.
3,15 : 29, 32, 37, 255.
3,16 : 32.
3,17 : 29, 34.
3,17-18 : 33.
3,18 : 29, 32, 33, 255.
3,19-21 : 71, 76, 84, 219, 252.
3,20-21 : 29, 31, 106.
3,20b : 32.
3,21 : 126, 194, 195.
3,22-24 : 29.
3,25 : 32, 34.
3,25-26 : 32.
3,26 : 25, 74, 226, 239.
4,8-12 : 28.
4,9-12 : 30.
4,10 : 30, 32, 255.
4,10-11 : 33, 34.
4,11 : 34.
4,12 : 30.
4,25b-26 : 34.
4,27-28 : 33.
4,30 : 32.
5,29-30 : 34.
5,30 : 33, 255.
5,30-31 : 44.
5,31 : 32, 37, 50, 246.
5,32 : 31, 32.
6,5 : 35.
7,2-53 : 70.
7,9 : 37.
7,12 : 156.
7,17-43 : 37.
7,20-40 : 115.
7,27 : 37.
7,35 : 37.

7,36-37 : 37.
7,38 : 37.
7,39 : 37.
7,44 : 37.
7,48 : 37.
7,51 : 37.
7,52 : 38.
8,3 : 40.
8,12 : 181.
8,26-40 : 35.
8,35 : 35.
8,37 : 35.
9,1 : 40.
9,3 ff : 41 f.
9,3-19 : 41.
9,10-19 : 42.
9,13 : 40.
9,15 : 43.
9,15-16 : 50.
9,16 : 43, 46.
9,17 : 44, 250.
9,17-18 : 181.
9,20 : 32, 35, 53, 58, 84, 162, 266.
9,26 : 40.
9,27 : 53.
9,28 : 53, 57.
9,30 : 156, 251.
10,9 ff : 30.
10,23 : 246.
10,34-35 : 30, 52.
10,34-43 : 30.
10,34-43 : 28.
10,35 : 32.
10,36 : 30, 32, 51.
10,37 : 30, 32.
10,38 : 32, 37.
10,38-39 : 32.
10,38-39a : 30.
10,39 : 255.
18,39b : 30.
10,40 : 33, 255.
10,40-41 : 30, 34.
10,40-42 : 85.
10,41 : 32.
10,42 : 30, 32, 37, 121.
10,43 : 30.
10,46 : 24.
10,48 : 43, 181.

11,16-17 : 181.

11,19-21 : 71.

11,20 : 54.

11,22 : 156.

11,25 : 53, 70.

11,26 : 69, 70.

13,1 : 70.

13,1 ff : 70.

13,5 : 118.

13,5-12 : 71.

13,16 ff : 64.

13,16-41 : 50.

13,16-25 : 56.

13,17 : 50.

13,19 : 51.

13,21 : 51.

13,22 : 51, 87.

13,23 : 58, 87.

13,24 : 51.

13,24-25 : 32, 51, 58.

13,26 : 51.

13,26-27 : 51.

13,27 : 51.

13,28 : 255.

13,28-29 : 51.

13,29 : 184.

13,30 : 51, 255.

13,31 : 32, 51, 57.

13,31-37 : 247.

13,32 f : 251.

13,32-33 : 58, 149.

13,33 : 32, 42, 58, 84.

13,33a : 51.

13,33b : 51.

13,34-37 : 51, 119.

13,37 : 42, 255.

13,38-41 : 52, 58.

13,42-48 : 71.

14,1 ff : 71.

14,15-17 : 54, 57, 78.

14,22 : 54, 57, 71.

14,23 : 71.

14,28 : 69.

15,1 ff : 20, 71.

15,25 ff : 71.

15,35 : 53, 54, 57, 69.

16,9 : 72.

16,17 : 54, 57, 118.

16,19-39 : 73.

16,32 : 54.

17,2 : 162.

17,2-3 : 54.

17-3 : 42, 118, 255.

17,5-10 : 73.

17,7 : 54, 57.

17,14 : 156.

17,18 : 42, 53.

17,18-20 : 73.

17,22-23 : 52.

17,22-31 : 50, 78.

17,24-25 : 52.

17,24-31 : 57.

17,26 : 78.

17,26a : 52.

17,26b : 52.

17,28-29 : 52.

17,30 : 52, 58, 59.

17,31 : 37, 42, 52, 255.

17,32 f : 53.

17,42 : 52.

18,11 : 69.

18,19 : 75.

18,20 : 75.

18,20-21 : 54.

19,1-7 : 75.

19,2-3 : 68.

19,6 : 24.

19,8 : 54, 57.

19,8-9 : 75.

19,8-12 : 66.

19,10 : 69.

19,11 : 75.

19,12 : 67.

19,20 : 65.

20,1 : 65.

20,2 : 66.

20,3 : 68.

20,6 : 66, 68.

20,18-35 : 53.

20,21 : 55.

20,24b : 55.

20,25 : 55, 57.

20,28 : 90, 241.

20,31 : 65, 69.

22,4 : 40.

22,6-16 : 43 ff.

22,6-16 :   41.

22,11 :   44.

22,12 :   42.

22,14 :   44.

22,17-21 :   43, 70.

22,18-19 :   40.

22,19-20 :   40.

22,20-21 :   40.

22,21 :   156.

23,6 :   42, 55.

24,15 :   42, 55, 86.

25,19 :   55, 184.

26,6-8 :   55.

26,8 :   42.

26,11 :   40.

26,12 ff :   43.

26,12-18 :   45 f.

26,12-18 :   41.

26,16 :   45.

26,16-18 :   50.

26,17 :   45.

26,22 :   45.

26,22-23 :   55, 162.

26,23 :   42, 226.

28,23 :   55, 57, 162.

28,29 :   69.

28,30 :   70.

28,31 :   55, 57.

Rom

1,1 :   162.

1,1 :   50, 162.

1,1-2 :   56.

1,1-3 :   267.

1,1-4 :   161.

1,1-4 :   57.

1,1-7 :   161.

1,2-3 :   260.

1,3 :   162.

1,3 :   254, 262.

1,3-4 :   247.

1,4 :   163.

1,4 :   42, 51, 55, 58, 79, 84, 114, 121, 126, 146, 184, 198, 212, 227, 238, 254, 262, 271, 272, 274, 278, 283.

1,7 :   255.

1,9 :   267.

1,13 :   115.

1,14 :   73.

1,16 :   161, 167, 217, 220, 247, 281.

1,17 :   52.

1,17-4,25 :   59, 166, 249.

1,18-32 :   57.

1,18-3,20 :   167, 175.

1,23 :   134.

2-3 :   188.

2,4 :   87, 223.

2,5 :   175.

2,7 :   134, 247, 249.

2,16 :   37, 56, 57.

2,29 :   212, 281.

3,2 :   220.

3,3-4 :   249.

3,4 :   249.

3,12 :   224.

3,21 :   167.

3,21 :   173, 196.

3,21-25 :   260.

3,21-26 :   166.

3,21-26 :   79, 189, 232.

3,21-30 :   110.

3,22 :   167.

3,23 :   167.

3,23 :   134, 272.

3,24 :   166, 271.

3,24 :   169, 186, 189, 227, 273.

3,24-25 :   169, 173.

3,25 :   167.

3,25 :   4, 141, 173, 227, 229, 233.

3,25 f :   8.

3,26 :   169.

3,26 :   167, 168.

3,27 :   158.

3,31 :   225.

4,16 :   170.

4,17 :   170, 223.

4,23-24 :   170.

4,24 :   262.

4,25 :   170, 261.

4,25 :   14, 15, 20, 33, 42, 46, 79, 88, 101, 102, 114, 121, 144, 161, 170, 175, 188, 229, 241, 242, 261, 263, 268, 271, 274, 278.

4,1-25 : 170.
5 : 184.
5-8 : 195.
5,1 : 180, 207.
5,1-2 : 227.
5,1 ff : 286.
5,1-7,25 : 78.
5,1-11,36 : 166.
5,2 : 166, 176, 248.
5,5 : 161, 176, 188, 192, 206, 225.
 264, 283.
5,5b : 174.
5,8 : 174.
5,8 : 59, 184, 227, 269.
5,8-9 : 264.
5,8-10 : 190, 267.
5,8-11 : 174.
5,8-11 : 79.
5,9 : 175.
5,9 : 8, 175.
5,9b : 174.
5,9-10 : 176, 195, 222.
5,10 : 259.
5,10 : 4, 175, 197, 263, 268, 278.
5,10b : 174, 175, 227.
5,10-11 : 227.
5,11 : 176.
5,11 : 121.
5,12 : 78.
5,12 ff : 124, 125, 126, 127, 186, 214,
 272.
5,12-15 : 12.
5,12-21 : 49, 78, 172, 188.
5,14 : 180.
5,15 : 178, 179.
5,15a : 179.
5,15c : 179.
5,15 ff : 102.
5,16 : 179.
5,16b : 185.
5,17 : 179, 180.
5,18 : 179, 180, 268.
5,19 : 176, 268, 274.
5,19 : 46, 178, 227.
5,21 : 276.
5,21 : 176, 180, 184, 268.
6-8 : 4.
6,1 : 182.

6,1-11 : 187.
6,2-11 : 137.
6,3 : 182.
6,3 ff : 139, 212, 215.
6,3-4 : 21.
6,3-5 : 88.
6,3-6 : 278.
6,3-11 : 181.
6,3-11 : 244, 249.
6,4 : 184.
6,4 : 44, 134, 173, 184, 186, 212,
 262, 272, 278.
6,4 ff : 87.
6,4-6 : 265.
6,4-6 : 227.
6,4-11 : 199.
6,5 : 184.
6,5 : 184, 213.
6,5-7 : 186.
6,6 : 185.
6,6 : 114, 184, 199, 214, 246.
6,7 : 185.
6,7-10 : 190.
6,8 : 186, 265.
6,8 : 184.
6,8-10 : 186.
6,9 : 42.
6,9-10 : 186.
6,10 : 112, 173, 183, 246, 271.
6,10b : 178.
6,10-11 : 87.
6,11 : 186.
6,11 : 188, 271.
6,12 : 78.
6,17 : 59.
6,23 : 176, 191.
7,1-3 : 187.
7,1-6 : 187.
7,4 : 188.
7,4 : 188, 209, 227, 261, 273.
7,4-6 : 186.
7,4-6 : 189.
7,5-6 : 114, 188.
7,6 : 114, 225, 282.
7,7-24 : 188, 189.
7,10 : 187.
7,11 : 78.
7,12 : 187.

7,13 : 187.
7,14 : 187.
7,18 : 78.
7,22 : 187.
7,25 : 176.
8 : 188, 189, 191, 192.
8,1 : 189, 191.
8,1-2 : 263.
8,1 ff : 225.
8,2 : 191, 282.
8,2-4 : 227.
8,3 : 8, 13, 15, 84, 98, 144, 145, 146, 153, 178, 186, 188, 190, 209, 225, 258, 267, 272.
8,3 f : 141.
8,3-4 : 189.
8,3-4 : 79, 143, 233, 263.
8,3 ff : 114.
8,4 : 191.
8,4 : 225.
8,5 : 191.
8,7 : 187.
8,9 : 191, 242, 282, 283.
8,9b : 228.
8,9-10 : 278, 283.
8,9-11 : 157, 188, 199.
8,10 : 271.
8,10 : 173, 191, 210, 242.
8,11 : 283.
8,11 : 42, 114, 151, 190, 192, 223, 228, 262.
8,13 : 237.
8,14 : 87, 190, 262.
8,14 ff : 157, 192, 220.
8,14-16 : 285.
8,14-16 : 103.
8,15 : 151, 176, 195, 228, 257, 284.
8,17 : 88, 184, 244, 248.
8,18 : 166.
8,18-22 : 49, 78.
8,19 : 193.
8,19-22 : 192, 278.
8,19-23 : 192.
8,20 : 194.
8,20 : 78.
8,21 : 194.
8,21 : 166.
8,22 : 194.

8,23 : 195.
8,23 : 79, 167, 174, 176, 192, 193, 194, 222, 223, 269, 270, 283.
8,24 : 195, 222.
8,24-25 : 249.
8,26 : 195.
8,26-27 : 285.
8,26-27 : 126.
8,27 : 195.
8,29 : 285.
8,29 : 133, 184, 205, 207, 219, 262, 264, 267.
8,30 : 166.
8,31 : 190.
8,31-39 : 189.
8,32 : 260.
8,32 : 33, 46, 102, 184, 190, 192, 219, 227, 229, 267, 268.
8,34 : 42, 189, 192, 235, 252, 270.
8,34-39 : 206.
8,35 : 192.
8,37 : 264.
8,39 : 59, 176, 189, 192, 264.
9,4 : 284.
9-11 : 79, 195.
9,22 : 122.
9,27 : 222.
10,4 : 150, 195.
10,6 : 196.
10,7 : 196.
10,8 : 196.
10,8-9 : 230.
10,9 : 195.
10,9 : 42, 57, 100, 222, 262.
10,17 : 92.
11,1-36 : 197.
11,14-26 : 222.
11,15 : 197.
11,15 : 278.
11,16 : 122.
11,22 : 223.
11,25 : 115.
11,25-26 : 197, 235.
11,25 ff : 76.
11,25-27 : 31.
11,30-32 : 249.
11,36 : 108, 141, 257.
12,1 : 92, 209.

12,1-2 :   210.
12,2 :   132, 243.
12,4-6 :   42.
12,4-8 :   206.
12,5 :   206.
12,7 :   211.
12,9 ff :   206.
13,8-10 :   192, 225.
13,11 :   222.
13,11-12 :   79.
14,1 ff :   68.
14,2 :   78.
14,7 : 198.
14,7-8 :   88.
14,7-9 : 198.
14,7-9 :   79, 114, 228, 248.
14,7-12 :   101.
14,8 : 199.
14,8-9 :   246.
14,9 : 199, 278.
14,9 :   57, 101, 165.
14,17 :   281.
15,6 :   256.
15,7 :   134.
15,14 :   211.
15,16 :   281.
15,18 :   68.
15,19 :   281.
15,20 :   67.
15,30 : 280.
16,1-2 :   68.
16,5 :   91.
16,20 :   78.
16,25 :   219.
16,25-26 :   56, 79, **227**, 236.

1 Cor

1,3 :   255.
1,7 :   55, 193.
1,8 :   75.
1,8-9 :   266.
1,9 :   108, 249.
1,10-6,20 :   108.
1,11 :   67.
1,13 :   181.
1,17-31 :   108.

1,18 :   122, 222.
1,18-25 :   73.
1,21 :   108.
1,22-23 :   109.
1,23 :   55, 108, 270.
1,24 :   51, 108, 114.
1,26-28 :   108.
1,29 :   108.
1,30 : 258, 271.
1,30 :   73, 104, 108.
2,1 ff :   52.
2,1 :   188, 219.
2,2 :   55, 270.
2,3 :   72.
2,4 :   281.
2,6 ff :   211.
2,6-9 :   73.
2,6-16 :   53.
2,7 :   134.
2,7-8 :   236.
2,8 :   114, 134, 258.
2,10-11 :   281.
3,5 :   67.
3,11 :   209.
3,13 :   75.
3,16 :   282, 283.
3,18-20 :   73.
3,21-22 :   67.
4,7 :   158.
4,14 :   211.
4,16 :   228.
4,17 :   65, 211.
5,1-13 :   110.
5,2 :   67.
5,4 :   51, 146.
5,5 :   75, 222.
5,6b : 111.
5,6b-8 : 110.
5,7 : 111.
5,7 :   226, 229.
5,8 : 112.
5,11 :   67.
6,1-11 :   113.
6,9 :   137.
6,11 :   108, 243, 281.
6,12 :   113.
6,12-20 :   113.
6,13 :   101, 113.

6,13b :   113.
6,13b-15a :   113.
6,13-14 :   274.
6,14 :   51, 105, 107, 146, 176, 184,
     262, 271, 272.
6,14 :   114.
6,15 :   115.
6,16 :   78.
6,17 :   114, 132, 181, 199, 228, 282.
6,19 :   282.
6,19-20 :   114.
6,20 :   8.
7,1-14,40 :   108.
7,11 :   141.
7,18 :   67.
7,23 :   8.
8,1-11,1 :   115.
8,6 :   108, 141, 256, 257.
8,8 :   209.
9,1 :   50.
9,14 :   118.
9,20-22 :   67.
9,22 :   222.
9,25 :   247.
10,1 :   115.
10,1-2 :   181.
10,1-4 :   115.
10,1-11 :   115.
10,2 :   116.
10,2 :   183.
10,3-4 :   116.
10,5 ff :   37.
10,5 :   116.
10,6 :   115.
10,13 :   249.
10,16 :   117.
10,17 :   77, 115, 206, 217.
10,21 :   116.
10,33 :   222.
11,1 :   228.
11,3 :   78, 127.
11,7 :   78, 127.
11,8 :   78.
11,9 :   78.
11,12 :   141.
11,23 :   46, 47, 56, 260.
11,23-25 :   117.
11,23-26 :   56.

11,23-27 :   117.
11,26 :   117.
11,26 :   75, 210.
11,27 :   116.
11,28 :   118.
11,29 :   118.
12,1 :   115.
12,3 :   281.
12,4 :   228, 280.
12,4-31 :   181.
12,12 :   42, 181, 206.
12,12-28 :   42.
12,12-30 :   77.
12,12-31 :   206.
12,13 :   181.
13,1 ff :   206.
13,4 :   137.
14,34 :   78.
15 :   88.
15,1 ff :   278.
15,1-8 :   58.
15,1-9 :   54.
15,1-34 :   118.
15,1-58 :   108.
15,2 :   118, 222.
15,3 :   119.
15,3 :   8, 47, 56, 175, 255, 260.
15,3-4 :   118.
15,3-4 :   75, 86, 102, 120.
15,4 :   119.
15,4 :   30, 184, 261.
15,5-7 :   47.
15,5-8 :   43.
15,5-11 :   120.
15,8 :   47.
15,8 :   50.
15,8-9 :   41.
15,9 :   40, 47.
15,12 :   126, 261.
15,12-19 :   120.
15,13-14 :   15.
15,13-17 :   20.
15,14 :   121.
15,14-18 :   120.
15,14 ff :   274.
15,15 :   121.
15,15 :   262.
15,16 :   121.

15,17 : 121.
15,17 : 271.
15,17-18 : 15.
15,18 : 122.
15,18 : 88.
15,20 : 122.
15,20a : 123.
15,20b : 123.
15,20 : 21, 42, 87, 101, 165, 246, 261, 271, 273.
15,20-21 : 125.
15,20-22 : 122.
15,20-22 : 9, 78, 105, 121, 176, 205.
15,21 : 123.
15,21 : 78, 114.
15,21-22 : 274.
15,21-22 : 49, 177, 180, 214.
15,22 : 123.
15,22 : 223, 246.
15,23-28 : 124, 204.
15,24 : 257, 266.
15,25-28 : 215.
15,26 : 246.
15,28 : 31, 215, 216, 257, 266.
15,32 : 75.
15,35 : 124.
15,35-53 : 118.
15,36 : 223.
15,37-38 : 125.
15,38 : 78.
15,42 : 194, 247.
15,42-44a : 125.
15,43 : 51, 134.
15,44 : 116.
15,44*b* : 125.
15,44b-45 : 13.
15,44b-46 : 188.
15,44*b*-49 : 124.
15,45 : 125, 274.
15,45 : 15, 20, 78, 114, 126, 132, 223, 227, 228, 278, 283.
15,45 ff : 133.
15,45-47 : 214.
15,45-49 : 49, 78, 125, 133, 177, 180.
15,46 : 126.
15,46 : 116, 143.
15,47 : 126.
15,47 : 78.

15,48 : 127.
15,49 : 127.
15,49 : 78, 180, 205.
15,50 : 247.
15,51 : 277.
15,53-54 : 247.
15,54-55 : 87.
15,54-58 : 118.
15,55-57 : 185.
15,57 : 269.
16,1 : 67.
16,8 : 111.
16,10 : 65.
16,15 : 91.
16,22 : 89.

2 Cor

1,1 : 65, 202.
1,2 : 255.
1,3 : 256.
1,3-11 : 129.
1,5 : 77, 105, 146.
1,5-7 : 209.
1,6 : 77.
1,6-8 : 249.
1,8 : 75, 115, 278.
1,8-9 : 66, 128.
1,9 : 129.
1,9 : 77, 262.
1,9-10 : 129.
1,9-10 : 278.
1,10 : 130.
1,10 : 227.
1,10 ff : 75.
1,12-7,16 : 129.
1,14 : 77, 129.
1,18 : 249.
1,21 : 141.
1,22 : 12.
2,1 : 75.
2,3 : 188.
2,3 ff : 75.
2,5-10 : 68.
2,12-13 : 65.
2,14 : 141.
2,15 : 222.

3,4-11 : 131.
3,5 : 68.
3,6 : 225.
3,6 : 282.
3,12 : 132.
3,13 : 132.
3,12-4,6 : 131.
3,13 : 132.
3,14-15 : 76.
3,16 : 132.
3,16-18 : 188.
3,17 : 114, 126, 134, 164, 228, 283.
3,17a : 131.
3,18 : 131.
3,18 : 12, 48, 129, 184, 185, 215, 248.
4,4 : 48, 133, 232, 246.
4,5 : 55.
4,6 : 48.
4,6 : 41, 42, 78, 141, 184.
4,7 : 134.
4,8-9 : 135.
4,10 : 135.
4,10 : 77, 185, 246, 269.
4,10-11 : 278.
4,10-11 : 129, 176, 248.
4,10-12 : 105.
4,10-14 : 134.
4,10-14 : 129.
4,11 : 136.
4,11 : 136.
4,11-12 : 77.
4,12 : 137.
4,12 : 145, 269.
4,13 : 137.
4,14 : 138.
4,14 : 42, 88, 136, 176, 184, 262.
4,14-18 : 77.
4,16 : 12.
5,1-10 : 77.
5,3 : 129.
5,4 f : 12.
5,5 : 141, 195.
5,8 : 269.
5,10 : 77, 129, 138.
5,12 : 68.
5,14 : 139, 269.
5,14 : 8, 9, 87, 140, 143, 183, 188, 273.
5,14-15 : 236, 248.

5,14 ff : 4.
5,14-21 : 138.
5,14-21 : 102.
5,15 : 139, 278.
5,15 : 14, 15, 101, 114, 143, 144, 185, 198, 228, 261, 270, 278.
5,15-17 : 136.
5,16 : 140.
5,16b : 48, 58.
5,17 : 140.
5,17 : 49, 50, 78, 108, 114, 140, 155, 158, 159, 227.
5,18 : 141.
5,18 : 142, 176, 268.
5,18 ff : 4, 174.
5,18-19 : 259.
5,18-20 : 197.
5,18-21 : 174.
5,19 : 142.
5,19 : 207, 228, 268.
5,19-20 : 227.
5,20 : 142.
5,20 : 77, 176.
5,21 : 143, 258.
5,21 : 8, 190, 263, 272.
6,1-2 : 83.
6,1-10 : 77.
6,6 : 224.
6,7 : 256.
6,16 : 282.
7,3 : 88.
7,5-7 : 65.
7,8 ff : 75.
7,10 : 77.
8,1-9, 15 : 129, 144.
8,6 : 66.
8,9 : 144, 272.
8,9 : 101.
8,16-17 : 66.
8,23-24 : 66.
10,1-13,10 : 129.
10,2 : 68.
10,10 : 278.
10,10-11 : 75.
10,10-18 : 68.
11,3 : 78.
11,5 : 68.
11,13 : 68.

11,22-23 : 68.
11,31 : 256.
12,9 : 146.
12,11 : 68.
12,19-13,10 : 145.
13,1-2 : 75.
13,3-6 : 77.
13,4 : 145, 258.
13,4 : 42, 51, 105, 138, 272.
13,11 : 264.
13,13 : 280.
13,13 : 228, 264.
13,46 : 136.

Gal

1,1 : 148.
1,1 : 262.
1,1-5 : 147.
1,3 : 255.
1,3-4 : 149, 259.
1,4 : 8, 77, 85, 102, 241, 227, 229, 268.
1,6 f : 147.
1,6-9 : 210.
1,7 : 48.
1,7-9 : 56.
1,9 : 147.
1,11-2,21 : 150.
1,14 : 40.
1,15 : 50.
1,15-16 : 41.
1,15-17 : 46.
1,16 : 42, 50, 84, 256, 267.
1,23 : 40.
2,1-9 : 53.
2,17 : 228.
2,17 f : 151.
2,19 : 150.
2,19 : 72, 78, 88, 149, 227, 265.
2,19-20 : 136, 185, 248.
2,19-21 : 150.
2,19-21 : 77.
2,20 : 151, 269.
2,20 : 33, 46, 102, 114, 184, 227, 229, 241, 261, 267, 268.
2,20-21 : 234.
2,21 : 72, 151.

2,21 : 152.
3-4 : 152.
3,1 : 55, 72, 149, 270.
3,3 : 282.
3,3 ff : 157, 195, 220.
3,3-5 : 72, 77, 103, 154.
3,5 : 282.
3,6 ff : 155.
3,6-4,31 : 77.
3,8 : 153.
3,10 : 4.
3,11 : 52.
3,13 : 4, 8, 72, 78, 102, 143, 149, 157, 263, 268, 272.
3,13 : 153.
3,13-14 : 152.
3,14 : 153.
3,14 : 157, 228.
3,14 ff : 220.
3,15-18 : 154.
3,16 : 149, 152, 155.
3,19 : 187.
3,21 : 187.
3,22 : 260.
3,23 : 155.
3,23-4,7 : 192.
3,24 : 187.
3,25 : 155, 260.
3,26 : 154.
3,26 : 263, 284.
3,26-29 : `77.
3,26-29 : 154.
3,27 : 155.
3,27 : 182.
3,27-28 : 214.
3,28 : 155.
3,28 : 214, 273.
3,29 : 155.
4,2 : 156.
4,4 : 78, 84, 153, 157, 185, 225, 260, 272.
4,4 : 156.
4,4 ff : 15, 141, 176, 233.
4,4-5 : 262, 284.
4,4-5 : 143.
4,4-6 : 178, 267.
4,4-7 : 155.
4,4-7 : 77.

4,5 : 156.
4,5 : 4, 219, 227, 268, 284.
4,6 : 157.
4,6 : 72, 133, 155, 156, 188, 195, 220,
257, 262, 283, 284.
4,7 : 157.
4,7 : 244.
4,8-11 : 72.
4,12 : 228.
4,13-14 : 72.
4,28-31 : 77.
5,2 : 72, 77.
5,6 : 159.
5,9 : 111.
5,11 : 149, 158.
5,11-12 : 72.
5,16-25 : 77.
5,18 : 87, 282.
5,21 : 72, 77.
5,22 : 224.
5,24 : 78, 149, 199.
6,7-10 : 75.
6,8 : 194.
6,9-10 : 77.
6,12 : 78, 149.
6,12-15 : 72.
6,13 : 158.
6,14 : 158.
6,14 : 77, 78, 149.
6,14-15 : 158.
6,15 : 159.
6,15 : 49, 78, 114, 227.
6,17 : 149.

Eph

1,2 : 255.
1,3 : 218.
1,3 : 256, 263.
1,3-14 : 216.
1,3-14 : 216, 217, 230.
1,4 : 218.
1,5 : 218, 285.
1,5 : 227, 264, 284.
1,5-7 : 264.
1,6 : 219.
1,6 : 248, 264.

1,7 : 219.
1,7 : 227, 271.
1,8 : 219.
1,9 : 219.
1,9-10 : 78, 227, 236.
1,10 : 219.
1,10 : 216, 227, 267.
1,11 : 219.
1,12 : 219.
1,12 : 219.
1,13 : 220.
1,13 : 217, 226.
1,13 f : 12.
1,13-14 : 241.
1,14 : 220, 271, 285.
1,14 : 90, 219.
1,15 ff : 217, 220.
1,17 : 134, 257, 262.
1,19 : 51.
1,19b : 221.
1,19b-22 : 227.
1,19 b-23 : 220.
1,20 : 221.
1,20 : 42, 262.
1,20-23 : 78.
1,21 : 221.
1,22 : 221.
1,22 : 206, 219.
1,23 : 206.
2,1-2 : 78.
2,1-3 : 222.
2,1-21 : 230.
2,3-10 : 243.
2,4 : 222.
2,4 f : 14.
2,4-6 : 266.
2,4-7 : 264.
2,4-7 : 227.
2,4-8 : 222.
2,5 : 222.
2,5 : 13, 217, 220.
2,6 : 223.
2,6 : 88, 184.
2,7 : 223.
2,8 : 13, 217, 220, 222, 223.
2,8-10 : 224.
2,10 : 225.
2,11-12 : 224.

2,13 :   224.
2,14 :   224.
2,14 :   227, 237.
2,14-16 :   276.
2,14-18 :   224.
2,14-18 :   153.
2,15 :   225.
2,15 :   213, 226, 227.
2,16 :   225.
2,16 :   4, 225, 268.
2,17 :   226.
2,18 :   226, 286.
2,18 :   257, 281.
2,20 :   216.
2,21-22 :   282.
3,1-13 :   56.
3,3-4 :   219.
3,3-10 :   227.
3,5 :   281.
3,7 :   51, 146.
3,8 :   145.
3,8-12 :   236.
3,10 :   78.
3,14 :   257.
3,16-17 :   286.
3,18-19 :   78.
3,20 :   146.
4,1-16 :   228.
4,1-6,22 :   228.
4,3 :   280.
4,3-4 :   228.
4,4 :   280.
4,4-13 :   230.
4,6 :   216, 256.
4,7-10 :   78.
4,7-13 :   226.
4,8 ff :   239.
4,10 :   44, 79.
4,11-13 :   276.
4,11-16 :   42.
4,13 :   267.
4,14-15 :   207.
4,15 :   206, 219.
4,17-31 :   228.
4,21 :   211.
4,22 :   214.
4,24 :   78, 225.
4,30 :   270.

4,32 :   228.
4,32 :   229.
4,32 f :   259.
4,32-5,2 :   228.
5,1 :   228.
5,1 :   227, 269.
5,2 :   229, 269.
5,2 :   33, 46, 102, 226, 228, 229, 241,
        261, 268.
5,14 :   83, 236.
5,18 :   282.
5,18-20 :   217.
5,21-6,9 :   229.
5,21-6,12 :   78.
5,23 :   106, 206, 230, 246.
5,25 :   230.
5,25 :   33, 102, 241, 261, 268.
5,25-26 :   229.
5,25-27 :   269.
5,26 :   230.
5,26 :   243.
5,30-31 :   78.
6,9 :   236.
6,12 :   216.
6,15 :   226, 281.
6,19 :   219.
6,24 :   247.

Phil

1,2 :   255.
1,3-11 :   66.
1,6 :   75, 95.
1,9 :   95.
1,10 :   75.
1,11 :   95.
1,12-13 :   66.
1,12-26 :   95.
1,15-17 :   75.
1,17 :   118.
1,18-19 :   95.
1,19 :   75, 222, 283.
1,20-23 :   95.
1,21 :   234.
1,21-23 :   269.
1,21-26 :   66.
1,27 :   106, 280.

1,27-30 : 95.
1,28 :   122, 222.
1,28-29 : 75.
1,29 : 209.
2,1 : 181, 264.
2,1-2 :   280.
2,1-5 : 95.
2,5-11 : 46, 105, 248.
2,6 :   97.
2,6 : 78, 97, 133.
2,6-7 : 98.
2,6 ff : 17, 165.
2,6-11 :   95.
2,6-11 : 9, 102, 107, 120, 145, 227, 268, 273, 280.
2,7 :   272.
2,7 : 97, 145.
2,8 :   98.
2,8 : 97, 178, 179.
2,8-9 : 42.
2,9 :   98.
2,9 : 50, 97.
2,9-11 : 54.
2,10 :   99.
2,10 : 97, 238.
2,11 :   100.
2,11 : 97.
2,12 : 66, 222.
2,14-17 : 95.
2,15 : 256.
2,16 : 75.
2,17 : 95.
2,19 : 65.
2,19-30 : 102.
2,20-21 : 75.
3,1-3 : 102.
3,2-6 : 67.
3,3 : 281, 283.
3,3-14 : 105.
3,4-9 : 130.
3,4-17 : 102.
3,6 : 40.
3,7-8 : 152.
3,8 : 95, 102, 103.
3,9 : 95, 144.
3,9-11 : 103.
3,10 :   104.
3,10 : 51, 75, 88, 95, 136, 146, 209, 233.

3,10-11 :   102.
3,10-11 : 227, 248, 277.
3,10-12 : 185.
3,11 :   104.
3,11 : 75, 95.
3,12 :   49.
3,12 : 41, 50, 103.
3,14 : 49, 75.
3,15-16 : 105.
3,17 : 105, 228.
3,18-19 : 76, 105.
3,19 : 122.
3,20 :   106.
3,20 : 95, 222, 246.
3,20-21 :   105.
3,20-21 : 75, 277.
3,21 : 95, 106, 127, 134, 248.
3,21b : 107.
4,1 : 75, 95.
4,1-20 : 66.
4,5 : 75, 95.
4,10 : 66.
4,15 : 91.
4,16 : 66.
4,19 : 134, 248.
4,20 : 256.

Col

1,2 : 255.
1,3 : 256.
1,3 ff : 202.
1,7 : 67, 208, 227.
1,8 : 280.
1,9 ff : 202.
1,11 : 184.
1,12 : 202, 257.
1,13 :   204.
1,13 : 59, 76, 227, 259, 267.
1,13-14 : 203, 204, 219.
1,13-20 :   202.
1,13-28 : 230.
1,14 : 204, 227, 271.
1,15 :   205.
1,15 : 78, 215.
1,15-17 : 204.
1,15-20 : 78, 203.

1,3 : 256.
1,4 : 264.
1,4-5 : 82.
1,5 : 73, 91, 281.
1,6 : 228.
1,6-7 : 82.
1,8 : 82, 210.
1,9 : 83.
1,9-10 : 82.
1,9-10 : 82.
1,10 : 42, 55, 57, 58, 73, 74, 95, 149, 266.
1,10 : 84, 261.
2,7-12 : 73.
2,12 : 74, 92, 134.
2,13-14 : 73.
2,15 : 258.
2,18 : 74.
3,1 : 73.
3,11 : 256.
3,13 : 74, 256.
3,30 : 92.
4,3 : 92, 110.
4,3 ff : 92.
4,4 : 92.
4,7 : 92, 110.
4,8 : 91, 283.
4,13 : 90, 115.
4,13-16 : 74.
4,13-17 : 82, 90.
4,13-18 : 86.
4,13-5,11 : 85.
4,14 : 85.
4,14 : 42, 74, 105, 121, 127, 138, 174, 176, 184, 199, 227, 248, 261, 269, 277.
4,15 : 38, 86.
4,15-18 : 124.
4,16 : 90.
4,17 : 90, 95, 277.
5,1-3 : 74, 82.
5,1-11 : 89.
5,9 : 74, 89, 92, 222.
5,9-10 : 89, 258.
5,9-10 : 241, 284.
5,10 : 90, 277.
5,10 : 184, 199, 246, 248, 278.
5,12 : 211.

5,19 : 281.
5,23 : 74, 92.
5,24 : 249.
5,27 : 202.

2 Thes

1,1 : 255.
1,4-5 : 249.
1,5 : 74.
1,7 : 193.
1,9-10 : 248.
1,10 : 184.
2,1-2 : 31.
2,1-3 : 74.
2,2 : 82.
2,3-12 : 82.
2,6 : 74.
2,13 : 91.
2,13 : 74, 92, 110, 181, 222, 228.
2,13-14 : 284.
2,13-14 : 89, 241, 248.
2,14 : 92.
2,14 : 90, 134, 184.
2,16 : 264.
2,17 : 256.
3,3 : 249.
3,7 : 228.
3,10 : 78.
3,15 : 211.

1 Tm

1,1 : 231.
1,2 : 256.
1,3 : 69.
1,11 : 232, 246.
1,12 : 232.
1,13 : 40.
1,15 : 232.
1,15-16 : 232.
1,15-16 : 57, 59.
1,16 : 233.
1,16 : 232.
1,17 : 247.

2 :   234.
2,1-8 :   234.
2,3 :   234.
2,3 :   231.
2,3-7 :   234.
2,4-5 :   240.
2,5 :   235.
2,5 :   236, 252.
2,5-6 :   235.
2,6 :   235.
2,6 :   102, 229, 241.
2,7 :   236.
2,7 :   245.
2,9-15 :   234.
2,14 :   78.
3,9 :   236.
3,16 :   236.
3,16 :   14, 44, 258.
4,4 :   78.
4,10 :   231.
5,11 :   233.
6,13-14 :   **56.**
6,20 :   80.

2 Tm

1,2 :   256.
1,8 :   245.
1,8-11 :   244.
1,9 :   245.
1,9 :   233.
1,9-10 :   245.
1,10 :   245.
1,10 :   231, 233, 237, 240, 246.
1,14 :   80, 281.
1,17 :   69.
2,3-7 :   247.
2,8 :   247.
2,8 :   55, 80, 248, 249, 261.
2,8-10 :   247.
2,8-13 :   247.
2,9 :   69.
2,9-10 :   248.
2,10 :   231, 233.
2,11 :   248.
2,11-12 :   88.
2,11-13 :   247.

2,11-13 :   248.
2,12 :   249.
2,13 :   249.
4,1 :   231.
4,18 :   231, 233.

Ti

1,3 :   231.
1,4 :   231, 246, 256.
1,9 :   232.
2,10 :   231.
2,11 :   59, 231, 237, 240.
2,11-14 :   239.
2,11-14 :   242.
2,12 :   240.
2,13 :   240.
2,13 :   231, 233, 237, 246.
2,14 :   241.
2,14 :   102, 229.
3,1-3 :   242.
3,4 :   243.
3,4 :   231, 237.
3,4-6 :   240.
3,4-7 :   242.
3,4-7 :   233.
3,5 :   243.
3,5 :   231, 233, 242, 281.
3,6 :   231, 246.
3,6-7 :   244.
3,6-7 :   242.

Phlm

12 :   68.
23-24 :   68.
24 :   41, 68.

Heb

1,2 :   254.
1,3 :   44.
1,5 :   52.
1,13 :   44.
2,4 :   52.

20. - D. M. STANLEY.

2,7 ff :   44.

2,9 :   253.

2,10 :   29,   37,   87,   253,   254.

2,14 :   221,   246.

2,17 :   253.

3,6 :   254.

4,14 :   253,   254.

4,15 :   190,   253.

5,5 ff :   253.

5,7-10 :   254.

5,8 :   98,   253.

5,9 :   253.

6,5 :   230.

6,20 :   253.

7,16 :   253.

7,17 :   254.

7,22 :   253.

7,26 :   253.

7,27 :   253.

7,28 :   254.

8,1 :   252.

8,5 :   37.

8,6 :   253.

8,6-13 :   253.

9,11-12 :   226,   253.

9,11-14 :   253.

9,15 :   253.

9,24-28 :   226.

9,26 :   253.

10,5-9 :   253.

10,10 :   253.

10,12 :   253.

10,15-18 :   253.

10,19-22 :   226.

10,38 :   52.

11,1-40 :   70.

12,2 :   37,   44,   253,   254.

12,4 :   254.

12,5-9 :   254.

12,24 :   253.

13,20 :   253.

1 Pt

2,4-8 :   30.

2,20 :   246.

2,20-25 :   35.

2 Pt

1,1 :   246.

1,11 :   246.

3,2 :   246.

3,18 :   246.

1 Jn

4,14 :   246.

Ap

5,6 :   111.

14,1-5 :   111.

20,4-5 :   223.

21,1 :   194.

21,5 :   141.

22,20 :   89.

AUTHORS

GENERAL INDEX

STAMPATO CON I TIPI DELLO
STABILIMENTO TIPOGRAFICO
« PLINIANA » - SELCI UMBRO
LUGLIO 1961

Photomechanischer Nachdruck der
Akademischen Druck - u. Verlagsanstalt
Graz / Austria

Printed in Austria
187. 63 / 13